Lecture Notes in Computer Science 7115

Commenced Publication in 1973
Founding and Former Series Editors:
Gerhard Goos, Juris Hartmanis, and Jan van Leeuwen

Souhwan Jung   Moti Yung (Eds.)

Information Security Applications

12th International Workshop, WISA 2011
Jeju Island, Korea, August 22-24, 2011
Revised Selected Papers

 Springer

Volume Editors

Souhwan Jung
Soongsil University
School of Electronic Engineering
Hyungnam Memorial Engineering Building 1105
Sangdo-Dong, Dongjak-Gu, Seoul 156-743, Korea
E-mail: souhwanj@ssu.ac.kr

Moti Yung
Google Inc. and
Columbia University, Computer Science Department
1214 Amsterdam Ave.
New York, NY 10025, USA
E-mail: moti@cs.columbia.edu

ISSN 0302-9743   e-ISSN 1611-3349
ISBN 978-3-642-27889-1   e-ISBN 978-3-642-27890-7
DOI 10.1007/978-3-642-27890-7
Springer Heidelberg Dordrecht London New York

Library of Congress Control Number: 2011944973

CR Subject Classification (1998): C.2, K.6.5, E.3, D.4.6, H.4, J.1

LNCS Sublibrary: SL 4 – Security and Cryptology

Typesetting: Camera-ready by author, data conversion by Scientific Publishing Services, Chennai, India

Printed on acid-free paper

Springer is part of Springer Science+Business Media (www.springer.com)

Preface

The 12th international Workshop on Information Security Applications (WISA 2011) was held on Jeju Island, Korea, during August 22–24, 2011. The workshop is hosted annually by the Korea Institute of Information Security and Cryptology (KIISC), supported by the Electronics and Telecommunications Research Institute (ETRI) and the Korea Internet & Security Agency (KISA), and sponsored by the Ministry of Public Administration and Security (MoPAS) and the Korea Communications Commission (KCC).

The objective of this workshop is to cover all technical and practical aspects of security applications, representing both cryptographic and non-cryptographic works. The workshop serves as a forum for presentations of new results from the academic research community as well as from industry.

It was our great pleasure and honor to serve as the Program Committee Co-chairs of WISA 2011. The current proceedings of the workshop continue the tradition of earlier years which were also published as part of the LNCS series of Springer. The WISA 2011 Program Committee received 74 papers form 11 countries. This year the submissions were exceptionally strong, and the committee accepted 21 papers for the full-paper presentation track. All the papers were carefully evaluated through blind peer review, wherein at least three members of the Program Committee reviewed each submitted work. The numbers above indicate that the selection process was highly competitive, and, unfortunately, due to time limitation, many good papers were not accepted.

In addition to the contributed papers, the workshop had two invited talks: Kanta Matsuura and Shyhtsun Felix Wu presented distinguished special talks entitled "Passive and Active Measurements of Cybersecurity Risk Parameter" and "On Leveraging Social Informatics for Cyber Security," respectively.

Many people helped and worked hard to make WISA 2011 successful. We would like to thank all the people involved in the technical program and in organizing the workshop. We are very grateful to the Program Committee members and the external referees for their time and efforts in reviewing the submissions and selecting the accepted papers. We should also express our special thanks to the Organizing Committee members and the General Chair, Heungyoul Youm, for their hard work in managing the workshop.

Finally, on behalf of all those involved in organizing the workshop, we would like to thank the authors of all the submitted papers, for sending and contributing their interesting research results to the workshop, and the invited speakers. Without their submissions and support, WISA 2011 could not have been a success.

October 2011

Souhwan Jung
Moti Yung

Organization

Advisory Committee

ManYoung Rhee	Kyung Hee University, Korea
Hideki Imai	Chuo University, Japan
Bart Preneel	Katholieke University Leuven, Belgium
KilHyun Nam	Korea National Defense University, Korea
SangJae Moon	Kyungpook National University, Korea
DongHo Won	Sungkyunkwan University, Korea
SeHun Kim	KAIST, Korea
PilJoong Lee	POSTEC, Korea
DaeHo Kim	NSRI, Korea
JooSeok Song	Yonsei University, Korea
MinSub Rhee	Dankook University, Korea
HongSub Lee	Soonchunhyang University, Korea
KwanJo Kim	SKAIST, Korea

General Committee

Heung-Youl Youm	Soonchunhyang University, Korea

Steering Committee

ChangSub Park	Dankook University, Korea
KyoIl Chung	ETRI, Korea
JaeCheol Ryou	Chungnam National University, Korea
Kiwook Sohn	NSRI, Korea
KyungHyune Rhee	Pukyoung National University, Korea
JungDuk Kim	Chungang University, Korea
DaeWoo Park	Hoseo University, Korea
BeomSoo Kim	Yonsei University, Korea
SungTaek Chi	NSRI, Korea
JinHo Hahm	ETRI, Korea
HongGeun Kim	KISA, Korea

Organizing Committee

Chair

Jihong Kim	Semyung University, Korea

Members

TaeNam Cho	Woosuk University, Korea
HeuiSu Ryu	Gyeongin National University of Education, Korea
JaeMo Seung	Financial Security Agency, Korea
DaeSung Kwon	NSRI, Korea
JeongSik Park	TTA, Korea
JungTae Kim	Mokwon University, Korea
HaeSuk Kim	MOPAS, Korea
ChangKyu Kim	Dongeui University, Korea
JongSoo Jang	ETRI, Korea
SukLae Lee	KISA, Korea
DongGook Park	Sunchon National University, Korea
Seok Lae Lee	KISA, Korea

Program Committee

Co-chairs

Souhwan Jung	Soongsil University, Korea
Moti Yung	Columbia University and Google Inc., USA

Members

Gail-Joon Ahn	Arizona State University, USA
Joonsang Baek	Institute for Infocomm Research, Singapore
Rodrigo Roman Castro	University of Malaga, Spain
Kefei Chen	Shanghai Jiaotong University, China
Yongwha Chung	Korea University, Korea
Debbie Cook	Telcordia Technologies Inc., USA
Ed Dawson	University of Technology, Australia
Jun Furukawa	NEC, Japan
David Galindo	University of Luxembourg, Luxembourg
Dieter Gollmann	TU Hamburg, Germany
JaeCheol Ha	Hoseo University, Korea
Seokhie Hong	CIST, Korea
Jiankun Hu	RMIT, Australia
Seung Wook Jung	KISA, Korea
Namhi Kang	Duksung Women's University, Korea
Hiroaki Kikuchi	Tokai University, Japan
Dong Kyue Kim	Hanyang University, Korea
Howon Kim	Pusan National University, Korea
Kwangjo Kim	KAIST, Korea
Seungjoo Kim	CIST, Korea University, Korea
Brian King	Indiana University, Purdue University, Indianapolis, USA
Seungjoo Kim	CIST, Korea University, Korea

Table of Contents

Practical Attacks on a Cryptosystem Proposed in Patent WO/2009/066313*

Gautham Sekar[1,**] and Bart Preneel[2,3]

[1] Temasek Laboratories, National University of Singapore,
5A, Engineering Drive 1, Singapore 117411, Singapore
[2] Department of Electrical Engineering ESAT/SCD-COSIC,
Katholieke Universiteit Leuven, Kasteelpark Arenberg 10, B-3001 Heverlee, Belgium
[3] Interdisciplinary Institute for BroadBand Technology (IBBT), Belgium
tslgs@nus.edu.sg, Bart.Preneel@esat.kuleuven.be

Abstract. A new cryptosystem is proposed in the international patent WO/2009/066313 by Artus. The symmetric-key primitive in the cryptosystem resembles a stream cipher. The system differs markedly from cryptosystems used today in that the secret key is changed with the plaintext. The patent does not discuss key management (generation, transmission) in sufficient detail. Some of the proposed methods for transmission of keys are highly insecure and an algorithm for key generation is missing. In this paper, we find that related-key attacks of negligibly low complexity (data/time) can result when certain (flawed) key generation algorithms are used. We also present a negligibly-low-complexity attack in a non-related-key setting. We hope that the results caution potential users of the cryptosystem.

Keywords: Cryptosystem, stream cipher, public-key cryptography, chaffing-and-winnowing, key management, cryptanalysis, related-key attack.

1 Introduction

A new cryptosystem is proposed by Artus in [2]. The design is covered by the following patents: international (WO/2009/066313), US (US 2010/0153723), European (EP 2183875), Australian (AU 2008327506), Canadian (CA 2695019), Indian (1456/MUM/2007) and Russian (national reference number 2010104728). The Russian patent document is not yet publicly available. So far, to the best of our knowledge, there is no cryptanalysis result on this cryptosystem in the open literature.

---

* This work was supported in part by the IAP Program P6/26 BCRYPT of the Belgian State (Belgian Science Policy), and in part by the European Commission through the ICT program under contract ICT-2007-216676 ECRYPT II.
** Part of this work was performed during the authors PhD research at ESAT/SCD-COSIC, Katholieke Universiteit Leuven.

S. Jung and M. Yung (Eds.): WISA 2011, LNCS 7115, pp. 1–12, 2012.
© Springer-Verlag Berlin Heidelberg 2012

The cryptosystem (as it is not named in [2], we call it Γ) consists of a key distribution mechanism and a symmetric-key primitive. The latter is a stream cipher-like construction; for conciseness, henceforth, we shall call it a stream cipher. The system significantly differs from cryptosystems used today. The secret key of the stream cipher is changed with every new message (plaintext). It is not clear to us what the designer means by 'new message' – there is no specific message length mentioned in [2]. The designer proposes some means for the initial key exchange between the sender and the receiver (e.g., via SMS, without any mention about encryption) and assumes that these are secure. Even though the designer notes that one could use "other means" (see [2]) to securely initiate communication, there is not a single mention of public-key cryptography (PKC).

Besides, the patent just mentions that the keys are changed in a random manner but fails to mention how. Performance estimates are also missing. Since keys are changed so often, the key generation algorithm and performance figures are extremely vital. Also required in [2] are the targeted applications for which the cryptosystem has been designed, and a more detailed security evaluation. Looking at the design, we presume that the proposed system is intended for software-oriented applications.

In this paper, we first point out problems associated with some of the proposed methods in [2] to initiate communication between the sender and the receiver. Following this, we present other attacks assuming that PKC is used to exchange the initial keys. The attacks work in both a related-key setting and otherwise, under some very reasonable assumptions.

In the non-related-key setting, we present an attack that recovers one plaintext bit from the corresponding ciphertext bit in nearly zero time. This attack results from the way in which decimal-to-binary conversions are performed in [2]. When decimal numbers are converted to binary and stored in (fixed-length) registers, some of the most significant bits may be zeroes (we call them *leading zeroes*). In [2], leading zeroes are discarded while converting decimal numbers to binary, thereby ensuring that the most significant bits of the (truncated) binary numbers are all ones.

The related-key attacks result when certain key generation algorithms are used (the patent does not provide any algorithm for key generation). Each of these attacks requires only 2 plaintext-ciphertext pairs[1] and negligible time to recover a key or key-dependent information with guaranteed success. As the key is changed with every new message, related-key attacks are important to be addressed. In a way, this paper tells one how not to use the proposed cryptosystem, especially with respect to key management.

Another motive behind this work is to caution potential users of the cryptosystem. The practical nature of the attacks presented in this paper seems to suggest that WO/2009/066313 has no industrial applicability, as opposed to what the international search report of the patent claims. Given that the system is covered by 7 patents, it may not be unreasonable to imagine that there

---

[1] Here, the term *plaintext* or *ciphertext* may have a connotation. This point is explained further in the paper.

would be several potential buyers (and maybe even current users). To further substantiate this point, we take the example of KeeLoq [9]. The block cipher KeeLoq is a proprietary algorithm used in remote keyless entry systems. It was designed in South Africa in the mid 1980's by researchers who had little or no prior record of designing cryptographic algorithms. The cipher was sold to Microchip Technology Inc. and subsequently used by companies such as Chrysler, Daewoo, Fiat, General Motors, Honda, Toyota, Volvo, Volkswagen Group, Clifford and Jaguar [9,15]. In the last few years, several researchers had analysed the cipher [15], and a practical attack was published in 2008 [6].

Organisation: The paper is organised as follows. Section 2 lists the notation and convention used throughout the paper. In Sect. 3, we detail the specifications of the cryptosystem Γ. In Sect. 4, we discuss the issue of initial key exchange between the sender and the receiver. Assuming the exchange has been performed securely, Sect. 5 presents some observations which are converted into practical attacks in Sect. 6. Finally, we conclude in Sect. 7 where we also provide some directions for future work.

2   Notation and Convention

The notation and convention used in this paper are listed in Table 1.

Table 1. Notation and convention

Symbol / Notation	Meaning
$\oplus$	Bitwise XOR
$\|$	Concatenation
LSB	Least significant bit
MSB	Most significant bit
$\beta_{i(x)}$	Bit x of β_i, $x = 0$ denotes the LSB of β_i
$\beta_{i(x)}^c$	Bit-complement of $\beta_{i(x)}$
$len(m)$	Length of m in bits[†]
KP	Known plaintext
CP	Chosen plaintext

[†]It is not mentioned in [2] whether the leading zeroes are discarded while coding $len(m)$ in binary.

3   Description of the Cryptosystem

The stream cipher (as it is not named in [2], we call it E) uses keys that are sufficiently long to thwart brute force attacks. The designer, however, does not recommended any particular key size. The internal state of E consists of an array A that stores N digits chosen arbitrarily from the decimal representation of π. We denote the array by $A[0, \ldots, N-1]$. It is not mentioned in [2] whether this array is secret or not. Despite this, we present in this paper attacks that recover the secret key or plaintext without the attacker knowing $A[0, \ldots, N-1]$. The key (or seed) is a 4-tuple (K_1, K_2, K_3, K_4) where:

1. K_1 is an arbitrarily chosen array index such that $0 \leq K_1 \leq N - 1$,
2. K_2 is a number that uniquely corresponds to a subset of r elements ($r \geq \sqrt{N}$) of $A[0, \ldots, N-1]$ (i.e., $1 \leq K_2 \leq C(N, r)$),
3. K_3 is a number that uniquely corresponds to an ordering of the r elements determined by K_2 (i.e., $1 \leq K_3 \leq r!$)
4. K_4 determines how consecutive decimal digits in the r-element ordered list are concatenated; $1 \leq K_4 \leq 2^{r-1}$.

We call each of these four components of the seed as subkey. According to [2], the seed is "dynamically" changed, in a random manner, for every message sent. To initiate communication between the sender (Alice) and the receiver (Bob), a mechanism is proposed. The text in the paper, that describes this mechanism, is not entirely clear to us and we believe that the designer may have been inspired by chaffing-and-winnowing [12]. The technique proposed in [2] does not employ a MAC algorithm; so it is definitely not chaffing-and-winnowing.

Alice first sends a file (a pilot-file according to [2]) to Bob. This file contains a long string of random-looking numbers of which the initial seed is a part. The following assumption is made by the designer.

Assumption 1: An algorithm to locate the initial seed, using four numbers, in the string of random numbers of the pilot-file is known to both Alice and Bob, but not to an eavesdropper (Mallory). ☐

We denote the Algorithm in Assumption 1 by L and the four numbers by the tuple $(\alpha_1, \alpha_2, \alpha_3, \alpha_4)$. This 4-tuple is now sent by Alice, separately, by "Text, SMS or other means" [2].

The seed for the second message is encrypted using the first seed and then sent to Bob. The seed for the third message is encrypted using the second seed, and so on.

Figure 1 shows the working of the cipher E. The key (K_1, K_2, K_3, K_4) first produces an ordered decimal number list (ODNL). The numbers in the list are converted to binary and the resultant bit strings are concatenated to give a single concatenated bit string (CBS). Let *extended message (plaintext)* denote the message (plaintext) concatenated with the seed that is intended to be used to encrypt the next message. The CBS is truncated if it is longer than the ex- tended message.[2] The (truncated) keystream is then XOR-ed with the extended message to yield the *extended ciphertext*. Figure 2 illustrates, with an example, the generation of the extended ciphertext. The extended ciphertext is split into two parts of variable lengths. A concatenation is then performed, where the length (in bits) of the plaintext is placed between the two parts of the extended

---

[2] Details on how the truncation is done are missing in [2].

ciphertext. The resultant bitstream is transmitted to Bob. It is assumed by the designer that Bob (not Mallory) knows

- where the length of the plaintext is placed, i.e., the starting point of the bit string representing the length of the plaintext (*starting point*, hereafter) in the bit string of the extended ciphertext,
- the length (in bits) of the length of the plaintext.

Again, it is not mentioned in [2] whether the leading zeroes are discarded while coding the length of the length of the plaintext (from the length of the plaintext) in binary. Since it is an algorithm that is a part of Γ, by the Shannon's maxim [14], it is known to Mallory. Similarly, Mallory knows whether the leading zeroes are discarded while coding the length of the plaintext (from the plaintext) in binary.

Figure 3 shows the working of the cryptosystem Γ with a fixed starting point that immediately follows the LSB of the extended ciphertext. In this figure, $E_{\beta_1}(m_1\|\beta_2)$ is the output of stream cipher encryption, using the key β_1, of the message m_1 concatenated with the key β_2 (which is used to encrypt the next message m_2).

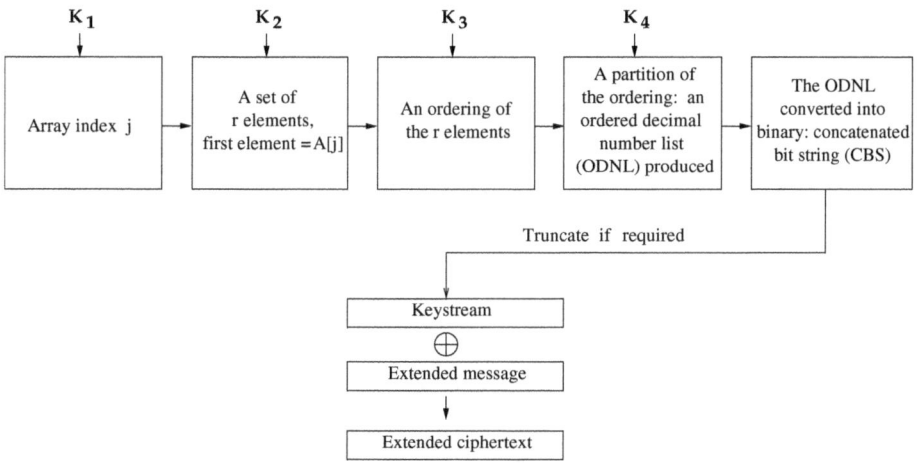

Fig. 1. Encrypting a plaintext message with E under key (K_1, K_2, K_3, K_4)

4 A Trivial Attack on the Cryptosystem Γ

In this section, we outline a trivial attack on the cryptosystem Γ. Recall that the algorithm L is known only to Alice and Bob. A risk that this poses is when the secret algorithm is reverse engineered later and found to be insecure. For example, the stream cipher RC4 was a trade secret for several years before it was reverse engineered in 1994 and leaked to the Cypherpunks mailing list and

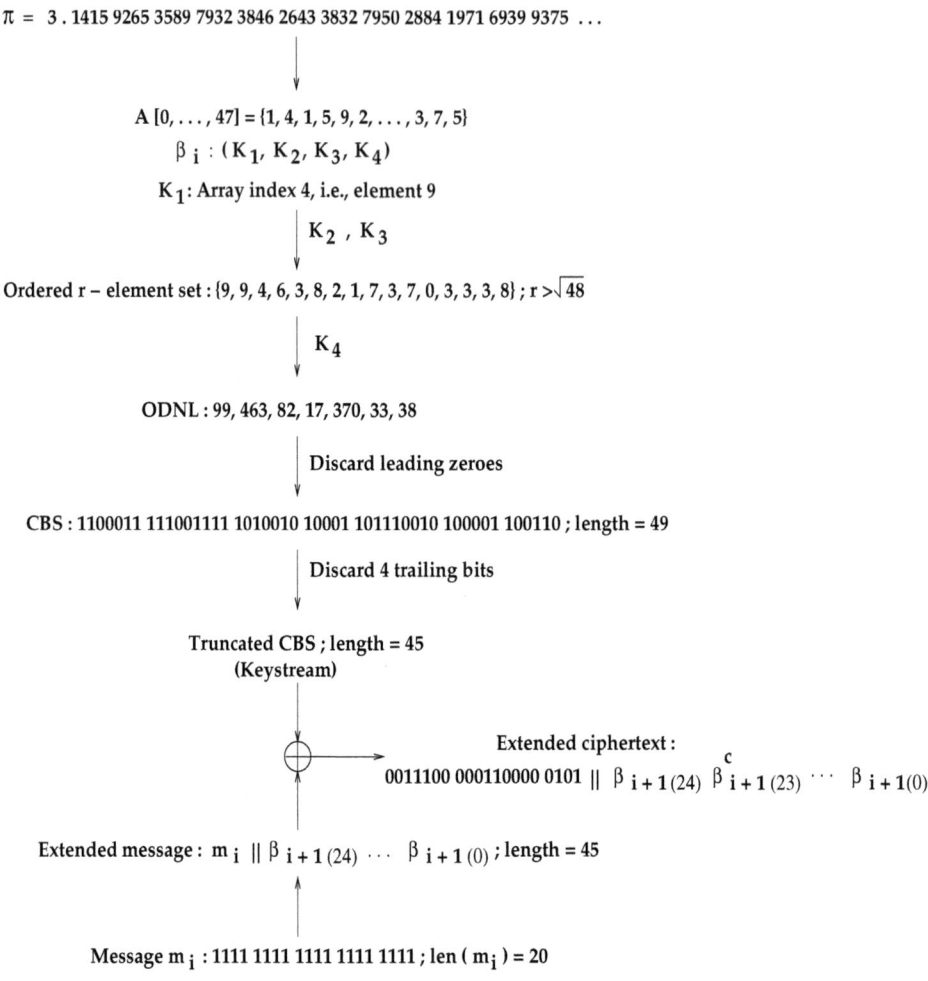

Fig. 2. An example (similar to the example in [2]) to illustrate the generation of the extended ciphertext; in this example, while truncating the CBS, the redundant trailing bits are discarded (while 4 leading bits could have instead been discarded)

the Usenet newsgroup sci.crypt [1]. Following this, the cipher witnessed several attacks some of which are listed in [8].

By Shannon's maxim, L is known to Mallory. Given this, she can obtain the initial seed from the pilot-file using $(\alpha_1, \alpha_2, \alpha_3, \alpha_4)$. The pilot-file and $(\alpha_1, \alpha_2, \alpha_3, \alpha_4)$ may be obtained by Mallory if these are sent through an insecure channel by Alice without encrypting properly. This sometimes applies to, for example, sending raw data by SMS. Though GSM phones support ciphers like A5/1, A5/2 and A5/3, in some countries encryption is disabled. Besides, practical attacks have been found in the A5/1 and A5/2 ciphers [3,5]. Messaging via SMS has some other security vulnerabilities due to its store-and-forward feature.

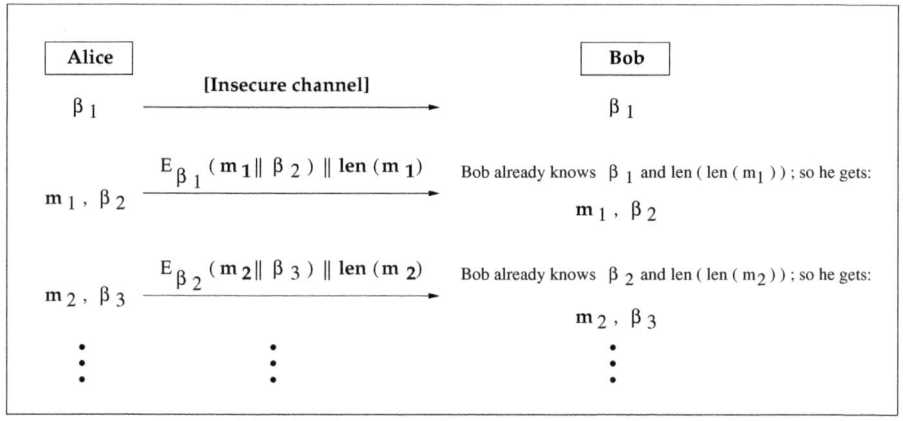

Fig. 3. Working of the cryptosystem Γ; β_1 may be securely transmitted across the insecure channel through the use of PKC

The problem can be overcome if PKC (Diffie-Hellman protocol [4], RSA [11], or elliptic curve cryptography [7,10]) is one of the "other means" (see Sect. 3) of communicating the initial seed to Bob in [2]. Chaffing-and-winnowing is another technique that could be used to achieve confidentiality without performing encryption. However, if this technique were to be used, a MAC algorithm is required (HMAC-SHA1 has been suggested in [12]) and its secret key is shared by the sender and receiver using PKC (e.g., authenticated Diffie-Hellman key exchange). Chaffing-and-winnowing is primarily used to thwart attempts by law enforcement to regulate confidentiality by regulating encryption.

Even when the initial keys are exchanged securely, regardless of the technique used, we find the system Γ to contain serious weaknesses. We describe these in Sects. 5 and 6.

In this paper, we construct a couple of attacks (in Sect. 6) under the following assumption.

Assumption 2: The bit string representing the length of the plaintext trails the LSB of the extended ciphertext.   □

With every message, if Alice were to provide the corresponding starting point securely to Bob, then she needs to use PKC. But doing so would make the scheme very slow for practical usage. To solve this, Alice and Bob can, alternatively, agree on one fixed starting point – for example, immediately following the LSB of the extended ciphertext (as in Figure 3). To agree on a single starting point value, Alice can enter it into the pilot file, extend the tuple $(\alpha_1, \alpha_2, \alpha_3, \alpha_4)$ to $(\alpha_1, \alpha_2, \alpha_3, \alpha_4, \alpha_5)$ and modify the algorithm L accordingly. Now,

- if the pilot file and the 5-tuple $(\alpha_1, \alpha_2, \alpha_3, \alpha_4, \alpha_5)$ are sent to Bob through an insecure channel without encrypting properly (e.g., via SMS), then Mallory may obtain the starting point when she knows L.

– Assume that PKC is used to transmit the pilot file and $(\alpha_1, \alpha_2, \alpha_3, \alpha_4, \alpha_5)$. Even then, for a transmitted bit string of length d, the probability that Mallory correctly guesses the starting point, without knowing the length of the plaintext, is at least $1/d$. The probability is high when d is small.
– In the preceding case, if Mallory knows the length of the plaintext $(len(m)$, say), then she can search for the bit string in the string of bits transmitted by Alice. There are at most $d - len(len(m)) + 1$ matches;[3] therefore, the probability that Eve correctly guesses the starting point is at least $1/(d - len(len(m)) + 1)$. Again, the probability is high when d is small.

In these scenarios, therefore, Assumption 2 is reasonable. But even if this assumption is not made, it is possible to attack Γ. We present this attack in Sect. 6.

5   Motivational Observations

We continue our analysis, starting with the following observations. Let m_i and β_i $(i \geq 1)$ respectively denote the i-th message and the seed used to encrypt it. The initial seed is β_1.

Observation 1: Let $\beta_i \leftarrow (K_1, K_2, K_3, K_4)$ and $\beta_j \leftarrow (K_1, K_2, K_3, K_4')$, where $K_4' \neq K_4$. Then, regardless of relation between K_4 and K_4', the LSBs of the CBSs produced by the two keys are identical.

Observation 2: Let us consider the following two scenarios.

Scenario 1: Consider $\beta_i \leftarrow (K_1, K_2, K_3, K_4)$ and $\beta_j \leftarrow (K_1, K_2', K_3', K_4')$, $j > i$, where K_2', K_3' and K_4' are such that the ODNL obtained using β_j is a list that is formed by appending numbers to the ODNL obtained using β_i. Let $len(m_i||\beta_{i+1}) = len(m_j||\beta_{j+1})$. Then, we have the following observation.

Observation: If the truncation of the CBS is such that the redundant trailing bits are discarded, the keystreams corresponding to β_i and β_j are identical.

Scenario 2: Consider $\beta_i \leftarrow (K_1, K_2, K_3, K_4)$ and $\beta_j \leftarrow (K_1', K_2', K_3', K_4')$, $j > i$, where K_1', K_2', K_3' and K_4' are such that the ODNL obtained using β_j is a list that is formed by prefixing numbers to the ODNL obtained using β_i. Let $len(m_i||\beta_{i+1}) = len(m_j||\beta_{j+1})$. Then, we have the following observation.

Observation: If the truncation of the CBS is such that the redundant leading bits are discarded, the keystreams corresponding to β_i and β_j are identical.[4]

---

[3] This upper bound is reached only when the transmitted bits are all ones or all zeroes; hence, one *expects* fewer matches. Our analysis, therefore, is worst-case with respect to the attacker.

[4] Since [2] does not discuss how the truncation of the CBS is done, it is not possible to tell which of the two scenarios results in identical keystreams. This is also the reason why we rule out the possibility that bits are discarded from the middle of a CBS.

Observation 3: Given Assumption 2, if β_i and $len(len(m_i))$ are known to Mallory, she can obtain m_i and β_{i+1} (see Figure 3).

6   Attacks Due to Weaknesses in the Stream Cipher

In this section, we present several attacks on the cryptosystem that stem from flawed key management techniques and weaknesses in the underlying stream cipher. We use the observations of Sect. 5.

6.1   Attacks in a Related-Key Setting

In a related-key setting, we present the following two attacks.

Attack 1: In this attack, Mallory obtains key-dependent information from message-dependent information. We begin with Observation 1. Suppose that the identical LSBs (denote them by b) of the CBSs produced by β_i and β_j are in the keystream (i.e., only the redundant leading bits of the CBS are discarded).[5] Given Assumption 2, if $len(len(m_i))$ and $len(len(m_j))$ are known to Mallory, she knows $\beta_{i+1(0)} \oplus b$ and $\beta_{j+1(0)} \oplus b$. From these two values, she obtains key-dependent information in the form of $\beta_{i+1(0)} \oplus \beta_{j+1(0)}$. Often, in practice, Mallory knows $len(m_i)$ or m_i, so she can compute $len(len(m_i))$. Therefore, to mount this attack, Mallory only requires the lengths of two plaintexts, or 2 KPs and the corresponding intercepted texts (i.e., extended ciphertexts concatenated respectively with the lengths of the plaintexts).

Attack 2: This attack works as follows. Consider the case when β_1 and β_2 are such that the keystreams they produce are identical (i.e., as in Observation 2). First, Mallory collects $E_{\beta_1}(m_1 || \beta_2)$, using the knowledge of $len(m_1)$ or m_1 itself. Now, Mallory forces Alice to encrypt a message of Mallory's choice, of length equal to $len(m_1 || \beta_2)$ (e.g., message with $len(m_1 || \beta_2)$ zero-bits).[6] Alice encrypts this new message with the key β_2. Since Mallory has chosen the plaintext message, she has its length and hence obtains the keystream that is produced by β_1 (since the keystreams produced by β_2 and β_1 are identical). Using this, the $len(m_1)$ and $E_{\beta_1}(m_1 || \beta_2)$, she recovers β_2. The attack requires 1 KP (or 1 message length), 1 CP (in which the 'plaintext' is actually 'extended plaintext'), the corresponding intercepted texts, and negligible time.

The attacker can continue recovering subsequent messages and keys. For example, after recovering β_2, given the message length $len(m_2)$, the message m_2 and the key β_3 can be obtained. Subsequently, using β_3 and $len(m_3)$, she can recover m_3 and β_4; and so on.

---

[5] The manner in which the CBS is truncated would normally be a part of the algorithm that is known to the attacker; hence, it is reasonable to assume that Mallory knows whether the leading or the trailing bits are discarded.

[6] In this paper, we use the placeholder name *Mallory* in place of the more common *Eve* because the attacker is not completely passive in Attack 2 (see also [13]).

6.2   Attacks in a Non-Related-Key Setting

The stream cipher can also be attacked in a non-related-key setting. The attack works as follows.

Attack 3: In the example given in [2], while the CBS is formed from the ODNL, the leading zeroes of each number in the ODNL are discarded. When Γ works this way, the MSB of the keystream is 1 if the leading bits of the CBS are not discarded while forming the keystream (i.e., only the redundant trailing bits of the CBS are discarded). Given that the MSB of the keystream is 1, Mallory computes the MSB of the plaintext by complementing the MSB of the intercepted text. This attack recovers only one plaintext bit from the corresponding ciphertext bit, but requires practically zero time.

Even if Mallory does not know where the $len(m_i)$ is inserted in the intercepted text (i.e., Assumption 2 is not made), she can mount Attack 3. If she knows $len(len(m_i))$ or $len(m_i)$, she can conclude that the recovered bit is a plaintext bit with probability $p \geq 1-1/(d-len(len(m_i))+1)$ (see Sect. 4). This probability is high because of the following argument. The minimum length of β_{i+1} is 4 bits because it has 4 subkeys. Since $d = len(len(m_i)) + len(m_i) + len(\beta_{i+1})$, for a zero-length message, $d \geq 5$. Therefore, for any message, $d - len(len(m_i)) + 1 \geq 5 \Rightarrow p \geq 0.8$. This attack, in addition to the requirements of Attack 3, requires message-dependent information in the form of $len(len(m_i))$ or $len(m_i)$. The success probability is at least 0.8.

Attack 3 works regardless of whether the array $A[0, \ldots, N-1]$ is secret or not. The same is the case with the attack in Sect. 4 and Attacks 1 and 2. However, for Mallory to recover a message m_i using a recovered key β_i, she needs to know $A[0, \ldots, N-1]$ to compute the keystream.

Attacks Due to a Poor Choice of the Array: Depending on how the array $A[0, \ldots, N-1]$ is chosen, we may have more attacks. For example, let us consider the following array containing elements from around the Feynman point in the decimal number sequence of π:

$$A[0, \ldots, 20] = \{9, 9, 6, 0, 5, 1, 8, 7, 0, 7, 2, 1, 1, 3, 4, 9, 9, 9, 9, 9, 9\}.$$

Let $r = 17$. The number of possibilities for the key is $21 \cdot C(21, 17) \cdot 17! \cdot 2^{16} \approx 2^{81.3}$ – this is high enough to make a straightforward exhaustive key search nearly infeasible in practice. Suppose that the array is public. Since there are 6 even numbers in the array and $r = 17$, the number of odd numbers in the ODNL is at least 11. If there are exactly t odd numbers ($1 \leq t \leq 11$) in the ODNL, the probability that an odd number is the last digit in the ODNL is $t/17$. Therefore, the probability that the last digit in the ODNL is odd is at least $11/17$. In other words, given that redundant trailing bits are not discarded during truncation of the CBS, the probability that the LSB of the extended ciphertext is complemented during transmission is at least $11/17$. One may, alternatively, exploit the presence of the unusually many 9's in the array in some clever manner. It may not be common for the users of the system to choose such number sequences, but a smaller bias may result when the array contains unequal numbers of even and odd digits (note that the array need not contain contiguous digits from the decimal representation of π).

7   Conclusions and Open Problems

In this paper, we presented several attacks on a cryptosystem patented by Artus [2]. The attacks are of extremely low data complexity and require nearly zero time. We also point out a major weakness in the key exchange scheme proposed in [2]. It is hoped that the results of this paper have shed light on how not to design ciphers and how the proposed cryptosystem has to be used in practice.

The patent also proposes a so-called "embodiment" of the cryptosystem in which Alice, instead of encrypting keys along with plaintexts, transmits the keys as pilot-messages. One can immediately see that this embodiment is also vulnerable to the attack of Sect. 4 and Attack 3 of Sect. 6.

While it seems that some of the attacks presented in this paper could be easily averted (e.g., by using PKC for key exchange), it is also possible that there are better attacks in a non-related-key setting. As the flaws pointed out in this paper are serious enough, there was not enough motivation for us to work further in the non-related-key setting. However, if the cryptosystem is tweaked in future, so as to thwart the attacks in this paper, a more detailed analysis may be worthwhile carrying out.

Acknowledgements. The authors would like to thank Vincent Rijmen and Nicky Mouha for their useful comments and suggestions.

References

1. Anonymous, Thank you Bob Anderson, Cypherpunks mailing list (1994), `http://web.archive.org/web/20080120083537/`, `http://cypherpunks.venona.com/date/1994/09/msg00304.html`
2. Artus, R.G.C.: Method and System for Encryption of Data. International Patent, publication number WO/2009/066313 (May 28, 2009), `http://www.wipo.int/pctdb/en/wo.jsp?WO=2009066313`
3. Barkan, E., Biham, E., Keller, N.: Instant Ciphertext-Only Cryptanalysis of GSM Encrypted Communication. In: Boneh, D. (ed.) CRYPTO 2003. LNCS, vol. 2729, pp. 600–616. Springer, Heidelberg (2003)
4. Diffie, W., Hellman, M.E.: New Directions in Cryptography. IEEE Transactions on Information Theory 22, 644–654 (1976)
5. Goldberg, I., Wagner, D., Green, L.: The (Real-Time) Cryptanalysis of A5/2. In: rump session CRYPTO 1999 (1999)
6. Indesteege, S., Keller, N., Dunkelman, O., Biham, E., Preneel, B.: A Practical Attack on KeeLoq. In: Smart, N.P. (ed.) EUROCRYPT 2008. LNCS, vol. 4965, pp. 1–18. Springer, Heidelberg (2008)
7. Koblitz, N.: Elliptic curve cryptosystems. Mathematics of Computation 48, 203–209 (1987)

8. Mantin, I.: RC4 (2002),
   http://www.wisdom.weizmann.ac.il/~itsik/RC4/rc4.html
9. Microchip Technology Inc., KeeLoq Authentication Products (2009),
   http://www.microchip.com/keeloq/
10. Miller, V.S.: Use of Elliptic Curves in Cryptography. In: Williams, H.C. (ed.)
    CRYPTO 1985. LNCS, vol. 218, pp. 417–426. Springer, Heidelberg (1986)
11. Rivest, R.L., Shamir, A., Adleman, L.M.: A Method for Obtaining Digital Signa-
    tures and Public-Key Cryptosystems. Communications of the ACM 21(2), 120–126
    (1978)
12. Rivest, R.L.: Chaffing and Winnowing: Confidentiality without Encryption (April
    1998), http://people.csail.mit.edu/rivest/Chaffing.txt
13. Schneier, B.: Applied Cryptography, 2nd edn. John Wiley & Sons (1996)
14. Shannon, C.E.: Communication Theory of Secrecy Systems. Bell System Technical
    Journal 28-4, 656–715 (1949)
15. Wikipedia, KeeLoq (July 2010), http://en.wikipedia.org/wiki/KeeLoq

Generalized Security Analysis of the Random Key Bits Leakage Attack

Jun Kogure[1], Noboru Kunihiro[2], and Hirosuke Yamamoto[2]

[1] Fujitsu Laboratories Ltd.,
4-1-1 Kamikodanaka, Nakahara-ku, Kawasaki, 211-8588, Japan
[2] The University of Tokyo
5-1-5 Kashiwanoha, Kashiwa-shi, Chiba, 277-8561, Japan

Abstract. In CRYPTO 2009, Heninger and Shacham presented a new method of recovering RSA private keys bit by bit given a fraction of private data, and analyzed resistance of RSA against the attack. They obtained a system of relations between RSA private variables and calculated the expected number of solution candidates. As they dealt with only RSA case, we consider the case that the system of equations is given in more general linear form. We show that the complexity of their attack depends only on the number of variables, the number of *ambiguous* variables, and the *degree of freedom*. As concrete examples, we apply the attack to Paillier cryptosystem and Takagi's variant of RSA, and analyze their resistance against the attack. In Pailiier's case, its resistance is almost the same as the case when a fraction of three private RSA keys are leaked. In Takagi's case, we find that the asymmetricity in two factors of the modulus give some effects on the resistance against the attack.

Keywords: Cold boot attack, random key bits leakage attack, Paillier cryptosystem, Takagi's variant of RSA.

1 Introduction

In USENIX security 2008, Halderman et al.[4] reported that memory remanence times can be increased with simple cooling techniques and that successful attacks on popular disk encryption systems can be mounted using the techniques. In the scenario of their "cold boot attack", it is assumed that some random part of secret data, e.g. private key bits, are leaked, and the attacker can utilize them to reveal the whole secret.

In CRYPTO 2009, Heninger and Shacham[6] presented a new method of recovering RSA private keys bit by bit, when random 27% of private key bits are given. Their method is based on multivariate Hensel's lemma, and they calculated the expected number of possible solution bit assignments generated from assignments at previous bit slice level, using theory of probability generating function.

There are two main directions in this research area, one of which is to construct a cryptosystem that is resilient to key leakage, and the other is to evaluate

S. Jung and M. Yung (Eds.): WISA 2011, LNCS 7115, pp. 13–27, 2012.

the security of existing cryptosystems against this kind of attack[9,2,6,7,5]. This paper belongs to the latter way. By applying Heninger-Shacham method to other cryptosystems, we can get relations of the variables corresponding to the private keys of those cryptosystems. Heninger and Shacham[6] only deal with the case of RSA cryptosystems in their security analysis. In cases of other cryptosystems, the system of equations differs from that of RSA, and this could cause differences in the analysis of their attack complexity.

Our Contributions : We make analysis of their attack complexity when the system of equations is given by linear equations of more general form. We show that the expected number of solution candidates generated from the correct assignment at previous bit slice level is determined by the degree of freedom and the number of variables that have freedom. We also show that the expected number of solution candidates generated from wrong solution candidates at previous bit slice level is determined by the number of variables and the degree of freedom. Using our results, we can immediately calculate the attack complexity once we get linear equations of other cryptosystems. Further, as the complexity of this attack is dominated by the expected number of solution candidates generated from wrong solution candidates at previous bit slice level, we know that the number of variables and the degree of freedom are crucial to determine the total complexity of the attack.

As concrete examples, we apply the attack to Paillier cryptosystem[8] and Takagi's variant of RSA[10], and make analysis of the attack complexity. Paillier cryptosystem draws much attention recently because of its additive homomorphic property and its potential in cloud computing environment, hence it would be worthwhile to analyze its security against various kinds of recent attacks. In Paillier cryptosystem's case, we need four variables to describe the relations of private keys. By showing a method to find the value of one of the variables, we can reduce the number of variables to three and can launch the attack if we assume that these three keys are partially leaked. Hence the resistance of Paillier cryptosystem against the attack is almost the same as the case that three private keys of RSA (two factors of its modulus and one private exponent) are partially leaked.

Takagi's variant of RSA and some other cryptosystems attract interests because of their asymmetricity in two factors of the modulus. By applying Heninger-Shacham attack to Takagi's variant of RSA, we find that different phenomenon arises because of its asymmetricity. It uses the modulus $p^m q$ instead of pq for the improvement of decryption performance. When m is even, one of the relations of unknown variables differs from corresponding relation of RSA case, because we consider the relation modulo 2 and partial differentiation of $p^m q$ regarding p vanishes when m is even. This makes the complexity of the attack larger than RSA case. When m is odd, the relations of unknown variables are almost the same as RSA, and the smaller bit length of the secret factor p, q of Takagi's case reduces total complexity of the attack. These phenomena indicate that from the view point of resistance against Heninger-Shacham attack, we had better use even number m in Takagi's variant of RSA.

In Section 2 we briefly look over the previous results and mathematical background. In Section 3 we give a proof to our statement, and in Section 4 we apply the attack to Paillier cryptosystem and analyze its security. In Section 5, we also apply the attack to Takagi's variant of RSA and compare the security of RSA and Takagi's variant against the attack.

2 Preliminaries

2.1 Random Key Bits Leakage Attack

In this subsection we look over Heninger-Shacham method [6] of reconstructing RSA private key bits. Let N be an RSA n-bit modulus and let p, q be its prime factors. Let e be the public exponent, d be the private exponent, d_p and d_q denote $d \pmod{p-1}$ and $d \pmod{q-1}$ respectively. We have four equations as follows

$$N = pq \tag{1}$$
$$ed = k(N - p - q + 1) + 1 \tag{2}$$
$$ed_p = k_p(p-1) + 1 \tag{3}$$
$$ed_q = k_q(q-1) + 1. \tag{4}$$

Here k, k_p, k_q are unknowns, but in case e is small enough these values can be obtained. Let $\tau(x)$ denote the exponent of the largest power of 2 that divides x. And let $x[i]$ denote the $(i+1)$-st least significant bit (hereafter LSB for short) of variable x. We know first $1, 1, 2 + \tau(k), 1 + \tau(k_p), 1 + \tau(k_q)$ bits of p, q, d, d_p, d_q, respectively. Let $p[i], q[i], d[i + \tau(k)], d_p[i + \tau(k_p)], d_q[i + \tau(k_q)]$ be the i-th bit slice of these unknown variables. Once i LSB's of p and q, $i + \tau(k)$ LSB's of d, $i + \tau(k_p)$ LSB's of d_p, $i + \tau(k_q)$ LSB's of d_q are obtained, we can have the $(i+1)$-st bit slice by using Hensel's lemma below. We can represent the $(i+1)$-st bit slice with the i-th bit slice as follows

$$p[i] + q[i] \equiv (N - p'q')[i] \tag{5}$$
$$d[i + \tau(k)] + p[i] + q[i] \equiv (k(N+1) + 1 - k(p' + q') - ed')[i + \tau(k)] \tag{6}$$
$$d_p[i + \tau(k_p)] + p[i] \equiv (k_p(p'-1) + 1 - ed_p')[i + \tau(k_p)] \tag{7}$$
$$d_q[i + \tau(k_q)] + q[i] \equiv (k_q(q'-1) + 1 - ed_q')[i + \tau(k_q)], \tag{8}$$

where equivalences are considered modulo 2, and x' denotes the i LSB's of variable x.

For example, as to equation (3), we use Hensel's lemma by defining function f as $f(p, d_p) = k_p(p-1) + 1 - ed_p$. By multiplying k_p, i-th bit of p affects $(i + \tau(k_p))$-th bit of $f(p, d_p)$. Hence, if we get i LSB's of p, we have a relation modulo $2^{i+\tau(k_p)}$ instead of modulo 2^i. Let $\mathbf{r} = (p', d_p')$ be a partial solution up to i LSB's of p and $i + \tau(k_p)$ LSB's of d_p. Then

$$f(\mathbf{r}) = f(p', d_p') \equiv 0 \pmod{2^{i+\tau(k_p)}},$$

and

$$\frac{f(\mathbf{r})}{2^{i+\tau(k_p)}} \pmod 2 = \frac{f(p', d_p')}{2^{i+\tau(k_p)}} \pmod 2$$

corresponds to $(i + \tau(k_p) + 1)$-st bit of $f(p', d_p')$, that is,

$$(k_p(p'-1) + 1 - ed_p')[i + \tau(k_p)].$$

And we have

$$f(p' + b_1 2^i, d_p' + b_2 2^{i+\tau(k_p)}) = k_p(p' + b_1 2^i - 1) + 1 - e(d_p' + b_2 2^{i+\tau(k_p)})$$
$$= k_p(p' - 1) + 1 - ed_p' + b_1 k_p 2^i - eb_2 2^{i+\tau(k_p)}.$$

In order that this is equivalent to $0 \pmod{2^{i+\tau(k_p)+1}}$,

$$f(p', d_p')[i + \tau(k_p)] + b_1 + b_2$$
$$\equiv (k_p(p'-1) + 1 - ed_p')[i + \tau(k_p)] + p[i] + d_p[i + \tau(k_p)]$$
$$\equiv 0 \pmod 2.$$

Hence we get the relation

$$d_p[i + \tau(k_p)] + p[i] \equiv (k_p(p'-1) + 1 - ed_p')[i + \tau(k_p)] \pmod 2,$$

as e is odd and k_p is a product of $2^{\tau(k_p)}$ and some odd number.

Together with the leaked information of private key bits, they claim that they can determine the remaining bits if the leakage ratio is more than 27%.

Lemma 1 (Hensel's Lemma (multivariate version)[6])
Let $f(x_1, x_2, ..., x_n) \in \mathbb{Z}[x_1, x_2, ..., x_n]$ be a multivariate polynomial with integer coefficients. Let π be a positive integer and $\mathbf{r} = (r_1, r_2, ..., r_n) \in \mathbb{Z}^n$ be a solution for $f(x_1, x_2, ..., x_n) \equiv 0 \pmod{\pi^i}$. Then $\mathbf{r}$ can be lifted to a root $\mathbf{r} + \mathbf{b} \pmod{\pi^{i+1}}$, if $\mathbf{b} = (b_1 \pi^i, b_2 \pi^i, ..., b_n \pi^i)$, $0 \leq b_j \leq \pi - 1$, satisfies

$$f(\mathbf{r}) + \sum_{j=1}^n b_j \pi^i f_{x_j}(\mathbf{r}) \equiv 0 \pmod{\pi^{i+1}}$$

where f_{x_j} is the partial derivative of f with respect to x_j, or equivalently

$$\frac{f(\mathbf{r})}{\pi^i} + \sum_{j=1}^n b_j f_{x_j}(\mathbf{r}) \equiv 0 \pmod{\pi}.$$

2.2   Branching Behavior

Heninger and Shacham made following considerations regarding as the branching behavior of solutions of the equations obtained in the first step of their RSA attack.

First we see how many incorrect solutions will be generated from a correct partial assignment. If the solution assignment up to level i is correct, the next bit of d is uniquely determined, hence this bit is correct. The variable p, q, d_p and d_q are ambiguous, but specified correctly from leakage information with probability δ respectively and independently. If none of the values are specified, we have two solutions as there are four variables and three equations. In this case one of them is the correct solution and the other is a wrong solution. If at least one of the values is specified, we have only the correct solution. Hereafter for a random variable X we denote the expected value of X by EX.

So if we let Z_g be a random variable that denotes the number of wrong solution at level $i+1$ generated from the correct assignment at level i, the expected value of Z_g is

$$EZ_g = 1 \times (1 - \delta)^4 + 0 \times (2\delta - \delta^2) = (1 - \delta)^4.$$

We also have $EZ_g^2 = (1 - \delta)^4$.

Next we consider how many wrong solutions are generated from wrong assignment at previous level. In order to analyze the probability of the existence of solutions, Heninger and Shacham made an assumption that the solution bit values appearing in the relations are uniformly distributed. We let W_b be a random variable denoting the number of wrong solutions at level $i + 1$ generated from a wrong solution at level i. The situation changes depending on which variable is specified by the leakage information. For example, in the case when one value is specified, if the specified variable is d, the probability that the value is correct is $\frac{1}{2}$ according to their assumption. If the value is correct, we have two solutions, and otherwise we have no solution. If the specified variable is p or d_p or q or d_q, one of two solutions will satisfy the constraint. So we have only one wrong solution. They did not give details, but calculated the value

$$EW_b = \frac{(2 - \delta)^5}{16},$$

which can be confirmed through minute classification.

Let X_i be a random variable that denotes the number of wrong assignments at level i. Using the theory of probability generating function, they proved

$$EX_i = \frac{EZ_g}{1 - EW_b}(1 - (EW_b)^i). \tag{9}$$

Hence when $EW_b < 1$, they can bound EX_i as

$$EX_i \leq \frac{EZ_g}{1 - EW_b}. \tag{10}$$

3 The Expected Number of Solution Candidates in General Cases

When we apply the attack to other cryptosystems, the equations obtained differ from those of RSA, hence we need another examinations of the expected values in the previous section, each time we obtain new equations. In order to avoid such examinations for each cryptosystem, we would like to know what determine these expected values, and would like to express the expected values explicitly when the system of equations is given in general form.

First we assume that the system of equations is given by linear equations of general form and that some of the unknown variables are determined uniquely from the previous bit slice level, and the others have the same *ambiguity*. That is, all these ambiguous variables can have any value (0 or 1) and if some fixed number of these variables are determined, the rest of these variables are uniquely determined. We call this fixed number as *degree of freedom*. Let r be the number of unknown variables, l be the number of ambiguous variables, and k be the degree of freedom. In order to describe this statement precisely, we can use the Dulmage-Mendelsohn decomposition of bipartite graph [3], which is a classical tool and is sometimes re-discovered. However, as the statement will get too complicated, we refer it to appendix A.

More generally, there may be cases that some of ambiguous variables have no relations with the other ambiguous variables. In these cases we can reduce the problem to the situation we consider now. See remark 1.

As to the number of wrong solutions generated from a correct solution, we have the following proposition.

Proposition 1. *Let the notations be as above. Let Z_g be a random variable that represents the number of wrong solutions at level $i + 1$ generated from a correct solution at level i. Let δ be the probability that a bit of one variable is correctly specified. Then the expected value of Z_g is*

$$\mathrm{E}Z_g = \sum_{j=0}^{k-1} \delta^j (1 - \delta)^{l-j} \binom{l}{j} (2^{k-j} - 1).$$

In particular, if $k = 1$, $\mathrm{E}Z_g = (1 - \delta)^l$.

Proof. Let j be the number of ambiguous variables whose bit at level $i + 1$ is specified. Then the number of solutions at level $i + 1$ generated from correct solution at level i is 2^{k-j}, among which there is only one correct solution. As the probability that the bit at level $i + 1$ of j variables out of l variables are specified, is $\delta^j (1 - \delta)^{l-j} \binom{l}{j}$. Hence the result holds.   □

In RSA case, only d is determined uniquely from previous bit slice level, and p, q, d_p, d_q are ambiguous variables. If one of these four values is specified, the rest of these values are uniquely determined. Hence we have $l = 4$, $k = 1$, and $\mathrm{E}Z_g = (1 - \delta)^4$.

As to the number of wrong solutions generated from a wrong solution at previous level, we have the following theorem if we make an assumption that the solution bit values appearing in the relations are uniformly distributed.

Theorem 1. *Let the notations be as above. Let W_b be a random variable that represents the number of wrong solutions at level $i+1$ generated from one wrong solution at level i. Let δ be the probability that a bit of one variable is correctly specified. We assume that when the assignment at level i is wrong, the probability of each variable of the concerning equations at level $i+1$ to be 0 is $\frac{1}{2}$. Then the expected value of W_b is*

$$\mathrm{E}W_b = \frac{(2-\delta)^r}{2^{r-k}}.$$

Proof. Let j be the number of variables whose bit at level $i+1$ is specified. Then the number of solutions at level $i + 1$ generated from a wrong solution at level i depends on how many of above j variables are ambiguous. Let j_0 denote the number. The probability that the level $i + 1$ bit of j_0 ambiguous variables and $j - j_0$ unambiguous variables are specified is

$$\binom{l}{j_0} \times \binom{r-l}{j-j_0} \times \delta^j (1-\delta)^{r-j}.$$

As we have correct values of j_0 ambiguous variables, the number of solutions is decreased to 2^{k-j_0}. We further have correct values of $j - j_0$ unambiguous variables. From the assumption the number of solutions will decreased to the factor $\frac{1}{2^{j-j_0}}$, and the number of solutions will be

$$2^{k-j_0} \times \frac{1}{2^{j-j_0}} = 2^{k-j}.$$

Hence the expected number of solutions when j variables are specified is

$$\sum_{j_0=0}^{j} 2^{k-j} \times \binom{l}{j_0} \times \binom{r-l}{j-j_0} \times \delta^j (1-\delta)^{r-j}$$

$$= 2^{k-j} \delta^j (1-\delta)^{r-j} \times \binom{r}{j}.$$

The total expected number of wrong solutions $\mathrm{E}W_b$ is

$$\sum_{j=0}^{r} 2^{k-j} \delta^j (1-\delta)^{r-j} \times \binom{r}{j} = 2^k ((\frac{\delta}{2}) + (1-\delta))^r = \frac{(2-\delta)^r}{2^{r-k}}.$$

□

In RSA case, as $r = 5$ and $k = 1$, $\mathrm{E}W_b = \frac{(2-\delta)^5}{2^4}$.

We showed that the expected number of solution candidates generated from the correct assignment at previous bit slice level is determined by the degree of freedom and the number of variables that have freedom. We also showed that the expected number of solution candidates generated from wrong solution candidates at previous bit slice level is determined by the number of variables and the degree of freedom. The difference between these cases is interpreted as follows. When the solution of previous bit level is correct, the next bit of unambiguous variable is already obtained, and it is useless if we get the next bit of unambiguous variable by leakage information. Hence the number of ambiguous variables matters in this case. In the latter case, as the solution of previous bit level is incorrect, generated solutions are also incorrect, and it doesn't matter which variables are specified by leakage information. When unambiguous variable is specified by the correct value, the probability it coincides with the solution candidate is $\frac{1}{2}$, hence it reduces the number of solution candidates with the same probability of ambiguous variable case.

Using these results, we can immediately calculate the attack complexity once we get linear equations of other cryptosystems. As the complexity of this attack is dominated by the expected number of solution candidates generated from wrong solution candidates at previous bit slice level, we know that the number of variables and the degree of freedom are crucial to determine the total complexity of the attack.

Remark 1. More generally, there may be cases some of ambiguous variables have no relations with the other ambiguous variables. For example, consider the case that relations are given in the following two equations

$$x_1[i] + x_2[i] = f_1(x_1', x_2', x_3', x_4', x_5')$$
$$x_3[i] + x_4[i] + x_5[i] = f_2(x_1', x_2', x_3', x_4', x_5').$$

We have two groups of ambiguous variables $\{x_1, x_2\}$ and $\{x_3, x_4, x_5\}$. The degree of freedom of the former is 1 and that of the latter is 2. In such cases, we let v be the number of these groups, l_u be the number of ambiguous variables in the u-th group, k_u be the degree of freedom of the u-th group, and $l = \sum_{u=1}^{v} l_u$. Theorem 1 holds if we replace k with $\sum_{u=1}^{v} k_u$. As to proposition 1 we have

$$EZ_g = \sum_{j=0}^{l} \delta^j (1-\delta)^{l-j} \sum_{\substack{(j_1,\cdots,j_v): \\ j_1+\cdots+j_v=j, 0 \le j_u \le k_u}} (\prod_{u=1}^{v} \binom{l_u}{j_u})(\prod_{u=1}^{v} 2^{k_u-j_u} - 1).$$

4 Application of the Attack to Paillier Cryptosystem

As a concrete example, we apply the attack to Paillier cryptosystem [8] in this section. Paillier cryptosystem draws much attention recently because of its homomorphic property, which will be useful in cloud computing environment. It would be worthwhile to apply the random key bits leakage attack to Paillier cryptosystem and analyze its security against the attack.

Let p and q be large primes of the same size, and let $N = pq$. Let $\lambda = \text{lcm}(p-1, q-1)$ and $c = \gcd(p-1, q-1)$. Usually p, q, and λ are kept private, and we assume that some random bits of these three parameters are leaked. A new relation we have in this case is

$$c\lambda = (p-1)(q-1). \tag{11}$$

Here we have another variable c and would like to eliminate it. In order to avoid the $p-1$ method, p and q are selected so that $p-1$ and $q-1$ are not smooth. Hence we can assume that c is fairly small. When c is small, we can determine the value of c as follows. From (11),

$$\lambda = \frac{(p-1)(q-1)}{c} = \frac{N+1-(p+q)}{c}.$$

Let $\hat{\lambda}(u) = \frac{N+1}{u}$ be a function of integer u. As

$$\hat{\lambda}(c) - \lambda = \frac{p+q}{c}$$

is much smaller than λ, we can exhaustively search c if c is small. Namely, if the leaked bits of λ coincide with $\hat{\lambda}(u)$ in the upper half for some u, that u will give the value of c.

Let $p-1 = cp_1$ and $q-1 = cq_1$, then $\lambda = cp_1q_1$. Let $c = 2^{\tau(c)}c_1$ and $\lambda = 2^{\tau(c)}\lambda_1$, then $\lambda_1 = c_1p_1q_1$ and c_1 is odd. If we put $p_2 = c_1p_1$ and $q_2 = c_1q_1$, then we have $p_2[i] = p[i+\tau(c)]$, $q_2[i] = q[i+\tau(c)]$, $\lambda_1[i] = \lambda[i+\tau(c)]$, and

$$c_1\lambda_1 = p_2q_2.$$

By applying Hensel's lemma, we have the relation

$$\lambda_1[i] + q_2'p_2[i] + p_2'q_2[i] \equiv (c_1\lambda_1' - \ddot{p}_2'q_2')[i] \pmod{2}.$$

In cases, where p_1 and q_1 are both odd, we have

$$\lambda_1[i] + p_2[i] + q_2[i] \equiv (c_1\lambda_1' - p_2'q_2')[i] \pmod{2}, \tag{12}$$

and this is equivalent to

$$\lambda[i+\tau(c)] + p[i+\tau(c)] + q[i+\tau(c)] \equiv (c_1\frac{\lambda'}{2^{\tau(c)}} - \frac{p'-1}{2^{\tau(c)}}\frac{q'-1}{2^{\tau(c)}})[i] \pmod{2}.$$

Together with the same relation (5) as RSA

$$p[i] + q[i] \equiv (N - p'q')[i],$$

we have three variables and two linear relations, and we see that λ is uniquely determined from the previous bit slice level. Applying our proposition 1 and theorem 1, we have the expected values $EZ_g = (1-\delta)^2$ and $EW_b = \frac{(2-\delta)^3}{2^2}$. In cases either p_1 or q_1 is even, $q_2[i]$ or $p_2[i]$ in the relation (12) vanishes respectively. In this case the expected value $EZ_g = (1-\delta)^3$.

Hence the resistance of Paillier cryptosystem against the attack is almost the same as the case that three private keys of RSA (two factors p,q of its modulus $N = pq$ and one private exponent d) are partially leaked.

5   Application of the Attack to Takagi's Variant of RSA

As another example, we consider applying the attack to a variant of RSA due to Takagi[10] in this section. It uses the modulus $N = p^m q$ instead of $N = pq$ for the improvement of decryption performance. Takagi's variant and some other cryptosystems attract interests because of their asymmetricity in two factors of the modulus. By applying the attack to Takagi's variant, we look into if this asymmetricity affects the security.

5.1   Relations of Variables

In Takagi's variant, we have four equations as follows

$$N = p^m q \tag{13}$$
$$ed = k(pq - p - q + 1) + 1 \tag{14}$$
$$ed_p = k_p(p - 1) + 1 \tag{15}$$
$$ed_q = k_q(q - 1) + 1. \tag{16}$$

As to equation (14), e and d are generated so that they satisfy the relation $ed \equiv 1 \pmod{L}$, where $L = \text{lcm}(p-1, q-1)$. Particularly, if $ed \equiv 1 \pmod{(p-1)(q-1)}$, the relation $ed \equiv 1 \pmod{L}$ is satisfied, and we consider this case hereafter for simplicity.

For equation (13), we apply Hensel's lemma (lemma 1). If we put $f(p, q) = N - p^m q$, then $f_p(p, q) = -mp^{m-1}q$, and $f_q(p, q) = -p^m$, where f_x denotes the partial differential of f with respect to x. Let $\mathbf{r} = (p', q')$ be a partial solution up to i LSB's of p and q. Then $\frac{f(\mathbf{r})}{2^i} \pmod 2 = \frac{f(p', q')}{2^i} \pmod 2$ corresponds to $(N - p'^m q')[i]$, that is, $(i+1)$-st bit of $(N - p'^m q')$.

$$p[i] f_p(p', q') = p[i](-mp'^{m-1}q')$$
$$\equiv \begin{cases} 0 \pmod 2 & \text{if } m \text{ is even} \\ p[i] \pmod 2 & \text{if } m \text{ is odd} \end{cases}$$

and $q[i] f_q(p', q') = q[i](-p'^m) \equiv q[i] \pmod 2$. If m is even, we get the relation

$$q[i] \equiv (N - p'^m q')[i] \pmod 2. \tag{17}$$

If m is odd, we get the relation

$$p[i] + q[i] \equiv (N - p'^m q')[i] \pmod 2. \tag{18}$$

Equation (7) and (8) are obtained from equation (15) and (16) in the same way as RSA case. For equation (14), we apply Hensel's lemma to function f defined as $f(p, q, d) = k(p-1)(q-1) + 1 - ed$. By multiplying k, i-th bit of p affects $(i + \tau(k))$-th bit of $f(p, q, d)$. Hence, if we get i LSB's of p, we have a relation modulo $2^{i+\tau(k)}$ instead of modulo 2^i. As $(q - 1)$ is also divided by 2, i-th bit of

p actually affect $(i + \tau(k) + 1)$-st bit of $f(p, q, d)$ or higher, but this is dependent on $f()$ and in any case we have a relation modulo $2^{i+\tau(k)}$.

Let $\mathbf{r} = (p', q', d')$ be a partial solution up to i LSB's of p and q, and $i + \tau(k)$ LSB's of d. Then $f(\mathbf{r}) = f(p', q', d') \equiv 0 \pmod{2^{i+\tau(k)}}$, and we expect that

$$f(p' + b_1 2^i, q' + b_2 2^i, d' + b_3 2^{i+\tau(k)}) \equiv 0 \pmod{2^{i+\tau(k)+1}}$$

holds in the next level. The left term is represented as follows

$$
\begin{aligned}
&f(p' + b_1 2^i, q' + b_2 2^i, d' + b_3 2^{i+\tau(k)}) \\
&= k(p' - 1 + b_1 2^i)(q' - 1 + b_2 2^i) + 1 - e(d' + b_3 2^{i+\tau(k)}) \\
&= f(p', q', d') - k(p' - 1)b_2 2^i - k(q' - 1)b_1 2^i - k b_1 b_2 2^{2i} + e b_3 2^{i+\tau(k)}.
\end{aligned}
$$

In order that this is equivalent to 0 $\pmod{2^{i+\tau(k)+1}}$, we first divide the equation by $2^{i+\tau(k)}$. As to the first term,

$$\frac{f(\mathbf{r})}{2^{i+\tau(k)}} \pmod 2 = \frac{f(p', q', d')}{2^{i+\tau(k)}} \pmod 2$$

corresponds to $(i + \tau(k) + 1)$-st bit of $f(p', q', d')$, that is

$$(k(p' - 1)(q' - 1) + 1 - ed')[i + \tau(k)].$$

As p' and q' are odd, the second and third term vanishes modulo 2 even after divided by $2^{i+\tau(k)}$, and same for the fourth term. As e is odd, we finally get the following relation.

$$d[i + \tau(k)] \equiv (k(p'q' + 1) + 1 - k(p' + q') - ed')[i + \tau(k)] \pmod 2. \qquad (19)$$

In particular, if $pq = N$, this relation is equivalent to the relation (6) of RSA.

In Takagi's variant case, if m is even, the variable q is determined uniquely. This affects the freedom of the variables in the next bit level. We see that usual RSA has the relation $p[i] + q[i] \equiv (N - p'q')[i] \pmod 2$, while Takagi's case has the relation $q[i] \equiv (N - p'^m q')[i] \pmod 2$. In RSA case, when i LSB's of p and q are determined, $p[i]$ and $q[i]$ can be 0 or 1 as long as their sum modulo 2 is the value determined by the right hand side of the relation. However, in Takagi's case, $q[i]$ is uniquely determined by the i LSB's of p and q, and thus $q[i]$ has no ambiguity nor $d_q[i + \tau(k_q)]$ has. $d[i + \tau(k)]$ does not have ambiguity either. Only $p[i]$ and $d_p[i + \tau(k_p)]$ have ambiguity as long as they satisfy the relation (7). This difference has some effects on the branching behavior.

Table 1 summarizes the relations of private variables. We have five variables and four equations. If m is even, two variables p and d_p are ambiguous and the degree of freedom is 1. From proposition 1 and theorem 1, we have $EZ_g = (1 - \delta)^2$ and $EW_b = \frac{(2-\delta)^5}{2^4}$.

5.2 Security Comparison of RSA and Takagi's Variant against Random Key Bits Leakage Attack

The security of RSA cryptosystem and Takagi's variant are based on the hardness of integer factoring problem. There are several methods to factor integers:

Table 1. Relations of Private Key Bits

RSA	Takagi's variant
$N = pq$	$N = p^m q$
$ed = k(N + 1 - p - q) + 1$	$ed = k(pq + 1 - p - q) + 1$
$ed_p = k_p(p - 1) + 1$	$ed_p = k_p(p - 1) + 1$
$ed_q = k_q(q - 1) + 1$	$ed_q = k_q(q - 1) + 1$
$p[i] + q[i] \equiv (N - p'q')[i]$	$q[i] \equiv (N - p'^m q')[i]$ (m:even)
	$p[i] + q[i] \equiv (N - p'^m q')[i]$ (m:odd)
$d[i + \tau(k)] + p[i] + q[i] \equiv$	$d[i + \tau(k)] \equiv$
$(k(N + 1) + 1 - k(p' + q') - ed')$	$(k(p'q' + 1) + 1 - k(p' + q') - ed')$
$[i + \tau(k)]$	$[i + \tau(k)]$
$d_p[i + \tau(k_p)] + p[i] \equiv$	$d_p[i + \tau(k_p)] + p[i] \equiv$
$(k_p(p' - 1) + 1 - ed'_p)[i + \tau(k_p)]$	$(k_p(p' - 1) + 1 - ed'_p)[i + \tau(k_p)]$
$d_q[i + \tau(k_q)] + q[i] \equiv$	$d_q[i + \tau(k_q)] + q[i] \equiv$
$(k_q(q' - 1) + 1 - ed'_q)[i + \tau(k_q)]$	$(k_q(q' - 1) + 1 - ed'_q)[i + \tau(k_q)]$

number field sieve method, elliptic curve method, and lattice reduction method. For relatively small m and relatively large p, q of cryptographic use size, general number field sieve method is the fastest one among these methods[1]. As the complexity of general number field sieve method depends on the size of the composite number to be factored, we compare RSA and Takagi's variant with modulus of the same size.

Let s be the bit length of smallest private key, i.e. p and q in our situation. For $n = 1024$-bit RSA we have $s = \frac{n}{2} = 512$, and $s = \frac{1024}{m+1}$ for Takagi's variant of the same strength. In particular if $m = 2$, $s = 341$ for Takagi's case. From inequality (10), the total number of keys examined is bounded by

$$\sum_{i=0}^{s-1} \mathrm{EX}_i \leq \frac{\mathrm{EZ}_g}{1 - \mathrm{EW}_b} s,$$

which indicates the total complexity of the attack using key leakage information. From the condition $\mathrm{EW}_b < 1$, we have $\delta > 2 - 2^{\frac{4}{5}} \approx 0.2589$ in RSA case. By using the analysis of previous subsection, we can actually calculate the value of $\frac{\mathrm{EZ}_g}{1-\mathrm{EW}_b} s$ for some values of δ. If m is even, these values are different between RSA and Takagi's variant cases. Table 2 shows the comparison of this value.

If $n = 1024$ and m is even, the number of wrong assignments at each bit level of Takagi's RSA is almost 80 % greater than that of RSA. However, the bit length of private key of Takagi's variant, which corresponds to the number of total bit levels to be searched, is $\frac{2}{3}$ when $m = 2$ compared with that of RSA, hence the total complexity of this attack against Takagi's variant is almost 20 % greater than RSA. If $m \geq 4$, the complexity is smaller than RSA case. When m is odd, EZ_g and EW_b take the same values, and total complexity of the attack against Takagi's variant is $\frac{2}{m+1}$ compared with that of RSA, because of the shorter bit length of p, q. These phenomena indicate that from the view point

Table 2. Comparison of total complexity of key leakage attack

δ	$\frac{EZ_g}{1-EW_b}$ (RSA)	$\times 512$	$\frac{EZ_g}{1-EW_b}$ (Takagi)	$\times 341$
			m : even	$m = 2$
0.2589	93239	47738368	169762	57888842
0.26	95	48640	173	58943
0.27	9	4608	17	5797
0.28	4.5	2304	9	3069

of resistance against the attack, we had better use even number m, especially $m = 2$, in Takagi's variant.

Another difference we have to note is that the value of k in (19) is not easy to find beforehand in Takagi's case. In RSA case, when e is fairly small, we can exhaustively search k using public value N. In Takagi's case we have to know the value pq for the same exhaustive search, which is not equal to N. However, if e is small, we can exhaustively search k in another way, as k is bounded by e. Similarly k_p and k_q can be searched exhaustively, and because $k+k_pk_q \equiv 0 \pmod{e}$ holds, we are able to mount the attack with $O(e^2)$ overhead. This increases the total complexity of the attack in Takagi's variant case.

6   Conclusion

We made analysis of the security of cryptosystems against random key bits leakage attack, when the system of equations is given in general linear form. We showed that the expected value of solutions generated from the correct solution is determined by the number of ambiguous variables, which can have any values, and the degree of freedom of these variables. We also showed that the expected value of solutions generated from incorrect solutions is determined by the number of variables and the degree of freedom. Hence we can calculate the complexity of the attack once we get these three values.

As concrete examples, we applied the attack to Paillier cryptosystem and Takagi's variant of RSA, and analyzed their resistance against the attack. In Pailiier case, we showed a method to eliminate one variable, and obtained two relations between three private variables p, q, and λ. Hence we have almost the same security as the case three private variables p, q, and d of RSA are leaked. In Takagi's case, which uses the modulus p^mq, the value of m has some effects on the security against the attack. When m is even, one of the relations differs from corresponding relation of RSA, because we consider the relation modulo 2 and partial differentiation of p^mq regarding p vanishes when m is even. This makes the complexity of the attack larger than the RSA case. When m is odd, the relations are almost the same as RSA, and the smaller bit length of the secret factor p, q of Takagi's case reduces total complexity of the attack. These phenomena indicate that from the view point of resistance against the attack, we had better use even number m, especially $m = 2$, in Takagi's variant of RSA.

References

1. Boneh, D., Durfee, G., Howgrave-Graham, N.: Factoring $N = pq$ for Large r. In: Wiener, M. (ed.) CRYPTO 1999. LNCS, vol. 1666, pp. 326–337. Springer, Heidelberg (1999)
2. Coppersmith, D.: Small Solutions to Polynomial Equations, and Low Exponent RSA Vulnerabilities. Journal of Cryptology, 233–260 (1997)
3. Dulmage, A.L., Mendelsohn, N.S.: Two Algorithms for Bipartite Graphs. J. Soc. Indust. Appl. Math. 11(1), 183–184 (1963)
4. Halderman, J.A., Schoen, S.D., Heninger, N., Clarkson, W., Paul, W., Calandrino, J.A., Feldman, A.J., Appelbaum, J., Felten, E.W.: Lest We Remember: Cold Boot Attacks on Encryption Keys. In: Proceedings of the 17th USENIX Security Symposium, pp. 45–60. USENIX Association (2008)
5. Henecka, W., May, A., Meurer, A.: Correcting Errors in RSA Private Keys. In: Rabin, T. (ed.) CRYPTO 2010. LNCS, vol. 6223, pp. 351–369. Springer, Heidelberg (2010)
6. Heninger, N., Shacham, H.: Reconstructing RSA Private Keys from Random Key Bits. In: Halevi, S. (ed.) CRYPTO 2009. LNCS, vol. 5677, pp. 1–17. Springer, Heidelberg (2009)
7. Maitra, S., Sarkar, S., Sen Gupta, S.: Factoring RSA Modulus Using Prime Reconstruction from Random Known Bits. In: Bernstein, D.J., Lange, T. (eds.) AFRICACRYPT 2010. LNCS, vol. 6055, pp. 82–99. Springer, Heidelberg (2010)
8. Paillier, P.: Public-Key Cryptosystems Based on Composite Degree Residuosity Classes. In: Stern, J. (ed.) EUROCRYPT 1999. LNCS, vol. 1592, pp. 223–238. Springer, Heidelberg (1999)
9. Rivest, R.L., Shamir, A.: Efficient Factoring Based on Partial Information. In: Pichler, F. (ed.) EUROCRYPT 1985. LNCS, vol. 219, pp. 31–34. Springer, Heidelberg (1986)
10. Takagi, T.: Fast RSA-type Cryptosystem Modulo $p^k q$. In: Krawczyk, H. (ed.) CRYPTO 1998. LNCS, vol. 1462, pp. 318–326. Springer, Heidelberg (1998)

A   Dulmage-Mendelsohn Decomposition of Bipartite Graph

Let $A = (a_{ij})$ be an $n \times m$-matrix, and $Ax = b$ be linear equations of $x = {}^t(x_1, ..., x_m)$, where ^{t} denotes the transpose of matrix. Let $R = \{e_1, ..., e_n\}$ be vertices set of equations, and $C = \{x_1, ..., x_m\}$ be vertices set of variables. Bipartite graph of A is defined as $G(A) = (R, C, E)$, where edges are $E = \{(i, j) | a_{ij} \neq 0\}$. Let $\{R_0; R_1, ..., R_K; R_\infty\}$ and $\{C_0; C_1, ..., C_K; C_\infty\}$ be partitions of R and C. They are called properly block triangularized when they satisfy following three conditions

$$B1 : |R_0| < |C_0| \text{ or } |R_0| = |C_0| = 0$$
$$|R_i| = |C_i| \text{ for } 1 \leq i \leq K$$
$$|R_\infty| > |C_\infty| \text{ or } |R_\infty| = |C_\infty| = 0$$
$$B2 : A[R_i, C_j] = O \text{ for } 0 \leq j < i \leq \infty$$
$$B3 : \text{rank } A[R_i, C_i] = \min(|R_i|, |C_i|) \text{ for } 0 \leq i \leq \infty,$$

where $|S|$ denotes the cardinality of a finite set S, and $A[R_i, C_j]$ denotes the submatrix of A corresponding to the rows R_i and the columns C_j. Dulmage and Mendelsohn showed that there exists a unique finest proper block triangularization, which is called Dulmage-Mendelsohn (DM for short) decomposition.

Let $G(A)$ be a bipartite graph generated by the linear equations represented by a matrix A. We consider the relations (5)-(8) of RSA private keys and (17)-(19) of Takagi's variant. As d is uniquely determined, we replace relation (6) with the relation obtained by subtracting (5) from (6). We consider the case p's exponent m is even for Takagi's variant. Then the matrix A_R of RSA case, A_T of Takagi's case, and the equations will be represented as follows

$$A_R = \begin{pmatrix} 1 & 1 & 0 & 0 & 0 \\ 0 & 0 & 1 & 0 & 0 \\ 1 & 0 & 0 & 1 & 0 \\ 0 & 1 & 0 & 0 & 1 \end{pmatrix}, \quad A_T = \begin{pmatrix} 0 & 1 & 0 & 0 & 0 \\ 0 & 0 & 1 & 0 & 0 \\ 1 & 0 & 0 & 1 & 0 \\ 0 & 1 & 0 & 0 & 1 \end{pmatrix}, \quad A \begin{pmatrix} p \\ q \\ d \\ d_p \\ d_q \end{pmatrix} = \mathbf{b}.$$

The graph $G(A_R)$ and $G(A_T)$ are as follows.

Let $\{C_0; C_1, ..., C_K; C_\infty\}$ be the DM decomposition of the graph $G(A)$. Let $r = \sum_{i < \infty} |C_i|$ be the number of variables, $k = |C_0| - |R_0|$ be the degree of freedom of variables, $l = |C_0|$ be number of variables belonging to C_0. The DM decompositions of RSA and Takagi's variant in concern are as follows.

$$A_R = \begin{array}{c|cccc|c} & \multicolumn{4}{c|}{C_0} & C_1 \\ & p & d_p & q & d_q & d \\ \hline e_3 & 1 & 1 & 0 & 0 & \\ R_0\ e_1 & 1 & 0 & 1 & 0 & \\ e_4 & 0 & 0 & 1 & 1 & \\ \hline R_1\ e_2 & & & & & 1 \end{array}, \quad A_T = \begin{array}{c|cc|cc|c} & \multicolumn{2}{c|}{C_0} & \multicolumn{2}{c|}{C_1} & C_2 \\ & p & d_p & q & d_q & d \\ \hline R_0\ e_3 & 1 & 1 & & & \\ \hline R_1\ e_1 & & & 1 & 0 & \\ e_4 & & & 1 & 1 & \\ \hline R_2\ e_2 & & & & & 1 \end{array}$$

Thus we can represent r, k, and l, using the DM decomposition.

Improved Integral Attacks on Reduced-Round CLEFIA Block Cipher

Yanjun Li[1,2,3], Wenling Wu[1,2], and Lei Zhang[1,2]

[1] State Key Laboratory of Information Security,
Institute of Software, Chinese Academy of Sciences, Beijing 100190, P.R. China
[2] Graduate University of Chinese Academy of Sciences, Beijing 100049, P.R. China
[3] Beijing Electronic Science and Technology Institute, Beijing 100070, P.R. China
{liyanjun,wwl,zhanglei1015}@is.iscas.ac.cn

Abstract. In this paper a new 9-round integral distinguisher of CLE-FIA is proposed based on byte-pattern, which is proved in detail. Then by using the partial sum technique we improve the previous result on 11-round CLEFIA and proposed integral attack on 12-, 13- and 14- round CLEFIA with the whitening keys. The 12-round CLEFIA-128/192/256 is attacked with data complexity 2^{113} and time complexity $2^{116.7}$, 13-round CLEFIA-192/256 is attacked with data complexity 2^{113} and time complexity $2^{180.5}$, and 14-round CLEFIA-256 is breakable with data complexity 2^{113} and time complexity $2^{244.5}$. These results demonstrate that based on the byte-pattern we can improve the integral attacks on CLE-FIA two more rounds than those given by the designers.

Keywords: Block cipher, Distinguisher, Integral attack, CLEFIA, Partial sum technique.

1 Introduction

The block cipher CLEFIA was developed by Sony Corporation [10]. It has the block length of 128 bits and a variable key length of 128/192/256 bits. The security of CLEFIA was initially analyzed by the algorithm designers, including differential cryptanalysis, linear cryptanalysis, impossible differential cryptanalysis and square attack, in which the impossible differential cryptanalysis is most effective[9]. In FSE 2008 Tsunoo *et al.* improved impossible differential cryptanalysis to 12 rounds of CLEFIA-128 with $2^{118.9}$ chosen plaintexts and 2^{119} encryptions [11]. Later by using the same impossible differential distinguisher, Zhang *et al.* presented an attack on 14-round CLEFIA-128 considering the weakness in the key schedule[13]. But CLEFIA design team pointed out a flaw in their attack and showed that it is not successful[2]. In IndoCrypt 2010, Tezcan proposed improbable differential cryptanalysis and applied it on 13-, 14-, and 15-round CLEFIA-128/192/256 by the advantage of the relation of round keys [1]. However, compared with these differential cryptanalysis, integral attack is still an important attack because of its advantages[6, 8, 14]. The basic idea of integral attack comes from square attack, which was first proposed by Daemen about the

S. Jung and M. Yung (Eds.): WISA 2011, LNCS 7115, pp. 28–39, 2012.
© Springer-Verlag Berlin Heidelberg 2012

analysis of block cipher SQUARE[3,4]. Later Ferguson *et al.* improved this attack to 8 rounds version of Rijndael-128 with the partial sum technique and the herd technique[7]. In the same year Knudsen and Wagner analyzed this cryptanalysis as a dual to differential attacks particularly applicable to block ciphers with bijective components, and they first proposed the definition of integral[5]. So far the best results of square attack on CLEFIA is presented by Wang *et al.*. They has attacked 11-round CLEFIA-128/192/256 with the same distinguisher given by the algorithm designers[12].

In this paper we use the definition of integral attack instead of square attack. According to the structure properties of CLEFIA, a new 9-round integral distinguisher is proposed. Then by using the partial sum technique we proposed integral attacks on 12-, 13- and 14- round CLEFIA. The detail results are as follows: 12-round CLEFIA- 128/192/256 is attacked with data complexity 2^{113} and time complexity $2^{116.7}$, 13-round CLEFIA-192/256 is attacked with data complexity 2^{113} and time complexity $2^{180.5}$, and 14-round CLEFIA-256 is breakable with data complexity 2^{113} and time complexity $2^{244.5}$. The results demonstrate that based on the byte-pattern we can improve the integral attack on CLEFIA two more rounds than those given by the designers. Moreover, the results also present that in the condition of random round keys integral attack is no less effective than differential cryptanalysis on evaluating the security of encryption structure.

This paper is organized as follows: Section 2 provides a brief outline of CLEFIA, the definition of integral attack and the notations used throughout this paper. Section 3 gives the new 9-round distinguisher in detail. Section 4 describes the integral attacks on the reduced-round CLEFIA. Finally, Section 5 concludes this paper.

2   Preliminaries

2.1   Description of CLEFIA

CLEFIA is designed based on generalized Feistel structure as shown in Fig.1, and the number of rounds are 18/22/26 corresponding to key length of 128/192/256 bits. The round function of CLEFIA includes two different functions: F_0 and F_1. An N-round CLEFIA iterates the round function N times, and in the first round and the last round there are 4 whitening key bytes.

F_0 and F_1 have the same SP structure and include three basic operations: Round Key Addition, Substitution Layer and Diffusion Layer. However, in the Substitution Layer the order of S_0 and S_1 is different and the Permutation Layers are also different, which are shown in Fig.2. M_0 and M_1 are shown as follows:

$$M_0 = \begin{bmatrix} 01 & 02 & 04 & 06 \\ 02 & 01 & 06 & 04 \\ 04 & 06 & 01 & 02 \\ 06 & 04 & 02 & 01 \end{bmatrix} \quad M_1 = \begin{bmatrix} 01 & 08 & 02 & 0a \\ 08 & 01 & 0a & 02 \\ 02 & 0a & 01 & 08 \\ 0a & 02 & 08 & 01 \end{bmatrix}$$

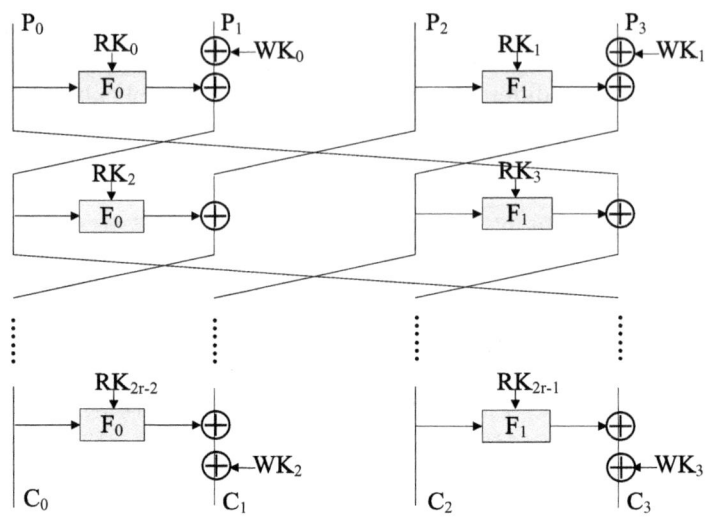

Fig. 1. The Block Cipher: CLEFIA

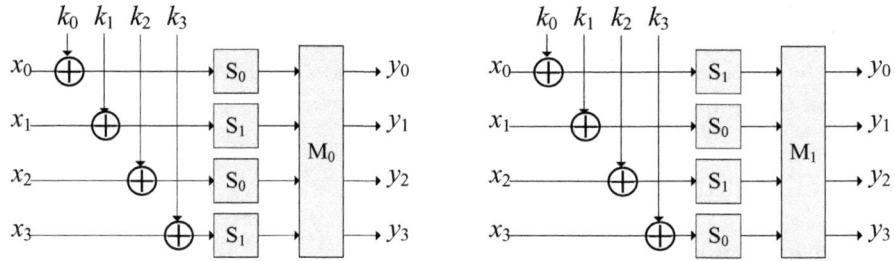

Fig. 2. The Function of F_0 and F_1

In the encryption procedure of CLEFIA, since the relations between the round subkeys will not help in our attacks, we will omit the key scheduling algorithm here and interested readers can refer to [10].

2.2 Integral Attack

The integral attack has many interesting features. It can saturate S-Box Layer, and Round Key Addition Layer will not affect this property of saturation. However, Diffusion Layer influences the length of the integral distinguisher. Integral attack considers a particular collection of m bytes in the plaintexts and cipher-texts. The aim of this attack is to predict the values in the sums (i.e. the integral) of the chosen bytes after a certain number of rounds of encryption. In [5], Knudsen and Wagner also generalized this approach to higher order integrals: the original set to consider becomes a set of vectors which differ in d components and where the sum of this set is predictable after a certain number of rounds. The sum of this set is called a dth-order integral. The following definitions are essential:

Active Set. A set $\{x_i | x_i \in F_{2^n}, 0 \leq i \leq 2^n - 1\}$ is active, if for any $0 \leq i < j \leq 2^n - 1$, $x_i \neq x_j$.

Passive Set. A set $\{x_i | x_i \in F_{2^n}, 0 \leq i \leq 2^n - 1\}$ is passive, if for any $0 < i \leq 2^n - 1$, $x_i = x_0$.

Balanced Set. A set $\{x_i | x_i \in F_{2^n}, 0 \leq i \leq 2^n - 1\}$ is balanced, if the sum of all element of the set is 0, that is $\sum_{i=0}^{2^n - 1} x_i = 0$.

Usually, Active Set is denoted as A. Passive Set is denoted as C. And Balanced Set is denoted as B.

2.3   Notations

In the following, we introduce some notations used throughout this paper. The plaintext and ciphertext are denoted as $P = P_0 | P_1 | P_2 | P_3$ and $C = C_0 | C_1 | C_2 | C_3$ respectively. WK_0, WK_1, WK_2, WK_3 denote four whitening keys. Other notations that will be used in this paper are described as follows:

$m_{r,i}$: the (i+1)-th byte of the input of the r-th round;
c_i: the (i+1)-th byte of the ciphertext;
$RK_{i,j}$: the (j+1)-th byte of the (i+1)-th round subkey;
$RK'_{i,j}$: This is a simple linear function of the round key $RK_{i,j}$ and WK.
x, y, z, w, v: the active bytes needed in the proofs.

3   New 9-Round Distinguisher of CLEFIA

The integral attack on reduced-round CLEFIA was initially proposed by the algorithm designers, where the text (the data being encrypted) is neatly partitioned into small component words. In this paper we will explore the SP structure of the round function of CLEFIA and partition the text into smaller component bytes. Instead of 8-round integral distinguisher presented by the designers, a new 9-round distinguisher is depicted in Fig.3. In order to prove it, two lemmas are described as follows.

Lemma 1. If $m_{1,4}$ is an active byte and other bytes of the input are constants, after 5 rounds of CLEFIA encryption the c_4, c_5, c_6, c_7 are balance bytes.

Proof. According to Fig.3, 5 rounds of CLEFIA encryption correspond to the rounds from Round 5 to Round 9. The byte $m_{5,4}$ is the only active byte of input of Round 5, which is denoted as x.

After 2 rounds encryption, we will obtain the output state as follows:

$$[y, 2y, 4y, 6y, c, c, c, c, c, c, c, c, x, c, c, c],$$

where $y = s_0(x \oplus RK_{11,0}) \oplus c$, and the value of byte ky is $ky \oplus c, k = 2, 4, 6$.

After 3 rounds encryption, we will obtain the output state as follows:

$$[f_0(y), f_1(y), f_2(y), f_3(y), c, c, c, c, x, c, c, c, y, 2y, 4y, 6y],$$

where $[f_0(y), f_1(y), f_2(y), f_3(y)] = F_0([y, 2y, 4y, 6y], RK_{13})$, and each $f_i(y), 0 \leq i \leq 3$ is balance.

After 4 rounds encryption, we will obtain the output state as follows:

$$[?, ?, ?, ?, ?, ?, ?, ?, z \oplus y, 8z \oplus 2y, 2z \oplus 4y, az \oplus 6y, f_0(y), f_1(y), f_2(y), f_3(y)],$$

where $z = s_0(x \oplus RK_{16,0}) \oplus c$. We can easily deduce that each byte of $[z \oplus y, 8z \oplus 2y, 2z \oplus 4y, az \oplus 6y]$ is balance.

After 5 rounds encryption, only c_4, c_5, c_6, c_7 are balanced bytes, and other bytes are uncertain due to those unknown key bytes.

$$c_4 = z \oplus y, c_5 = 8z \oplus 2y, c_6 = 2z \oplus 4y, c_7 = az \oplus 6y. \qquad \square$$

Lemma 2. If $m_{1,4}, m_{1,5}, m_{1,6}$, and $m_{1,7}$ take the values of $v \oplus w, 2v \oplus 8w, 4v \oplus 2w, 6v \oplus aw$, where v and w are two active bytes, and other 12 bytes of the first round input are active, after 4 rounds of CLEFIA encryption we will obtain 2^{104} sets, and in each set, only byte c_4 is active and other bytes are constant.

Proof. According to Fig.3, $(AAAA)$ denotes 4 active bytes (or an active word), and $(BBBB)$ denotes 4 balanced bytes (or a balanced word). The 4 rounds of CLEFIA encryption described in **Lemma 2** correspond to the rounds from Round 1 to Round 4 in Fig.3. we will proof this lemma in four steps as follows.

1. (Round 4 → 5)Let the input byte pattern be $[c, c, c, c, c, c, c, c, x, c, c, c, w, 8w, 2w, aw]$, where x and w are active bytes. After one round encryption we will get 2^8 sets and in each set $c_4 = x$ is active and other bytes are constants.
2. (Round 3 → 4)Let the input byte pattern be $[w, 8w, 2w, aw, u_0, u_1, u_2, u_3, c, c, c, c, x, c, c, c]$, where w, u_0, u_1, u_2, u_3 and x are active bytes. After one round encryption we will get 2^{32} sets and in each set the byte pattern is $[c, c, c, c, c, c, c, c, x, c, c, c, w, 8w, 2w, aw]$, where x and w are active bytes.

3. (Round $2 \to 3$)Let the input byte pattern be $[x, c, c, c, v \oplus w, 2v \oplus 8w, 4v \oplus 2w, 6v \oplus aw, u_0, u_1, u_2, u_3, \lambda_0, \lambda_1, \lambda_2, \lambda_3]$, where x, v, w and $u_i, \lambda_j, 0 \le i, j \le 3$ are active bytes. One round encryption can be described as the following equation.

$$P_0 \begin{bmatrix} s_0(x \oplus RK_{3,0}) \oplus v \\ c' \oplus 0 \\ c' \oplus 0 \\ c' \oplus 0 \end{bmatrix} \oplus \begin{bmatrix} w \\ 8w \\ 2w \\ aw \end{bmatrix} = \begin{bmatrix} w \oplus i \\ 8w \oplus 2i \\ 2w \oplus 4i \\ aw \oplus 6i \end{bmatrix} \tag{1}$$

$$P_1 \begin{bmatrix} s_1(u_0 \oplus RK_{4,0}) \\ s_0(u_1 \oplus RK_{4,1}) \\ s_1(u_2 \oplus RK_{4,2}) \\ s_0(u_3 \oplus RK_{4,3}) \end{bmatrix} \oplus \begin{bmatrix} \lambda_0 \\ \lambda_1 \\ \lambda_2 \\ \lambda_3 \end{bmatrix} = \begin{bmatrix} c'_0 \\ c'_1 \\ c'_2 \\ c'_3 \end{bmatrix} \tag{2}$$

Without loss of generality, let $c' = 0$. For each value of x, there is $v = v_0$ satisfying the equation (1), and the value of v_0 is unknown due to the unknown RK_3. So when $v = v_0 \oplus t, 0 \le t \le 255$ take all 2^8 values, we will obtain 2^8 sets. They are indexed by the value of t. It means that 2^{24} values of $[x, c, c, c, v \oplus w, 2v \oplus 8w, 4v \oplus 2w, 6v \oplus aw]$ will lead to 2^8 sets, and in each set the byte pattern is $[w, 8w, 2w, aw, x, c, c, c]$. Similarly, 2^{64} values of $[u_0, u_1, u_2, u_3, \lambda_0, \lambda_1, \lambda_2, \lambda_3]$ will lead to 2^{32} sets, and in each set the byte pattern is $[u_0, u_1, u_2, u_3, c, c, c, c]$. The sets are different in 4 constant bytes. Therefore, after one round encryption we will get 2^{40} sets from 2^{88} input values, and in each set the byte pattern is $[w, 8w, 2w, aw, u_0, u_1, u_2, u_3, c, c, c, c, x, c, c, c]$.
4. (Round $1 \to 2$)Let the input byte pattern be $[\lambda_0, \lambda_1, \lambda_2, \lambda_3, v \oplus w, 2v \oplus 8w, 4v \oplus 2w, 6v \oplus aw, \lambda_4, \lambda_5, \lambda_6, \lambda_7, \lambda_8, \lambda_9, \lambda_{10}, \lambda_{11}]$, where v, w and $\lambda_i, 0 \le i \le 11$ are active bytes, after one round encryption we will get 2^{24} sets and in each set the byte pattern is $[x, c, c, c, v \oplus w, 2v \oplus 8w, 4v \oplus 2w, 6v \oplus aw, u_0, u_1, u_2, u_3, \lambda_0, \lambda_1, \lambda_2, \lambda_3]$.

By the steps 1 to 4, we conclude that if $m_{1,4}, m_{1,5}, m_{1,6}$, and $m_{1,7}$ take the values of $v \oplus w, 2v \oplus 8w, 4v \oplus 2w, 6v \oplus aw$, where v and w are two active bytes, and other 12 bytes of the first round input are active, after 4 rounds of CLEFIA encryption we will obtain 2^{104} sets. In each set, the byte c_4 is active and other bytes are constant. $\qquad \square$

In line with Lemma 1 and Lemma 2, we can construct 14th-order 9-round integral distinguisher as depicted in Theorem 1(Fig.3).

Theorem 1. If $m_{1,4}, m_{1,5}, m_{1,6}$, and $m_{1,7}$ take the values of $v \oplus w, 2v \oplus 8w, 4v \oplus 2w, 6v \oplus aw$, where v and w are two active bytes, and other 12 bytes of the first round input are all active, then after 9 rounds of CLEFIA encryption the bytes of c_4, c_5, c_6, c_7 are balanced.

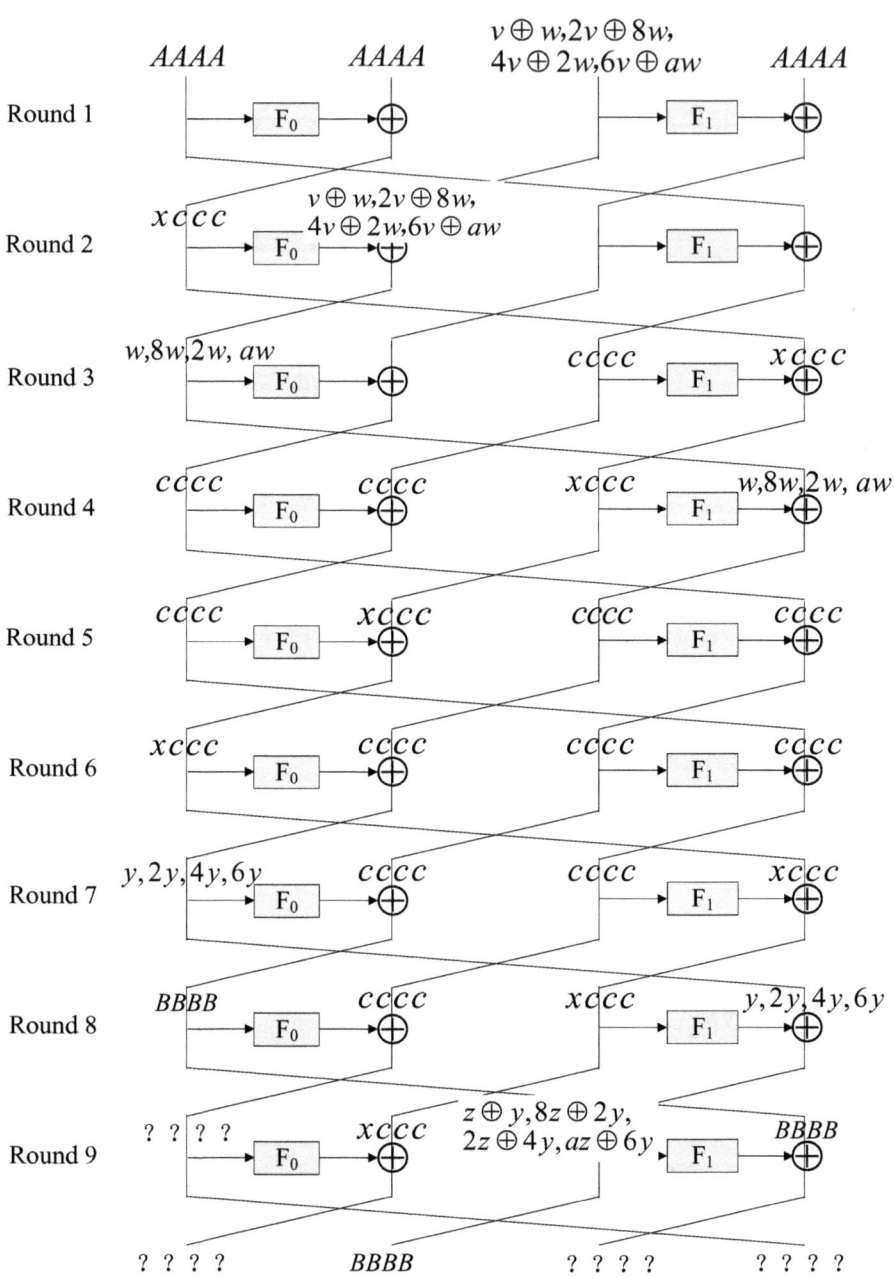

Fig. 3. The 9-Round Integral Distinguisher of CLEFIA

4   Attacks to Reduced Rounds of CLEFIA

4.1   The 11-Round Attack

In this subsection, we describe the integral attack on 11-round CLEFIA based on byte-pattern. It is based on the above 9-round distinguisher with additional two rounds at the end as shown in Fig.4. In the last round there are two whitening keys should be considered. We denote that WK_2 will not affect the attack and $WK_{3,0} \oplus RK_{18,0}$ will be replaced by $RK'_{18,0}$. For 11-round CLEFIA, the following equation can be established:

$$\oplus_{i=1}^{2^{112}} [S_0(S_1(c_8 \oplus RK_{21,0}) \oplus 08 S_0(c_9 \oplus RK_{21,1})$$
$$\oplus 02 S_1(c_{10} \oplus RK_{21,2}) \oplus 0a S_0(c_{11} \oplus RK_{21,3}) \oplus c_{12} \oplus RK'_{18,0})] = \oplus_{i=1}^{2^{112}} c' \tag{3}$$

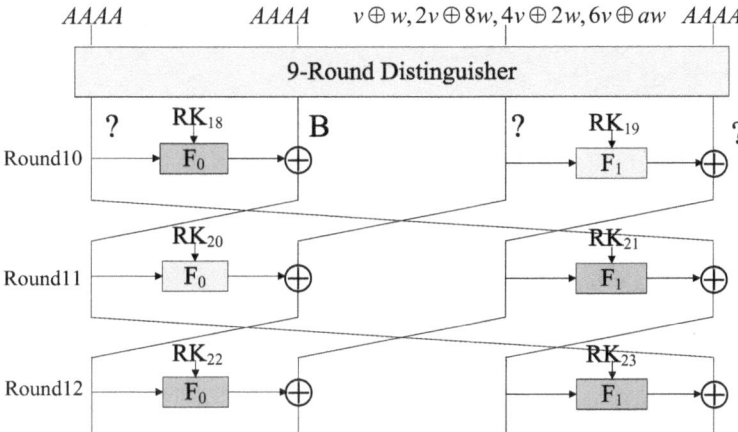

Fig. 4. The Integral Attack on Reduced Rounds of CLEFIA

Using the equation(3), we can attack 11-round CLEFIA as follows:

1. Choose a structure of 2^{112} plaintexts. Let $m_{1,4}, m_{1,5}, m_{1,6}$, and $m_{1,7}$ take the values of $v \oplus w, 2v \oplus 8w, 4v \oplus 2w, 6v \oplus aw$, where v and w are two active bytes, and other 12 bytes of the plaintexts are active. Encrypt all these plaintexts and set 2^{48} counters for six bytes of $c_8, c_9, c_{10}, c_{11}, c_{12}$, and c', where $c' = c_0 \oplus 02c_1 \oplus 04c_2 \oplus 06c_3$, and then the corresponding counter is increased by 1. For all the values of ciphertexts, there are 2^{48} values at most in the six bytes. We choose those values that the counters are odd times $(a \oplus a = 0)$.

2. Guess the value of $RK_{21,0}, RK_{21,1}, RK_{21,2}, RK_{21,3}, RK'_{18,0}$, and compute the left value of the equation(3) for all 2^{48} values, where we will use the partial sum technique to compute. Let $t_0, t_1, t_2, \cdots, t_l$ and $r_0, r_1, r_2, \cdots, r_l$ denote the bytes of the ciphertext and the corresponding bytes of RK. We define

$$x_i := \sum_{j=0}^{i} S[t_j \oplus r_j],$$

where i, j satisfy $l \geq i > j \geq 0$.

Now we operate four substeps to compute the left value of the equation(3):

(a) Guessing the two bytes of $RK_{21,0}$ and $RK_{21,1}$, and computing the partial sum, then we get the corresponding 4 bytes value:

$$(x_1, c_{10}, c_{11}, c_{12}).$$

(b) Guessing the value of $RK_{21,2}$, and computing the partial sum, then we get 3 bytes value:

$$(x_2, c_{11}, c_{12}).$$

(c) Guessing the value of $RK_{21,3}$, and computing the partial sum, then we get 2 bytes value:

$$(x_3, c_{12}).$$

(d) Guessing the value of $RK'_{18,0}$, and computing the partial sum, then we get 1 byte value:

$$(x_4).$$

The sum of all x_4 is equal to the right value of the equation(3). If the equation(3) holds, the $RK'_{18,0}, RK_{21,0}, RK_{21,1}, RK_{21,2}, RK_{21,3}$ might be right, otherwise it is a wrong guess.

3. Repeat Step 1 and Step 2 until $RK'_{18,0}, RK_{21,0}, RK_{21,1}, RK_{21,2}, RK_{21,3}$ is uniquely determined.

In Step 2, computing the right value of the equation(3) needs 4×2^{32} times XOR operation at most. To get the left value of the equation(3) needs no more than $2^{40} \times 2^{16} \times 4 = 2^{58}$ table lookups. For a wrong key, the probability that it satisfies the equation(3) is 2^{-8}, and thus after analyzing a structure, the number of wrong keys that can pass the equation(3) is $(2^{40} - 1) \times 2^{-8} \approx 2^{32}$. Hence to uniquely determine 5 bytes key, we need to analyze 6 structures. Similarly, the key bytes of $RK'_{18,1}, RK'_{18,2}$ and $RK'_{18,3}$ also can be determined. Accordingly, the data complexity of the attack is about $2^{114.6}$ chosen plaintexts, and the time complexity is $6 \times 2^{58}/(11 \times 2^3) = 2^{54}$ encryptions. Guessing the remaining key bytes of RK_{19} and RK_{20}, the total time complexity is about 2^{64} encryptions (the time cost of searching RK_{19} and RK_{20}).

4.2   The 12-Round Attack

The integral attack on 12 rounds CLEFIA is similar to the attack described above. In the last round there are two white key should be considered. We denote that WK_3 is a constant which will not affect the sum value and $WK_2 \oplus RK_{21}$

will be replaced by RK'_{21}. The equation of integral attack on 12-round CLEFIA is as follows

$$\oplus_{i=1}^{2^{112}} \{S_0[S_1(b_0 \oplus RK'_{21,0}) \oplus 08S_0(b_1 \oplus RK'_{21,1}) \oplus 02S_1(b_2 \oplus RK'_{21,2})$$
$$\oplus 0aS_0(b_3 \oplus RK'_{21,3}) \oplus c_8 \oplus RK_{18,0}] \oplus [S_1(c_8 \oplus RK_{23,0})$$
$$\oplus S_0(c_9 \oplus RK_{23,1}) \oplus S_1(c_{10} \oplus RK_{23,2}) \oplus S_0(c_{11} \oplus RK_{23,3})]\} = \oplus_{i=1}^{2^{112}} c', \tag{4}$$

where

$$\begin{bmatrix} b_0 \\ b_1 \\ b_2 \\ b_3 \end{bmatrix} = P_0 \begin{bmatrix} S_0(c_0 \oplus RK_{22,0}) \\ S_1(c_1 \oplus RK_{22,1}) \\ S_2(c_2 \oplus RK_{22,2}) \\ S_3(c_3 \oplus RK_{22,3}) \end{bmatrix} \oplus \begin{bmatrix} c_4 \\ c_5 \\ c_6 \\ c_7 \end{bmatrix}.$$

For those 2^{112} ciphertexts just as in Sec 4.1, we need set 2^{104} counters for 13 bytes of C_0, C_1, C_2, and c', where $c' = c_{12} \oplus 02c_{13} \oplus 04c_{14} \oplus 06c_{15}$, and then the corresponding counter plus one. For all the values of ciphertexts, there are 2^{104} values at most in the 13 bytes. We attack 12-round CLEFIA in 2 steps as follows.

1. We need the precomputation of b_0, b_1, b_2, b_3 in the eqution(4). Guessing the four bytes of RK_{22}, and performing $F_0(C_0, RK_{22})$, then Xoring C_1, we will obtain the corresponding 2^{32} values of (b_0, b_1, b_2, b_3).
2. For the 2^{64} values of $(b_0, b_1, b_2, b_3, C_2)$, do the following operations.
   (a) Guess the value of $RK'_{21,0}, RK'_{21,1}$, and compute the partial sum, then we get 2^{56} values of (x_1, b_2, b_3, C_2). Guess the values of $RK'_{21,2}, RK'_{21,3}$ respectively, 2^{40} values of (x_3, C_2) will be obtained after 2 substeps.
   (b) Guess the value of $RK_{18,0}$ and $RK_{23,0}$, and we get 2^{32} values of $(x_4, c_9, c_{10}, c_{11})$. Guess the remaining 3 key bytes of RK_{23} respectively, the only 2^8 values will be obtained after 3 substeps.

In Step 1, for each value of (C_0, C_1, RK_{22}), there is a corresponding (b_0, b_1, b_2, b_3). So 16×2^{96} bytes memory is needed. The time complexity is about $2^{96}/(2 \times 12) \approx 2^{91.4}$, which can be ignored compared with that in Step 2. In Step 2-(a), it cost $2^{32} \times 2^{16} \times [2^{64} + 2^8 \times (2^{56} + 2^8 \times (2^{48} + 2^8 \times 2^{40}))] = 2^{114}$ S-box lookups. In Step 2-(b), the cost is $2^{64} \times 2^{16} \times [2^{40} + 2^8 \times (2^{32} + 2^8 \times (2^{24} + 2^8 \times (2^{16} + 2^8 \times 2^8)))] = 2^{120} \times 5$ S-box lookups, which is the main cost. The Xoring of c' in each step also can be ignored. There are 13 bytes of key needs to be guessed at all, and after analyzing two structures, the number of keys that can pass the eqution(4) is $(2^{104}) \times (2^{-8})^2 = 2^{88}$. We search these 2^{88} and the remaining 2^{24} keys exhaustively. The total time complexity is about $2 \times 2^{120} \times 5/(2^3 \times 12) \approx 2^{116.7}$ encryptions.

4.3   The 13-Round and 14-Round Attacks

For 13-round CLEFIA we decrypt the last round at first, and then attack 12-round. In this attack we guess 8 more key bytes than in the attack on 12-round CLEFIA. If the data complexity is still 2^{113}, we need to search $2^{192-16} = 2^{172}$

keys. The main time complexity is $2^{176} + 2^{64} \times 2^{116.7} \times 12/13 = 2^{180.5}$. This result is fit to CLEFIA with 192 bits key and 256 bits key. For 14-round CLEFIA, our integral attack needs 2^{113} plaintexts and about $2^{256-16} + 2^{128} \times 2^{116.7} \times 12/14 = 2^{244.5}$ encryptions, which is only fit to CLEFIA with 256 bits key.

5   Conclusion

The integral attacks on reduced-round CLEFIA was described in this paper. Firstly, based on byte-pattern a new 9-round integral distinguisher was proposed, which was also be proved in detail. Secondly, by using the partial sum technique we improved integral attack result on 11-round CLEFIA and proposed integral attack on 12-, 13- and 14-round CLEFIA. Table 1 summarizes our integral attacks together with the previously known integral attacks on CLEFIA.

Table 1. Results of integral attacks on CLEFIA

Attack type	D-Rounds	Rounds	Data	Time	Source
Integral Attack	8	10	$2^{97.6}$	$2^{123.7}$	[9]
	8	11	$2^{99.8}$	$2^{111.4}$	[12]
	8	12	$2^{100.5}$	$2^{176.1}$	[12]
	8	13	$2^{100.9}$	$2^{240.3}$	[12]
	9	12	2^{113}	$2^{116.7}$	Sec.4.2
	9	13	2^{113}	$2^{180.5}$	Sec.4.3
	9	14	2^{113}	$2^{244.5}$	Sec.4.3

Time complexity is measured in encryption units.
D-Rounds is Distinguisher Rounds.

According to Table 1, the integral attacks presented in this paper make significant improvements on both data and time complexities. However, the full rounds CLEFIA provides sufficient safety margin against integral attack.

Without considering the relation of round keys the improbable differential and impossible differential cryptanalysis can only attack on 12-, 13-, and 14-round CLEFIA-128/192/256. So our results also present that in the condition of random round keys integral attack is no less effective than the front two kinds of differential cryptanalysis on evaluating the security of encryption structure. For block cipher cryptanalysis, how to study the relation of differential and integral is more significant, which will be our future work.

References

1. Tezcan, C.: The Improbable Differential Attack: Cryptanalysis of Reduced Round CLEFIA. In: Gong, G., Gupta, K.C. (eds.) INDOCRYPT 2010. LNCS, vol. 6498, pp. 197–209. Springer, Heidelberg (2010)
2. CLEFIA design team, Sony Corporation, Comments on the Impossible Differential Analysis of Reduced Round CLEFIA. Presented at Inscrypt 2008 (Jannuary 8, 2009)

3. FIPS 197. Advanced Encryption Standard. Federal Information Processing Standards Publication 197, U.S. Department of Commerce, N.I.S.T (2001)
4. Daemen, J., Knudsen, L.R., Rijmen, V.: The Block Cipher Square. In: Biham, E. (ed.) FSE 1997. LNCS, vol. 1267, pp. 149–165. Springer, Heidelberg (1997)
5. Knudsen, L., Wagner, D.: Integral Cryptanalysis. In: Daemen, J., Rijmen, V. (eds.) FSE 2002. LNCS, vol. 2365, pp. 112–127. Springer, Heidelberg (2002)
6. Duo, L., Li, C., Feng, K.: Square Like Attack on Camellia. In: Qing, S., Imai, H., Wang, G. (eds.) ICICS 2007. LNCS, vol. 4861, pp. 269–283. Springer, Heidelberg (2007)
7. Ferguson, N., Kelsey, J., Lucks, S., Schneier, B., Stay, M., Wagner, D., Whiting, D.: Improved Cryptanalysis of Rijndael. In: Schneier, B. (ed.) FSE 2000. LNCS, vol. 1978, pp. 213–230. Springer, Heidelberg (2001)
8. Galice, S., Minier, M.: Improving Integral Attacks Against Rijndael-256 upto 9 Rounds. In: Vaudenay, S. (ed.) AFRICACRYPT 2008. LNCS, vol. 5023, pp. 1–15. Springer, Heidelberg (2008)
9. Sony Corporation. The 128-bit Blockcipher CLEFIA. Security and Performance Evaluation. Revision 1.0 (June 1, 2007)
10. Shirai, T., Shibutani, K., Akishita, T., Moriai, S., Iwata, T.: The 128-Bit Block Cipher CLEFIA. In: Biryukov, A. (ed.) FSE 2007. LNCS, vol. 4593, pp. 181–195. Springer, Heidelberg (2007)
11. Tsunoo, Y., Tsujihara, E., Shigeri, M., Saito, T., Suzaki, T., Kubo, H.: Impossible Differential Cryptanalysis of CLEFIA. In: Nyberg, K. (ed.) FSE 2008. LNCS, vol. 5086, pp. 398–411. Springer, Heidelberg (2008)
12. Wei, W., Wang, X.: Saturation cryptanalysis of CLEFIA. Journal on Communications 29(10), 88–92 (2008)
13. Zhang, W., Han, J.: Impossible Differential Analysis of Reduced Round CLEFIA. In: Yung, M., Liu, P., Lin, D. (eds.) Inscrypt 2008. LNCS, vol. 5487, pp. 181–191. Springer, Heidelberg (2009)
14. Li, Y., Wu, W., Zhang, L.: Integral Attacks on Reduced-Round ARIA Block Cipher. In: Kwak, J., Deng, R.H., Won, Y., Wang, G. (eds.) ISPEC 2010. LNCS, vol. 6047, pp. 19–29. Springer, Heidelberg (2010)

Preimage Attacks on Full-ARIRANG: Analysis of DM-Mode with Middle Feed-Forward

Chiaki Ohtahara[1], Keita Okada[1], Yu Sasaki[2], and Takeshi Shimoyama[3]

[1] Chuo-University
{cohtahara,kokada}@chao.ise.chuo-u.ac.jp
[2] NTT Information Sharing Platform Laboratories, NTT Corporation
3-9-11 Midori-cho, Musashino-shi, Tokyo, 180-8585 Japan
NTT Corporation
sasaki.yu@lab.ntt.co.jp
[3] Fujitsu Laboratories LTD
shimo@labs.fujitsu.com

Abstract. In this paper, we present preimage attacks on hash function ARIRANG, which is one of the first round candidates in the SHA-3 competition. Although ARIRANG was not chosen for the second round, the vulnerability as a hash function has not been discovered yet. ARIRANG has an unique design where the feed-forward operation is computed not only after the last step but also in a middle step. In fact, this design prevents previous preimage attacks from breaking full steps. In this paper, we apply a framework of meet-in-the-middle preimage attacks to ARIRANG. Specifically, we propose a new initial-structure technique optimized for ARIRANG that overcomes the use of the feed-forward to the middle. This enables us to find preimages of full steps ARIRANG-256 and ARIRANG-512 with 2^{254} and 2^{505} compression function operations and 2^6 and 2^{16} amount of memory, respectively. These are the first results breaking the security of ARIRANG as a hash function.

Keywords: ARIRANG, SHA-3, hash function, middle feed-forward, preimage.

1 Introduction

Hash functions are widely used in various information processing applications. After the surprising breakthrough on MD5 and SHA-1 by Wang *et al.* [1,2], NIST started the competition to determine a new standard hash function called SHA-3 [3].

In October 2008, 64 algorithms were submitted to the SHA-3 competition, and 51 algorithms were accepted as the first round candidates. ARIRANG [4] designed by Chang *et al.* is one of the first round candidates. NIST then determined 14 second round candidates in August 2009 and 5 third round candidates in December 2010. ARIRANG could not go into the second round, however, even today, its security as a hash function is not broken yet.

S. Jung and M. Yung (Eds.): WISA 2011, LNCS 7115, pp. 40–54, 2012.

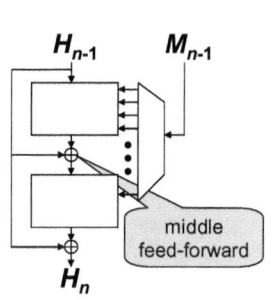

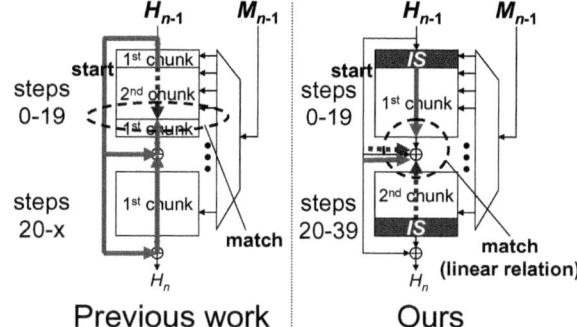

Fig. 1. DM-mode with middle feed-forward

Fig. 2. Strategy to overcome the middle feed-forward. IS represents "Initial Structure."

ARIRANG's structure is based on a Davies-Meyer construction. Although the standard Davies-Meyer construction computes the feed-forward operation only after the last step, ARIRANG also computes it in a middle step (middle feed-forward) as shown in Fig. 1. Regarding the effect of the middle feed-forward, the designers give the following statement [4, Section 6.6].

> *The compression function of ARIRANG uses the Feedforward operation twice, which makes it very difficult to invert a given hash value.*

In fact, the middle feed-forward seems to increase the security against preimage attacks. However, its impact is not clearly evaluated and understood.

There are several previous research reporting cryptanalyses on ARIRANG, e.g. a pseudo-collision (free-start collision) attack on full (40) steps of ARIRANG-224 and ARIRANG-384 by Guo *et al.* [5]. This attack exploits the use of the middle feed-forward, however, it requires to make differences in the initial value (IV) and truncates one or two registers at the end of the computation. Therefore, this attack cannot be applied to the hash function scenario where IV is fixed, nor ARIRANG-256 and ARIRANG-512 where the truncation is not performed. In fact, in the hash function setting, this attack only can work up to 26 steps. Therefore, although it points out a cetain vulnerability of ARIRANG, [5] is not enough to learn the effect of the use of the middle feed-forward in general.

In terms of the attacks on the hash function, Hong *et al.* proposed preimage attacks on reduced steps [6,7]. Both attacks are based on the meet-in-the-middle preimage attack [8]. In this framework, how to separate the computation into two independent parts called *chunks* is the most important step. In both of ref. [6,7], there is one strong limitation, that is, the first step and the step where the middle feed-forward is computed must be included in the same chunk as depicted in Fig. 2. Due to this limitation, previous work principally cannot attack full steps. In this sense, the designers' statement on the impact of the middle feed-forward to the preimage resistance seems correct.

Our Contributions

In this paper, we propose preimage attacks on full ARIRANG-256 and ARIRANG-512. Our approach follows the framework of the meet-in-the-middle preimage

Table 1. Summary of attack results

Target	Attack	Steps	Complexity (Time, Mem.) for each output size				Ref.
			224 bits	256 bits	384 bits	512 bits	
CF	FS coll	40 (full)	$(2^{24}, Neg)$		$(1, Neg)$		[5]
CF	FS near-coll	40 (full)		$(1, Neg)$		$(1, Neg)$	[5]
CF	Collision	26		$(1, Neg)$		$(1, Neg)$	[5]
Hash	Preimage	33		$(2^{241}, 2^{32})$		$(2^{481}, 2^{64})$	[6]
Hash	Preimage	35		$(2^{240.94}, 2^{32})$		$(2^{480.94}, 2^{64})$	[7]
Hash	Preimage	40 (full)		$(2^{254}, 2^6)$		$(2^{505}, 2^{16})$	Ours

CF and FS represent compression function and free-start, respectively. Note that the attacks become more efficient for step-reduced variants. For example, 38 steps are attacked with almost the same complexity as previous best attack on 35 steps [7].

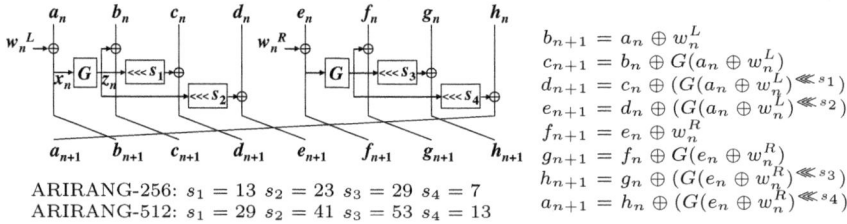

$$b_{n+1} = a_n \oplus w_n^L$$
$$c_{n+1} = b_n \oplus G(a_n \oplus w_n^L)$$
$$d_{n+1} = c_n \oplus (G(a_n \oplus w_n^L) \lll s_1)$$
$$e_{n+1} = d_n \oplus (G(a_n \oplus w_n^L) \lll s_2)$$
$$f_{n+1} = e_n \oplus w_n^R$$
$$g_{n+1} = f_n \oplus G(e_n \oplus w_n^R)$$
$$h_{n+1} = g_n \oplus (G(e_n \oplus w_n^R) \lll s_3)$$
$$a_{n+1} = h_n \oplus (G(e_n \oplus w_n^R) \lll s_4)$$

ARIRANG-256: $s_1 = 13$ $s_2 = 23$ $s_3 = 29$ $s_4 = 7$
ARIRANG-512: $s_1 = 29$ $s_2 = 41$ $s_3 = 53$ $s_4 = 13$

Fig. 3. Step function of ARIRANG

attack. We introduce an improved matching technique which checks the match of linear relations among several variables. The effect of this technique is depicted in Fig. 2. Different from the previous work, when we check the match of two chunks, impact from both chunks are propagated through the middle feed-forward. However, we can still perform an efficient match by analyzing the linear relations of the step function and the middle feed-forward operation. This enables us to apply the initial-structure technique [9], and thus full steps are attacked. Our attacks can find pseudo-preimages of full ARIRANG-256 and -512 with 2^{250} and 2^{496} compression function operations and 2^6 and 2^{16} amount of memory, respectively. They are then converted to preimage attacks with 2^{254} and 2^{505} compression function operations. Attack results are compared in Table 1. Note that our attacks can also generate second preimages.

From this research, we can learn the effect of the middle feed-forward operation against the meet-in-the-middle preimage attacks. In Sect. 5, we show that 4 rounds are not enough to keep the preimage resistance.

2   Description of ARIRANG

ARIRANG is a family of hash functions ARIRANG-224, -256, -384 and -512, and each algorithm outputs 224-bit, 256-bit, 384-bit and 512-bit message digests,

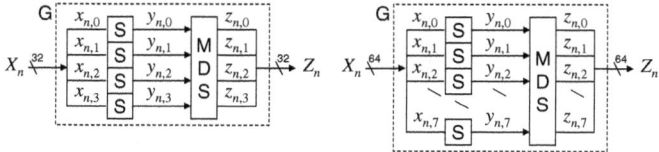

Fig. 4. Function G of ARIRANG-256 and ARIRANG-512

$$w_i = (w_{r_0} \oplus w_{r_1} \oplus w_{r_2} \oplus w_{r_3} \oplus K_{i-16})^{\lll t(i \bmod 4)} \quad (i = 16, \ldots, 31)$$

ARIRANG-256: $t_0 = 5$ $t_1 = 11$ $t_2 = 19$ $t_3 = 31$
ARIRANG-512: $t_0 = 11$ $t_1 = 23$ $t_2 = 37$ $t_3 = 59$

i	r_0	r_1	r_2	r_3	i	r_0	r_1	r_2	r_3	i	r_0	r_1	r_2	r_3	i	r_0	r_1	r_2	r_3
16	9	11	13	15	20	14	4	10	0	24	13	15	1	3	28	10	0	6	12
17	8	10	12	14	21	11	1	7	13	25	4	6	8	10	29	15	5	11	1
18	1	3	5	7	22	6	12	2	8	26	5	7	9	11	30	2	8	14	4
19	0	2	4	6	23	3	9	15	5	27	12	14	0	2	31	7	13	3	9

Fig. 5. Message schedule of ARIRANG

respectively. In this paper, we deal with ARIRANG-256 and ARIRANG-512. ARIRANG takes arbitrary length messages as input. ARIRANG uses a narrow-pipe Merkle-Damgård structure and its compression function uses a modified Davies-Meyer construction. In the preprocessing phase, the message is padded by a rule. We only note that the last 65 bits in the final message block is fixed by the padding string and thus is uncontrollable for the preimage attack. The compression function of ARIRANG consists of forty "Step function" and two "Feed-forward function." The feed-forward function is located every 20 steps.

The step function of ARIRANG updates eight working variables $a_n, b_n, c_n, d_n,$ e_n, f_n, g_n and h_n on n-th step as shown in Fig. 3. In each step, two message words w_n^L and w_n^R, which are XORed to variables a_n and e_n, respectively, are used. Then, the bijective function G randomizes the variables a_n and e_n and the outputs are rotated and XORed to the remaining 6 variables. The function G is composed of the S-box which is defined as SubBytes of AES and a linear mapping MDS. Fig. 4 shows the function G of ARIRANG-256 and -512.

The structures of the compression functions of ARIRANG-256 and -512 are the same except for the word size of working variables, the numbers of rotation bits and the MDS matrix in the function G. The word size of ARIRANG-256 is 32 bits and the word size of ARIRANG-512 is 64 bits. The function G of ARIRANG-512 splits the input word into eight bytes then each byte is run through the S-box and is gathered. The MDS transformation in the function G of ARIRANG-512 mixes 8 bytes by using an 8×8 matrix. (See Fig.12.)

The message schedule of ARIRANG generates 16 extra words $w_i(16 \leq i \leq 31)$ from the 16 input message words $w_i(0 \leq i \leq 15)$ and 16 constant values $K_i(0 \leq i \leq 15)$. For the ordering of the expanded message words w_n^L, w_n^R of the step n, the index in Fig. 6 is used. (In step 0, $w_0^L = w_{16}$ and $w_0^R = w_{17}$.)

3   Related Work

3.1   Converting Pseudo-preimage Attack to Preimage Attack

Given a hash value H_N, a pseudo-preimage is a pair of (H_{N-1}, M_{N-1}) such that $CF(H_{N-1}, M_{N-1}) = H_N$, and $H_{N-1} \neq IV$. For an n-bit narrow-pipe iterated hash function like ARIRANG, if pseudo-preimages with appropriate padding string can be generated with a complexity of 2^m, where $m < n - 2$, preimages can be generated with a complexity of $2^{\frac{m+n}{2}+1}$ [10, Fact9.99].

The above conversion works in general. In addition, if pseudo-preimage attacks can satisfy certain special properties, more efficient conversions are possible; tree approach [11], $\mathbf{P}^3$-graph [12], and multi-target pseudo-preimage [13]. Because our attacks cannot satisfy such special properties, we omit their details.

3.2   Meet-in-the-Middle Preimage Attack

Preimage attacks on hash functions with a meet-in-the-middle approach have been discussed many times. For example, Leurent applied it to MD4 [11] and Khovratovich et al. applied it to several round-one SHA-3 candidates [14]. As is explained later, ARIRANG is also analyzed [6,7].

Previous preimage attacks on ARIRANG and our attacks are based on the framework of the meet-in-the-middle preimage attack developed by Aoki and Sasaki [8]. The attack divides the compression function into two *chunks* of steps so that each chunk includes independent message words called *neutral words*. Then, pseudo-preimages are obtained by the meet-in-the-middle attack, namely, computing each chunk independently and matching the partially-computed intermediate chaining variables. The framework is illustrated in Fig. 13 in Appendix. Refer to [8] for more details such as terminologies and the procedure.

Assume that the first chunk has d_1 free bits and the second chunk has d_2 free bits, where $d_1 \leq d_2$. Also assume that each chunk computes d_3 bits of intermediate chaining variables used for the match, where $d_3 \geq min(d_1, d_2) = d_1$. In this framework, an attacker computes d_3 match bits of the first chunk for 2^{d_1} possible values and store the results in a table. The table is sorted in time 2^{d_1} using the hash table so that look-up can later be carried out in time 1. Then, for each of 2^{d_2} possible values, compute the d_3 match bits of the second chunk and check if they exist in the table. If exist, compute and check the match of the other $n - d_3$ bits with the matched message words, where n is the state size. Using 2^{d_2} computations of the second chunk, $2^{d_1+d_2-d_3}$ pairs whose d_3 bits match are obtained. Finally, by iterating the procedure $2^{n-(d_1+d_2)}$ times, a pseudo-preimage will be obtained. The attack complexity is 2^{n-d_1} in time, and 2^{d_1} in memory.

Several auxiliary techniques were proposed in this framework. The *splice-and-cut* technique [8] regards the first and last steps of the Davies-Meyer compression function as consecutive steps. The partial-matching/-fixing and indirect partial-matching techniques [8,15] match the values of two steps located in a few steps away. The *local-collision* and *initial-structure* techniques [16,9] exchange the positions of several message words in neighboring steps around the starting step of each chunk. Aoki and Sasaki introduced *linear algebra* on message schedules to search for independent message words [17], which works in general for hash functions with a linear message schedule.

3.3 Previous Works of Preimage Attacks on ARIRANG

Hong *et al.* proposed preimage attacks on reduced steps of ARIRANG hash function using the framework of the meet-in-the-middle preimage attack [6,7]. However, due to the existence of the middle feed-forward, the possibility of separating the compression function into two chunks is very limited compared to the original Davies-Mayer mode. For example, let the fist step (IV) is included in the first chunk and the step where the middle feed-forward is computed is included in the second chunk. Then, the middle feed-forward breaks the independence of two chunks and thus the attack cannot succeed. [6] summarizes patterns of the chunk separation which the attacker can perform the meet-in-the-middle attack even if the middle feed-forward is used. Briefly speaking, the idea is including the first step (IV) and the step for the middle feed-forward in the same chunk. This strategy is illustrated on the left side of Fig. 2.

By following this strategy, in [6], the authors assigned one message word as neutral words, and attacked 33 steps. In [7], the authors further analyzed linear relations of expanded message-words, and attacked 35 steps.

Note that to follow the strategy of [6], the range of the second chunk in the left of Fig. 2 must be completely included in the first half (steps 0–19) or completely included in the last half (steps 20–39). In either case, the neutral word to compute the second chunk must not appear in the other half. However, because the message schedule of ARIRANG always uses each message word in every 10 steps, achieving this condition on full-steps is principally impossible. Hence, unless several steps are removed from the attack target, the strategy of [6] cannot work. In other words, full ARIRANG is secure against previous work.

4 Preimage Attacks on Full ARIRANG-256 and -512

We firstly search for many pseudo-preimages (preimages of the compression function) by meet-in-the-middle attack. We then convert generated pseudo-preimages into a preimage of the hash function with the conversion method in Sect. 3.1.

4.1 Chunk Separation

Chooseing only one of w_0 to w_{15} as a neutral word is not a reasonable strategy. This is because changing one of them will activate four of expanded message words, which appear in every 5 steps. Hence, separating full steps into two independent chunks becomes difficult. To evade this obstacle, as [7], we choose two original message words as neutral words so that the impact on some expanded message words can cancel each other. Let us consider choosing w_0 and w_4 as neutral words. According to Fig. 5, six expanded message words will be influenced from w_0 and w_4. If we choose w_0 and w_4 so that $w_0 \oplus w_4$ always becomes

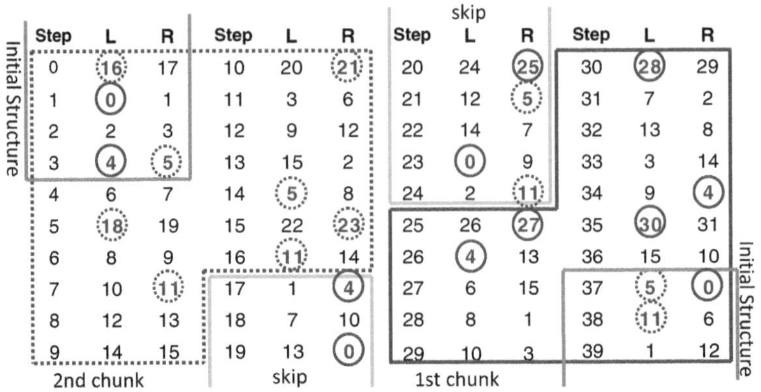

Fig. 6. Message scheculde and chunk separation for full ARIRANG

a certain constant e.g. 0, the impact on w_{19} and w_{20} will disappear, and only 4 expanded message words will be influenced. With this effort, the positions of influenced words can be gathered in a small range (Four influenced words w_{25}, w_{27}, w_{28}, and w_{30} lie within only 6 steps). This is a useful property to separate long steps into two independent chunks.

We coded the neutral-word-search algorithm and searched exhaustively for the neutral words that could generate chunks which were effective for the attack. In this algorithm, the search area includes the cases that neutral words are on the opposite chunk, since such neutral words in the opposite chunk can be moved to the suitable chunk area by using the Initial Structure technique based on equivalent transformation of the positions of XORing messages. Obviously, it is necessary to consider the influence to partial-bits for matching via feed-forward by executing Initial Structure. In our search, the variables which will be influenced via this feed-forward are treated as unknown words, and these variables are assumed not to able to use it for match of the partial-bits. Then, the number of match bits is checked so that the attack might succeed.

As a result, we choose (w_0, w_4), where $w_0 = w_4$ and (w_5, w_{11}), where $w_5 = w_{11}$ as neutral words. The chunk separation is shown in Fig. 6. Expanded message words influenced from the neutral words are circled in Fig. 6. Note that we use the same neutral words for ARIRANG-256 and -512.

4.2 Preimage Attacks on ARIRANG-256

In Fig. 6, neutral words w_0 and w_4 of the first chunk are included in the second chunk and neutral words w_5 and w_{11} of the second chunk are included in the first chunk. In the meet-in-the-middle attack, we need to compute each chunk independently, and we thus need to exchange the positions of these words. In this section, we firstly explain how to move the positions of these words into suitable chunks by using the initial-structure. In Fig. 6, steps 17 to 24 in total 8 steps are skipped. We then explain how to match the results from two chunks with with eight steps that are skipped.

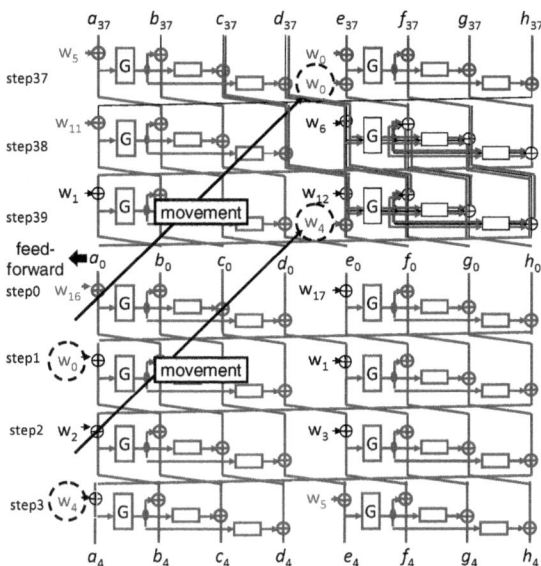

Fig. 7. Overview of initial structure

Initial Structure. The purpose of the initial-structure is ensuring the independence of the computations of each chunk even if neutral words for the opposite chunk are included in each chunk. To achieve this, we first apply equivalent transformations in order to move the positions of XOR operations so that impacts from neutral words for each chunk can be computed independently.

The overview of the initial structure is shown in Fig. 7. Note that several variables are affected from both chunks. In such a case, we only use a part of bits of neutral words as the freedom degree so that the impact from two chunks never reach the same bit position in those variables.

However, if input variables to the G function is affected from both chunks, the strategy of separating the active bits cannot work because values of all bits are mixed inside the G function. To solve this problem, we use a characteristic of the G function, where we can independently compute the impact on G from each input byte. For example, assume that the neutral words in the first chunk impact to the lower 2 bytes of the input variable to G in step 39, which are represented by $x_{39,0}$ and $x_{39,1}$. Similarly, the second chunk impacts to the higher 2 bytes of the input variable to G, which are $x_{39,2}$ and $x_{39,3}$. Then, functions to compute the impacts from the first and second chunks become $G_L = MDS(S(x_{39,0})\|S(x_{39,1})\|0\|0)$ and $G_H = MDS(0\|0\|S(x_{39,2})\|S(x_{39,3}))$, respectively, which can be computed independently in each chunk. This is illustrated in Fig. 14 in Appendix.

We apply the above separation to step 39. However, we also need to apply the similar separation to step 38. This is complicated because we need to control the bit positions of impacts from the first chunk after the computation of G in

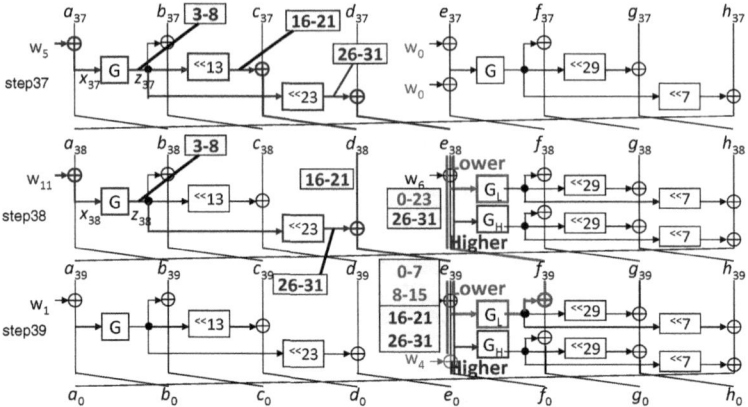

Fig. 8. Details of initial-structure construction for step 37 to step 39

step 39, and because the impacts from the second chunk (w_5 and w_{11}) will reach different bit positions between steps 38 and 39 due to the different bit rotations. The details of how we separate these steps is described in Fig. 8.

In the following, we explain computations in each chunk and show that bit positions influenced in each chunk are always in different positions, and thus two chunks can be computed independently.

First Chunk (Backward). We choose the values of neutral words w_0 and w_4 so that only the lower 2 bytes and the lower 3 bytes of the input variable to G in steps 39 and 38 are influenced, respectively. Therefore, considering step 39, we only use the lower 2 bytes of w_4 as the freedom degree. Furthermore, considering the G function in step 38, we need to ensure that the impacts never goes to the highest byte ($z_{39,3}$) through the G function in step 39. This is possible by looking the details of an MDS matrix as shown in Fig. 15 in Appendix, where the impacts to $z_{39,3}$ from $MDS(y_{39,0}\|y_{39,1}\|0\|0)$ is computed as $z_{39,3} = (03 \cdot y_{39,0}) \oplus y_{39,1}$. Therefore, every time we choose the value of $y_{39,0}$, we set $y_{39,1}$ to be identical with $(03 \cdot y_{39,0})$. In summary, in the first chunk, we choose the value of $y_{39,0}$ and then calculate $y_{39,1}$. Next, we compute the inverse of S-boxes for these two bytes to obtain the value of w_4, and then fix w_0 such that $w_0 = w_4$. We stress that the freedom degree for the first chunk is 8 bits.

Second Chunk (Forward). At first, we fix the values of a_{37} and a_{38} to an identical value.

We choose bit positions 3 to 8 of z_{37} as freedom degree. This will impact to bit positions 26 to 31 of the input of G in step 38 after the left rotation by 23 bits and impact to bit positions 16 to 21 of the input of G in step 39 after the left rotation by 13 bits.

After we choose z_{37}, we compute the inverse of G to obtain x_{37}, and then compute w_5 by $x_{37} \oplus a_{37}$. In step 38, because $w_{11} = w_5$ and $a_{37} = a_{38}$, $x_{38} = x_{37}$ is always satisfied and thus $z_{38} = z_{37}$. Namely, only bit positions

3–8 of z_{38} are influenced in the second chunk. This will impact to bit positions 26 to 31 of the input of G in step 38 after the left rotation by 23 bits.

Finally, we can guarantee that only the highest byte of z_{38} and higher 2 bytes of z_{39} are influenced in the second chunk. We stress that the freedom degree for the second chunk is 6 bits.

Finally, all computations inside the initial structure can be performed independently, and thus meet-in-the-middle attack is possible.

Skip. We cannot compute steps 17–24 because of the neutral words for the other chunk. Hence, we skip these steps, which means that we perform the meet-in-the-middle attack without fully computing these steps. Fig. 9 shows the partial computations in these steps. During these steps, w_0, w_4 and w_{25} are the neutral words of the first chunk, and w_5 and w_{11} are the neutral words of the second chunk. At a first glance, computing these steps independently in each chunk seems impossible due to the middle feed-forward. However, we show that independent computations and an efficient match of the results from two chunks are possible by carefully considering the linear relations among several variables.

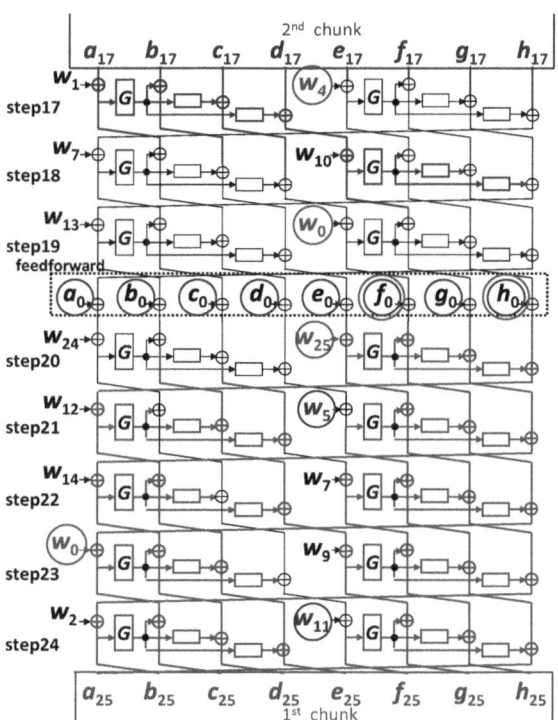

Fig. 9. Partial-matching with skipping 8 steps

In this section, to make the explanation clear, we denote variables just before the middle feed-forward by $a_{20}, b_{20}, \ldots, h_{20}$ and variables immediately after the middle feed-forward by $a_*, b_*, \ldots, h_*$.

In the backward computation from step 24 in the first chunk, after we compute the inverse of the step function in step 20, we know the values of 4 right most variables $(e_*, f_*, g_*,$ and $h_*)$. Then, initial value p_0 is added by the middle feed-forward operation. Therefore we must consider the influence caused by the initial structure. From Fig. 7, two variables f_0 and h_0 are influenced by the first chunk and all variables are influenced by the second chunk. Hence, more independent computations are impossible.

We similarly consider the forward computation in the second chunk and obtain the values of several variables as shown in Fig 9. We need to match the results from two chunks. However, it is impossible to compute the values of identical variables in both chunks. Hence, instead of the direct match, we consider the match of a linear-relation among several variables. The indirect partial-matching technique [15] can be applied to perform this match.

We show the details of the computation from step 17 to step 19 in Fig. 10. In the following, we denote the impact on h_0 from the first and second chunks by h_0^{1st} and h_0^{2nd}, respectively. Then, the equations to compute the values of g_* and h_* can be written as follows. Note that notations $\underline{V}_1$ and $\underline{V}_2$ represent that a variable V is computed in the first and second chunks, respectively.

$$\underline{g_*}_1 = \underline{f_{19}}_2 \oplus z_{19} \oplus \underline{g_0}_2, \quad \underline{h_*}_1 = \underline{z_{18}}_2 \oplus \underline{e_{17}}_2 \oplus \underline{w_4}_1 \oplus (z_{19})^{\lll 29} \oplus \underline{h_0^{2nd}}_2 \oplus \underline{h_0^{1st}}_1.$$

With rotating the first equation by 29 bits, we can cancel $(z_{19})^{\lll 29}$.

$$\underline{f_{19}}^{\lll 29}_2 \oplus \underline{g_0}^{\lll 29}_2 \oplus \underline{z_{18}}_2 \oplus \underline{e_{17}}_2 \oplus \underline{h_0^{2nd}}_2 = \underline{g_*}^{\lll 29}_1 \oplus \underline{w_4}_1 \oplus \underline{h_0^{1st}}_1 \oplus \underline{h_*}_1. \qquad (1)$$

By computing each side of Eq. 1 in each chunk independently, we can efficiently match the 32-bit linear relations of the results from two chunks.

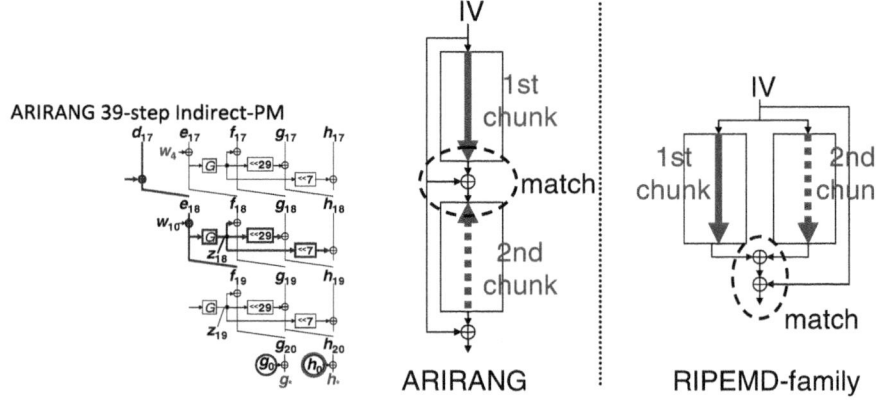

Fig. 10. Indirect partial-matching   **Fig. 11.** Another look of middle feed-forward

4.3   The Attack Procedure

The procedure for our pseudo-preimage attack is as follows.

1. We fix the message words w_{13}, w_{14}, and w_{15} so that the padding string for a 2-block message is satisfied. We also fix other message words that are not chosen as neutral words and several chaining variables inside the initial structure to randomly chosen constants.
2. In the second chunk, for all 2^6 choices of bit positions 3 to 8 of z_{37}, we compute the initial structure by the method in Sect. 4.2. Then, we compute the step function from step 0 to 16.
3. For the match, we calculate the left side of Eq. 1 and store it in a table T.
4. In the first chunk, for all 2^8 choices of $y_{39,0}$ we compute the initial structure, and then compute the step function from step 39 to 25.
5. We calculate the right side of Eq. 1 and check if that value is stored in T.
6. If it matches, we check the match of other bits with corresponding message words. Otherwise, we repeat the attack from stage 1 of this procedure.

With one iteration of stage 1, the dominant complexity is 2^8 for stage 4. Then, we check the match of $2^6 \cdot 2^8 = 2^{14}$ pairs in 32 bits. Hence, $2^{14} \cdot 2^{-32} = 2^{-18}$ pair that 32 bits match will remain. To obtain a pseudo-preimage (a pair that matches all 256 bits), Stage 1 needs to be repeated $2^{256-32+18} = 2^{242}$ times. The complexity of the pseudo-preimage attack is $2^8 \cdot 2^{242} = 2^{250}$ operations, and we use 2^6 memory for table T. Finally, with the conversion in Sect. 3.1, we find preimages of a hash function with $2^{\frac{256+250}{2}+1} = 2^{254}$ operations.

4.4   Preimage Attacks on ARIRANG-512

The important points of the difference between the compression functions of ARIRANG-256 and ARIRANG-512 are the size of an internal variable, and the values of rotation shifts in the step function. For attacking ARIRANG-512, the strategy is almost the same as that of ARIRANG-256 described in the previous section, except for the number of active bits in the neutral words. The pairs of neutral words are (w_0, w_4) and (w_5, w_{11}) for the first chunk and second chunk, respectively. In order to optimize the selection of active bits, it is necessary to consider the difference of the values of two rotation shifts s_1 and s_2 in the step function, that is $41 - 29 = 12$.

As the results, we reached that, for the first chunk, the bit positions 0 to 31 of the neutral words w_0 and w_4 should be used as the active bits so that the highest 2 bytes of the output of $MDS(y_{39,0}|| \cdots ||y_{39,3}||0||0||0||0)$ (see Fig. 12) in step 39 can not be influenced by $y_{39,0}, \cdots, y_{39,3}$, and for the second chunk, the neutral word $w_5 = w_{11}$ according to the active bit positions 7 to 22 of $z_{37} = z_{38}$, should be used, by using the same method of ARIRANG-256. In both chunks, the numbers of freedom degree is 16, and the number of match bits becomes at least 16. By the above setting, pseudo-preimages can be obtained by using $2^{512-16} = 2^{496}$ complexity and 2^{16} memory. With the conversion in Sect. 3.1, preimages are obtained with $2^{\frac{496+512}{2}+1} = 2^{505}$ complexity and 2^{16} memory.

5   Effect of the Middle Feed-Forward Operation

We can learn the effect of the middle feed-forward against MitM preimage attacks. The middle feed-forward limits the possibility of the chunk separation. The best attack strategy seems to regard the computation from the first step to the middle as one chunk and the computation from the last step to the middle as the other chunk, and finally checking the match by considering the effect of the middle feed-forward. In fact, all of [6,7] and ours adopted this strategy. This strategy can be regarded to be the same as the one for the double-branch structure (e.g. RIPEMD-family). This observation is illustrated in Fig. 11.

Assume that a hash function with the middle feed-forward consists of r rounds. The number of rounds in each chunk is $\frac{r}{2}$. Hence, the r-round middle feed-forward structure is as secure as the $\frac{r}{2}$-round double-branch structure.

ARIRANG consists of 4 rounds, and thus its security is the same as 2-round double-branch structure. On the other hand, several papers successfully attacked RIPEMD-family reduced to 2 rounds [18,19,20]. Moreover, [20] attacks almost all of 3 rounds. Hence, the preimage resistance of ARIRANG is suspectable from this viewpoint. In fact, our attacks have a certain similarity as [19].

A simple countermeasure against our attacks is increasing the number of rounds. Taking into account that [20] reaches almost all 3 rounds of RIPEMD, computing 6 rounds in ARIRANG is temporary secure but the security margin seems very thin. We recommend computing 8 rounds in ARIRANG instead.

6   Concluding Remarks

In this paper, we proposed preimage attacks on full ARIRANG-256 and -512 using the meet-in-the-middle preimage attack. We introduced the initial-structure technique in order to exchange positions of message-words over the initial value. This makes the middle feed-forward value to be influenced from both chunks and makes the matching procedure difficult. We then proposed the new matching technique which checks the match of linear relations so that the efficient match can be carried out even if the middle feed-forward value is influenced from both chunks. As a result, we finally succeeded in attacking full steps. As far as we know, these are the first results that break the security of ARIRANG as a hash function.

References

1. Wang, X., Yu, H.: How to Break MD5 and other Hash Functions. In: Cramer, R. (ed.) EUROCRYPT 2005. LNCS, vol. 3494, pp. 19–35. Springer, Heidelberg (2005)
2. Wang, X., Yin, Y.L., Yu, H.: Finding Collisions in the Full SHA-1. In: Shoup, V. (ed.) CRYPTO 2005. LNCS, vol. 3621, pp. 17–36. Springer, Heidelberg (2005)
3. U.S. Department of Commerce, National Institute of Standards and Technology: Federal Register, vol. 72(212) (November 2, 2007)

4. Chang, D., Hong, S., Kang, C., Kang, J., Kim, J., Lee, C., Lee, J., Lee, J., Lee, S., Lee, Y., Lim, J., Sung, J.: Arirang : Sha-3 proposal, http://cist.korea.ac.kr/~arirang/Arirang.pdf
5. Guo, J., Matusiewicz, K., Knudsen, L.R., Ling, S., Wang, H.: Practical Pseudo-Collisions for Hash Functions ARIRANG-224/384. In: Jacobson Jr., M.J., Rijmen, V., Safavi-Naini, R. (eds.) SAC 2009. LNCS, vol. 5867, pp. 141–156. Springer, Heidelberg (2009)
6. Hong, D., Kim, W.H., Koo, B.: Preimage attack on ARIRANG. Cryptology ePrint Archive, Report 2009/147 (2009)
7. Hong, D., Koo, B., Kim, W.-H., Kwon, D.: Preimage Attacks on Reduced Steps of ARIRANG and PKC98-Hash. In: Lee, D., Hong, S. (eds.) ICISC 2009. LNCS, vol. 5984, pp. 315–331. Springer, Heidelberg (2010)
8. Aoki, K., Sasaki, Y.: Preimage Attacks on One-Block MD4, 63-Step MD5 and More. In: Avanzi, R.M., Keliher, L., Sica, F. (eds.) SAC 2008. LNCS, vol. 5381, pp. 103–119. Springer, Heidelberg (2009)
9. Sasaki, Y., Aoki, K.: Finding Preimages in Full MD5 Faster than Exhaustive Search. In: Joux, A. (ed.) EUROCRYPT 2009. LNCS, vol. 5479, pp. 134–152. Springer, Heidelberg (2009)
10. Menezes, A.J., van Oorschot, P.C., Vanstone, S.A.: Handbook of applied cryptography. CRC Press (1997)
11. Leurent, G.: MD4 is Not One-Way. In: Nyberg, K. (ed.) FSE 2008. LNCS, vol. 5086, pp. 412–428. Springer, Heidelberg (2008)
12. De Cannière, C., Rechberger, C.: Preimages for Reduced SHA-0 and SHA-1. In: Wagner, D. (ed.) CRYPTO 2008. LNCS, vol. 5157, pp. 179–202. Springer, Heidelberg (2008)
13. Guo, J., Ling, S., Rechberger, C., Wang, H.: Advanced Meet-in-the-Middle Preimage Attacks: First Results on Full Tiger, and Improved Results on MD4 and SHA-2. In: Abe, M. (ed.) ASIACRYPT 2010. LNCS, vol. 6477, pp. 56–75. Springer, Heidelberg (2010)
14. Khovratovich, D., Nikolić, I., Weinmann, R.-P.: Meet-in-the-Middle Attacks on SHA-3 Candidates. In: Dunkelman, O. (ed.) FSE 2009. LNCS, vol. 5665, pp. 228–245. Springer, Heidelberg (2009)
15. Aoki, K., Guo, J., Matusiewicz, K., Sasaki, Y., Wang, L.: Preimages for Step-Reduced SHA-2. In: Matsui, M. (ed.) ASIACRYPT 2009. LNCS, vol. 5912, pp. 578–597. Springer, Heidelberg (2009)
16. Sasaki, Y., Aoki, K.: Preimage Attacks on 3, 4, and 5-Pass HAVAL. In: Pieprzyk, J. (ed.) ASIACRYPT 2008. LNCS, vol. 5350, pp. 253–271. Springer, Heidelberg (2008)
17. Aoki, K., Sasaki, Y.: Meet-in-the-Middle Preimage Attacks Against Reduced SHA-0 and SHA-1. In: Halevi, S. (ed.) CRYPTO 2009. LNCS, vol. 5677, pp. 70–89. Springer, Heidelberg (2009)
18. Sasaki, Y., Aoki, K.: Meet-in-the-Middle Preimage Attacks on Double-Branch Hash Functions: Application to RIPEMD and Others. In: Boyd, C., González Nieto, J. (eds.) ACISP 2009. LNCS, vol. 5594, pp. 214–231. Springer, Heidelberg (2009)
19. Ohtahara, C., Sasaki, Y., Shimoyama, T.: Preimage Attacks on Step-Reduced RIPEMD-128 and RIPEMD-160. In: Lai, X., Yung, M., Lin, D. (eds.) Inscrypt 2010. LNCS, vol. 6584, pp. 169–186. Springer, Heidelberg (2011)
20. Wang, L., Sasaki, Y., Komatsubara, W., Ohta, K., Sakiyama, K. (Second) Preimage Attacks on Step-Reduced Ripemd/Ripemd-128 with a New Local-Collision Approach. In: Kiayias, A. (ed.) CT-RSA 2011. LNCS, vol. 6558, pp. 197–212. Springer, Heidelberg (2011)

A   Auxiliary Figures

$$
\begin{pmatrix} z_0 \\ z_1 \\ z_2 \\ z_3 \end{pmatrix} = \begin{pmatrix} 02 & 03 & 01 & 01 \\ 01 & 02 & 03 & 01 \\ 01 & 01 & 02 & 03 \\ 03 & 01 & 01 & 02 \end{pmatrix} \begin{pmatrix} y_0 \\ y_1 \\ y_2 \\ y_3 \end{pmatrix} \qquad \begin{pmatrix} z_0 \\ z_1 \\ z_2 \\ z_3 \\ z_4 \\ z_5 \\ z_6 \\ z_7 \end{pmatrix} = \begin{pmatrix} 01 & 02 & 0A & 09 & 08 & 01 & 04 & 01 \\ 01 & 01 & 02 & 0A & 09 & 08 & 01 & 04 \\ 04 & 01 & 01 & 02 & 0A & 09 & 08 & 01 \\ 01 & 04 & 01 & 01 & 02 & 0A & 09 & 08 \\ 08 & 01 & 04 & 01 & 01 & 02 & 0A & 09 \\ 09 & 08 & 01 & 04 & 01 & 01 & 02 & 0A \\ 0A & 09 & 08 & 01 & 04 & 01 & 01 & 02 \\ 02 & 0A & 09 & 08 & 01 & 04 & 01 & 01 \end{pmatrix} \begin{pmatrix} y_0 \\ y_1 \\ y_2 \\ y_3 \\ y_4 \\ y_5 \\ y_6 \\ y_7 \end{pmatrix}
$$

Fig. 12. MDS functions in function G of ARIRANG-256 and ARIRANG-512

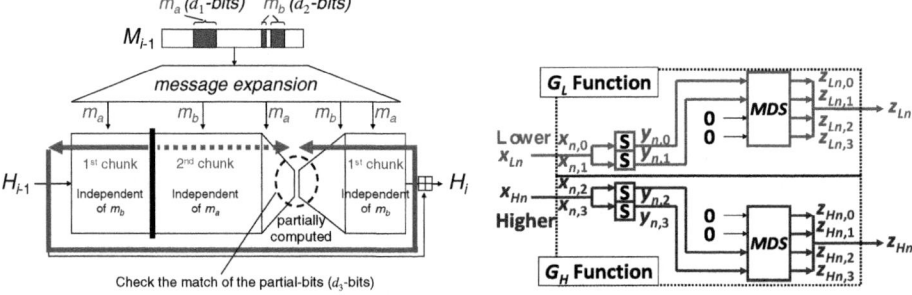

Fig. 13. MitM preimage attack framework

Fig. 14. Separation for G function

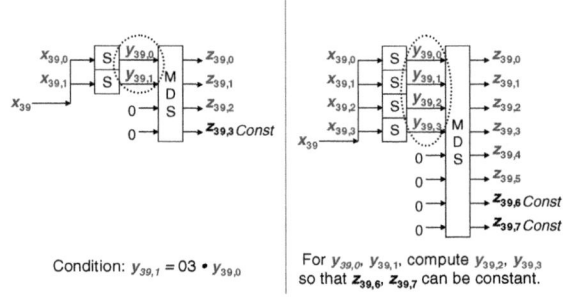

Condition: $y_{39,1} = 03 \cdot y_{39,0}$

For $y_{39,0}$, $y_{39,1}$, compute $y_{39,2}$, $y_{39,3}$ so that $z_{39,6}$, $z_{39,7}$ can be constant.

Fig. 15. G function of step 39 for ARIRANG-256 (left) and ARIRANG-512 (right)

Known-Key Distinguisher on Round-Reduced 3D Block Cipher

Le Dong[1,2], Wenling Wu[1], Shuang Wu[1], and Jian Zou[1,2]

[1] State Key Lab of Information Security
Institute of Software, Chinese Academy of Sciences, Beijing 100190, China
[2] Graduate University of Chinese Academy of Sciences, Beijing 100149, China
{dongle,wwl,wushuang,zoujian}@is.iscas.ac.cn

Abstract. 3D block cipher is an AES-based block cipher which has a three-dimensional state. Besides some traditional attacks, Knudsen and Rijmen introduced a new tool, known-key distinguisher, to identify the weak pseudo-randomness of a block cipher. In this paper, we present a known-key distinguisher on 15-round 3D cipher, which has 22 rounds in total. In our attack, we use the rebound attack to construct two differential paths, and integrate them by a technique of solving a system of nonlinear equations. It can be done with a negligible complexity and sufficient random degrees are provided for the subsequent attack. We extend the differential trail to 15 rounds and give a known-key distinguisher based on the 15-round differential path. The complexity of finding a right pair is 2^{200}, which is clearly lower than the complexity of generic attack.

Keywords: 3D block cipher, distinguisher, rebound attack, limited birthday problem.

1 Introduction

AES [1] is an SPN block cipher announced by NIST in 2001. It has a fixed block size of 128 bits and a key size of 128, 192, or 256 bits. In 2008, Jorge Nakahara Jr introduced a three-dimension block cipher called 3D which is designed based on AES and has a larger state [2]. The 3D block cipher also has an SPN structure. It operates on 512-bit blocks and uses 512-bit keys. The reason to use 512-bit size user key is against the key-recovery attacks, i.e. they must recover 512 subkey bits with an expensive complexity. The recommended number of rounds for 3D is 22. In the AES, the state can be represented by a two-dimensional 4×4 state matrix of bytes. In contrast, the plaintext, ciphertext, subkeys and intermediate data blocks of 3D block cipher are denoted by a three-dimensional cube or a 4×16 matrix with bytes inserted columnwise. In [2], Nakahara constructed a multiset distinguisher on 5.75-round 3D. Applying the missing-in-the-middle technique and the inside-out technique, he gave a 6-round impossible differential path and a 9.75-round known-key distinguisher [3].

In 2007, Knudsen and Rijmen raised a question [4]: should we recommend the use of a block cipher where if one is given any key, one can distinguish the

S. Jung and M. Yung (Eds.): WISA 2011, LNCS 7115, pp. 55–69, 2012.

cipher from an ideal function, but no efficient attacks are known in the traditional black-box model? The authors gave a negative answer and constructed an attack called known-key distinguisher for some block ciphers. Chosen-key distinguisher is another model to attack block ciphers. This model assumes that the attacker can choose both the key and the plaintext. The known-key model and the chosen-key model can be called the open key security model [5]. Both of them exploit the weak properties of some block ciphers. Knudsen and Rijmen presented a 7-round known-key integral distinguisher for AES in [4]. Minier et al. gave some known-key distinguishers for Rijndael with large blocks up to 7 and 8 rounds [6]. In [5], Biryukov et al. constructed a chosen-key distinguisher on the full AES-256. All of them are attacks of analyzing AES or its predecessor.

Our Contributions. In this paper, we show an attack for 15-round 3D block cipher in the known-key model. In the attack, we can distinguish the round-reduced cipher from a random permutation. First we identify some properties of the operations and the round function of 3D and then give an equivalent presentation of the round function. Using rebound attack, we construct a 6-round differential path with 64 active S-boxes, and we extend it to 15-round. This allows us to construct a distinguisher based on the limited-birthday problem. In order to integrate two differential paths into a new one, we apply a new technique, i.e. constructing an equation system and solving it to get a match.

This paper is organized as follows: in Section 2, we give a description of 3D block cipher. In Section 3, we show 4 properties of the operations used in the cipher and an equivalent presentation of the round function of 3D. In Section 4, the 15-round differential path is given. In Section 5, we introduce the limited-birthday problem and show how to distinguish the round-reduced cipher from a random function. Section 6 concludes the paper.

2   Preliminaries

2.1   Description of 3D Block Cipher

The 3D block cipher operates on 512-bit blocks and the same size key. It is an iterated cipher and the number of rounds is 22. The state of 3D can be denoted by a 3-dimensional cube ($4 \times 4 \times 4$ state of bytes) or a 4×16 matrix as follows,

$$
State = \begin{pmatrix}
a_0 & a_4 & a_8 & a_{12} & a_{16} & a_{20} & a_{24} & a_{28} & a_{32} & a_{36} & a_{40} & a_{44} & a_{48} & a_{52} & a_{56} & a_{60} \\
a_1 & a_5 & a_9 & a_{13} & a_{17} & a_{21} & a_{25} & a_{29} & a_{33} & a_{37} & a_{41} & a_{45} & a_{49} & a_{53} & a_{57} & a_{61} \\
a_2 & a_6 & a_{10} & a_{14} & a_{18} & a_{22} & a_{26} & a_{30} & a_{34} & a_{38} & a_{42} & a_{46} & a_{50} & a_{54} & a_{58} & a_{62} \\
a_3 & a_7 & a_{11} & a_{15} & a_{19} & a_{23} & a_{27} & a_{31} & a_{35} & a_{39} & a_{43} & a_{47} & a_{51} & a_{55} & a_{59} & a_{63}
\end{pmatrix}. \quad (1)
$$

In this paper, we use some names of parts of the 3D state illustrated in Figure 6 in Appendix A. Furthermore, we call one 4×4 submatrix separated by lines in (1) a *substate*.

The round transformations in 3D include four basic operations:

- κ_i: the operation is similar to the AddRoundKey in AES. A 512-bit subkey state XORs bytewise to the i-th round state;
- γ: the only nonlinear operation consists of the bytewise applications of the AES S-box to all bytes of the state in 3D;
- θ_1, θ_2: the two operations are the same as ShiftRows in AES and applied in alternate rounds in 3D. θ_1 operates on the slices in one round and θ_2 operates in the sheets on the next round.
- π: a 4×4 MDS matrix is applied to every column in the similar way to the MixColumn transformation in the AES. The matrix is used in Anubis cipher [7] and has branch number 5. Let an input column of π be denoted by $(a_0, a_1, a_2, a_3)^T$, and the output column be $(b_0, b_1, b_2, b_3)^T$. We can represent the operation π with the equation (2),

$$\begin{pmatrix} 01_x & 02_x & 04_x & 06_x \\ 02_x & 01_x & 06_x & 04_x \\ 04_x & 06_x & 01_x & 02_x \\ 06_x & 04_x & 02_x & 01_x \end{pmatrix} \begin{pmatrix} a_0 \\ a_1 \\ a_2 \\ a_3 \end{pmatrix} = \begin{pmatrix} b_0 \\ b_1 \\ b_2 \\ b_3 \end{pmatrix}, \tag{2}$$

where the subscript denotes hexadecimal notation.

The i-th round of 3D can be denoted by

$$\tau_i(X) = \pi \circ \theta_{i \bmod 2 + 1} \circ \gamma \circ \kappa_i(X).$$

For r-round 3D the round function is iterated $r - 1$ times, and in the last round the Diffusion Layer is replaced by the Round Key addition κ_r.

We omit the key schedule of 3D here, because our attack does not involve it. For the detail of key scheduling algorithm, the interested readers can refer to [2].

2.2   Notations

3D is an AES-like block cipher with a larger state than AES. We can denote its state by a three-dimensional cube. However, it is also convenient to view it with two-dimensional perspective. In our attack, we usually denote the 512-bit state of 3D by four 128-bit substates.

We recall that $\kappa_i, \gamma, \theta_i, \pi$ denote the four operations of 3D. For more intuitive, we use the same names as used in the AES to express them, namely, AddRoundKey (AK), SubBytes (SB), ShiftRows (SR_i), MixColumns (MC) denote $\kappa_i, \gamma, \theta_i, \pi$ respectively. Therefore, the two consecutive rounds of 3D can be presented by

$$MC \circ SR_2 \circ SB \circ AK \circ MC \circ SR_1 \circ SB \circ AK(X).$$

3   Some Properties of the Round Function of 3D

3.1   An Alternative Description of Round Function of 3D

In our attack, we use another description of round function of 3D and demonstrate that it is equivalent to the original one in this section. First, we can define a new transformation acting on every column for mixing the parallel substates.

Definition 1. *Let x_{i-1} denote the i-th column of the state of 3D block cipher. SwapColumns (SC) is given by*

$$Swapcolumns(x_0\|x_1\|\cdots\|x_{15}) =$$
$$x_0\|x_4\|x_8\|x_{12}\|x_1\|x_5\|x_9\|x_{13}\|x_2\|x_6\|x_{10}\|x_{14}\|x_3\|x_7\|x_{11}\|x_{15}.$$

Figure 1 shows the SwapColumns transformation. We can easily obtain a property of the new operation from its definition.

Proposition 1. *SwapColumns is equivalent to its inverse, namely $SC = SC^{-1}$.*

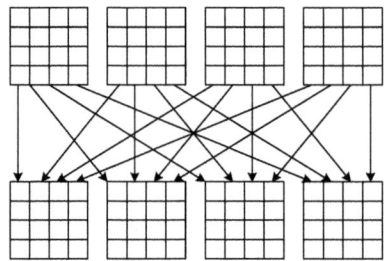

Fig. 1. The SwapColumns transformation

The following properties of the relationship between SC and other operations are also easy to verify.

Proposition 2. *For the operations SC, SB, MC, and AK, we have*

1. *$SC \circ SB = SB \circ SC$,*
2. *$SC \circ MC = MC \circ SC$,*
3. *$SC \circ AK = AK^* \circ SC$,*

where AK^* denotes the AddRoundKey transformation whose subkey bytes are in a different order.

Proposition 3. *For the two transformations SR_1 and SR_2, we have $SR_1 = SC \circ SR_2 \circ SC$. Since $SC = SC^{-1}$, we also have $SR_2 = SC \circ SR_1 \circ SC$.*

Proof. We use the three-dimension cube presentation in this proof. For convenience, Slice[0][1][2][3] denotes the four slices from the front to the back and Sheet[0][1][2][3] denotes the four sheets from the right to the left. Actually, Swap-Columns transforms Slice[0][1][2][3] into Sheet[3][2][1][0]. Hence the next transformation SR_2 is equivalent to the transformation SR_1 acting on the sheets. And then the second SC bring the Slice[0][1][2][3] back. As a result, $SC \circ SR_2 \circ SC$ acts on a state of 3D as the operation SR_1.   □

Proposition 4. *The two rounds of 3D can be presented by another form*

$$SC \circ MC \circ SR_1 \circ SB \circ AK^* \circ SC \circ MC \circ SR_1 \circ SB \circ AK.$$

Proof. From the three propositions mentioned before, we have

$$MC \circ SR_2 \circ SB \circ AK \circ MC \circ SR_1 \circ SB \circ AK$$
$$= MC \circ SC \circ SR_1 \circ SC \circ SB \circ AK \circ MC \circ SR_1 \circ SB \circ AK$$
$$= SC \circ MC \circ SR_1 \circ SB \circ AK^* \circ SC \circ MC \circ SR_1 \circ SB \circ AK.$$

□

We omit the footnotes of the operation ShiftRows in the following text for convenience.

4   The Differential Path Used in the Attack

In this section firstly we give a short overview of the rebound attack in general and then, construct a 4-round truncated differential path of 3D. Next, we present the core of the truncated differential path for 6-round 3D block cipher and show how to find a matching point. At last, we show the 15-round differential trail. We present the states of 3D by its longitudinal form. In this form, we move the right substates to underneath.

4.1   The Rebound Attack

The rebound attack [8] is a new tool to analyze hash functions by using the available freedom degrees efficiently. We can construct truncated differential paths with some active bytes in the middle rounds. The two main steps of the attack are called inbound phase and subsequent outbound phase. The inbound phase exploits the available degrees of freedom in the middle of a differential path by using the efficient match-in-the-middle technique. In the outbound phase, the matching states in the middle are computed backwards and forwards to obtain desired collisions or near-collisions.

This attack has been used for the cryptanalysis of some hash functions and some compression functions of hash algorithms such as Whirlpool [8,9], Grøstl [8,10,11,12], LANE [13,14], Twister [15], ECHO [10,11,12], JH [16], Cheetah [17], and Luffa [18]. However, one can also use the technique to analyze some AES-like block ciphers.

4.2   Primary Truncated Differential Path

The primary of the attack is a 4-round truncated differential trail from round 3 to round 6, and the number of active S-Boxes in each round is:

$$4 \xrightarrow{r_3} 16 \xrightarrow{r_4} 4 \xrightarrow{r_5} 16 \xrightarrow{r_6} 4.$$

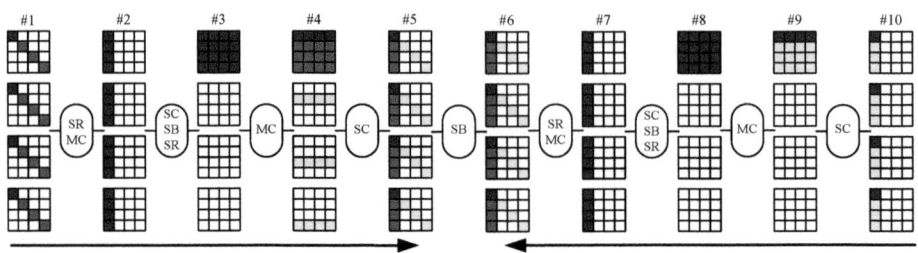

Fig. 2. The primary truncated differential path in our attack. Black bytes are active, red bytes and yellow bytes denote the bytes whose values can be determined after the first three steps.

The truncated differential path is given in Figure 2. The attack can be presented as follows:

Step 1. Firstly, choose 4-byte differences for state #1 and state #10, and then the differences of state #2 and state #8 are determined. The attack steps in the forward and backward directions are similar, so we only give the details of the forward direction.

Step 2. For each active byte in state #5, there are about 2^8 differences. The differences of four columns in state #3 can be independently determined by the four active bytes in state #5, so we can find possible candidates for each active byte in state #5 separately. From one difference of the first active byte in state #5, we can obtain the difference of the first column in state #3, which can be matched with four corresponding bytes in state #2 with a probability of 2^{-4}. So, only 2^4 differences are possible for the first active byte in state #5. For each possible difference d_i, 2^4 values $V_{i,j}$ are possible for the first column of state #5, including the red bytes. Then, there are 2^8 possible difference-value pairs $(d_i, V_{i,j})$ for each active byte in state #5, which are computed and stored in four look-up tables with 2^8 computations and 2^8 memory separately.

Step 3. With the same technique, we can compute 2^8 difference-value pairs for each active byte in state #6. Then we check if any of them is in the corresponding look-up table. The probability to match a bytewise difference-value pair is 2^{-16}, so we expect to find one match for all the four active bytes. This step has a complexity of 2^8 computations.

In total, it has a complexity of 2^8 and 2^8 memory requirement. Note that the differences and values of black bytes are matched. In addition, the values of the yellow bytes can also be obtained after these steps, and we discuss the values of yellow and red bytes later.

4.3   Core of the Truncated Differential Path

The core of the truncated path described in this subsection is composed of 6 rounds, with the following number of active bytes at SubBytes:

$$4 \xrightarrow{r_3} 16 \xrightarrow{r_4} 4 \xrightarrow{r_5} 16 \xrightarrow{r_6} 4 \xrightarrow{r_7} 16 \xrightarrow{r_8} 4.$$

We can see the details of the truncated differential path on r_7 and r_8 in Figure 3. The attack can be summarized as follows:

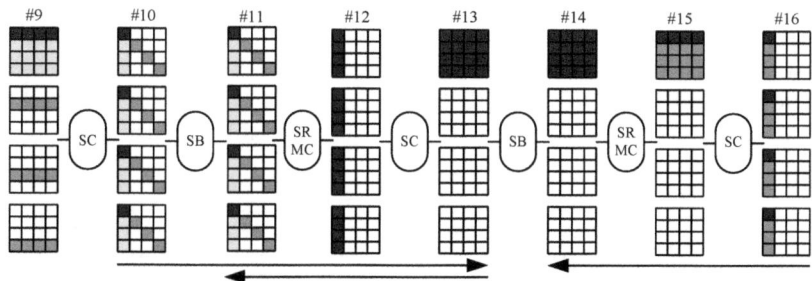

Fig. 3. The last two rounds of the core of the truncated differential path in our attack. Black bytes are active, green bytes denote the bytes whose value can be determined after the fifth steps.

Step 4. Recall that the differences and values of the black bytes in state #10 are determined in previous steps. Hence, when they pass the SubBytes layer, the differences and values of the black bytes in state #11 are determined. The 4-byte difference propagates forward to the state #13 with a full active substate. Then, randomly choose a 4-byte difference at the state #16, and it propagates backward to the state #14 whose first substate is active. Furthermore, we can find a differential match for the SubBytes layer between state #13 and #14 with a probability of about 2^{-16}. Since we get at least two state values for each S-box match, we get about 2^{16} starting points for the outbound phase. In other words, we can obtain a starting point at state #13 for each 4-byte difference at the state #16 on average. Therefore, we get 2^{32} starting points in total.

Step 5. Computing back from these starting points, the values of the four black bytes of #11 can be determined. Recall that we have got the values of these bytes in step 4. Then we only need to find a match at this state. Since the probability of matching the four bytes is 2^{-32}, we expect to find one by trying all 2^{32} 4-byte differences at the state #16.

Note that we cannot obtain the matched values for each substate independently. Thus, it has a complexity of 2^{32} and 1 memory requirement.

The values of the green bytes can be determined after these steps. In addition, we find that the right three columns of the four substates of #10 are also related to the red bytes in Figure 2. So it needs to match these 48 bytes, i.e. find appropriate 35 white bytes in the state #10. We can find them by solving a system of equations. Note that the yellow bytes are free.

4.4 Solving the Conforming State

In this subsection, we first construct the system of equations mentioned in the last subsection and then solve it. Note that there are two MixColumns layers between #6 and #10 and we must consider the subkeys used in these rounds. Let the white bytes in state #10 be $(x_0, x_1, \cdots, x_{35})$, r_i, g_i are respectively red and green bytes whose values are known. k_i denotes a subkey byte. Note that all subkeys are constant in the known-key model. $S(\cdot)$ is the S-box. We can obtain the system with 12 equations (see Appendix B).

We notice that the equations (i), (iv), (vii), (x) only involve the variables x_0, x_1, x_2, x_{27}, x_{28}, x_{29}, x_{18}, x_{19}, x_{20}, x_9, x_{10}, x_{11}. The four equations are given as follows:

$$r_0 = \begin{pmatrix} 6 & 4 & 2 & 1 \end{pmatrix} \begin{pmatrix} S^{-1}(x_0 + k_{16} + 2g_0 + k_{20} + 4x_1 + k_{24} + 6x_2 + k_{28}) + k_1 \\ S^{-1}(2x_{27} + k_{19} + g_9 + k_{23} + 6x_{28} + k_{27} + 4x_{29} + k_{31}) + k_5 \\ S^{-1}(4x_{18} + k_{18} + 6g_6 + k_{22} + x_{19} + k_{26} + 2x_{20} + k_{30}) + k_9 \\ S^{-1}(6x_9 + k_{17} + 4g_3 + k_{21} + 2x_{10} + k_{25} + x_{11} + k_{29}) + k_{13} \end{pmatrix}, \text{(i)}$$

$$r_3 = \begin{pmatrix} 6 & 4 & 2 & 1 \end{pmatrix} \begin{pmatrix} S^{-1}(x_9 + k_{17} + 2g_3 + k_{21} + 4x_{10} + k_{25} + 6x_{11} + k_{29}) + k_{17} \\ S^{-1}(2x_0 + k_{16} + g_0 + k_{20} + 6x_1 + k_{24} + 4x_2 + k_{28}) + k_{21} \\ S^{-1}(4x_{27} + k_{19} + 6g_9 + k_{23} + x_{28} + k_{27} + 2x_{29} + k_{31}) + k_{25} \\ S^{-1}(6x_{18} + k_{18} + 4g_6 + k_{22} + 2x_{19} + k_{26} + x_{20} + k_{30}) + k_{29} \end{pmatrix}, \text{(iv)}$$

$$r_6 = \begin{pmatrix} 6 & 4 & 2 & 1 \end{pmatrix} \begin{pmatrix} S^{-1}(x_{18} + k_{18} + 2g_6 + k_{22} + 4x_{19} + k_{26} + 6x_{20} + k_{30}) + k_{33} \\ S^{-1}(2x_9 + k_{17} + g_3 + k_{21} + 6x_{10} + k_{25} + 4x_{11} + k_{29}) + k_{37} \\ S^{-1}(4x_0 + k_{16} + 6g_0 + k_{20} + x_1 + k_{24} + 2x_2 + k_{28}) + k_{41} \\ S^{-1}(6x_{27} + k_{19} + 4g_9 + k_{23} + 2x_{28} + k_{27} + x_{29} + k_{31}) + k_{45} \end{pmatrix}, \text{(vii)}$$

$$r_9 = \begin{pmatrix} 6 & 4 & 2 & 1 \end{pmatrix} \begin{pmatrix} S^{-1}(x_{27} + k_{19} + 2g_9 + k_{23} + 4x_{28} + k_{27} + 6x_{29} + k_{31}) + k_{49} \\ S^{-1}(2x_{18} + k_{18} + g_6 + k_{22} + 6x_{19} + k_{26} + 4x_{20} + k_{30}) + k_{53} \\ S^{-1}(4x_9 + k_{17} + 6g_3 + k_{21} + x_{10} + k_{25} + 2x_{11} + k_{29}) + k_{57} \\ S^{-1}(6x_0 + k_{16} + 4g_0 + k_{20} + 2x_1 + k_{24} + x_2 + k_{28}) + k_{61} \end{pmatrix} . \text{(x)}$$

Therefore, they can be solved independently.

For the sake of convenience, $A_i, B_i, C_i, D_i, 1 \le i \le 4$, denote the inputs of the inverse of S-boxes in these equations. Specifically, A_i, B_i, C_i, D_i denote the linear combinations of $\{x_0, x_1, x_2\}$, $\{x_{27}, x_{28}, x_{29}\}$, $\{x_{18}, x_{19}, x_{20}\}$, and $\{x_9, x_{10}, x_{11}\}$, respectively. For instance, the inputs of the inverse of S-boxes in equation (i) can be defined by the equations:

$$x_0 + k_{16} + 2g_0 + k_{20} + 4x_1 + k_{24} + 6x_2 + k_{28} = A_1,$$
$$2x_{27} + k_{19} + g_9 + k_{23} + 6x_{28} + k_{27} + 4x_{29} + k_{31} = B_1,$$
$$4x_{18} + k_{18} + 6g_6 + k_{22} + x_{19} + k_{26} + 2x_{20} + k_{30} = C_1,$$
$$6x_9 + k_{17} + 4g_3 + k_{21} + 2x_{10} + k_{25} + x_{11} + k_{29} = D_1.$$

We find that if we guess the values of A_1, B_1, C_1, the value of D_1 can be obtained by the equation (i). Similarly, if the values of A_i, B_i, C_i, $2 \le i \le 3$, are guessed, we can compute the values of D_2 and D_3 by the equations (iv) and (vii) respectively. Hence, we can compute the values of x_9, x_{10}, x_{11} from D_1, D_2, D_3 so that the value of D_4 can be obtained. Furthermore, there are only three variables, x_0, x_1, x_2, in A_1, A_2, A_3, and A_4. If we guess the values of A_1, A_2, A_3, we can get the values of x_0, x_1, x_2. Substituting them into A_4, we can get its value. Similarly, we compute B_4 and C_4 by guessing the values of B_1, B_2, B_3 and C_1, C_2, C_3. At last, we can obtain another value of D_4 by substituting A_4, B_4, C_4 into equation (x). As a result, there are two ways to get the value of D_4 (see Figure 4). And if the values of D_4 obtained by the two ways are equal, we can get a solution for the unknown bytes x_0, x_1, x_2, x_{27}, x_{28}, x_{29}, x_{18}, x_{19}, x_{20}, x_9, x_{10}, x_{11}. Note that the probability that we get the same D_4 by the two ways is 2^{-8}. Therefore, the complexity of solving the four equations is 2^8.

Fig. 4. The two ways to get the value of D_4

Moreover, all the twelve equations can be divided into three parts, (1) equations (i), (iv), (vii), (x), (2) equations (ii), (v), (viii), (xi), and (3) equations (iii), (vi), (ix), (xi). We notice that the equations in the second part involve only $x_3, x_4, x_5,$ $x_{12}, x_{13}, x_{14}, x_{21}, x_{22}, x_{23}, x_{30}, x_{31}, x_{32}$, and the equations in the third part involve only x_6, x_7, x_8, x_{15}, x_{16}, x_{17}, x_{24}, x_{25}, x_{26}, x_{33}, x_{34}, x_{35}. Thus, besides the first part, two other parts can also be solved independently. Furthermore, the method to solve them is similar to the one we used before. Consequently, the complexity to find a solution for the whole system of equations is 2^8.

4.5   The 15-Round Truncated Differential Path

The core of the truncated differential path can be extended by adding two rounds at the beginning and seven rounds at the end of the trail (see Figure 5).

The output differences of the S-boxes on the round 3 propagate backward to the starting point on the first round with probability 1. However, a portion 2^{-96} will follow a MixColumns transition $16 \longrightarrow 4$, because we have a probability of 2^{-24} for each column. Since we have two $16 \longrightarrow 4$ MixColumns transitions at round 10 and round 12(namely the differences are zero at the blue bytes in Figure 5) and consider them to be independent, the probability of differential propagating from round 9 to round 15 is 2^{-192}.

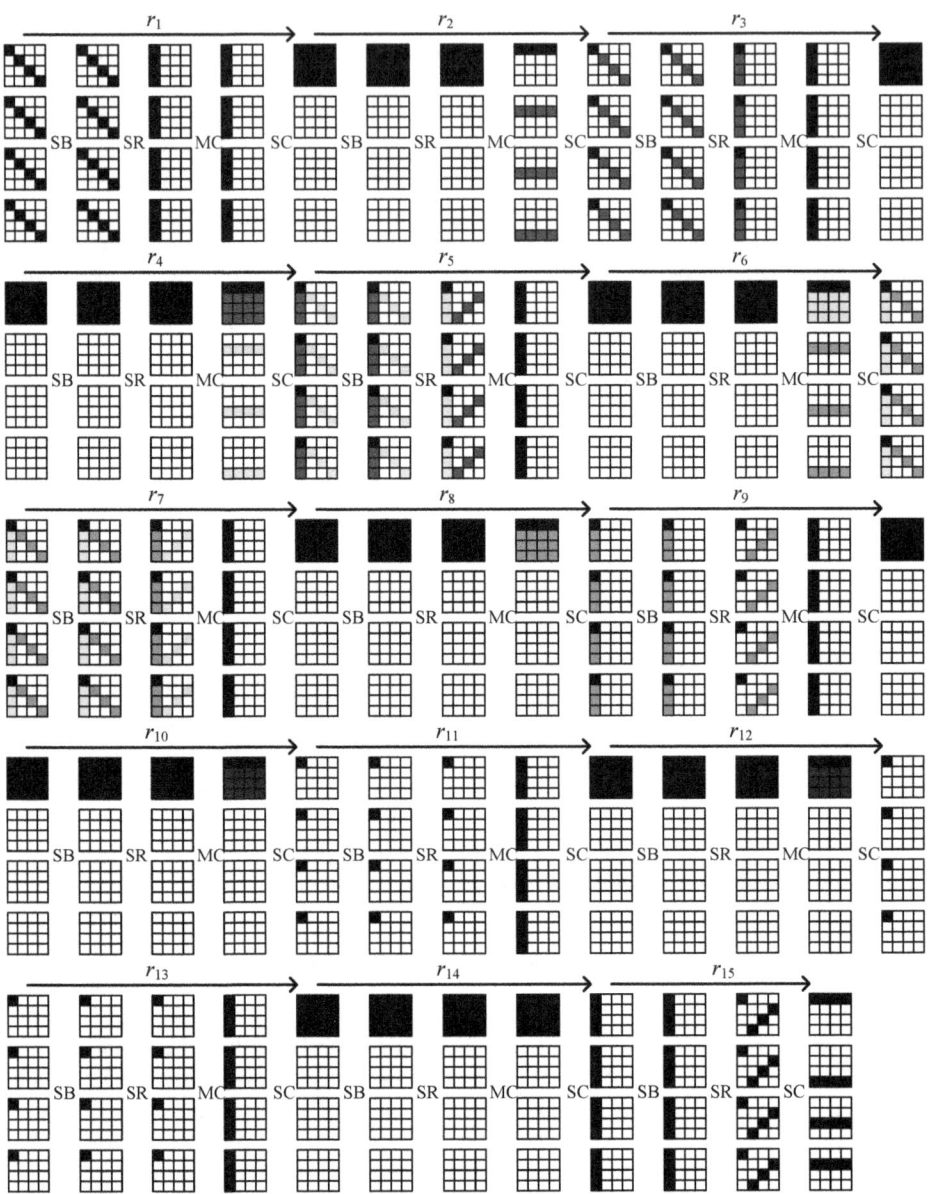

Fig. 5. The 15-round truncated differential path of 3D

5   Known-Key Distinguisher on 15-Round 3D

In this section, we start with the description of the limited-birthday problem. Next, we apply the truncated differential trail presented in the last section to construct a known-key distinguisher on 15-round 3D block cipher.

5.1   The Limited-Birthday Problem

The limited-birthday problem was introduced by Henri Gilbert and Thomas Peyrin [10]. The problem is: what is the generic attack complexity of finding a pair of plaintext/ciphertext couples with a zero difference at i prescribed input bit positions and a zero difference value at j prescribed output bit positions for an ideal (random) permutation?

Firstly, the attacker can choose to study the permutation or its inverse. Assume that $i \geq j$ and n is the bit size of the function. Secondly, each structure of 2^{n-i} input values with a zero difference at i prescribed positions allows providing a difference with at most $2(n - i)$ zero bits in prescribed positions of the output value.

- if $j \leq 2(n - i)$, there are enough freedom degrees to achieve a collision on the j target positions. Thus, we only need to choose $2^{j/2}$ input values from one single structure. The complexity is $2^{j/2}$.
- if $j > 2(n - i)$, since one structure of 2^{n-i} input value can achieve at most $2(n-i)$ zero difference bits, we need to select $j - 2(n-i)$ structures to provide j collision bits. As a result, the complexity is $2^{n-i} \times 2^{j-2(n-i)} = 2^{i+j-n}$.

5.2   The Known-Key Distinguisher on 15-Round 3D

In this subsection, we construct a known-key distinguisher by using the 15-round differential path shown in Section 4. We already showed that one can get a pair of input fulfilling this path with a computation complexity and memory. Specifically, a pair of plaintexts can be obtained, which have a zero difference at 384 prescribed bit positions, and the corresponding ciphertexts have a zero difference value at 384 prescribed bit positions. It's a limited birthday problem in the case of $j > 2(n-i)$. For an ideal (random) permutation, the complexity is $2^{384+384-512} = 2^{256}$. If we use the differential trail from Figure 5, we can achieve the target with a lower complexity.

Recall that the complexity from **Step 1** to **Step 3** is 2^8, and the complexity from **Step 4** to **Step 5** is 2^{32}. These steps can be done by pre-computing, because we have sufficient freedom degrees for the subsequent attack. Recall that we have 2^{216} available freedom degrees when solving the system of equations shown in Appendix B, since we can guess the values of 27 bytes. In addition, the complexity to solve the system of equations is 2^8, and it increases to $2^8 \times 2^{192}$ if we want to get 7 more rounds. In total, we need $2^8 + 2^{32} + 2^8 \times 2^{192} \approx 2^{200}$ computations and 2^8 memories, which is much lower than the generic attack.

6 Conclusion

In this paper, we presented the cryptanalysis results of 3D block cipher by using rebound attack technique. We study the operations used in 3D and provide some properties of the round function. We further construct a 15-round differential path by using the method of rebound attack and solving a system of equations. We show that one can use a system of nonlinear equations to integrate two differential paths into get a new one with more rounds. Our main result is a 15-round known-key distinguisher with a complexity of 2^{200} and 2^8 memory. The complexity is obviously lower than generic attack.

Acknowledgments. This work is supported by the National Natural Science Foundation of China (No.60873259), and the Knowledge Innovation Project of The Chinese Academy of Sciences. Moreover, the authors are very grateful to the anonymous referees for their comments and editorial suggestions.

References

1. National Institute of Standards and Technology: Specification for the advanced encryption standard (AES). Federal Information Processing Standards Publication 197 (2001), http://csrc.nist.gov/publications/fips/fips197/fips-197.pdf
2. Nakahara Jr., J.: 3D: A Three-Dimensional Block Cipher. In: Franklin, M.K., Hui, L.C.K., Wong, D.S. (eds.) CANS 2008. LNCS, vol. 5339, pp. 252–267. Springer, Heidelberg (2008)
3. Nakahara Jr., J.: New Impossible Differential and Known-Key Distinguishers for the 3D Cipher. In: Bao, F., Weng, J. (eds.) ISPEC 2011. LNCS, vol. 6672, pp. 208–221. Springer, Heidelberg (2011)
4. Knudsen, L.R., Rijmen, V.: Known-Key Distinguishers for Some Block Ciphers. In: Kurosawa, K. (ed.) ASIACRYPT 2007. LNCS, vol. 4833, pp. 315–324. Springer, Heidelberg (2007)
5. Biryukov, A., Khovratovich, D., Nikolić, I.: Distinguisher and Related-Key Attack on the Full AES-256. In: Halevi, S. (ed.) CRYPTO 2009. LNCS, vol. 5677, pp. 231–249. Springer, Heidelberg (2009)
6. Minier, M., Phan, R.C.-W., Pousse, B.: Distinguishers for Ciphers and Known Key Attack against Rijndael with Large Blocks. In: Preneel, B. (ed.) AFRICACRYPT 2009. LNCS, vol. 5580, pp. 60–76. Springer, Heidelberg (2009)
7. Rijmen, V., Barreto, P.S.L.M.: The ANUBIS Block Cipher. Submission to NESSIE (2000)
8. Mendel, F., Rechberger, C., Schläffer, M., Thomsen, S.S.: The Rebound Attack: Cryptanalysis of Reduced Whirlpool and Grøstl. In: Dunkelman, O. (ed.) FSE 2009. LNCS, vol. 5665, pp. 260–276. Springer, Heidelberg (2009)
9. Lamberger, M., Mendel, F., Rechberger, C., Rijmen, V., Schläffer, M.: Rebound Distinguishers: Results on the Full Whirlpool Compression Function. In: Matsui, M. (ed.) ASIACRYPT 2009. LNCS, vol. 5912, pp. 126–143. Springer, Heidelberg (2009)
10. Gilbert, H., Peyrin, T.: Super-Sbox Cryptanalysis: Improved Attacks for AES-like Permutations. In: Hong, S., Iwata, T. (eds.) FSE 2010. LNCS, vol. 6147, pp. 365–383. Springer, Heidelberg (2010)

11. Peyrin, T.: Improved Differential Attacks for ECHO and Grøstl. In: Rabin, T. (ed.) CRYPTO 2010. LNCS, vol. 6223, pp. 370–392. Springer, Heidelberg (2010)
12. Mendel, F., Peyrin, T., Rechberger, C., Schläffer, M.: Improved Cryptanalysis of the Reduced Grøstl Compression Function, Echo Permutation and Aes Block Cipher. In: Jacobson Jr., M.J., Rijmen, V., Safavi-Naini, R. (eds.) SAC 2009. LNCS, vol. 5867, pp. 16–35. Springer, Heidelberg (2009)
13. Matusiewicz, K., Naya-Plasencia, M., Nikolić, I., Sasaki, Y., Schläffer, M.: Rebound Attack on the Full Lane Compression Function. In: Matsui, M. (ed.) ASIACRYPT 2009. LNCS, vol. 5912, pp. 106–125. Springer, Heidelberg (2009)
14. Wu, S., Feng, D., Wu, W.: Cryptanalysis of the LANE Hash Function. In: Jacobson Jr., M.J., Rijmen, V., Safavi-Naini, R. (eds.) SAC 2009. LNCS, vol. 5867, pp. 126–140. Springer, Heidelberg (2009)
15. Mendel, F., Rechberger, C., Schläffer, M.: Cryptanalysis of Twister. In: Abdalla, M., Pointcheval, D., Fouque, P.-A., Vergnaud, D. (eds.) ACNS 2009. LNCS, vol. 5536, pp. 342–353. Springer, Heidelberg (2009)
16. Rijmen, V., Toz, D., Varıcı, K.: Rebound Attack on Reduced-Round Versions of JH. In: Hong, S., Iwata, T. (eds.) FSE 2010. LNCS, vol. 6147, pp. 286–303. Springer, Heidelberg (2010)
17. Wu, S., Feng, D., Wu, W.: Practical Rebound Attack on 12-Round Cheetah-256. In: Lee, D., Hong, S. (eds.) ICISC 2009. LNCS, vol. 5984, pp. 300–314. Springer, Heidelberg (2010)
18. Khovratovich, D., Naya-Plasencia, M., Röck, A., Schläffer, M.: Cryptanalysis of *Luffa* v2 Components. In: Biryukov, A., Gong, G., Stinson, D.R. (eds.) SAC 2010. LNCS, vol. 6544, pp. 388–409. Springer, Heidelberg (2011)

A Naming Conventions for Parts of the 3D State

B Equations of Finding a Match at Round 7

$$r_0 = \begin{pmatrix} 6 & 4 & 2 & 1 \end{pmatrix} \begin{pmatrix} S^{-1}(x_0 + k_{16} + 2g_0 + k_{20} + 4x_1 + k_{24} + 6x_2 + k_{28}) + k_1 \\ S^{-1}(2x_{27} + k_{19} + g_9 + k_{23} + 6x_{28} + k_{27} + 4x_{29} + k_{31}) + k_5 \\ S^{-1}(4x_{18} + k_{18} + 6g_6 + k_{22} + x_{19} + k_{26} + 2x_{20} + k_{30}) + k_9 \\ S^{-1}(6x_9 + k_{17} + 4g_3 + k_{21} + 2x_{10} + k_{25} + x_{11} + k_{29}) + k_{13} \end{pmatrix} \quad \text{(i)}$$

$$r_1 = \begin{pmatrix} 4 & 6 & 1 & 2 \end{pmatrix} \begin{pmatrix} S^{-1}(x_3 + k_{32} + 2x_4 + k_{36} + 4g_1 + k_{40} + 6x_5 + k_{44}) + k_2 \\ S^{-1}(2x_{30} + k_{35} + x_{31} + k_{39} + 6g_{10} + k_{43} + 4x_{32} + k_{47}) + k_6 \\ S^{-1}(4x_{21} + k_{34} + 6x_{22} + k_{38} + g_7 + k_{42} + 2x_{23} + k_{46}) + k_{10} \\ S^{-1}(6x_{12} + k_{33} + 4x_{13} + k_{37} + 2g_4 + k_{41} + x_{14} + k_{45}) + k_{14} \end{pmatrix} \quad \text{(ii)}$$

$$r_2 = \begin{pmatrix} 2 & 1 & 6 & 4 \end{pmatrix} \begin{pmatrix} S^{-1}(x_6 + k_{48} + 2x_7 + k_{52} + 4x_8 + k_{56} + 6g_2 + k_{60}) + k_3 \\ S^{-1}(2x_{33} + k_{51} + x_{34} + k_{55} + 6x_{35} + k_{59} + 4g_{11} + k_{63}) + k_7 \\ S^{-1}(4x_{24} + k_{50} + 6x_{25} + k_{54} + x_{26} + k_{58} + 2g_8 + k_{62}) + k_{11} \\ S^{-1}(6x_{15} + k_{49} + 4x_{16} + k_{53} + 2x_{17} + k_{57} + g_5 + k_{61}) + k_{15} \end{pmatrix} \quad \text{(iii)}$$

$$r_3 = \begin{pmatrix} 6 & 4 & 2 & 1 \end{pmatrix} \begin{pmatrix} S^{-1}(x_9 + k_{17} + 2g_3 + k_{21} + 4x_{10} + k_{25} + 6x_{11} + k_{29}) + k_{17} \\ S^{-1}(2x_0 + k_{16} + g_0 + k_{20} + 6x_1 + k_{24} + 4x_2 + k_{28}) + k_{21} \\ S^{-1}(4x_{27} + k_{19} + 6g_9 + k_{23} + x_{28} + k_{27} + 2x_{29} + k_{31}) + k_{25} \\ S^{-1}(6x_{18} + k_{18} + 4g_6 + k_{22} + 2x_{19} + k_{26} + x_{20} + k_{30}) + k_{29} \end{pmatrix} \quad \text{(iv)}$$

$$r_4 = \begin{pmatrix} 4 & 6 & 1 & 2 \end{pmatrix} \begin{pmatrix} S^{-1}(x_{12} + k_{33} + 2x_{13} + k_{37} + 4g_4 + k_{41} + 6x_{14} + k_{45}) + k_{18} \\ S^{-1}(2x_3 + k_{32} + x_4 + k_{36} + 6g_1 + k_{40} + 4x_5 + k_{44}) + k_{22} \\ S^{-1}(4x_{30} + k_{35} + 6x_{31} + k_{39} + g_{10} + k_{43} + 2x_{32} + k_{47}) + k_{26} \\ S^{-1}(6x_{21} + k_{34} + 4x_{22} + k_{38} + 2g_7 + k_{42} + x_{23} + k_{46}) + k_{30} \end{pmatrix} \quad \text{(v)}$$

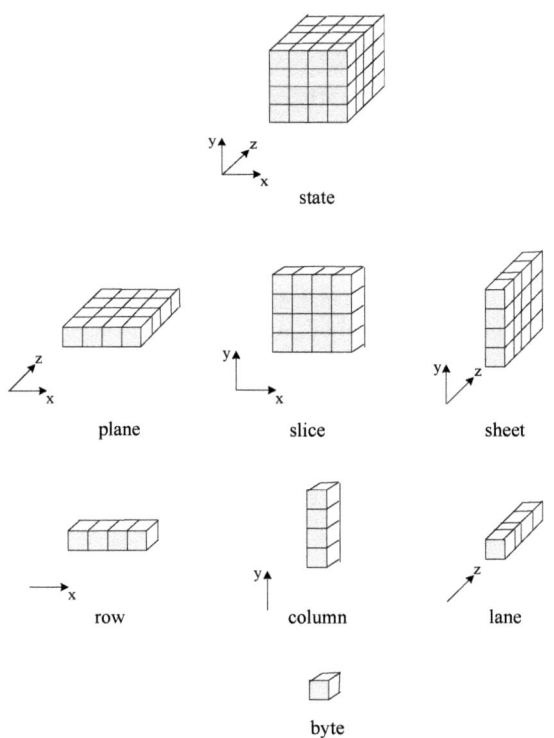

Fig. 6. Naming conventions for parts of the 3D state

$$r_5 = \begin{pmatrix} 2 & 1 & 6 & 4 \end{pmatrix} \begin{pmatrix} S^{-1}(x_{15} + k_{49} + 2x_{16} + k_{53} + 4x_{17} + k_{57} + 6g_5 + k_{60}) + k_{19} \\ S^{-1}(2x_6 + k_{48} + x_7 + k_{52} + 6x_8 + k_{56} + 4g_2 + k_{60}) + k_{23} \\ S^{-1}(4x_{33} + k_{51} + 6x_{34} + k_{55} + x_{35} + k_{59} + 2g_{11} + k_{63}) + k_{27} \\ S^{-1}(6x_{24} + k_{50} + 4x_{25} + k_{54} + 2x_{26} + k_{58} + g_8 + k_{62}) + k_{31} \end{pmatrix} \quad \text{(vi)}$$

$$r_6 = \begin{pmatrix} 6 & 4 & 2 & 1 \end{pmatrix} \begin{pmatrix} S^{-1}(x_{18} + k_{18} + 2g_6 + k_{22} + 4x_{19} + k_{26} + 6x_{20} + k_{30}) + k_{33} \\ S^{-1}(2x_9 + k_{17} + g_3 + k_{21} + 6x_{10} + k_{25} + 4x_{11} + k_{29}) + k_{37} \\ S^{-1}(4x_0 + k_{16} + 6g_0 + k_{20} + x_1 + k_{24} + 2x_2 + k_{28}) + k_{41} \\ S^{-1}(6x_{27} + k_{19} + 4g_9 + k_{23} + 2x_{28} + k_{27} + x_{29} + k_{31}) + k_{45} \end{pmatrix} \quad \text{(vii)}$$

$$r_7 = \begin{pmatrix} 4 & 6 & 1 & 2 \end{pmatrix} \begin{pmatrix} S^{-1}(x_{21} + k_{34} + 2x_{22} + k_{38} + 4g_7 + k_{42} + 6x_{23} + k_{46}) + k_{34} \\ S^{-1}(2x_{12} + k_{33} + x_{13} + k_{37} + 6g_4 + k_{41} + 4x_{14} + k_{45}) + k_{38} \\ S^{-1}(4x_3 + k_{32} + 6x_4 + k_{36} + g_1 + k_{40} + 2x_5 + k_{44}) + k_{42} \\ S^{-1}(6x_{30} + k_{35} + 4x_{31} + k_{39} + 2g_{10} + k_{43} + x_{32} + k_{47}) + k_{46} \end{pmatrix} \quad \text{(viii)}$$

$$r_8 = \begin{pmatrix} 2 & 1 & 6 & 4 \end{pmatrix} \begin{pmatrix} S^{-1}(x_{24} + k_{50} + 2x_{25} + k_{54} + 4x_{26} + k_{58} + 6g_8 + k_{62}) + k_{35} \\ S^{-1}(2x_{15} + k_{49} + x_{16} + k_{53} + 6x_{17} + k_{57} + 4g_5 + k_{61}) + k_{39} \\ S^{-1}(4x_6 + k_{48} + 6x_7 + k_{52} + x_8 + k_{56} + 2g_2 + k_{60}) + k_{43} \\ S^{-1}(6x_{33} + k_{50} + 4x_{34} + k_{55} + 2x_{35} + k_{59} + g_{11} + k_{63}) + k_{47} \end{pmatrix} \quad \text{(ix)}$$

$$r_9 = \begin{pmatrix} 6 & 4 & 2 & 1 \end{pmatrix} \begin{pmatrix} S^{-1}(x_{27} + k_{19} + 2g_9 + k_{23} + 4x_{28} + k_{27} + 6x_{29} + k_{31}) + k_{49} \\ S^{-1}(2x_{18} + k_{18} + g_6 + k_{22} + 6x_{19} + k_{26} + 4x_{20} + k_{30}) + k_{53} \\ S^{-1}(4x_9 + k_{17} + 6g_3 + k_{21} + x_{10} + k_{25} + 2x_{11} + k_{29}) + k_{57} \\ S^{-1}(6x_0 + k_{16} + 4g_0 + k_{20} + 2x_1 + k_{24} + x_2 + k_{28}) + k_{61} \end{pmatrix} \quad \text{(x)}$$

$$r_{10} = \begin{pmatrix} 4 & 6 & 1 & 2 \end{pmatrix} \begin{pmatrix} S^{-1}(x_{30} + k_{35} + 2x_{31} + k_{39} + 4g_{10} + k_{43} + 6x_{32} + k_{47}) + k_{50} \\ S^{-1}(2x_{21} + k_{34} + x_{22} + k_{38} + 6g_7 + k_{42} + 4x_{23} + k_{46}) + k_{54} \\ S^{-1}(4x_{12} + k_{33} + 6x_{13} + k_{37} + g_4 + k_{41} + 2x_{14} + k_{45}) + k_{58} \\ S^{-1}(6x_3 + k_{32} + 4x_4 + k_{36} + 2g_1 + k_{40} + x_5 + k_{44}) + k_{62} \end{pmatrix} \quad \text{(xi)}$$

$$r_{11} = \begin{pmatrix} 2 & 1 & 6 & 4 \end{pmatrix} \begin{pmatrix} S^{-1}(x_{33} + k_{51} + 2x_{34} + k_{55} + 4x_{35} + k_{59} + 6g_{11} + k_{63}) + k_{51} \\ S^{-1}(2x_{24} + k_{50} + x_{25} + k_{54} + 6x_{26} + k_{58} + 4g_8 + k_{62}) + k_{55} \\ S^{-1}(4x_{15} + k_{49} + 6x_{16} + k_{53} + x_{17} + k_{57} + 2g_5 + k_{61}) + k_{59} \\ S^{-1}(6x_6 + k_{48} + 4x_7 + k_{52} + 2x_8 + k_{56} + g_2 + k_{60}) + k_{63} \end{pmatrix} \quad \text{(xii)}$$

Identity-Based Signcryption from Identity-Based Cryptography*

Woomyo Lee, Jae Woo Seo, and Pil Joong Lee

Information Security Lab. POSTECH, Republic of Korea
{wmlee,jwseo,pjlee}@postech.ac.kr

Abstract. A signcryption scheme encrypts and signs data in a single operation which is more efficient than using an encryption scheme combined with a signature scheme. Identity-based cryptography (IBC) does not require users to pre-compute key pairs and obtain certificates for their public keys. Identity-based signcryption (IBSC) applies the idea of IBC to signcryption. IBSC involves five security notions: message confidentiality, signature non-repudiation, ciphertext anonymity, ciphertext unlinkability, and ciphertext authentication. Recently, the Pandey scheme has been proposed; the scheme uses an identity-based encryption scheme and an identity-based signature scheme. However, this scheme only achieves message confidentiality and signature non-repudiation. In this work, we improve the scheme to achieve additional security notions, ciphertext anonymity and ciphertext authentication, with no loss in efficiency.

Keywords: Identity-based signcryption, identity-based cryptography.

1   Introduction

Encryption and signature have been considered the fundamental cryptographic tools of public key cryptography for providing private and authenticated communications. An encryption scheme ensures that an adversary cannot learn any information about a plaintext from ciphertexts (i.e., confidentiality) and a signature scheme ensures that an adversary cannot forge a new valid signature on a new plaintext (i.e., non-repudiation). Nowdays, many applications require two distinct goals to be simultaneously achieved. When applying two distinct tools to applications sequentially, both confidentiality and non-repudiation can be achieved easily. However, it performs unnecessary operations, thus wastes resource in space and computation complexities. Encryption and signature can be efficiently combined to provide both confidentiality and non-repudiation simultaneously. Zheng [11] proposed a primitive which is called signcryption. A signcryption scheme is to encrypt and sign data in a single operation which

---

* This research was supported by the MKE(The Ministry of Knowledge Economy), Korea, under the ITRC support program supervised by the NIPA(National IT Industry Promotion Agency)(NIPA-2011-C1090-1001-0004) and by the Brain Korea 21 Project in 2011.

S. Jung and M. Yung (Eds.): WISA 2011, LNCS 7115, pp. 70–83, 2012.

is more efficient than using an encryption scheme combined with a signature scheme.

In identity-based cryptography, an arbitrary string can be used as public keys and private keys are derived from these pubic keys. Therefore, a sender uses an identity information (e.g., mail address, name, and phone number) of a receiver as a public key and the receiver can get a corresponding private key from the private key generator (PKG) after receiving a ciphertext from the sender. In the system, users do not need to obtain certificates. The concept of identity-based cryptography was first introduced by Shamir [9]. He presented an identity-based signature (IBS) scheme but the construction for encryption had been an open issue. The first practical identity-based encryption (IBE) scheme was introduced by [2], which was based on bilinear maps. After the introduction of this bilinear map, many works have been proposed in the field of the identity-based cryptography.

Identity-based signcryption (IBSC) is to apply the idea of identity-based cryptography to signcryption. The first IBSC scheme was proposed in [6]. Their scheme considered two security notions: confidentiality and non-repudiation. confidentiality requires indistinguishability against adaptive chosen-ciphertext attacks and non-repudiation requires existential unforgeability against chosen-message insider attacks. Boyen [3] supplemented three security requirements for IBSC: ciphertext anonymity, ciphertext unlinkability, and ciphertext authentication. Ciphertext anonymity requires that authorship not be transmitted in the clear, ciphertext unlinkability requires that authorship remain unverifiable by anyone, and ciphertext authentication requires that a ciphertext comes from a legitimate user that originally generates the ciphertext. Note that ciphertext unlinkability and ciphertext authentication cannot be achieved simultaneously. Since then, much research has been proceeded on IBSC [1,4,5,8,10]. Recently, Pandey et al. [7] proposed an efficient construction of IBSC using an IBE scheme and an IBS scheme. However, their scheme only achieves confidentiality and non-repudiation.

In this work, we improve the scheme of Pandey et al. [7]. The proposed scheme achieves confidentiality, non-repudiation, ciphertext anonymity, and ciphertext authentication. The security of the proposed scheme is proved in the random oracle model. Our construction achieves more security notions but does not make a loss in efficiency; our scheme reduced one hash operation when comparing with the Pandey's scheme.

2   Preliminaries

2.1   Identity-Based Encryption

Formal Model. An IBE scheme consists of the following four algorithms:

- $\mathsf{Setup}_{\mathsf{IBE}}$. On input of a security parameter 1^k, private key generator (PKG) uses this algorithm to produce a pair $(msk_{\mathsf{IBE}}, \mathsf{param}_{\mathsf{IBE}})$, where msk_{IBE} is the master secret key and $\mathsf{param}_{\mathsf{IBE}}$ is the set of the global parameters for the system. We assume that $\mathsf{param}_\mathsf{IBE}$ are publicly known so that we do not need to explicitly provide them as input to other algorithms.

- $\mathsf{KeyGen}_\mathsf{IBE}$. On input of the master secret key msk_IBE and an identity ID, the PKG uses this algorithm to compute a private key $SK_\mathsf{IBE.ID}$ corresponding to ID.
- E_IBE. Given a message m and an identity ID, this algorithm returns a ciphertext $C \leftarrow \mathsf{E}_\mathsf{IBE}(m, \mathsf{ID})$.
- D_IBE. Given a ciphertext C and a private key $SK_\mathsf{IBE.ID}$, this algorithm returns a message $m = \mathsf{D}_\mathsf{IBE}(C, SK_\mathsf{IBE.ID})$.

Definition 1. *An IBE scheme is said to be adaptively chosen-ciphertext secure, or IND-CCA secure if no probabilistic polynomial-time (PPT) adversary has a non-negligible advantage in the following game:*

- **Initial:** The challenger runs $\mathsf{Setup}_\mathsf{IBE}$ to produce msk_IBE and $\mathsf{param}_\mathsf{IBE}$.
- **Phase 1:** The adversary makes queries adaptively to the challenger. The following queries are allowed:
  - . Private key extraction queries: The adversary submits an identity ID to the challenger. The challenger responds with the private key corresponding to the identity ID.
  - . Decryption queries: The adversary submits a ciphertext C and an identity ID to the challenger. The challenger returns either a message m if C is a valid ciphertext of m; otherwise, it return $\perp$ indicating an error.
- **Selection:** After the end of **Phase** 1, the adversary returns the identity ID^* and two distinct messages (m_0, m_1) to the challenger. The only constraint is that ID^* has not appeared in any private key extraction queries in **Phase** 1.
- **Challenge:** The challenger chooses a bit b uniformly at random and returns the challenge ciphertext $C^* \leftarrow \mathsf{E}_\mathsf{IBE}(m_b, \mathsf{ID}^*)$ to the adversary.
- **Phase 2:** The adversary makes queries adaptively to the challenger. But the adversary cannot have made the private key extraction query for the private key corresponding to ID^* and the decryption query for the challenge ciphertext C^*.
- **Response:** The adversary returns a bit b' and wins if $b = b'$.

Definition 2. *An IBE scheme is said to be adaptively chosen-ciphertext secure, or ANON-IND-CCA secure if no PPT adversary has a non-negligible advantage in the following game:*

- **Initial:** The same as in the IND-CCA game.
- **Phase 1:** The same as in the IND-CCA game.
- **Selection:** After the end of **Phase** 1, the adversary returns two distinct identity $(\mathsf{ID}_0, \mathsf{ID}_1)$ and two distinct messages (m_0, m_1) to the challenger. The only constraint is that private key extraction queries for ID_0 and ID_1 have not been issued.
- **Challenge:** The challenger chooses bits $a, b \in \{0, 1\}$ uniformly at random and returns the challenge ciphertext $C^* \leftarrow \mathsf{E}_\mathsf{IBE}(m_a, \mathsf{ID}_b)$ to the adversary.

- **Phase 2:** The adversary makes a number of queries adaptively to the challenger. But the adversary cannot have made the private key extraction queries for ID_0 and ID_1, and the decryption query for the challenge ciphertext C^*.
- **Response:** The adversary returns bits $a', b' \in \{0, 1\}$ and wins if $a = a'$ and $b = b'$.

2.2 Identity-Based Signature

Formal Model. An IBS scheme consists of the following four algorithms:

- $\mathsf{Setup_{IBS}}$. On input of a security parameter 1^k, PKG uses this algorithm to produce a pair $(msk_{IBS}, param_{IBS})$, where msk_{IBS} is the master secret key and $param_{IBS}$ is the set of the global parameters for the system. We assume that $param_{IBS}$ are publicly known so that we do not need to explicitly provide them as input to other algorithms.
- $\mathsf{KeyGen_{IBS}}$. On input of the master secret key msk_{IBS} and an identity ID, the PKG uses this algorithm to compute a signing key $SK_{IBS.ID}$ corresponding to ID.
- $\mathsf{S_{IBS}}$. Given a message m, an identity ID, and the signing key $SK_{IBS.ID}$, this algorithm returns a signature $s \leftarrow \mathsf{S_{IBS}}(m, ID, SK_{IBS.ID})$.
- $\mathsf{V_{IBS}}$. Given a message m and a signature s, this algorithm returns a message $m = \mathsf{V_{IBS}}(m, s)$ if s is a valid signature on m; otherwise, it returns $\perp$ indicating an error.

Definition 3. *An IBS scheme is said to be existentially unforgeable against chosen-message attacks, or EUF-CMA secure if no PPT adversary has a non-negligible advantage in the following game:*

- **Initial:** The challenger runs $\mathsf{Setup_{IBS}}$ to produce msk_{IBS} and $param_{IBS}$.
- **Query:** The adversary makes queries adaptively to the challenger. The following queries are allowed:

  . Private key extraction queries: The adversary submits an identity ID to the challenger. The challenger responds with the private key corresponding to the identity ID.
  . Sign queries: The adversary submits a message m and an identity ID to the challenger. The challenger responds with a signature s.

- **Forge:** After the end of **Query**, the adversary returns (m^*, ID^*, s^*). The constraints are as follows: (1) the sign query for (m^*, ID^*) has not been issued and (2) the private key extraction query for ID^* has not appeared. The adversary wins the game if s^* is the valid signature on message m^* associated to the identity ID^*.

3   Identity-Based Signcryption

3.1   Formal Model

An IBSC scheme consists of the following four algorithms:

- Setup. On input of a security parameter 1^k, PKG uses this algorithm to produce a pair (msk, param), where msk is the master secret key and param is the set of the global parameters for the system. We assume that param are publicly known so that we do not need to explicitly provide them as input to other algorithms.
- KeyGen. On input of the master secret key msk and an identity ID, the PKG uses this algorithm to compute a private key SK_{ID} corresponding to ID.
- Signcryption. Given a message m, a sender's identity $\mathsf{ID_S}$, a recipient's identity $\mathsf{ID_R}$, and a sender's private key $SK_{\mathsf{ID_S}}$, the sender S uses this algorithm to produce a ciphertext C.
- Designcryption. Given a ciphertext C, a recipient's identity $\mathsf{ID_R}$, and a recipient's private key $SK_{\mathsf{ID_R}}$, the recipient R uses this algorithm to return a message m if C is a valid ciphertext on m; otherwise, it returns $\bot$ indicating an error.

These algorithms should satisfy the following consistency requirement:

$$m = \mathsf{Designcryption}(\mathsf{Signcryption}(m, \mathsf{ID_S}, \mathsf{ID_R}, SK_{\mathsf{ID_S}}), \mathsf{ID_R}, SK_{\mathsf{ID_R}}).$$

3.2   Security Notions

In the field of IBSC, there are five security notions that were proposed in [3]: ciphertext authentication, ciphertext unlinkability, message confidentiality, signature non-repudiation, ciphertext anonymity. We describe the security notions of each below.

Ciphertext Authentication allows the legitimate recipient to be convinced that the message was encrypted by same sender who generated a signature. The legitimate recipient is sure that the ciphertext has not been decrypted by any other entities. In other words, the integrity of ciphertexts is guaranteed. Therefore, ciphertexts of IBSC satisfying ciphertext authentication should not be able to be the target of a man-in-the-middle interception.

Definition 4. *An IBSC scheme is said to be existentially ciphertext-unforgeable against chosen-message attacks, or AUTH-IBSC-CMA secure if no PPT adversary has a non-negligible advantage in the following game:*

- **Initial:** The challenger runs Setup algorithm to produce msk and param.
- **Query:** The adversary makes queries adaptively to the challenger. The following queries are allowed:

. Private key extraction queries: The adversary submits an identity ID
to the challenger. The challenger responds with the private key SK_{ID}
corresponding to the identity ID.
. Signcryption queries: The adversary submits a message m, a sender's
identity ID_S, and a recipient's identity ID_R to the challenger. The challenger responds with a ciphertext C that is encrypted under the recipient's identity ID_R and includes the signature on the message.
. Designcryption queries: The adversary submits a ciphertext C and a
recipient's identity ID_R to the challenger. The challenger returns either
a message m if C is a valid ciphertext of m; otherwise, it returns $\perp$
indicating an error.
- **Forge:** After the end of **Query**, the adversary returns (C^*, ID_R^*). The challenger decrypts C^* under the private key $SK_{ID_R^*}$ corresponding to ID_R^* and
gets the information about (m^*, ID_S^*, s^*). The constraints are as follows: (1)
the challenge ciphertext C^* has not been queried to the signcryption query
with ID_S^* and ID_R^*, and (2) the private key of ID_S^* and ID_R^* have not been
extracted during the private key extraction query. The adversary wins the
game if $\mathsf{Designcryption}(C^*, ID_R^*, SK_{ID_R^*})$ is not $\perp$ indicating an error, where
$SK_{ID_R^*} = SK_{IBE.ID_R^*}$.

Ciphertext Unlinkability is not compatible with ciphertext authentication.
The ciphertext unlinkability allows that a recipient decrypts ciphertexts under
the recipient's private key and once again encrypts the same messages under
the other entity's identity. That is, the signature does not guarantee that the
ciphertext is generated by the entity who generates the ciphertext. This security
notion is used in a particular application such as a subscription-based internet multimedia system. Thus, we focus on ciphertext authentication instead of
ciphertext unlinkability.

Message Confidentiality ensures that the communicating parties preserve
the secrecy of message when they exchange their messages.

Definition 5. *An IBSC scheme is said to be indistinguishable against adaptive chosen-ciphertext attacks, or IND-IBSC-CCA secure if no PPT algorithm
adversary has a non-negligible advantage in the following game:*

- **Initial:** The challenger runs Setup algorithm to produce msk, param.
- **Phase 1:** The adversary makes queries adaptively to the challenger and the
same queries (i.e., private key extraction queries, signcryption queries and
designcryption queries) in the game of ciphertext authentication are allowed.
- **Selection:** After the end of **Phase** 1, the adversary returns a sender's identity ID_S^*, a recipient's identity ID_R^* and two distinct messages (m_0, m_1) to the
challenger. The only constraint is that ID_R^* does not appear in any private
key extraction queries.
- **Challenge:** The challenger chooses a bit b uniformly at random and extracts
the private key corresponding to ID_S^*. Then the challenger signs m_b under

the private key of ID_S^* and encrypts the result under ID_R^* to produce the ciphertext C^*. The challenger returns the challenge ciphertext C^* to the adversary.

- **Phase 2:** The adversary makes queries adaptively to the challenger. But the adversary should not make the private key extraction query for the private key corresponding to ID_R^* and the designcryption query for the challenge ciphertext C^*.
- **Response:** The adversary returns a bit b' and wins if $b = b'$.

Signature Non-Repudiation makes it universally verifiable that a message speaks in the name of the signer (regardless of the ciphertext used to convey it, if any).

Definition 6. *An IBSC scheme is said to be existentially unforgeable against chosen-message attacks, or EUF-IBSC-CMA secure if no PPT adversary has a non-negligible advantage in the following game:*

- **Initial:** The challenger runs Setup algorithm to produce msk and param.
- **Query:** The adversary makes queries adaptively to the challenger and the same queries as in the game of ciphertext authentication are allowed.
- **Forge:** After the end of **Query**, the adversary returns (C^*, ID_R^*). The challenger decrypts the ciphertext C^* under the private key $SK_{ID_R^*}$ corresponding to ID_R^* and gets the information about (m^*, ID_S^*, s^*). The constraints are as follows: (1) the signcryption query for (m^*, ID_S^*, ID_R') has not been issued, where ID_R' can either be ID_R^* or not, and (2) the private key extraction query for ID_S^* has not appeared. The adversary wins the game if Designcryption$(C^*, ID_R^*, SK_{IBE.ID_R^*})$ is not $\perp$ indicating an error.

Ciphertext Anonymity makes a ciphertext hide an identities of both the sender and the recipient. In other words, the ciphertext contains no information identifies the sender or recipient of the ciphertext.

Definition 7. *An IBSC scheme is said to be ciphertext-anonymous against adaptive chosen-ciphertext attack, or ANON-IBSC-CCA secure if no PPT algorithm adversary has a non-negligible advantage in the following game:*

- **Initial:** The challenger runs Setup algorithm to produce msk and param.
- **Phase 1:** The adversary makes queries adaptively to the challenger and the same queries as in the game of ciphertext authentication are allowed.
- **Selection:** After the end of **Phase 1**, the adversary returns a message m^*, two distinct sender's identities (ID_{S0}, ID_{S1}), and two distinct recipient's identities (ID_{R0}, ID_{R1}). The only constraint is that the private keys corresponding to ID_{R0} and ID_{R1} should not be extracted during the private key extraction query.

- **Challenge:** The challenger chooses bits $a, b \in \{0, 1\}$ uniformly at random and computes the ciphertext C^* including a signature under the private key $SK_{\mathsf{ID}_{Sa}}$ corresponding to ID_{Sa} and encrypted message under the public key of ID_{Rb}. Then the challenger returns C^* to the adversary as a challenge.
- **Phase 2:** The adversary makes new queries adaptively to the challenger. The constraints are as follows: (1) the private key extraction queries for private keys corresponding to ID_{R0} and ID_{R1} have not appeared; and (2) the designcryption queries for the ciphertext C^* under ID_{R0} and ID_{R1} have not been issued.
- **Response:** The adversary returns bits a', b' and wins if $(a, b) = (a', b')$.

4 The Proposed Scheme

4.1 Notation

Let $H_1 : \{0, 1\}^{l_1} \to \{0, 1\}^{l_2}$ and $H_2 : \{0, 1\}^{l_3} \to \{0, 1\}^{l_4}$ are hash functions. We assume that e_1 is the bit-length of outputs of $\mathsf{E}_{\mathsf{IBE}}$, let e_2 be the bit-length of an identity, and let l_4 be the bit length of signature s where $l_1 = l_2 + e_1 + e_2$ and $l_3 = 2l_2 + e_2$. Moreover, we assume that $\mathsf{param}_{\mathsf{IBE}} \bigcap \mathsf{param}_{\mathsf{IBS}} = \Phi$.

4.2 Construction

This IBSC scheme is based on the ordinary IBE and IBS schemes.

- $\mathsf{Setup}(1^k) \to (msk_{\mathsf{IBE}}, \mathsf{param}_{\mathsf{IBE}}, msk_{\mathsf{IBS}}, \mathsf{param}_{\mathsf{IBS}}, H_1, H_2)$: Given a security parameter 1^k, output $(msk_{\mathsf{IBE}}, \mathsf{param}_{\mathsf{IBE}}, msk_{\mathsf{IBS}}, \mathsf{param}_{\mathsf{IBS}}, H_1, H_2)$ where the master key is $msk = (msk_{\mathsf{IBE}}, msk_{\mathsf{IBS}})$, the global parameter is $\mathsf{param} = (\mathsf{param}_{\mathsf{IBE}}, \mathsf{param}_{\mathsf{IBS}}, H_1, H_2)$.
- $\mathsf{KeyGen}(msk, \mathsf{ID}) \to SK_{\mathsf{ID}}$: Given the master secret key msk and an identity ID, output the private key SK_{ID} for ID. The private key is compute as follows:
  1) $SK_{\mathsf{IBE.ID}} \leftarrow \mathsf{KeyGen}_{\mathsf{IBE}}(\mathsf{ID})$;
  2) $SK_{\mathsf{IBS.ID}} \leftarrow \mathsf{KeyGen}_{\mathsf{IBS}}(\mathsf{ID})$;
  3) $SK_{\mathsf{ID}} = (SK_{\mathsf{IBE.ID}}, SK_{\mathsf{IBS.ID}})$.
- $\mathsf{Signcryption}(m, \mathsf{ID}_S, \mathsf{ID}_R, SK_{\mathsf{ID}_S}) \to C$: Given a message m, a sender's identity ID_S, a recipient's identity ID_R, and a sender's private key SK_{ID_S}, output a ciphertext $C = (c_1, c_2, d)$. The computation is as follows:
  1) $r \leftarrow \{0, 1\}^{l_2}$;
  2) $c_1 \leftarrow \mathsf{E}_{\mathsf{IBE}}((r\|\mathsf{ID}_S), \mathsf{ID}_R)$;
  3) $t_1 \leftarrow H_1(r\|c_1\|\mathsf{ID}_S)$;
  4) $t_2 \leftarrow H_2(m\|t_1\|\mathsf{ID}_R)$;
  5) $c_2 = t_1 \oplus m$;
  6) $s \leftarrow \mathsf{S}_{\mathsf{IBS}}((m\|\mathsf{ID}_R), SK_{\mathsf{IBS.ID}_S})$;
  7) $d = t_2 \oplus s$.
- $\mathsf{Designcryption}(C, \mathsf{ID}_R, SK_{\mathsf{ID}_R}) \to m$ or $\perp$: Given a ciphertext C, a recipient's identity ID_R, and a recipient's private key SK_{ID_R}, output a message m or $\perp$ indicating an error. The computation is as follows:

1) $r\|\mathsf{ID_S} = \mathsf{D_{IBE}}(c_1, SK_{\mathsf{IBE.ID_R}})$;
2) $t_1 \leftarrow H_1(r\|c_1\|\mathsf{ID_S})$;
3) $m = t_1 \oplus c_2$;
4) $t_2 \leftarrow H_2(m\|t_1\|\mathsf{ID_R})$;
5) $s = t_2 \oplus d$;
6) m or $\perp = \mathsf{V_{IBS}}((m\|\mathsf{ID_R}), s, \mathsf{ID_S})$.

5   Security

We assume that the underlying IBS and IBE schemes used in the construction of our IBSC scheme are IND-CCA secure and EUF-CMA secure respectively. For the proof, we use four oracles: $O_{\mathsf{K.IBE}}(\cdot)$, $O_{\mathsf{D.IBE}}(\cdot, \cdot)$, $O_{\mathsf{K.IBS}}(\cdot)$, and $O_{\mathsf{S.IBS}}(\cdot, \cdot)$.

- A private key extraction oracle in IBE takes as input an identity ID and outputs the private key corresponding to ID: $O_{\mathsf{K.IBE}}(\mathsf{ID}) \rightarrow SK_{\mathsf{IBE.ID}}$.
- A decryption oracle in IBE takes as input a ciphertext c_1 and an identity $\mathsf{ID_R}$ and outputs a plaintext $(r\|\mathsf{ID_S})$: $O_{\mathsf{D.IBE}}(c_1, \mathsf{ID_R}) \rightarrow (r\|\mathsf{ID_S})$.
- A private key extraction oracle in IBS takes as input an identity ID and outputs the signing key corresponding to ID: $O_{\mathsf{K.IBS}}(\mathsf{ID}) \rightarrow SK_{\mathsf{IBS.ID}}$.
- A signing oracle in IBS takes as input a plaintext $(m\|\mathsf{ID_R})$ and $\mathsf{ID_S}$ and outputs the signature on the plaintext $(m\|\mathsf{ID_R})$: $O_{\mathsf{S.IBS}}((m\|\mathsf{ID_R}), \mathsf{ID_S}) \rightarrow s$.

We assume that random oracles g_1 and g_2 simply return the truly random numbers t_1 and t_2, respectively. The simulator works as follows:

- g_1 (or g_2): Given a string with the length of l_1 (or l_3), outputs the truly random number t_1 (or t_2) with the length of l_2 (or l_4). The random oracle stores the input string and the output number in the list L_1 (or L_2). If the random oracle takes as input the same string in L_1 (or L_2), it returns the number corresponding to the input string.

5.1   Ciphertext Authentication

Theorem 1. *If there is an AUTH-IBSC-CMA adversary $\mathcal{A}$ that succeeds with probability ϵ, then there is an EUF-CMA adversary $\mathcal{B}$ against the underlying IBS scheme (used in the IBSC) with probability ϵ.*

Proof. We show how an AUTH-IBSC-CMA adversary $\mathcal{A}$ with ϵ may be used to construct an EUF-CMA adversary $\mathcal{B}$ with ϵ. To successfully simulate the adversary $\mathcal{A}$'s environment, we use a private key extraction oracle $O_{\mathsf{K.IBS}}(\cdot)$ and a signature oracle $O_{\mathsf{S.IBS}}(\cdot, \cdot)$ of IBS.

- **Initial:** An algorithm $\mathcal{B}$ is given $\mathsf{param_{IBS}}$. $\mathcal{B}$ chooses an IBE scheme and generates $(\mathsf{param_{IBE}}, msk_{\mathsf{IBE}})$. $\mathcal{B}$ chooses two random oracles g_1 and g_2. $\mathcal{B}$ sends global parameters $\mathsf{param} = (\mathsf{param_{IBE}}, \mathsf{param_{IBS}}, g_1, g_2)$ to $\mathcal{A}$.

- **Query:** $\mathcal{A}$ makes queries adaptively to $\mathcal{B}$ who plays the role of a challenger. $\mathcal{B}$ treats the queries as follows.
  - Private key extraction queries: $\mathcal{B}$ sends Private key extraction query on ID to $O_{\mathsf{K.IBS}}$ and receives $SK_{\mathsf{IBS.ID}}$. Then $\mathcal{B}$ generates the $SK_{\mathsf{IBE.ID}}$ corresponding to ID using msk_{IBE} generated by $\mathcal{B}$. $\mathcal{B}$ responds with the secret key $SK_{\mathsf{ID}} = (SK_{\mathsf{IBS.ID}}, SK_{\mathsf{IBE.ID}})$ corresponding to ID.
  - Signcryption queries: $\mathcal{B}$ chooses $r \leftarrow \{0,1\}^{l_2}$; computes $c_1 \leftarrow \mathsf{E}_{\mathsf{IBE}}((r\|ID_{\mathsf{S}}), \mathsf{ID}_{\mathsf{R}})$, $t_1 \leftarrow g_1(r\|c_1\|\mathsf{ID}_{\mathsf{S}})$, $t_2 \leftarrow g_2(m\|t_1\|\mathsf{ID}_{\mathsf{R}})$, and $c_2 = t_1 \oplus m$. $\mathcal{B}$ sends sign query for $((m\|\mathsf{ID}_{\mathsf{R}}), \mathsf{ID}_{\mathsf{S}})$ to $O_{\mathsf{S.IBS}}$ to get a signature s of $(m\|\mathsf{ID}_{\mathsf{R}})$. Then $\mathcal{B}$ computes $d = t_2 \oplus s$. $\mathcal{B}$ responds with the ciphertext $C = (c_1, c_2, d)$ to $\mathcal{A}$.
  - Designcryption queries: $\mathcal{B}$ runs $\mathsf{KeyGen}_{\mathsf{IBE}}(\mathsf{ID}_{\mathsf{R}})$ to computes $SK_{\mathsf{IBE.ID}_{\mathsf{R}}}$. $\mathcal{B}$ computes $r\|\mathsf{ID}_{\mathsf{S}} = \mathsf{D}_{\mathsf{IBE}}(c_1, SK_{\mathsf{IBE.ID}_{\mathsf{R}}})$, $t_1 \leftarrow g_1(r\|c_1\|\mathsf{ID}_{\mathsf{S}})$, $m = t_1 \oplus c_2$, $t_2 \leftarrow g_2(m\|t_1\|\mathsf{ID}_{\mathsf{R}})$, and $s = t_2 \oplus d$. Then $\mathcal{B}$ runs $\mathsf{V}_{\mathsf{IBS}}((m\|\mathsf{ID}_{\mathsf{R}}), s, \mathsf{ID}_{\mathsf{S}})$. If s is a valid signature, $\mathcal{B}$ returns m; otherwise, returns $\perp$ to $\mathcal{A}$.
- **Forge:** After the end of **Query**, $\mathcal{A}$ returns a pair $(C^*, \mathsf{ID}_{\mathsf{R}}^*)$ as a forgery. $\mathcal{B}$ decrypts C^* under the secret key corresponding to $\mathsf{ID}_{\mathsf{R}}^*$ and gets the information about $(m^*, \mathsf{ID}_{\mathsf{S}}^*, s^*)$. $\mathcal{B}$ returns $((m^*\|\mathsf{ID}_{\mathsf{R}}^*), \mathsf{ID}_{\mathsf{S}}^*, s^*)$ as a forgery. A pair $((m^*\|\mathsf{ID}_{\mathsf{R}}^*), s^*)$ is valid message-signature pair for $\mathsf{ID}_{\mathsf{S}}^*$ if C^* is valid ciphertext. At this time, (1) the secret key extraction queries for $\mathsf{ID}_{\mathsf{S}}^*$ and $\mathsf{ID}_{\mathsf{R}}^*$ have not been issued and (2) the signcryption queries for C^* with $\mathsf{ID}_{\mathsf{S}}^*$ and $\mathsf{ID}_{\mathsf{R}}^*$ have not appeared. In our IBSC scheme, C^* was not obtained as output of $\mathsf{Signcryption}(m', \mathsf{ID}_{\mathsf{S}}^*, \mathsf{ID}_{\mathsf{R}}^*, SK_{\mathsf{ID}_{\mathsf{S}}^*})$ with $m' \neq m^*$, because $(m\|\mathsf{ID}_{\mathsf{R}})$ is signed, not m. This means that the signcryption query for $(m^*, \mathsf{ID}_{\mathsf{S}}^*, \mathsf{ID}_{\mathsf{R}}^*)$ has not been queried by $\mathcal{A}$; i.e., $\mathcal{B}$ does not need to send the sign query $((m^*\|\mathsf{ID}_{\mathsf{R}}^*), \mathsf{ID}_{\mathsf{S}}^*)$ to $O_{\mathsf{S.IBS}}$ to get a signature s of $(m^*\|\mathsf{ID}_{\mathsf{R}}^*)$.

Hence, the advantage of $\mathcal{B} = Adv(\mathcal{B}) = \Pr[\mathcal{B} \text{ wins }] = \Pr[\mathcal{A} \text{ wins }] = \epsilon$. $\qquad\square$

5.2 Message Confidentiality

Theorem 2. *If there is an IND-IBSC-CCA adversary $\mathcal{A}$ that succeeds with probability ϵ, then there is an IND-CCA adversary $\mathcal{B}$ against the underlying IBE scheme (used in the IBSC) with probability $\epsilon/2$.*

Proof. We will show how an IND-IBSC-CCA adversary $\mathcal{A}$ of IBSC may be used to construct an IND-CCA adversary $\mathcal{B}$. To successfully simulate the adversary $\mathcal{A}$'s environment, we use a private key extraction oracle $O_{\mathsf{K.IBE}}(\cdot)$ and a signature oracle $O_{\mathsf{D.IBE}}(\cdot, \cdot)$ of IBE.

- **Initial:** An algorithm $\mathcal{B}$ is given $\mathsf{param}_{\mathsf{IBE}}$. $\mathcal{B}$ chooses an IBS scheme and generates $(\mathsf{param}_{\mathsf{IBS}}, msk_{\mathsf{IBS}})$. $\mathcal{B}$ chooses two random oracles g_1 and g_2. $\mathcal{B}$ sends global parameters $\mathsf{param} = (\mathsf{param}_{\mathsf{IBE}}, \mathsf{param}_{\mathsf{IBS}}, g_1, g_2)$ to $\mathcal{A}$.
- **Phase 1:** $\mathcal{A}$ makes queries adaptively to $\mathcal{B}$ who plays the role of a challenger. $\mathcal{B}$ treats the queries as follows.

- Private key extraction queries: $\mathcal{B}$ sends a Private key extraction query on ID to $O_{\text{K.IBE}}$ and receives $SK_{\text{IBE.ID}}$. Then $\mathcal{B}$ generates the $SK_{\text{IBS.ID}}$ corresponding to ID using msk_{IBS} generated by $\mathcal{B}$. $\mathcal{B}$ responds with the secret key $SK_{\text{ID}} = (SK_{\text{IBS.ID}}, SK_{\text{IBE.ID}})$.
- Signcryption queries: $\mathcal{B}$ chooses $r \leftarrow \{0,1\}^{l_2}$; computes $c_1 \leftarrow \mathsf{E}_{\text{IBE}}((r\|ID_\mathsf{S}), \mathsf{ID_R})$, $t_1 \leftarrow g_1(r\|c_1\|\mathsf{ID_S})$, $t_2 \leftarrow g_2(m\|t_1\|\mathsf{ID_R})$, and $c_2 = t_1 \oplus m$; generates the signature $s \leftarrow \mathsf{S}_{\text{IBS}}((m\|\mathsf{ID_R}), SK_{\text{IBS.ID}_\mathsf{S}})$; and computes $d = t_2 \oplus s$. $\mathcal{B}$ sends the ciphertext $C = (c_1, c_2, d)$ to $\mathcal{A}$.
- Designcryption queries: $\mathcal{B}$ sends the decryption query $(c_1, \mathsf{ID_R})$ to $O_{\text{D.IBE}}$ to get $(r\|\mathsf{ID_S})$. $\mathcal{B}$ Computes $t_1 \leftarrow g_1(r\|c_1\|\mathsf{ID_S})$, $m = t_1 \oplus c_2$, $t_2 \leftarrow g_2(m\|t_1\|\mathsf{ID_R})$, and $s = t_2 \oplus d$. Then $\mathcal{B}$ runs $\mathsf{V}_{\text{IBS}}((m\|\mathsf{ID_R}), s, \mathsf{ID_S})$. If s is a valid signature, $\mathcal{B}$ returns m; otherwise, returns $\perp$ to $\mathcal{A}$.
- **Selection:** After the end of **Phase** 1, $\mathcal{A}$ returns a sender's identity ID_S^*, a recipient's identity ID_R^* and two distinct messages (m_0, m_1) to $\mathcal{B}$.
- **Challenge:** $\mathcal{B}$ chooses two distinct random numbers (r_0, r_1) and sends the tuple $((r_0\|\mathsf{ID}_\mathsf{S}^*), (r_1\|\mathsf{ID}_\mathsf{S}^*), \mathsf{ID}_\mathsf{R}^*)$ (on which it wishes to be challenged in IND-CCA) to $O_{Challenge}$. $O_{Challenge}$ chooses a bit x uniformly at random and returns a challenge ciphertext $c_{1x} \leftarrow \mathsf{E}_{\text{IBE}}((r_x\|\mathsf{ID}_\mathsf{S}^*), \mathsf{ID}_\mathsf{R}^*)$ to $\mathcal{B}$. Then $\mathcal{B}$ chooses a bit b uniformly at random; computes $t_1 \leftarrow g_1(r_b\|c_{1x}\|\mathsf{ID}_\mathsf{S}^*)$, $t_2 \leftarrow g_2(m_b\|t_1\|\mathsf{ID}_\mathsf{R}^*)$, $c_2 = t_1 \oplus m$; generates the signature of m_b, $s = \mathsf{S}_{\text{IBS}}((m_b\|\mathsf{ID}_\mathsf{R}^*), SK_{\text{IBS.ID}_\mathsf{S}^*})$; and computes $d = t_2 \oplus s$. $\mathcal{B}$ sends the challenge ciphertext $C^* = (c_{1x}, c_2, d)$ to $\mathcal{A}$.
- **Phase 2:** $\mathcal{A}$ makes new queries adaptively to $\mathcal{B}$.
- **Response:** If $\mathcal{A}$ returns a bit b' then $\mathcal{B}$ also returns the same bit b'.

We have two cases to consider.

Case 1 $(x = b)$, $\mathcal{B}$ produced the valid ciphertext C^* of message m_b corresponding to ID_R^* and ID_S^*. Therefore, $\mathcal{A}$'s view is identical to its view in the real attack. $\Pr[\mathcal{B} \text{ wins } | x = b] = \Pr[\mathcal{A} \text{ wins } | C^* \text{ is a valid ciphertext}]$.

Case 2 $(x \neq b)$, In the $\mathcal{A}$'s view, c_{1x} can be considered that it is chosen uniformly at random from $(0,1)^{e_1}$ (because c_{1x} and r_b are independent); the t_1 and t_2 are considered that they are chosen uniformly chosen at random from $(0,1)^{l_2}$ and $(0,1)^{l_4}$ (because those inputs include c_{1x} and t_2).; The c_2 and d are considered that they are chosen uniformly chosen at random from $(0,1)^{l_2}$ and $(0,1)^{l_4}$ (because they are computed by XOR with t_1 and t_2). Therefore, $C^* = (c_1, c_2, d)$ is a random ciphertext chosen uniformly from the ciphertext space in the $\mathcal{A}$'s view. $\Pr[\mathcal{B} \text{ wins } | x \neq b] = \Pr[\mathcal{A} \text{ wins } | C^* \text{ is a valid ciphertext}] = 1/2$.

$$\begin{aligned}
\Pr[\mathcal{B} \text{ wins}] &= \Pr[\mathcal{B} \text{ wins } | x = b]\Pr[x = b] + \Pr[\mathcal{B} \text{ wins } | x \neq b]\Pr[x \neq b] \\
&= 1/2(\Pr[\mathcal{B} \text{ wins } | x = b] + 1/2) \\
&= 1/2(\Pr[\mathcal{A} \text{ wins } | C^* \text{ is a valid ciphertext}] + 1/2).
\end{aligned}$$

Hence, the advantage of $\mathcal{B} = Adv(\mathcal{B}) = |\Pr[\mathcal{B} \text{ wins}] - 1/2|$
$$\begin{aligned}
&= 1/2(|\Pr[\mathcal{A} \text{ wins}] - 1/2|) \\
&= 1/2(Adv(\mathcal{A})) = \epsilon/2. \qquad \square
\end{aligned}$$

5.3   Signature Non-repudiation

Theorem 3. *If there is an EUF-IBSC-CMA adversary $\mathcal{A}$ that succeeds with probability ϵ, then there is an EUF-CMA adversary $\mathcal{B}$ against the IBS scheme (used in the IBSC) with probability ϵ.*

Proof. We will show how an EUF-IBSC-CMA adversary $\mathcal{A}$ of IBSC may be used to construct an EUF-CMA adversary $\mathcal{B}$. To successfully simulate the adversary $\mathcal{A}$'s environment, we use a private key extraction oracle $O_{K.IBS}(\cdot)$ and a signature oracle $O_{S.IBS}(\cdot, \cdot)$ of IBS.

- **Initial:** The same as in Section 5.1
- **Query:** The same as in Section 5.1
- **Forge:** After the end of **Query**, $\mathcal{A}$ returns (C^*, ID_R^*) as a forgery. The $\mathcal{B}$ decrypts C^* under the secret key corresponding to ID_R^* and gets the information about (m^*, ID_S^*, s^*). $\mathcal{B}$ returns $((m^*||ID_R^*), ID_S^*, s^*)$ as a forgery. A pair $((m^*||ID_R^*), s^*)$ is a valid message-signature pair for ID_S^* if C^* is valid ciphertext. At this time, (1) the secret key extraction queries for ID_S^* have not been issued and (2) the signcryption queries for (m^*, ID_S^*, ID_R') have not appeared, and ID_R' can be either ID_R^* or not. This means that $\mathcal{B}$ does not need to send the sign query $((m^*||ID_R'), ID_S^*)$ to $O_{S.IBS}$ to get a signature s for $(m^*||ID_R')$. Of course, $\mathcal{B}$ does not need to send Sign query $((m^*||ID_R^*), ID_S^*)$.

Hence, the advantage of $\mathcal{B} = Adv(B) = \Pr[B \text{ wins }] = \Pr[A \text{ wins }] = \epsilon$.   □

5.4   Ciphertext Anonymity

Theorem 4. *If there is an ANON-IBSC-CCA adversary $\mathcal{A}$ that succeeds with probability ϵ, then there is an ANON-IND-CCA adversary $\mathcal{B}$ against the underlying IBE scheme (used in the IBSC) with probability $\epsilon/4$.*

Proof. We will show how an ANON-IBSC-CCA adversary $\mathcal{A}$ of IBSC may be used to construct an ANON-IND-CCA adversary $\mathcal{B}$. To successfully simulate the adversary $\mathcal{A}$'s environment, we use a private key extraction oracle $O_{K.IBE}(\cdot)$ and a signature oracle $O_{D.IBE}(\cdot, \cdot)$ of IBE.

- **Initial:** The same as in Section 5.2
- **Phase 1:** The same as in Section 5.2
- **Selection:** After the end of **Phase** 1, $\mathcal{A}$ returns a message m^*, two distinct sender's identities (ID_{S0}, ID_{S1}), and two distinct recipient's identities (ID_{R0}, ID_{R1}) to $\mathcal{B}$.
- **Challenge:** $\mathcal{B}$ chooses a random number $r \leftarrow (0,1)^{l_2}$ and sends the tuple $((r||ID_{S0}, r||ID_{S1}), (ID_{R0}, ID_{R1}))$, on which it wishes to be challenged in ANON-IND-CCA. $O_{Challenge}$ chooses two bits (x, y) uniformly at random and returns a challenge ciphertext $c_{1.x,y} \leftarrow E_{IBE}((r||ID_{Sx}), ID_{Ry})$ to $\mathcal{B}$. Then $\mathcal{B}$ chooses two bits (a, b) uniformly at random and computes $t_1 \leftarrow g_1(r||c_{1.x,y}||ID_{Sa})$, $t_2 \leftarrow g_2(m||t_1||ID_{Rb})$, and $c_2 = t_1 \oplus m^*$; and computes the signature

$s \leftarrow \mathsf{S}_{\mathsf{IBS}}((m^*||ID_{Rb}), SK_{IBS.ID_{Sa}})$, $d = t_2 \oplus s$. $\mathcal{B}$ sends the challenge ciphertext $C^* = (c_{1.x,y}, c_2, d)$ to $\mathcal{A}$.

- **Phase 2:** $\mathcal{A}$ makes new queries adaptively to $\mathcal{B}$.
- **Response:** If $\mathcal{A}$ returns two bits a', b' then $\mathcal{B}$ also returns same two bits.

We have four cases to consider.

Case 1 ($x = a \cap y = b$), $\mathcal{B}$ produced the valid ciphertext C^* of message m^* corresponding to ID_{Rb} and ID_{Sa}. therefore, $\mathcal{A}$'s view is identical to its view in the real attack.

$\Pr[\mathcal{B} \text{ wins } |x = a \cap y = b] = \Pr[\mathcal{A} \text{ wins } |C* \text{ is a valid ciphertext}].$

Case 2 ($x = a \cap y \neq b$), In the $\mathcal{A}$'s view, $c_{1.x,y}$ can be considered that it is chosen uniformly at random from $(0,1)^{e_1}$ (because $c_{1.x,y}$ and ID_{Rb} are independent); the h_1 and h_2 are considered that they are chosen uniformly chosen at random from $(0,1)^{l_2}$ and $(0,1)^{l_4}$ (because those inputs include $c_{1.x,y}$ and h_2); the c_2 and d are considered that they are chosen uniformly chosen at random from $(0,1)^{l_2}$ and $(0,1)^{l_4}$ (because they are computed XOR with h_1 and h_2). Therefore, $C^* = (c_1, c_2, d)$ is a random ciphertext chosen uniformly from the ciphertext space in the $\mathcal{A}$'s view.

$\Pr[\mathcal{B} \text{ wins } |x = a \cap y \neq b] = \Pr[\mathcal{A} \text{ wins } |C^* \text{ is a random ciphertext}] = 1/4.$

Case 3 ($x \neq a \cap y = b$),

$\Pr[\mathcal{B} \text{ wins } |x \neq a \cap y = b] = \Pr[\mathcal{A} \text{ wins } |C^* \text{ is a random ciphertext}] = 1/4.$

Case 4 ($x \neq a \cap y \neq b$),

$\Pr[\mathcal{B} \text{ wins } |x \neq a \cap y \neq b] = \Pr[\mathcal{A} \text{ wins } |C^* \text{ is a random ciphertext}] = 1/4.$

$$
\begin{aligned}
\Pr[\mathcal{B} \text{ wins }] &= \Pr[\mathcal{B} \text{ wins } |x = a \cap y = b]\Pr[x = a \cap y = b] \\
&+ \Pr[\mathcal{B} \text{ wins } |x = a \cap y \neq b]\Pr[x = a \cap y \neq b] \\
&+ \Pr[\mathcal{B} \text{ wins } |x \neq a \cap y = b]\Pr[x \neq a \cap y = b] \\
&+ \Pr[\mathcal{B} \text{ wins } |x \neq a \cap y \neq b]\Pr[x \neq a \cap y \neq b] \\
&= 1/4(\Pr[\mathcal{B} \text{ wins } |x = a \cap y = b] + 3/4).
\end{aligned}
$$

Hence, the advantage of $\mathcal{B} = Adv(\mathcal{B}) = |\Pr[\mathcal{B} \text{ wins}] - 1/4|$
$$
\begin{aligned}
&= 1/4(|\Pr[\mathcal{A} \text{ wins}] - 1/4|) \\
&= 1/4(Adv(\mathcal{A})) = \epsilon/4. \qquad \square
\end{aligned}
$$

6   Conclusion

We have improved the Pandey scheme to propose an efficient method of construction an IBSC scheme which satisfies ciphertext authentication, message confidentiality, signature non-repudiation, and ciphertext anonymity. The security of the proposed scheme was proved by using the random oracle model. Our construction achieves more security notions with no loss in efficiency; our scheme reduced one hash operation when comparing with the Pandey scheme.

References

1. Barreto, P.S.L.M., Libert, B., McCullagh, N., Quisquater, J.-J.: Efficient and Provably-Secure Identity-Based Signatures and Signcryption from Bilinear Maps. In: Roy, B. (ed.) ASIACRYPT 2005. LNCS, vol. 3788, pp. 515–532. Springer, Heidelberg (2005)
2. Boneh, D., Franklin, M.K.: Identity-based encryption from the weil pairing. SIAM J. Comput. 32(3), 586–615 (2003)
3. Boyen, X.: Multipurpose Identity-Based Signcryption (a Swiss Army Knife for Identity-Based Cryptography). In: Boneh, D. (ed.) CRYPTO 2003. LNCS, vol. 2729, pp. 383–399. Springer, Heidelberg (2003)
4. Chen, L., Malone-Lee, J.: Improved Identity-Based Signcryption. In: Vaudenay, S. (ed.) PKC 2005. LNCS, vol. 3386, pp. 362–379. Springer, Heidelberg (2005)
5. Gu, C., Zhu, Y.: An Efficient Id-Based Proxy Signature Scheme from Pairings. In: Pei, D., Yung, M., Lin, D., Wu, C. (eds.) Inscrypt 2007. LNCS, vol. 4990, pp. 40–50. Springer, Heidelberg (2008)
6. Malone-Lee, J.: Identity-based signcryption. Cryptology ePrint Archive, Report 2002/098 (2002), http://eprint.iacr.org/
7. Pandey, S.K., Barua, R.: Construction of Identity Based Signcryption Schemes. In: Chung, Y., Yung, M. (eds.) WISA 2010. LNCS, vol. 6513, pp. 1–14. Springer, Heidelberg (2011)
8. Selvi, S.S.D., Vivek, S.S., Srinivasan, R., Rangan, C.P.: An Efficient Identity-Based Signcryption Scheme for Multiple Receivers. In: Takagi, T., Mambo, M. (eds.) IWSEC 2009. LNCS, vol. 5824, pp. 71–88. Springer, Heidelberg (2009)
9. Shamir, A.: Identity-Based Cryptosystems and Signature Schemes. In: Blakely, G.R., Chaum, D. (eds.) CRYPTO 1984. LNCS, vol. 196, pp. 47–53. Springer, Heidelberg (1985)
10. Zhang, J., Gao, S., Chen, H., Geng, Q.: A Novel Id-Based Anonymous Signcryption Scheme. In: Li, Q., Feng, L., Pei, J., Wang, S.X., Zhou, X., Zhu, Q.-M. (eds.) APWeb/WAIM 2009. LNCS, vol. 5446, pp. 604–610. Springer, Heidelberg (2009)
11. Zheng, Y.: Digital Signcryption or How to Achieve Cost(Signature & Encryption) << Cost(Signature) + Cost(Encryption). In: Kaliski Jr., B.S. (ed.) CRYPTO 1997. LNCS, vol. 1294, pp. 165–179. Springer, Heidelberg (1997)

Order-Preserving Encryption for Non-uniformly Distributed Plaintexts

Dae Hyun Yum[1], Duk Soo Kim[2], Jin Seok Kim[1],
Pil Joong Lee[1], and Sung Je Hong[1]

[1] Electrical Engineering, POSTECH, Republic of Korea
{dhyum,treasure,pjl,sjhong}@postech.ac.kr
[2] Penta Security Systems, Inc., Republic of Korea
dskim@pentasecurity.com

Abstract. Order-preserving encryption (OPE) is a deterministic encryption scheme whose encryption function preserves numerical ordering of the plaintexts. While the concept of OPE was introduced in 2004, the first provably-secure OPE scheme was constructed by Boldyreva, Chenette, Lee, and O'Neill at Eurocrypt 2009. The BCLO scheme uses a sampling algorithm for the hypergeometric distribution as a subroutine and maps the Euclidean middle range gap to a domain gap. We study how to utilize the (non-uniform) distribution of the plaintext-space to reduce the number of sampling algorithm invocations in the BCLO scheme. Instead of the Euclidean middle range gap, we map the probabilistic middle range gap to a domain gap. Our simulation shows that the proposed method is effective for various distributions and especially for distributions with small variance.

Keywords: Order-preserving encryption, hypergeometric distribution, lazy sampling.

1 Introduction

The integration of ordinary encryption schemes with database systems causes undesirable performance degradation because ordinary encryption schemes do not preserve order of plaintexts. In order to allow comparison operations to be directly applied on encrypted data, order-preserving encryption (OPE) was proposed in the database community by Agrawal et al. [1]. When OPE is used in database systems, equality and range queries as well as the MAX, MIN, and COUNT queries can be directly processed over encrypted data. In addition to the database systems, OPE has also been used for concealed data aggregation in sensor networks [2] and signal processing on encrypted multimedia content [3].

At Eurocrypt 2009, Boldyreva, Chenette, Lee, and O'Neill introduced a security notion and proposed an efficient OPE scheme (which we call BCLO scheme) based on a sampling algorithm for the hypergeometric (HG) distribution. As a straightforward relaxation of standard security notions for encryption such as indistinguishability against chosen-plaintext attack is unachievable by a practical

S. Jung and M. Yung (Eds.): WISA 2011, LNCS 7115, pp. 84–97, 2012.
© Springer-Verlag Berlin Heidelberg 2012

OPE scheme, the security notion is defined to require that an OPE scheme look "as-random-as-possible" subject to the order-preserving constraint. To meet the proposed security notion, the encryption algorithm of the BCLO scheme behaves similarly to an algorithm that samples a random order-preserving function from a specified domain and range on-the-fly (often called "lazy sampling" [4]); it recursively maps the Euclidean middle range gap to a domain gap.

In modern cryptography, encryption transforms a plaintext into a ciphertext in such a way that anyone who does not know the corresponding key cannot extract any useful information on the plaintext from the ciphertext. The encryption algorithm essentially tries to destroy all relations between plaintexts and ciphertexts. Therefore, modern encryption algorithms such as AES [5] and RSA [6] have not used the knowledge of the plaintext-space distribution in any way; the knowledge of the plaintext-space distribution was considered useful only for cryptanalysis (e.g., frequency analysis of classical ciphers [7]). OPE is very special in that it preserves (or does not destroy) the order relation between plaintexts and ciphertexts.

In order to build a more efficient OPE scheme, we extend the BCLO scheme to make use of the plaintext-space distribution. Whereas the BCLO scheme always maps the Euclidean middle range gap to a domain gap, we map the probabilistic middle range gap to a domain gap; if the plaintext-space is uniformly distributed, two methods are equivalent. It turns out that mapping the probabilistic middle range gap reduces the expected number of sampling algorithm invocations for various plaintext-space distributions. Up to the authors' knowledge, this is the first example that the knowledge of the plaintext-space distribution is used in a constructive way by a provably-secure encryption scheme.

2   Preliminaries

In this section, we summarize the mathematical background and the BCLO scheme [8].

NOTATION. Let $\mathbb{N} = \{0, 1, 2, \ldots\}$ be the set of non-negative integers and $\mathbb{N}^+ = \{1, 2, \ldots\}$ be the positive integers. For $x, y \in \mathbb{N}^+$, $[x]$ denotes the set $\{1, 2, \ldots, x\}$ and $[x, y]$ denotes $\{x, x + 1, \ldots, y\}$. If S is a set, then $x \xleftarrow{\$} S$ denotes that x is selected uniformly at random from S and $x \xleftarrow{cc} S$ denotes that x is assigned a value sampled uniformly at random from S using coins cc. If $\mathcal{A}$ is a randomized algorithm, then $a \xleftarrow{\$} \mathcal{A}(x, y, \ldots)$ means that the output of $\mathcal{A}$ run on inputs $x, y, \ldots$ is assigned to a. For a set $\mathcal{D}$ (which is possibly exponential size), we sometimes abuse the notation $\mathcal{D}$ to mean a (short) description of $\mathcal{D}$ when $\mathcal{D}$ is an input to an algorithm (e.g., $\mathsf{Enc}(K, \mathcal{D}, \mathcal{R}, m)$) or is used as an index of an array (e.g., $F[\mathcal{D}, \mathcal{R}, m]$).

DETERMINISTIC ENCRYPTION. A deterministic symmetric encryption scheme $\mathcal{E} = (\mathsf{Kg}, \mathsf{Enc}, \mathsf{Dec})$ with associated plaintext-space $\mathcal{D}$ and ciphertext-space $\mathcal{R}$ consists of three algorithms.

- The randomized key generation algorithm Kg returns a secret key K.
- The deterministic encryption algorithm Enc takes the secret key K, descriptions of plaintext-space $\mathcal{D}$ and ciphertext-space $\mathcal{R}$, and a plaintext m to return a ciphertext c.
- The deterministic decryption algorithm Dec takes the secret key K, descriptions of plaintext-space $\mathcal{D}$ and ciphertext-space $\mathcal{R}$, and a ciphertext c to return a corresponding plaintext m or a special symbol $\bot$ indicating that the ciphertext is invalid.

We require the correctness condition, i.e., $\mathsf{Dec}(K, \mathcal{D}, \mathcal{R}, \mathsf{Enc}(K, \mathcal{D}, \mathcal{R}, m)) = m$ for all K output by Kg and all $m \in \mathcal{D}$.

ORDER-PRESERVING ENCRYPTION. For $A, B \subset \mathbb{N}$ with $|A| \leq |B|$, a function $f : A \to B$ is order-preserving if for all $i, j \in A$, $f(i) < f(j)$ iff $i < j$. A deterministic encryption scheme $\mathcal{E} = (\mathsf{Kg}, \mathsf{Enc}, \mathsf{Dec})$ with plaintext-space $\mathcal{D}$ and ciphertext-space $\mathcal{R}$ is order-preserving if $\mathsf{Enc}(K, \cdot)$ is an order-preserving function from $\mathcal{D}$ to $\mathcal{R}$ for all K output by Kg (with elements of $\mathcal{D}, \mathcal{R}$ interpreted as numbers, encoded as strings). For an adversary $\mathcal{A}$ against an OPE scheme $\mathcal{E} = (\mathsf{Kg}, \mathsf{Enc}, \mathsf{Dec})$, its popf-cca-advantage (or pseudorandom order-preserving function advantage under chosen-ciphertext attack), $\mathbf{Adv}_{\mathcal{E}}^{\mathrm{popf\text{-}cca}}(\mathcal{A})$ against $\mathcal{E}$ is defined as

$$\Pr\left[K \xleftarrow{\$} \mathsf{Kg} \ : \ \mathcal{A}^{\mathsf{Enc}(K,\cdot),\mathsf{Dec}(K,\cdot)} = 1 \right] - \Pr\left[g \xleftarrow{\$} \mathsf{OPF}_{\mathcal{D},\mathcal{R}} \ : \ \mathcal{A}^{g(\cdot),g^{-1}(\cdot)} = 1 \right]$$

where $\mathsf{OPF}_{\mathcal{D},\mathcal{R}}$ denotes the set of all order-preserving functions from $\mathcal{D}$ to $\mathcal{R}$. We say that an OPE scheme $\mathcal{E}$ is popf-cca secure if $\mathbf{Adv}_{\mathcal{E}}^{\mathrm{popf\text{-}cca}}(\mathcal{A})$ is negligible for any probabilistic polynomial-time algorithm $\mathcal{A}$.

HYPERGEOMETRIC DISTRIBUTION. The hypergeometric distribution is a discrete probability distribution that describes the number of successes in a sequence of draws from a finite population without replacement. Consider the following balls-and-bins model. Assume there are N balls in a bin out of which M balls are black and $N - M$ balls are white. At each step a ball is drawn at random, without replacement. Consider a random variable X that describes the number of black balls chosen after a sample size of y balls are picked. This random variable has a hypergeometric distribution, and the probability that $X = x$ for the parameters N, M, y is

$$P_{HGD}(x; N, M, y) = \frac{\binom{y}{x}\binom{N-y}{M-x}}{\binom{N}{M}} \tag{1}$$

where $x = 0, 1, \ldots, y$.

BCLO SCHEME. The BCLO scheme [8] is based on algorithms **LazySample**, **LazySampleInv** that sample a random order-preserving function from domain $\mathcal{D}$ to range $\mathcal{R}$ and its inverse, respectively. Both $\mathcal{D}$ and $\mathcal{R}$ are assumed to be sets of consecutive integers with $|\mathcal{D}| \leq |\mathcal{R}|$. The algorithms make use of two subroutines. The first, denoted HGD, takes inputs $\mathcal{D}$, $\mathcal{R}$, and $y \in \mathcal{R}$ to return $x \in \mathcal{D}$ such that for each $x^* \in \mathcal{D}$, we have $x = x^*$ with probability $P_{HGD}(x^* - d; |\mathcal{R}|, |\mathcal{D}|, y - r)$ over the coins of HGD, where $d = \min(\mathcal{D}) - 1$ and $r = \min(\mathcal{R}) - 1$. Let $\ell_1 = \ell(\mathcal{D}, \mathcal{R}, y)$ denote the number of coins needed by HGD on inputs $\mathcal{D}, \mathcal{R}, y$. The second, denoted GetCoins, takes inputs $1^\ell, \mathcal{D}, \mathcal{R}$, and $b\|z$, where $b \in \{0, 1\}$ and $z \in \mathcal{R}$ if $b = 0$ and $z \in \mathcal{D}$ otherwise, to return $cc \in \{0, 1\}^\ell$. The algorithms **LazySample** and **LazySampleInv** are given in Fig. 1 where the arrays F, I, initially empty, are global and shared between the algorithms.

LazySample$(\mathcal{D}, \mathcal{R}, m)$	**LazySampleInv**$(\mathcal{D}, \mathcal{R}, c)$
01 $M \leftarrow |\mathcal{D}|;\ N \leftarrow |\mathcal{R}|$	20 $M \leftarrow |\mathcal{D}|;\ N \leftarrow |\mathcal{R}|$
02 $d \leftarrow \min(\mathcal{D}) - 1;\ r \leftarrow \min(\mathcal{R}) - 1$	21 $d \leftarrow \min(\mathcal{D}) - 1;\ r \leftarrow \min(\mathcal{R}) - 1$
03 $y \leftarrow r + \lceil N/2 \rceil$	22 $y \leftarrow r + \lceil N/2 \rceil$
04 If $|\mathcal{D}| = 1$ then	23 If $|\mathcal{D}| = 1$ then $m \leftarrow \min(\mathcal{D})$
05 If $F[\mathcal{D}, \mathcal{R}, m]$ is undefined then	24 If $F[\mathcal{D}, \mathcal{R}, m]$ is undefined then
06 $cc \xleftarrow{\$} \text{GetCoins}(1^{\ell_\mathcal{R}}, \mathcal{D}, \mathcal{R}, 1\|m)$	25 $cc \xleftarrow{\$} \text{GetCoins}(1^{\ell_\mathcal{R}}, \mathcal{D}, \mathcal{R}, 1\|m)$
07 $F[\mathcal{D}, \mathcal{R}, m] \xleftarrow{cc} \mathcal{R}$	26 $F[\mathcal{D}, \mathcal{R}, m] \xleftarrow{cc} \mathcal{R}$
08 Return $F[\mathcal{D}, \mathcal{R}, m]$	27 If $F[\mathcal{D}, \mathcal{R}, m] = c$ then return m
	28 Else return $\perp$
09 If $I[\mathcal{D}, \mathcal{R}, y]$ is undefined then	29 If $I[\mathcal{D}, \mathcal{R}, y]$ is undefined then
10 $cc \xleftarrow{\$} \text{GetCoins}(1^{\ell_1}, \mathcal{D}, \mathcal{R}, 0\|y)$	30 $cc \xleftarrow{\$} \text{GetCoins}(1^{\ell_1}, \mathcal{D}, \mathcal{R}, 0\|y)$
11 $I[\mathcal{D}, \mathcal{R}, y] \xleftarrow{\$} \text{HGD}(\mathcal{D}, \mathcal{R}, y; cc)$	31 $I[\mathcal{D}, \mathcal{R}, y] \xleftarrow{\$} \text{HGD}(\mathcal{D}, \mathcal{R}, y; cc)$
12 $x \leftarrow I[\mathcal{D}, \mathcal{R}, y]$	32 $x \leftarrow I[\mathcal{D}, \mathcal{R}, y]$
13 If $m \leq x$ then	33 If $c \leq y$ then
14 $\mathcal{D} \leftarrow \{d+1, \dots, x\}$	34 $\mathcal{D} \leftarrow \{d+1, \dots, x\}$
15 $\mathcal{R} \leftarrow \{r+1, \dots, y\}$	35 $\mathcal{R} \leftarrow \{r+1, \dots, y\}$
16 Else	36 Else
17 $\mathcal{D} \leftarrow \{x+1, \dots, d+M\}$	37 $\mathcal{D} \leftarrow \{x+1, \dots, d+M\}$
18 $\mathcal{R} \leftarrow \{y+1, \dots, r+N\}$	38 $\mathcal{R} \leftarrow \{y+1, \dots, r+N\}$
19 Return **LazySample**$(\mathcal{D}, \mathcal{R}, m)$	39 Return **LazySampleInv**$(\mathcal{D}, \mathcal{R}, c)$

Fig. 1. The **LazySample**, **LazySampleInv** algorithms

To determine the image of input m, **LazySample** maps range gaps to domain gaps in a recursive, binary search manner where a gap means an imaginary barrier between two consecutive points. The algorithm maps the Euclidian middle range gap between y $(= r + \lceil N/2 \rceil)$ and $y + 1$ to the domain gap between x $(= I[\mathcal{D}, \mathcal{R}, y])$ and $x + 1$. The algorithms **LazySample** and **LazySampleInv** can be converted into encryption and decryption algorithms by implementing GetCoins as a length-flexible pseudorandom function and constructing entries of F and I on-the-fly as needed. The number of invocations of the sampling algorithm HGD by the encryption (or decryption) algorithm equals that of recursive calls made by **LazySample**.

3   OPE for Non-uniformly Distributed Plaintexts

3.1   Algorithm

When the probability mass function of the plaintext-space is given by $\mathsf{PMF}_{\mathcal{D}}(x)$ for $x \in \mathcal{D}$, the probabilistic middle point may be defined as x' such that

$$\sum_{z=d+1}^{x'} \mathsf{PMF}_{\mathcal{D}}(z) = \frac{1}{2} \sum_{z=d+1}^{d+M} \mathsf{PMF}_{\mathcal{D}}(z) \tag{2}$$

where $d = \min(\mathcal{D}) - 1$. However, the domain $\mathcal{D}$ consists of integers and thus a solution $x' \in \mathcal{D}$ to Eq. (2) does not always exist. Therefore, we define the probabilistic middle point as follows.

$$\hat{x} = \operatorname*{argmax}_{x \in \mathcal{D}} \left(\sum_{z=d+1}^{x} \mathsf{PMF}_{\mathcal{D}}(z) \leq \frac{1}{2} \sum_{z=d+1}^{d+M} \mathsf{PMF}_{\mathcal{D}}(z) \right). \tag{3}$$

We remark that the probabilistic middle point $\hat{x}$ is different from the center of mass (or mean) $\overline{x} = \sum_{x \in \mathcal{D}}(x \cdot \mathsf{PMF}_{\mathcal{D}}(x))$. For example, consider the following three probability mass functions $\mathsf{pmf}_1(\cdot)$, $\mathsf{pmf}_2(\cdot)$, and $\mathsf{pmf}_3(\cdot)$ for a domain $\mathcal{D} = \{1, 2, \ldots, 10\}$.

Table 1. Probability mass functions for $\mathcal{D} = \{1, 2, \ldots, 10\}$

x	1	2	3	4	5	6	7	8	9	10
$\mathsf{pmf}_1(x)$	0.4	0	0	0	0.1	0.1	0.1	0.1	0.1	0.1
$\mathsf{pmf}_2(x)$	0.1	0.1	0.1	0.1	0.1	0.1	0.1	0.1	0.1	0.1
$\mathsf{pmf}_3(x)$	0	0	0	0.4	0.1	0.1	0.1	0.1	0.1	0.1

For all three probability mass functions, the probabilistic middle point $\hat{x}$ is 5 because $\sum_{x=1}^{5} \mathsf{pmf}_i(x) = \frac{1}{2}$ and $\sum_{x=1}^{6} \mathsf{pmf}_i(x) = 0.6 > \frac{1}{2}$ where $i = 1, 2, 3$. The center of mass $\overline{x}$, by contrast, is 4.9 for pmf_1, 5.5 for pmf_2, and 6.1 for pmf_3.

In the definition of the probabilistic middle point (i.e., Eq. (3)), the function $\mathsf{PMF}_{\mathcal{D}}(\cdot)$ need not be a probability mass function. Specifically, the property $\sum_{x \in \mathcal{D}} \mathsf{PMF}_{\mathcal{D}}(x) = 1$ is unnecessary and any probability weight function $w_{\mathcal{D}}(\cdot)$ can be used instead of $\mathsf{PMF}_{\mathcal{D}}(\cdot)$ where for any $x_1, x_2 \in \mathcal{D}$, it should hold that $\Pr[X = x_1] : \Pr[X = x_2] = w_{\mathcal{D}}(x_1) : w_{\mathcal{D}}(x_2)$. Therefore, we use a generalized definition based on a probability weight function:

$$\hat{x} = \operatorname*{argmax}_{x \in \mathcal{D}} \left(\sum_{z=d+1}^{x} w_{\mathcal{D}}(z) \leq \frac{1}{2} \sum_{z=d+1}^{d+M} w_{\mathcal{D}}(z) \right). \tag{4}$$

This definition is useful when we consider a sub-domain with the probability mass function of the original domain.

Recall that the sampling algorithm HGD maps $y \in \mathcal{R}$ to $x \in \mathcal{D}$. Therefore, to use the probabilistic middle point $\hat{x} \in \mathcal{D}$, we need to find $y \in \mathcal{R}$ which HGD would map to $\hat{x}$ with high probability. We compute the expected value of $\mathrm{HGD}(\mathcal{D}, \mathcal{R}, y; cc)$ for $y \in \mathcal{R}$ over the coins cc. Assume $\mathcal{D} = [M]$ and $\mathcal{R} = [N]$ for some $M \leq N \in \mathbb{N}^+$. Then, the expected value can be computed as follows.

$$
\begin{aligned}
E(\mathrm{HGD}(\mathcal{D}, \mathcal{R}, y; cc)) &= \sum_{x=1}^{M} x P_{HGD}(x; N, M, y) \\
&= \sum_{x=1}^{M} x \frac{\binom{y}{x}\binom{N-y}{M-x}}{\binom{N}{M}} \\
&= \sum_{x=1}^{M} x \frac{\frac{y}{x}\binom{y-1}{x-1}\binom{N-y}{M-x}}{\frac{N}{M}\binom{N-1}{M-1}} \\
&= \frac{M}{N} y \sum_{x=1}^{M} \frac{\binom{y-1}{x-1}\binom{N-y}{M-x}}{\binom{N-1}{M-1}} \\
&= \frac{M}{N} y \sum_{\dot{x}=0}^{\dot{M}} \frac{\binom{\dot{y}}{\dot{x}}\binom{\dot{N}-\dot{y}}{\dot{M}-\dot{x}}}{\binom{\dot{N}}{\dot{M}}} \\
&= \frac{M}{N} y \sum_{\dot{x}=0}^{\dot{M}} P_{HGD}(\dot{x}; \dot{N}, \dot{M}, \dot{y}) \\
&= \frac{M}{N} y
\end{aligned}
\tag{5}
$$

where $\dot{x} = x - 1$, $\dot{y} = y - 1$, $\dot{M} = M - 1$, and $\dot{N} = N - 1$.

More generally, let $\mathcal{D}$ and $\mathcal{R}$ be sets of consecutive integers with $|\mathcal{D}| = M$, $|\mathcal{R}| = N$, and $M \leq N \in \mathbb{N}^+$. Then, Eq. (5) is translated into

$$
E(\mathrm{HGD}(\mathcal{D}, \mathcal{R}, y; cc)) = d + \frac{M}{N}(y - r) \tag{6}
$$

where $d = \min(\mathcal{D}) - 1$ and $r = \min(\mathcal{R}) - 1$. By solving $\hat{x} = d + \frac{M}{N}(y - r)$, we can get

$$
y = r + \frac{N}{M}(\hat{x} - d). \tag{7}
$$

As Eq. (7) does not always give an integer value, we define $\gamma(\mathcal{D}, \mathcal{R})$ as follows.

$$
\gamma(\mathcal{D}, \mathcal{R}) = r + \left\lceil \frac{N}{M}(\hat{x} - d) \right\rceil \tag{8}
$$

where $\hat{x} = \mathrm{argmax}_{x \in \mathcal{D}}\left(\sum_{z=d+1}^{x} w_{\mathcal{D}}(z) \leq \frac{1}{2}\sum_{z=d+1}^{d+M} w_{\mathcal{D}}(z)\right)$ from Eq. (4). Based on this observation, we extend the algorithms **LazySample** and **LazySampleInv** to **LazySample$^+$** and **LazySampleInv$^+$** as in Fig. 2; the difference is the selection of the range gap on line 03 and line 22 where instead of the Euclidean middle range gap, the probabilistic middle range gap is chosen.

LazySample$^+$($\mathcal{D}, \mathcal{R}, m$)

01 $M \leftarrow |\mathcal{D}|$; $N \leftarrow |\mathcal{R}|$
02 $d \leftarrow \min(\mathcal{D}) - 1$; $r \leftarrow \min(\mathcal{R}) - 1$
03 $\boxed{y \leftarrow \gamma(\mathcal{D}, \mathcal{R})}$
04 If $|\mathcal{D}| = 1$ then
05   If $F[\mathcal{D}, \mathcal{R}, m]$ is undefined then
06          $cc \xleftarrow{\$} \text{GetCoins}(1^{\ell_{\mathcal{R}}}, \mathcal{D}, \mathcal{R}, 1 || m)$
07          $F[\mathcal{D}, \mathcal{R}, m] \xleftarrow{cc} \mathcal{R}$
08   Return $F[\mathcal{D}, \mathcal{R}, m]$

09 If $I[\mathcal{D}, \mathcal{R}, y]$ is undefined then
10      $cc \xleftarrow{\$} \text{GetCoins}(1^{\ell_1}, \mathcal{D}, \mathcal{R}, 0 || y)$
11      $I[\mathcal{D}, \mathcal{R}, y] \xleftarrow{\$} \text{HGD}(\mathcal{D}, \mathcal{R}, y; cc)$
12 $x \leftarrow I[\mathcal{D}, \mathcal{R}, y]$
13 If $m \leq x$ then
14      $\mathcal{D} \leftarrow \{d + 1, \dots, x\}$
15      $\mathcal{R} \leftarrow \{r + 1, \dots, y\}$
16 Else
17      $\mathcal{D} \leftarrow \{x + 1, \dots, d + M\}$
18      $\mathcal{R} \leftarrow \{y + 1, \dots, r + N\}$
19 Return **LazySample$^+$**($\mathcal{D}, \mathcal{R}, m$)

LazySampleInv$^+$($\mathcal{D}, \mathcal{R}, c$)

20 $M \leftarrow |\mathcal{D}|$; $N \leftarrow |\mathcal{R}|$
21 $d \leftarrow \min(\mathcal{D}) - 1$; $r \leftarrow \min(\mathcal{R}) - 1$
22 $\boxed{y \leftarrow \gamma(\mathcal{D}, \mathcal{R})}$
23 If $|\mathcal{D}| = 1$ then $m \leftarrow \min(\mathcal{D})$
24   If $F[\mathcal{D}, \mathcal{R}, m]$ is undefined then
25          $cc \xleftarrow{\$} \text{GetCoins}(1^{\ell_{\mathcal{R}}}, \mathcal{D}, \mathcal{R}, 1 || m)$
26          $F[\mathcal{D}, \mathcal{R}, m] \xleftarrow{cc} \mathcal{R}$
27   If $F[\mathcal{D}, \mathcal{R}, m] = c$ then return m
28   Else return $\bot$
29 If $I[\mathcal{D}, \mathcal{R}, y]$ is undefined then
30      $cc \xleftarrow{\$} \text{GetCoins}(1^{\ell_1}, \mathcal{D}, \mathcal{R}, 0 || y)$
31      $I[\mathcal{D}, \mathcal{R}, y] \xleftarrow{\$} \text{HGD}(\mathcal{D}, \mathcal{R}, y; cc)$
32 $x \leftarrow I[\mathcal{D}, \mathcal{R}, y]$
33 If $c \leq y$ then
34      $\mathcal{D} \leftarrow \{d + 1, \dots, x\}$
35      $\mathcal{R} \leftarrow \{r + 1, \dots, y\}$
36 Else
37      $\mathcal{D} \leftarrow \{x + 1, \dots, d + M\}$
38      $\mathcal{R} \leftarrow \{y + 1, \dots, r + N\}$
39 Return **LazySampleInv$^+$**($\mathcal{D}, \mathcal{R}, c$)

Fig. 2. The **LazySample$^+$**, **LazySampleInv$^+$** algorithms

It can be shown that any (even computationally unbounded) adversary has no advantage in distinguishing oracle access to a random order-preserving function and its inverse from that to the algorithms **LazySample$^+$**, **LazySampleInv$^+$**.

Theorem 1. Suppose GetCoins returns truly random coins on each new input. Then for any algorithm $\mathcal{A}$, we have

$$\Pr\left[\mathcal{A}^{g(\cdot), g^{-1}(\cdot)} = 1\right] = \Pr\left[\mathcal{A}^{\mathbf{LazySample}^+(\mathcal{D}, \mathcal{R}, \cdot), \mathbf{LazySampleInv}^+(\mathcal{D}, \mathcal{R}, \cdot)} = 1\right]$$

where $g(\cdot)$, $g^{-1}(\cdot)$ denote an order-preserving function picked at random from $\text{OPF}_{\mathcal{D}, \mathcal{R}}$ and its inverse, respectively.

Proof. The security proof is almost identical to that of [8] because replacing the Euclidean middle gap with the probabilistic middle gap does not affect the main idea of the proof; actually, the proof is valid as long as the same range gap is selected on line 03 and line 22 of Fig. 1 (or Fig. 2).

Since unbounded adversaries are considered, an adversary can always query all points in the domain to learn all points in the image and therefore, the inverse oracle can be ignored in the analysis. Let $M = |\mathcal{D}|$, $N = |\mathcal{R}|$, $d = \min(\mathcal{D}) - 1$, and $r = \min(\mathcal{R}) - 1$. Two functions $g, h : \mathcal{D} \rightarrow \mathcal{R}$ are said to be equivalent if $g(m) = h(m)$ for all $m \in \mathcal{D}$. If $\mathcal{D} = \emptyset$, any two functions $g, h : \mathcal{D} \rightarrow \mathcal{R}$ are vacuously equivalent. Let f be a function in $\text{OPF}_{\mathcal{D}, \mathcal{R}}$. To show that the function defined by $\mathbf{LazySample}^+(\mathcal{D}, \mathcal{R}, \cdot)$ is equivalent to f with probability $1/|\mathsf{OPF}_{\mathcal{D},\mathcal{R}}|$, strong induction on M and N is used.

Consider the base case where $M = 1$, i.e., $\mathcal{D} = \{m\}$ for same m and $N \geq M$. When it is first called, $\mathbf{LazySample}^+(\mathcal{D}, \mathcal{R}, m)$ will choose an element c uniformly at random from $\mathcal{R}$ and set $F[\mathcal{D}, \mathcal{R}, m] = c$. As any future calls of $\mathbf{LazySample}^+(\mathcal{D}, \mathcal{R}, m)$ will return c that is chosen uniformly at random from $\mathcal{R}$, $c = f(m)$ with probability $1/|\mathcal{R}|$. Thus, $\mathbf{LazySample}^+(\mathcal{D}, \mathcal{R}, m)$ is equivalent to $f(m)$ with probability $1/|\mathcal{R}| = 1/|\mathsf{OPF}_{\mathcal{D},\mathcal{R}}|$.

Suppose $M > 1$ and $N \geq M$. As an induction hypothesis assume that for all domains $\mathcal{D}'$ of size M' and ranges $\mathcal{R}'$ of size $N' \geq M'$, where either $M' < M$ or ($M' = M$, $N' < N$), and for any function f' in $\mathsf{OPF}_{\mathcal{D}'\mathcal{R}'}$, $\mathbf{LazySample}^+(\mathcal{D}', \mathcal{R}', \cdot)$ is equivalent to f' with probability $1/|\mathsf{OPF}_{\mathcal{D}',\mathcal{R}'}|$. The first time it is called, $\mathbf{LazySample}^+(\mathcal{D}, \mathcal{R}, \cdot)$ computes $I[\mathcal{D}, \mathcal{R}, y] \xleftarrow{\$} \mathrm{HGD}(\mathcal{D}, \mathcal{R}, y; cc)$ where $y = r + \left\lceil \frac{N}{M}(\hat{x} - d) \right\rceil$ and $\hat{x} = \mathrm{argmax}_{x \in \mathcal{D}} \left(\sum_{z=d+1}^{x} w_{\mathcal{D}}(z) \leq \frac{1}{2} \sum_{z=d+1}^{d+M} w_{\mathcal{D}}(z) \right)$. Then, the algorithm sets $x \leftarrow I[\mathcal{D}, \mathcal{R}, y]$ and runs $\mathbf{LazySample}^+(\mathcal{D}_1, \mathcal{R}_1, m)$ if $m \leq x$, or $\mathbf{LazySample}^+(\mathcal{D}_2, \mathcal{R}_2, m)$ if $m > x$, where $\mathcal{D}_1 = \{d+1, \ldots, x\}$, $\mathcal{R}_1 = \{r+1, \ldots, y\}$, $\mathcal{D}_2 = \{x+1, \ldots, d+M\}$, $\mathcal{R}_2 = \{y+1, \ldots, r+N\}$. Let f_i be f restricted to the domain $\mathcal{D}_i$ for $i = 1, 2$, and let x_0 be the unique integer in $\mathcal{D} \cup \{d\}$ such that $f(z) \leq y$ for all $z \in \mathcal{D}$, $z \leq x_0$, and $f(z) > y$ for all $z \in \mathcal{D}$, $z > x_0$. $\mathbf{LazySample}^+(\mathcal{D}, \mathcal{R}, \cdot)$ is equivalent to f if and only if all three of the following events occur:

E_1: f restricted to range R_i stays within domain $\mathcal{D}_i$ for $i = 1, 2$.
E_2: $\mathbf{LazySample}^+(\mathcal{D}_1, \mathcal{R}_1, \cdot)$ is equivalent to f_1.
E_3: $\mathbf{LazySample}^+(\mathcal{D}_2, \mathcal{R}_2, \cdot)$ is equivalent to f_2.

$\Pr[E_1]$ is the hypergeometric probability that $\mathrm{HGD}(\mathcal{D}, \mathcal{R}, y; cc)$ for a truly random coin cc will return x_0, so

$$\Pr[E_1] = P_{HGD}\left(x_0 - d; N, M, \left\lceil \frac{N}{M}(\hat{x} - d) \right\rceil\right) = \frac{\binom{\lceil \frac{N}{M}(\hat{x}-d) \rceil}{x_0 - d} \binom{N - \lceil \frac{N}{M}(\hat{x}-d) \rceil}{M - (x_0 - d)}}{\binom{N}{M}}.$$

If neither $\mathcal{D}_1$ nor $\mathcal{D}_2$ are empty, both $\mathcal{R}_1$ and $\mathcal{R}_2$ are strictly less than $|\mathcal{R}|$, and $|\mathcal{D}_1|$ and $|\mathcal{D}_2|$ are less than or equal to $|\mathcal{D}|$, so the induction hypothesis holds for each. That is, for $i = 1, 2$, $\mathbf{LazySample}^+(\mathcal{D}_i, \mathcal{R}_i, \cdot)$ is equivalent to f_i with probability $1/|\mathsf{OPF}_{\mathcal{D}_i, \mathcal{R}_i}| = 1/\binom{|\mathcal{R}_i|}{|\mathcal{D}_i|}$. Thus, we have that

$$\Pr[E_2|E_1] = \frac{1}{\binom{\lceil \frac{N}{M}(\hat{x}-d) \rceil}{x_0 - d}} \quad \text{and} \quad \Pr[E_3|E_1] = \frac{1}{\binom{N - \lceil \frac{N}{M}(\hat{x}-d) \rceil}{M - (x_0 - d)}}.$$

If $\mathcal{D}_1 = \emptyset$, then $\Pr[E_2|E_1] = 1 = 1/\binom{\lceil \frac{N}{M}(\hat{x}-d) \rceil}{x_0 - d}$ since $x_0 = d$. Likewise, if $\mathcal{D}_2 = \emptyset$, then $\Pr[E_3|E_1]$ will be the same as above.

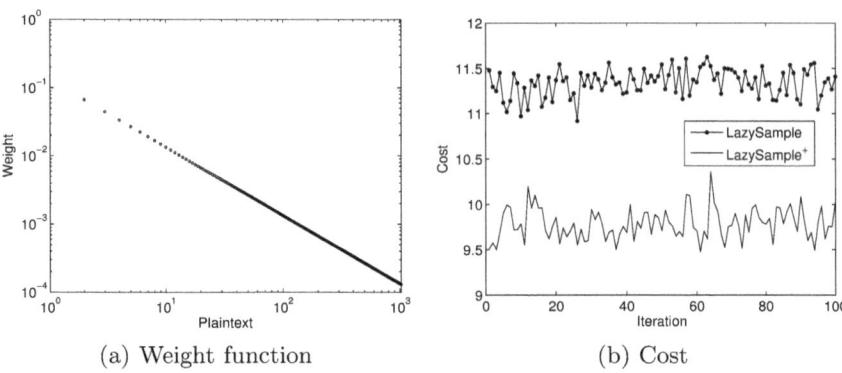

(a) Weight function   (b) Cost

Fig. 3. Monte Carlo simulation for Zipf distribution

By the law of conditional probability and since E_2 and E_3 are independent, we have that

$$\Pr[E_1 \cap E_2 \cap E_3] = \Pr[E_1] \cdot \Pr[E_2 \cap E_3|E_1] = \Pr[E_1] \cdot \Pr[E_2|E_1] \cdot \Pr[E_3|E_1]$$

$$= \frac{\binom{\lceil \frac{N}{M}(\hat{x}-d) \rceil}{x_0-d} \binom{N-\lceil \frac{N}{M}(\hat{x}-d) \rceil}{M-(x_0-d)}}{\binom{N}{M}} \cdot \frac{1}{\binom{\lceil \frac{N}{M}(\hat{x}-d) \rceil}{x_0-d}} \cdot \frac{1}{\binom{N-\lceil \frac{N}{M}(\hat{x}-d) \rceil}{M-(x_0-d)}} = \frac{1}{\binom{N}{M}}.$$

Therefore, **LazySample**$^+(\mathcal{D}_i, \mathcal{R}_i, \cdot)$ is equivalent to f with probability $1/\binom{N}{M} = 1/|\mathsf{OPF}_{\mathcal{D},\mathcal{R}}|$. Since f was an arbitrary element of $\mathsf{OPF}_{\mathcal{D},\mathcal{R}}$, the result follows. ∎

3.2   Experiments

To evaluate the performance of **LazySample**$^+$ (and **LazySampleInv**$^+$), we first consider the Zipf's law that has found many applications in the physical, biological, and behavioral sciences [9]. Popularized by the Harvard linguistic professor George Kingsley Zipf [10], it states that given some corpus of natural language utterances, the frequency of any word is inversely proportional to its rank in the frequency table. Formally, Zipf's law predicts that out of a population of M elements, the frequency of elements of rank x is

$$P_{\text{Zipf}}(x; s, M) = \left(x^s \sum_{z=1}^{M} \frac{1}{z^s} \right)^{-1} \tag{9}$$

where real number $s > 0$ is a parameter that characterizes the distribution. The Zipf's law is most easily observed by plotting the data on a log-log graph and the data conform to Zipf's law to the extent that plot is linear.

Fig. 3-(a) shows the probability mass function of the Zipf's law for $s = 1$ and $M = 2^{10}$ on a log-log scale. As the number of order-preserving functions from $\mathcal{D} = [M]$ to $\mathcal{R} = [N]$, which is given by $\binom{N}{M}$, is maximized when $M = N/2$, we choose $M = 2^{10} = 1024$ and $N = 2M = 2^{11} = 2048$. To estimate the average number of HGD invocations by **LazySample** and **LazySample$^+$**, we use Monte Carlo simulation with 100 iterations; each iteration consists of initializing the algorithm GetCoins with a fresh random seed and counting the number of HGD invocations. Let $\tau_i(m)$ be the number of HGD invocations for $m \in \mathcal{D}$ in the i-th iteration. Then, the cost of the i-th iteration is computed by

$$\mathsf{Cost}_{\mathcal{D}, w(\cdot)}(i) = \frac{\sum_{m \in \mathcal{D}} w(m)\tau_i(m)}{\sum_{m \in \mathcal{D}} w(m)} \tag{10}$$

where $\sum_{m \in \mathcal{D}} w(m)$ in the denominator is a normalization factor and redundant if the weight function $w(\cdot)$ is a probabilistic mass function (i.e., $\sum_{m \in \mathcal{D}} w(m) = 1$). Fig. 3-(b) shows $\mathsf{Cost}_{\mathcal{D}, w(\cdot)}(i)$ ($1 \leq i \leq 100$) for **LazySample** and **LazySample$^+$**. The average number of HGD invocations estimated by the Monte Carlo simulation is

$$E(\mathsf{Cost}) = \frac{\sum_{i=1}^{t} \mathsf{Cost}_{\mathcal{D}, w(\cdot)}(i)}{t} \tag{11}$$

where t is the number of iterations and thus $t = 100$ for our case. From the simulation results of Fig. 3, we obtain $E(\mathsf{Cost}) = 11.3415$ for **LazySample** and $E(\mathsf{Cost}) = 9.7859$ for **LazySample$^+$**; the ratio is $\frac{9.7859}{11.3415} \approx 0.8628$.

When the probabilistic middle point replaces the Euclidean middle point, two concerns may arise. First, the probabilistic middle point requires more computation than the Euclidean middle point. Second, a precise probability weight function (or probability mass function) is needed to compute the probabilistic middle point. For most practical cases, the first issue is not a serious obstacle because the computational cost of the sampling algorithm HGD (e.g., [11,12]) is far more expensive than that of $\gamma(\mathcal{D}, \mathcal{R})$. We, however, also admit that there might be some distributions for which the computation overhead of $\gamma(\mathcal{D}, \mathcal{R})$ is significant. Therefore, to address the two issues, we propose a simple technique based on linear interpolation. Fig. 4-(a) represents a domain with binomial distribution $P_{BD}(x; M, p) = \binom{M}{x} p^x (1-p)^{M-x}$ for $p = 1/2$. To simplify the computation of $\gamma(\mathcal{D}, \mathcal{R})$, we use linear interpolation with four lines in Fig. 4-(b); the connected points are where the cumulative weights are $0\%, 1\%, 50\%, 99\%, 100\%$. Fig. 4-(d) shows the number of HGD invocations for the original weight function and the interpolated weight function. The average cost is $E(\mathsf{Cost}) = 11.3797$ for **LazySample**, $E(\mathsf{Cost}) = 8.6801$ for **LazySample$^+$** with interpolation, and $E(\mathsf{Cost}) = 8.2524$ for **LazySample$^+$** with original weight function. The result shows that the linear interpolation with only four lines works fairly well for the binomial distribution. If more lines are employed for the linear

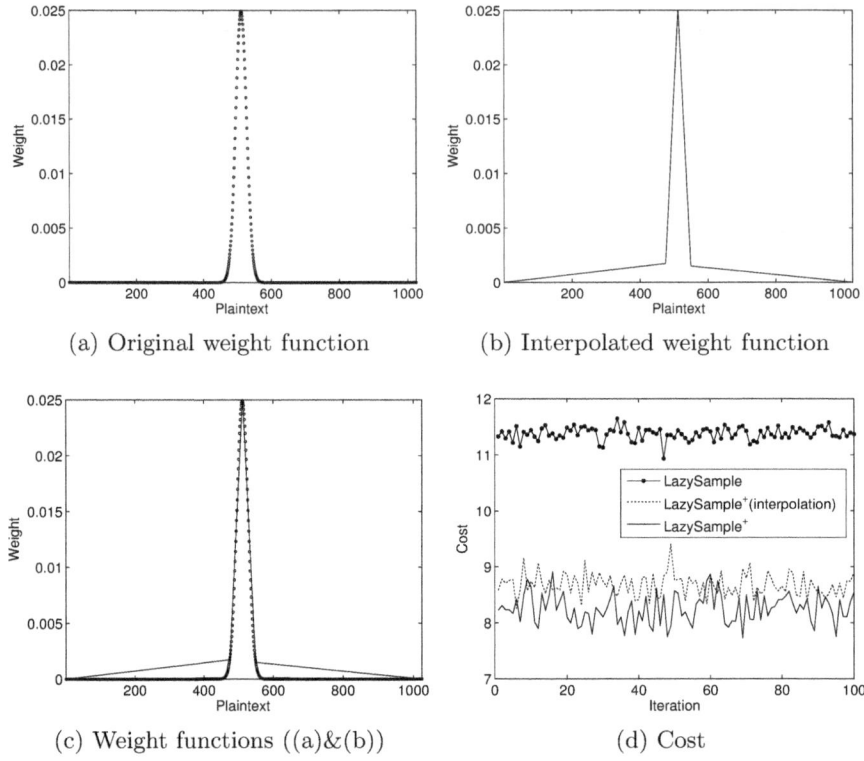

(a) Original weight function   (b) Interpolated weight function

(c) Weight functions ((a)&(b))   (d) Cost

Fig. 4. Monte Carlo simulation for binomial distribution

interpolation, better performance can be expected; the connected points can be chosen arbitrarily but inflection points (where a curve changes from being concave upwards to concave downwards, or vice versa) are good candidates. The linear interpolation is also very useful when the closed form of the probability weight function is unknown or only partial information is known for the distribution of the plaintext-space.

Remark 1. The interpolated weight function of Fig. 4.-(b) does not show perfect symmetry because of rounding error in computing the points of cumulative weight $= 0\%, 1\%, 50\%, 99\%, 100\%$.

From the above examples, one can see that the probabilistic middle point is an effective tool for plaintext-spaces of non-uniform distributions. Now, we explore, with Gaussian distributions, the relation between the efficiency of **LazySample**$^+$ and the standard deviation (or variance) of the plaintext-space distribution.

The Gaussian distribution is considered the most important (continuous) probability distribution in the entire field of statistics [13]. Its graph, called the Gaussian curve, is a bell-shaped cure, which approximately describes many phenomena that occur in nature, industry, and research. Physical measurements in areas such as meteorological experiments, rainfall studies, and measurements on manufactured parts are often more than adequately explained with a Gaussian distribution. The mathematical equation for the Gaussian distribution depends upon the two parameters μ and σ, its mean and standard deviation. The probability density function of the Gaussian variable X with parameters μ and σ is

$$G(x; \mu, \sigma) = \frac{1}{\sqrt{2\pi\sigma^2}} e^{-\frac{(x-\mu)^2}{2\sigma^2}} \tag{12}$$

where $\pi \simeq 3.141519$, $e \simeq 2.71824$, and $-\infty < x < \infty$. The Gaussian curve has the mode, which is the point on the horizontal axis where the curve is a maximum, at $x = \mu$ and is symmetric around the mode. The standard deviation shows how spread out or scattered the values around the mean. If they are tightly clustered, then the standard deviation is low and the Gaussian curve is tall and sharp. If they are very spread out, then the standard deviation is high and the Gaussian curve is low and wide.

σ	LazySample	LazySample$^+$
10	11.3882	7.6965
20	11.3760	8.5600
30	11.3720	9.0185
40	11.3716	9.4315
50	11.3718	9.7228
60	11.3719	9.9839
70	11.3717	10.2192
80	11.3714	10.3913
90	11.3711	10.5711
100	11.3707	10.7323

(a) Table

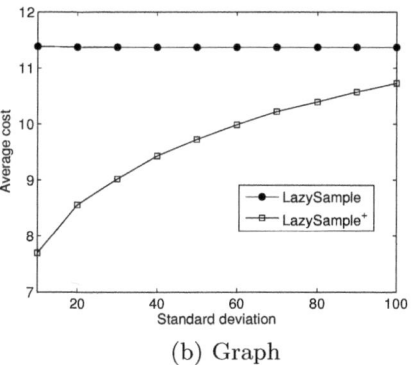

(b) Graph

Fig. 5. Average cost vs. standard deviation

Fig. 5 summarizes the result of Monte Carlo simulation for the weight function $w(x) = G(x; \mu, \sigma)$ with mean $\mu = 2^9 = 512$ and standard deviation $\sigma = 10k$ for $k = 1, 2, \ldots, 10$. While the average cost of **LazySample** remains almost unchanged, the average cost of **LazySample**$^+$ is highly dependent on the standard deviation; the probabilistic middle point works better for distributions with small standard deviation. Fig. 6 depicts the Monte Carlo simulation for $w(x) = G(x; \mu, \sigma)$ for $\mu = 512$ and $\sigma = 10, 40, 70, 100$.

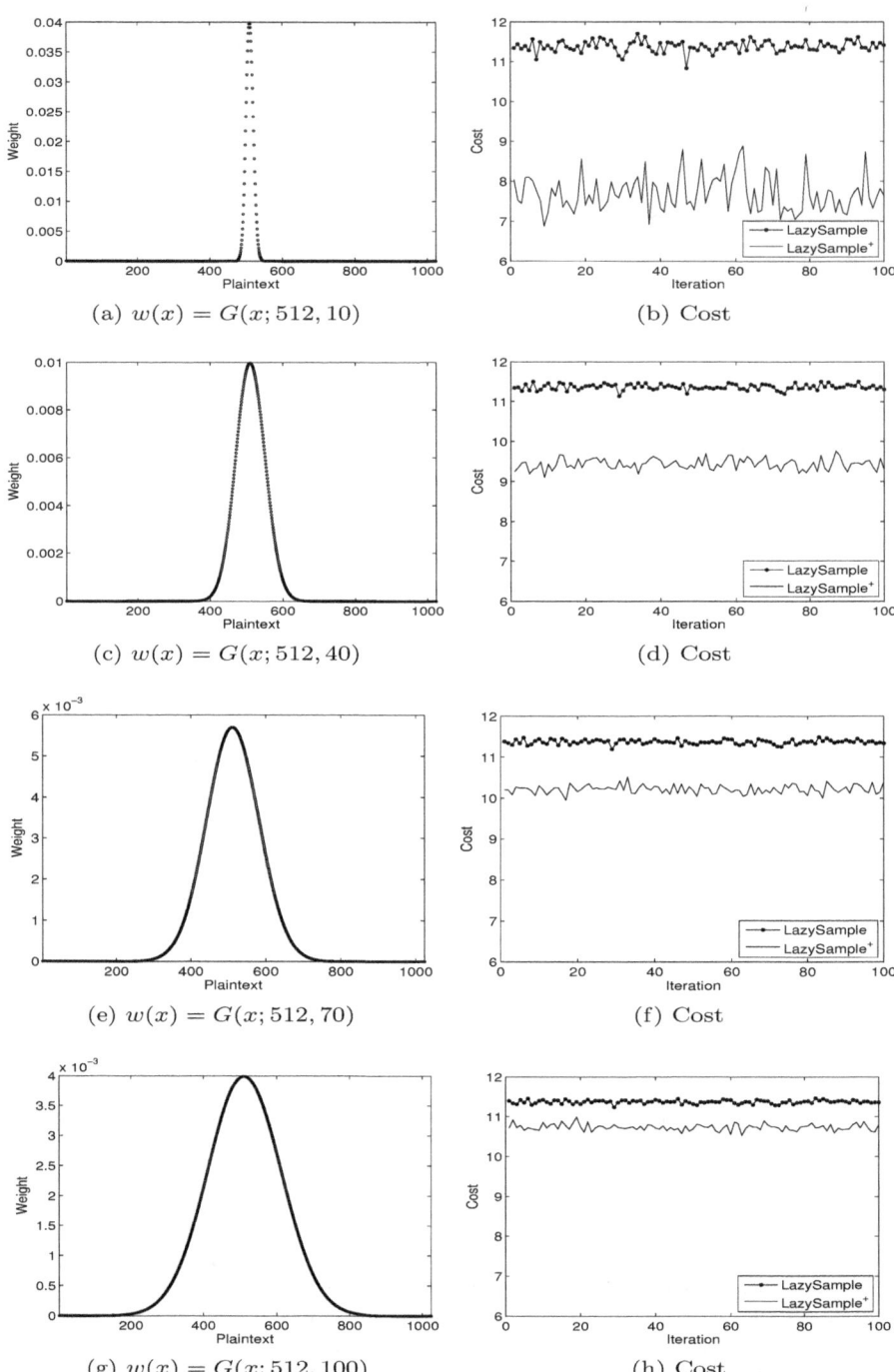

Fig. 6. Monte Carlo simulation for Gaussian distribution

4   Conclusion

Order-preserving encryption permits fast (i.e., logarithmic or at least sub-linear time) range queries on encrypted data. To reduce the computational cost of the BCLO scheme, we used the probabilistic middle gap instead of the Euclidean middle gap. The simulation showed that the proposed method is effective for various distributions and especially for distributions with small variance. As future work, we plan to derive a mathematical formula or upper bound for the average cost of **LazySample**$^+$ when a specific distribution of plaintext-space is given.

Acknowledgement. This research was supported by Penta Security Systems, Inc.

References

1. Agrawal, R., Kiernan, J., Srikant, R., Xu, Y.: Order-preserving encryption for numeric data. In: SIGMOD Conference, pp. 563–574. ACM (2004)
2. Westhoff, D., Girão, J., Acharya, M.: Concealed data aggregation for reverse multicast traffic in sensor networks: Encryption, key distribution, and routing adaptation. IEEE Trans. Mob. Comput. 5(10), 1417–1431 (2006)
3. Erkin, Z., Piva, A., Katzenbeisser, S., Lagendijk, R.L., Shokrollahi, J., Neven, G., Barni, M.: Protection and retrieval of encrypted multimedia content: When cryptography meets signal processing. EURASIP Journal on Information Security (2007); Article ID 78943
4. Bellare, M., Rogaway, P.: The Security of Triple Encryption and a Framework for Code-Based Game-Playing Proofs. In: Vaudenay, S. (ed.) EUROCRYPT 2006. LNCS, vol. 4004, pp. 409–426. Springer, Heidelberg (2006)
5. Daemen, J., Rijmen, V.: The Design of Rijndael: AES – The Advanced Encryption Standard. Springer, Heidelberg (2002)
6. Rivest, R.L., Shamir, A., Adleman, L.M.: A method for obtaining digital signatures and public-key cryptosystems. Commun. ACM 21(2), 120–126 (1978)
7. Menezes, A., van Oorschot, P.C., Vanstone, S.A.: Handbook of Applied Cryptography. CRC Press (1996)
8. Boldyreva, A., Chenette, N., Lee, Y., O'Neill, A.: Order-Preserving Symmetric Encryption. In: Joux, A. (ed.) EUROCRYPT 2009. LNCS, vol. 5479, pp. 224–241. Springer, Heidelberg (2009)
9. Kirby, G.: Zipf's law. UK Journal of Naval Science 10(3), 180–185 (1985)
10. Zipf, G.K.: Selected studies of the principle of relative frequency in language. Harvard University Press (1932)
11. Kachitvichyanukul, V., Schmeiser, B.W.: Computer generation of hypergeometric random variates. Journal of Statistical Computation and Simulation 22(2), 127–145 (1985)
12. Kachitvichyanukul, V., Schmeiser, B.W.: Algorithm 668: H2PEC: sampling from the hypergeometric distribution. ACM Trans. Math. Softw. 14(4), 397–398 (1988)
13. Walpole, R.E., Myers, R.H., Myers, S.L., Ye, K.E.: Probability and Statistics for Engineers and Scientists. Prentice-Hall (2011)

Solving a DLP with Auxiliary Input with the ρ-Algorithm

Yumi Sakemi, Tetsuya Izu, Masahiko Takenaka, and Masaya Yasuda

Fujitsu Laboratories Ltd.,
4-1-1, Kamikodanaka, Nakahara-ku, Kawasaki, 211-8588, Japan
{sakemi,izu,takenaka,myasuda}@labs.fujitsu.com

Abstract. The discrete logarithm problem with auxiliary input (DLP-wAI) is a problem to find a positive integer α from elements G, αG, $\alpha^d G$ in an additive cyclic group generated by G of prime order r and a positive integer d dividing $r - 1$. In 2011, Sakemi et al. implemented Cheon's algorithm for solving DLPwAI, and solved a DLPwAI in a group with 128-bit order r in about 131 hours with a single core on an elliptic curve defined over a prime finite field which is used in the TinyTate library for embedded cryptographic devices. However, since their implementation was based on Shanks' Baby-step Giant-step (BSGS) algorithm as a sub-algorithm, it required a large amount of memory (246 GByte) so that it was concluded that applying other DLPwAIs with larger parameter is infeasible. In this paper, we implemented Cheon's algorithm based on Pollard's ρ-algorithm in order to reduce the required memory. As a result, we have succeeded solving the same DLPwAI in about 136 hours by a single core with less memory (0.5 MByte).

1 Introduction

Let $\mathbb{G}$ be an additive cyclic group generated by G of prime order r. The discrete logarithm problem (DLP) in $\mathbb{G}$ is to find a positive integer $\alpha \in \mathbb{Z}/r\mathbb{Z}$ from elements G, $\alpha G \in \mathbb{G}$. In the general setting, the most efficient algorithms for solving DLP require $O(\sqrt{r})$ in time. In fact, Shanks' Baby-step Giant-step (BSGS) algorithm [18] requires $O(\sqrt{r})$ group operations in time and $O(\sqrt{r})$ group elements in space. On the other hand, Pollard's ρ-algorithm [16] also requires $O(\sqrt{r})$ in time, but much smaller numbers of elements in space. The security of ECC (Elliptic Curve Cryptosystems) relies on the infeasibility of DLP over elliptic curves (ECDLP).

The discrete logarithm problem with auxiliary input (DLPwAI) in $\mathbb{G}$ is a problem to find a positive integer $\alpha \in \mathbb{Z}/r\mathbb{Z}$ from elements G, αG, $\alpha^d G \in \mathbb{G}$ and a positive integer d dividing $r-1$. In 2006, Cheon proposed a novel algorithm for solving DLPwAI (Cheon's algorithm) [7,8]. The time complexity of Cheon's algorithm (together with the KKM improvement [13]) is $O\left(\sqrt{(r-1)/d} + \sqrt{d}\right)$, and especially when d can be chosen as $d \approx \sqrt{r}$, the complexity becomes $O(\sqrt[4]{r})$, which is much efficient than that for solving DLP in the general setting.

S. Jung and M. Yung (Eds.): WISA 2011, LNCS 7115, pp. 98–108, 2012.

Table 1. Required time for solving a DLPwAI (with a single core)

	Size of r	Required Time		Required Memory
		BSGS	ρ	
Jao, Yoshida [12]	60 bit	—	3 hours	—
Izu et al. [10,11]	83 bit	14 hours	11.5 hours	—
Sakemi et al. [17]	128 bit	131 hours	—	246 GByte
This paper	128 bit	—	**136 hours**	**0.5 MByte**

The infeasibility of DLPwAI assures the security of some cryptographic schemes including Boneh-Boyen's ID-based encryption scheme [3] and Boneh-Gentry-Waters' broadcast encryption scheme [5].

In 2011, Sakemi et al. implemented Cheon's algorithm and solved a DLPwAI in 45 hours with a single PC (131 hours with a single core) in a group with 128-bit order defined on an elliptic curve over a prime finite field with 256-bit elements, which is used in the TinyTate library [15] for implementing pairing-based cryptosystems in embedded devices. Since the implementation was based on Shanks' Baby-step Giant-step (BSGS) algorithm [18] as a sub-algorithm, it required a large amount of memory (246 GByte). The authors also estimated required time and memory for other DLPwAIs with larger parameters, and concluded that it is infeasible to solve such problems by their approach, namely, BSGS algorithm.

In this paper, we implemented Cheon's algorithm based on Pollard's ρ-algorithm [16] in order to reduce the required memory. We have succeeded solving the same DLPwAI (on the elliptic curve in the TinyTate library) in about 2.5 hours by 14 PCs (136 hours by a single core) with less memory, namely 0.5 MByte (see Table 1). Compared to previous results, our implementation requires almost same computing time with less memory. Note that since Pollard's ρ-algorithm is probabilistic, the computing time may vary according to parameters. In fact, BSGS algorithm works better than the ρ-algorithm when the order is 83-bit [10,11], while BSGS works worse than the ρ-algorithm when the order is 128-bit.

2   Preliminaries

This section introduces Cheon's algorithm for solving the discrete logarithm problem with auxiliary input (DLPwAI) [7,8].

2.1   DLP with Auxiliary Input (DLPwAI)

The discrete logarithm problem with auxiliary input (DLPwAI) was defined by Cheon in 2006 [7,8] as a variant of DLP, where DLPwAI in $\mathbb{G}$ is a problem to find a positive integer $\alpha \in \mathbb{Z}/r\mathbb{Z}$ from elements G, αG, $\alpha^d G \in \mathbb{G}$ and a positive integer d dividing $r - 1$, where $\mathbb{G}$ is an additive cyclic group generated by G of prime order r.

At the same time, Cheon also proposed a novel algorithm for solving DLPwAI in the same papers [7,8]. Cheon's algorithm (together with Kozaki-Kutsuma-Matsuo's improvement [13]) requires $O\left(\sqrt{(r-1)/d}+\sqrt{d}\right)$ group operations in time. Especially, when d can be chosen as $d \approx \sqrt{r}$, it only requires $O(\sqrt[4]{r})$ operations, which is much efficient than that required in the Baby-step Giant-step algorithm or in the ρ-algorithm for solving DLP.

2.2   Baby-Step Giant-Step Algorithm

The Baby-step Giant-step (BSGS) algorithm was introduced by Shanks in 1971 for solving DLP [18]. Instead of finding a positive integer $\alpha \in \mathbb{Z}/r\mathbb{Z}$ directly, from G and $G_1 = \alpha G$, BSGS searches two non-negative integers i, j such that $\alpha = i + jm$ and $0 \leq i,\ j < m := \lceil \sqrt{r} \rceil$. Here, such i, j are uniquely determined. Since $\alpha G = (i+jm)G = iG+jG'$ for $G' = mG$, we have a relation $G_1 - iG = jG'$.

BSGS consists of two steps: the Baby-step computes

$$G_1,\ G_1 - G,\ G_1 - 2G, \ldots, G_1 - (m-1)G$$

successively and stores them in a database. Similarly, the Giant-step computes

$$\mathcal{O},\ G',\ 2G', \ldots, (m-1)G'$$

successively and stores them in another database. Then, we search a collision $G_1 - iG = jG'$ among these databases and thus a solution $\alpha = i+jm$ is obtained. Since m group operations and $m \approx \sqrt{r}$ group elements are required in both steps, the time and space complexity of BSGS are $O(\sqrt{r})$ group operations and $O(\sqrt{r})$ group elements, respectively.

Algorithm 1. Cheon's Algorithm (Outline)

Input: : G, $G_1 = \alpha G$, $G_d = \alpha^d G \in \mathbb{G}$, $d \in \mathbb{Z}$ dividing $r-1$
Output: : $\alpha \in \mathbb{Z}/r\mathbb{Z}$
  1: Find a generator $\zeta \in (\mathbb{Z}/r\mathbb{Z})^*$
  2: Set $\zeta_d \leftarrow \zeta^d$
  3: [Step 1] Find $0 \leq k_1 < (r-1)/d$ such that $G_d = \zeta_d^{k_1} G$
  4: Set $\zeta_e \leftarrow \zeta^{(r-1)/d}$, $G_e \leftarrow \zeta^{-k_1} G_1$
  5: [Step 2] Find $0 \leq k_2 < d$ such that $G_e = \zeta_e^{k_2} G$
  6: Output $\zeta^{k_1+k_2(r-1)/d}$

2.3 ρ-Algorithm

The ρ-algorithm was introduced by Pollard in 1978 for solving DLP [16]. A strategy of the ρ-algorithm is to find a collided elements $P, Q \in \mathbb{G}$ such that $F^{(i)}(P) = F^{(j)}(Q)$ for a given efficiently computable function $F : \mathbb{G} \rightarrow \mathbb{G}$ (the random-walk function). If the function F is random enough, the ρ-algorithm requires $O(\sqrt{r})$ function evaluations in time because of the birthday paradox.

On the other hand, the naive ρ-algorithm requires $O(\sqrt{r})$ elements in space. However, the distinguished element technique [19] can reduce the number of elements to be stored. An element which satisfies the specific condition (the least significant 6-bit of an element is zero, for example) is called as the distinguished element. With this technique, one has to store elements $F^{(\ell)}(P)$, $F^{(\ell)}(Q)$ only when they are distinguished elements. Note that there exists a collision on the distinguished elements: in fact, for a collision $F^{(i)}(P) = F^{(j)}(Q)$, we have $F^{(i+1)}(P) = F^{(j+1)}(Q), F^{(i+2)}(P) = F^{(j+2)}(Q), \ldots$, and thus, we have a collision $F^{(i+w)}(P) = F^{(j+w)}(Q)$ on the distinguished elements for an integer w. The space complexity (also the number of elements) can be reduced to $1/w$ with arbitrary parameter w ($w = 2^6$ in the above example).

2.4   Cheon's Algorithm

Cheon's algorithm is an algorithm for solving DLPwAI, namely finding a positive integer $\alpha \in \mathbb{Z}/r\mathbb{Z}$ from elements G, $G_1 = \alpha G$, $G_d = \alpha^d G \in \mathbb{G}$ and a positive integer d dividing $r - 1$. Instead of finding $\alpha \in \mathbb{Z}/r\mathbb{Z}$ directly, Cheon's algorithm searches a positive integer $k \in \mathbb{Z}/r\mathbb{Z}$ satisfying $\alpha = \zeta^k$ for a generator of the multiplicative group $\zeta \in (\mathbb{Z}/r\mathbb{Z})^*$ (Note that finding the generator ζ is easy). Here, such k is uniquely determined. To do so, Cheon's algorithm searches two integers k_1, k_2 such that $k = k_1 + k_2(r - 1)/d$ satisfying $0 \le k_1 < (r - 1)/d :=$ e, $0 \le k_2 < d$ in the following two steps (see Algorithm 1). Step 1 searches an integer k_1 such that $G_d = \zeta_d^{k_1} G$ since k_1 satisfies $\alpha^d = \zeta_d^{k_1}$ for $\zeta_d = \zeta^d$. Similarly, Step 2 searches an integer k_2 such that $G_e = \zeta_e^{k_2} G$ since k_2 satisfies $\alpha = \zeta_1^k \zeta_e^{k_2}$ for $\zeta_e = \zeta^e$ and $G_e = \zeta^{-k_1} G_1$. Here, searching k_1 in Step 1 and searching k_2 in Step 2 require another sub-algorithm. Since these searching problems are very similar to DLP, the Baby-step Giant-step algorithm and the ρ-algorithm can be applied in the following ways.

Cheon's Algorithm with BSGS Algorithm. Searching an integer k_1 such that $\alpha^d = \zeta_d^{k_1}$ for $\zeta_d = \zeta^d$ in Step 1 in Cheon's algorithm is equivalent to searching two integers u_1, v_1 such that $\alpha^d \zeta_d^{-u_1} = \zeta_d^{v_1 d_1}$ satisfying $0 \le u_1, v_1 <$ $d_1 := \lceil \sqrt{(r - 1)/d} \rceil$. Here, such u_1, v_1 are uniquely determined. Since these u_1, v_1 satisfy $\zeta_d^{-u_1} G_d = \zeta_d^{v_1 d_1} G$, BSGS algorithm can be used in the following way: establish two databases

$$\zeta_d^{-0} G_d, \ \zeta_d^{-1} G_d, \ \zeta_d^{-2} G_d, \ \ldots, \ \zeta_d^{-(d_1 - 1)} G_d$$

and

$$\zeta_d^0 G, \ \zeta_d^{d_1} G, \ \zeta_d^{2d_1} G, \ \ldots, \ \zeta_d^{(d_1 - 1)d_1} G,$$

and searches a collision $\zeta_d^{-u_1} G_d = \zeta_d^{v_1 d_1} G$ among these databases. Thus, Step 1 in Cheon's algorithm with BSGS requires $2d_1 = 2\sqrt{(r - 1)/d}$ group operations in time, and $2d_1 = 2\sqrt{(r - 1)/d}$ elements in space (see also Algorithm 2).

Similarly, Step 2 in Cheon's algorithm with BSGS requires $2d_2 = 2\sqrt{d}$ group operations in time, and $2d_2 = 2\sqrt{d}$ elements in space. Since these group operations can be computed effectively by the KKM improvement [13], which will be

---

Algorithm 2. Cheon's Algorithm (with BSGS)

Input: : G, $G_1 = \alpha G$, $G_d = \alpha^d G \in \mathbb{G}$, $d \in \mathbb{Z}$ dividing $r - 1$

Output: : $\alpha \in \mathbb{Z}/r\mathbb{Z}$

  1: Find a generator $\zeta \in (\mathbb{Z}/r\mathbb{Z})^*$

  2: Set $\zeta_d \leftarrow \zeta^d$, $d_1 \leftarrow \left\lceil \sqrt{(r-1)/d} \right\rceil$

  3: [Step 1] Find $0 \le k_1 < (r-1)/d$ such that $G_d = \zeta_d^{k_1} G$

    3-1: Find $0 \le u_1$, $v_1 < d_1$ such that $\zeta_d^{-u_1} G_d = \zeta_d^{v_1 d_1} G$

    3-2: $k_1 \leftarrow u_1 + v_1 d_1$

  4: Set $\zeta_e \leftarrow \zeta^{(r-1)/d}$, $d_2 \leftarrow \left\lceil \sqrt{d} \right\rceil$, $G_e \leftarrow \zeta^{-k_1} G_1$

  5: [Step 2] Find $0 \le k_2 < d$ such that $G_e = \zeta_e^{k_2} G$

    5-1: Find $0 \le u_2$, $v_2 < d_2$ such that $\zeta_e^{-u_2} G_e = \zeta_e^{v_2 d_2} G$

    5-2: $k_2 \leftarrow u_2 + v_2 d_2$

  6: Output $\zeta^{k_1 + k_2 (r-1)/d}$

---

described later, the total time complexity of Cheon's algorithm T_{BSGS} and the total space complexity of Cheon's algorithm S_{BSGS} are evaluated by

$$T_{\mathrm{BSGS}} = O\left(\sqrt{(r-1)/d} + \sqrt{d}\right) \quad \text{(group operations)},$$

$$S_{\mathrm{BSGS}} = O\left(\max\left(\sqrt{(r-1)/d}, \sqrt{d}\right)\right) \quad \text{(group elements)}.$$

Cheon's Algorithm with ρ-Algorithm. When the ρ-algorithm is applied to Step 1 in Cheon's algorithm, the goal is to find a collision $F^{(i)}(G_d) = F^{(j)}(G)$ for the random-walk function

$$F(P) : P \mapsto \zeta_d^{f_e(P)} P$$

for a pseudo-random function $f_e : \mathbb{G} \rightarrow \mathbb{Z}/e\mathbb{Z}$, where $F^{(i)}(X) = F^{(i-1)}(X)$ $e = (r-1)/d$ and $\zeta_d = \zeta^d$ [7,8]. By the definition, we have

$$F^{(i)}(G_d) = \zeta_d^{\sum_{\ell=0}^{i-1} f_e(F^{(\ell)}(G_d))} G_d,$$

$$F^{(j)}(G) = \zeta_d^{\sum_{\ell=0}^{j-1} f_e(F^{(\ell)}(G))} G.$$

Thus, from a collision $F^{(i)}(G_d) = F^{(j)}(G)$, one can find k_1 by computing

$$k_1 = e_1 - f_1 \bmod (r-1)/d$$

for

$$e_1 = \sum_{\ell=0}^{i-1} f_e(F^{(\ell)}(G_d)) \bmod (r-1)/d$$

$$f_1 = \sum_{\ell=0}^{j-1} f_e(F^{(\ell)}(G)) \bmod (r-1)/d.$$

Algorithm 3. Cheon's Algorithm (with ρ-algorithm)

Input: : G, $G_1 = \alpha G$, $G_d = \alpha^d G \in \mathbb{G}$, $d \in \mathbb{Z}$ dividing $r - 1$
Output: : $\alpha \in \mathbb{Z}/r\mathbb{Z}$
1: Find a generator $\zeta \in (\mathbb{Z}/r\mathbb{Z})^*$
2: Set $\zeta_d \leftarrow \zeta^d$, $e \leftarrow (r - 1)/d$
3: [Step 1] Find $0 \le k_1 < (r - 1)/d$ such that $G_d = \zeta_d^{k_1} G$
  3-1: $F_e^{(0)}(G_d) \leftarrow G_d, F_e^{(0)}(G) \leftarrow G$
  3-2: Find $0 \le i_1, j_1$ such that $F_e^{(i_1)}(G_d) = F_e^{(j_1)}(G)$
  3-3: $e_1 \leftarrow \sum_{\ell=0}^{i_1} f_e(F_e^{(\ell)}(G_d))$ mod e,
     $f_1 \leftarrow \sum_{\ell=0}^{j_1} f_e(F_e^{(\ell)}(G))$ mod e
  3-4: $k_1 \leftarrow e_1 - f_1$ mod e
4: Set $\zeta_e \leftarrow \zeta^e$, $G_e \leftarrow \zeta^{-k_1} G_1$
5: [Step 2] Find $0 \le k_2 < d$ such that $G_e = \zeta_e^{k_2} G$
  5-1: $F_d^{(0)}(G_e) \leftarrow G_e, F_d^{(0)}(G) \leftarrow G$
  5-2: Find $0 \le i_2, j_2$ such that $F_d^{(i_2)}(G_e) = F_d^{(j_2)}(G)$
  5-3: $e_2 \leftarrow \sum_{\ell=0}^{i_2} f_d(F_d^{(\ell)}(G_e))$ mod d
     $f_2 \leftarrow \sum_{\ell=0}^{j_2} f_d(F_d^{(\ell)}(G))$ mod d
  5-4: $k_2 \leftarrow e_2 - f_2$ mod d
6: Output $\zeta^{k_1 + k_2 (r-1)/d}$

Since the image of the function F has $(r-1)/d$ elements, Step 1 with ρ-algorithm requires $O(\sqrt{(r - 1)/d})$ function evaluations by the birthday paradox. On the other hand, the space complexity of Step 1 is $O(2\sqrt{(r - 1)/d}/w)$ with the distinguished element technique, where w is the frequency parameter for distinguished elements (see also Algorithm 3).

Similarly, Step 2 in Cheon's algorithm with the ρ-algorithm requires $O(\sqrt{d})$ function evaluations in time, and $O(2\sqrt{d}/w)$ elements in space. Since the function is evaluated by a group operation, and a group operation is computed effectively with the KKM improvement, the total time complexity of Cheon's algorithm T_ρ and the total space complexity of Cheon's algorithm S_ρ are evaluated by

$$T_\rho = O\left(\sqrt{(r - 1)/d} + \sqrt{d}\right) \quad \text{(group operations)},$$

$$S_\rho = O\left(\max\left(\sqrt{(r - 1)/d}, \sqrt{d}\right)/w\right) \quad \text{(group elements)}.$$

2.5 KKM Improvement

Cheon's algorithm requires the number of group operations (scalar multiplications) for fixed elements (G, for example). In 2007, Kozaki, Kutsuma and Matsuo introduced a precomputation table for such scalar multiplications and reduced the time complexity of Cheon's algorithm by a factor of $\log r$.

Let us describe KKM improvement for a scalar multiplication γP ($\gamma \in \mathbb{Z}/r\mathbb{Z}$, $P \in \mathbb{G}$) in the followings. For a fixed integer c (which will be optimized later) and $n = \lceil \sqrt[c]{r} \rceil$, obtain the n-array expansion of the scalar $\gamma = \sum_{\ell=0}^{c-1} \gamma_\ell n^\ell$

$(0 \leq \gamma_\ell < n)$. For all $0 \leq i < c$ and $0 \leq j < n$, compute $S(i, j) = jn^i P$ and store them in a table in advance to the scalar multiplication. Then, the scalar multiplication γP is computed by the following way:

$$\gamma P = \gamma_0 P + \gamma_1 nP + \cdots + \gamma_{c-1} n^{c-1} P$$
$$= S(0, \gamma_0) + S(1, \gamma_1) + \cdots + S(c-1, \gamma_{c-1}). \tag{1}$$

Since the precomputation table can be computed by at most cn additions, the KKM improvement reduce the time complexity of Cheon's algorithm by a factor of $\log r$.

3   Implementation

This section describes our implementations of Cheon's algorithm with the ρ-algorithm.

3.1   Evaluating $F(X)$

In Cheon's algorithm with the ρ-algorithm, the most heavy operation is the evaluation of the function $F^{(\ell)}(P) = F(F^{(\ell-1)}(P))$, which consists of (1) Evaluate $f_e(F^{(\ell-1)}(P))$, (2) Compute $\zeta_d^{f_e(F^{(\ell-1)}(P))}$ as an exponentiation in $(\mathbb{Z}/r\mathbb{Z})^*$, and (3) Compute $\zeta_d^{f_e(F^{(\ell-1)}(P))} P$ as a scalar multiplication in $\mathbb{G}$. In our implementation, an element $P \in \mathbb{G}$ is represented by a pair of x-coordinate and y-coordinate, and the pseudo-random function $f_e(P) = x(P) \bmod e$ is used as a pseudo-random function, where $x(P)$ is the x-coordinate of P. Thus, procedure (1) is negligible compared to procedure (2) and (3).

Procedure (3) computes a scalar multiplication of a fixed element P independent from ℓ, so that the KKM improvement can be applied. Similar to procedure (3), procedure (2) also computes an exponentiation of a fixed element ζ_d independent from ℓ, so that the KKM improvement can be applied to procedure (2) in the same way.

3.2   Parallelization

The ρ-algorithm can be sped-up by parallelization. However, in order to make paths different, initial elements are randomized in the following way [8]: when a node (core) computes $F^{(\ell)}(G_d)$, $F^{(\ell)}(G)$ for Step 1, two random integers c_L, c_R are assigned to this node and initial points are converted to $G_d' = \zeta_d^{c_L} G_d$ and $G' = \zeta_d^{c_R} G$. Then, one can find k_1 by computing

$$k_1 = \left(\sum_{\ell=0}^{i-1} f_e(F^{(\ell)}(G_d')) + c_L \right) - \left(\sum_{\ell=0}^{j-1} f_e(F^{(\ell)}(G') + c_R \right) \bmod (r-1)/d$$

from a collision $F^{(i)}(G_d') = F^{(j)}(G')$. Note that since all converted initial points can be regarded as scalar multiple point of G, G_d, or G_e, the KKM improvement can be applied to the conversion.

3.3   KKM Improvement

In both implementations, the KKM improvement are also used for speeding-up Cheon's algorithm. Since our target group $\mathbb{G}$ is on an elliptic curve defined over a prime finite field with a mediate size, the affine coordinate system is used rather than the projective coordinate system. In the affine coordinate, every elliptic curve addition requires an inversion computation in the finite field. In order to avoid such heavy operations, we used the Montgomery trick [14], which converts N inversions into 1 inversion and $3(N-1)$ multiplications. When the Montgomery trick is used in the KKM improvement, only $O(\log_2 c)$ inversions are required.

4   Experimental Results

This section describes our experimental results of Cheon's algorithm for an elliptic curve used in the TinyTate library [15]. We successfully solved DLPwAI by our implementation in a group $\mathbb{G}$ with 128-bit order.

4.1   Parameters

We used an addition cyclic group $\mathbb{G} = \langle G \rangle$ with order r on an elliptic curve $y^2 = x^3 + x$ defined over a prime finite field $\mathbb{F}_p$ used in the TinyTate library [15] which was developed by Oliveria et al. for implementing the pairing-based cryptosystems in embedded devices. Concrete values of these parameters are summarized in the following:

$$
\begin{aligned}
p &= 37781606889598235856745576472658394721481625071533 \\
&\quad 3029839574761420382077746163 \ \ (256\text{-bit}) \\
\#E &= 37781606889598235856745576472658394721481625071533 \\
&\quad 3029839574761420382077746164 \ \ (256\text{-bit}) \\
&= 2^2 \cdot 3^2 \cdot 1227703 \cdot 50242951607062232327986689772851 \cdot r \\
r &= 170141188531071632644604909702696927233 \ \ (128\text{-bit}) \\
r - 1 &= 2^{102} \cdot 3 \cdot 11 \cdot 251 \cdot 4051 \ \ (128\text{-bit})
\end{aligned}
$$

where $\#E$ denotes the number of points in $E(\mathbb{F}_p)$. In our implementation of Cheon's algorithm, we used the following parameters:

$$
\begin{aligned}
d &= 12682136550675316736 \ \ (64\text{-bit}) \\
&= 2^{60} \cdot 11 \\
\zeta &= 5 \\
\zeta_d &= \zeta^d = 124313318310214169447902414199634645036 \\
d_1 &= \left\lceil \sqrt{(r-1)/d} \right\rceil = 3662760472 \ \ (32\text{-bit}) \\
d_2 &= \left\lceil \sqrt{d} \right\rceil = 3561198752 \ \ (32\text{-bit})
\end{aligned}
$$

Here, d is chosen to minimize the time complexity of Cheon's algorithm, and it is estimated that our implementation requires about $O(2^{32.75})$ group operations for solving DLPwAI. The generator ζ is chosen as the minimum generator of the multiplicative group $(\mathbb{Z}/r\mathbb{Z})^*$, and the smallness of this value does not reduce the time or space complexity of Cheon's algorithm.

A base point G is randomly chosen from points in $E(\mathbb{F}_p)$ with order r. Then, coordinate values of G, $G_1 = \alpha G$, $G_d = \alpha^d G$ for our solution $\alpha = 3$ are as follows:

$$
\begin{aligned}
x(G) &= 21200288773256318148725438778421364777705 \\
&\quad 53921599484324389949027229126693038 6 \\
y(G) &= 26761623705989368931204018789692655222293 \\
&\quad 12146143239140635788406897294957673 28 \\
x(G_1) &= 14065656213797322149877452698705463657 00 \\
&\quad 18530016497338926577641510030880161 4 \\
y(G_1) &= 38683308574106521926078235874461216295 91 \\
&\quad 29098892855061671768361458054835386 5 \\
x(G_d) &= 32496897821175066681382870355623859749 40 \\
&\quad 15599940749555201487620536516058802 30 \\
y(G_d) &= 20178499008260892062075798558988490926 92 \\
&\quad 37175542320859082745347459717376810 72.
\end{aligned}
$$

4.2   Results

In our experiment, Cheon's algorithm with ρ-algorithm was implemented on 14 PCs (7 PCs for evaluating $F^{(\ell)}(G_d)$ and the other 7 PCs for $F^{(\ell)}(G)$ in Step 1.

In Step 1, we found a collision $F^{(i_1)}(G_d) = F^{(j_1)}(G)$ and obtained exponents $e_1 = 5830677324892775306$, $f_1 = 2730878033043727388$, and thus a partial solution

$$k_1 = e_1 - f_1 \bmod (r-1)/d = 3099799291849047918$$

in about 73 minutes.

Similarly, in Step 2, we found a collision $F^{(i_2)}(G_e) = F^{(j_2)}(G)$ and obtained exponents $e_2 = 2482758160129538704$, $f_2 = 12605444724078073302$ and thus a partial solution

$$k_2 = e_2 - f_2 \bmod d = 2559449986726782138$$

in about 72 minutes.

In the experiment, we used the frequency parameter $w = 2^{18}$ so that the required memory is less than 0.5 MByte since 246 GByte/$2^{18}/2 \approx 0.5$ MByte.

4.3 Comparison

Both approaches require almost same computing time, while the required memory is quite different: 246 GByte for BSGS and 0.5 MByte for ρ-algorithm. When the order r becomes larger, both required computing time and memory grows in proportion to $\sqrt{r}$. Thus, when r is 140-bit, the required memory in BSGS case will be beyond 2 TByte which is infeasible for solving DLPwAI with this parameter. On the other hand, the ρ-algorithm only requires 4 MByte which will be feasible. Consequently, with the ρ-algorithm should be employed in order to solve such larger problems.

References

1. Aoki, K., Ueda, H.: Sieving Using Bucket Sort. In: Lee, P.J. (ed.) ASIACRYPT 2004. LNCS, vol. 3329, pp. 92–102. Springer, Heidelberg (2004)
2. Boneh, D., Boyen, X.: Short Signatures Without Random Oracles. In: Cachin, C., Camenisch, J.L. (eds.) EUROCRYPT 2004. LNCS, vol. 3027, pp. 56–73. Springer, Heidelberg (2004)
3. Boneh, D., Boyen, X.: Efficient Selective-ID Secure Identity-Based Encryption Without Random Oracles. In: Cachin, C., Camenisch, J.L. (eds.) EUROCRYPT 2004. LNCS, vol. 3027, pp. 223–238. Springer, Heidelberg (2004)
4. Boneh, D., Boyen, X., Goh, E.: Hierarchical Identity Based Encryption with Constant Size Ciphertext. In: Cramer, R. (ed.) EUROCRYPT 2005. LNCS, vol. 3494, pp. 440–456. Springer, Heidelberg (2005)
5. Boneh, D., Gentry, C., Waters, B.: Collusion Resistant Broadcast Encryption with Short Ciphertexts and Private Keys. In: Shoup, V. (ed.) CRYPTO 2005. LNCS, vol. 3621, pp. 258–275. Springer, Heidelberg (2005)
6. Box, R., et al.: A Fast Easy Sort. Computer Journal of Byte Magazine 16(4), 315–320 (1991)
7. Cheon, J.H.: Security Analysis of the Strong Diffie-Hellman Problem. In: Vaudenay, S. (ed.) EUROCRYPT 2006. LNCS, vol. 4004, pp. 1–11. Springer, Heidelberg (2006)
8. Cheon, J.H.: Discrete Logarithm Problems with Auxiliary Inputs. Journal of Cryptology 23(3), 457–476 (2010)
9. GNU MP, http://gmplib.org/
10. Izu, T., Takenaka, M., Yasuda, M.: Experimental Results on Cheon's Algorithm. In: WAIS 2010, The Proceedings of ARES 2010, pp. 625–630. IEEE Computer Science (2010)
11. Izu, T., Takenaka, M., Yasuda, M.: Experimental Analysis of Cheon's Algorithm against Pairing-Friendly Curves. In: AINA 2011, pp. 90–96. IEEE Computer Science (2011)
12. Jao, D., Yoshida, K.: Boneh-Boyen Signatures and the Strong Diffie-Hellman Problem. In: Shacham, H., Waters, B. (eds.) Pairing 2009. LNCS, vol. 5671, pp. 1–16. Springer, Heidelberg (2009)
13. Kozaki, S., Kutsuma, T., Matsuo, K.: Remarks on Cheon's Algorithms for Pairing-Related Problems. In: Takagi, T., Okamoto, T., Okamoto, E., Okamoto, T. (eds.) Pairing 2007. LNCS, vol. 4575, pp. 302–316. Springer, Heidelberg (2007)
14. Montgomery, P.: Speeding the Pollard and Elliptic Curve Methods of Factorization. Math. Comp. 48(177), 243–264 (1987)

15. Oliveira, L., López, J., Dahab, R.: TinyTate: Identity-Based Encryption for Sensor Networks. IACR Cryptology ePrint Archive, Report 2007/020 (2007)
16. Pollard, J.: Monte Carlo Methods for Index Computation (mod p). Math. Comp. 32, 918–924 (1978)
17. Sakemi, Y., Izu, T., Takenaka, M., Yasuda, M.: Solving DLP with Auxiliary Input over an Elliptic Curve Used in TinyTate Library. In: Ardagna, C.A., Zhou, J. (eds.) WISTP 2011. LNCS, vol. 6633, pp. 116–127. Springer, Heidelberg (2011)
18. Shanks, D.: Class Number, a Theory of Factorization, and Genera. In: Proc. of Symp. Math. Soc., vol. 20, pp. 41–440 (1971)
19. Teske, E.: Speeding Up Pollard's Rho Method for Computing Discrete Logarithms. In: Buhler, J.P. (ed.) ANTS 1998. LNCS, vol. 1423, pp. 541–554. Springer, Heidelberg (1998)

A General NTRU-Like Framework for Constructing Lattice-Based Public-Key Cryptosystems*

Yanbin Pan and Yingpu Deng

Key Laboratory of Mathematics Mechanization
Academy of Mathematics and Systems Science, Chinese Academy of Sciences
{panyanbin,dengyp}@amss.ac.cn

Abstract. As we know, one of the most difficult points of constructing a new public-key cryptosystem is to hide its trapdoor. By studying how NTRU hides its trapdoor, we present a general NTRU-like framework. The framework reduces constructing new lattice-based public-key cryptosystems to finding some certain kinds of easy closest vector problems (CVPs). We also show how to use the framework to reobtain NTRU. What's more, a new lattice-based public-key cryptosystem is proposed as an application of the framework.

Keywords: NTRU, Lattice, Public-Key Cryptosystem.

1 Introduction

In 1976, Diffie and Hellman [9] came up with a new idea that lead to a revolution in cryptography. They designed a key exchange protocol that allows two parties that have no prior knowledge of each other to jointly establish a shared secret key over an insecure communications channel. However, they did not give a public-key cryptosystem. The first public-key cryptosystem, RSA [26], was proposed by Rivest, Shamir and Adleman in 1978.

Merkle and Hellman [19] also proposed one of the first candidates for public-key cryptosystems. The Merkle-Hellman cryptosystem involves transforming an easy knapsack problem (with superincreasing weights) to a hard knapsack problem. It was hoped that to perform the inverse transformation without knowledge of the private key was hard. To hide the trapdoor of their cryptosystem, Merkle and Hellman used the following simple fact:

If $x = a \bmod p$, and $0 \leq x, a < p$, where $x, a, p \in \mathbb{Z}$, then $x = a$ holds over $\mathbb{Z}$.

The fact has been used widely in cryptography. For example, it is also involved in NTRU, one of the most efficient public-key cryptosystems.

Lattice-based cryptosystems are usually considered as one of the main post-quantum public-key cryptosystems. By now they have resisted the cryptanalysis

---

* This work was supported in part by the NNSF of China (No. 11071285 and No. 60821002) and in part by 973 Project (No. 2011CB302401).

S. Jung and M. Yung (Eds.): WISA 2011, LNCS 7115, pp. 109–120, 2012.

by quantum algorithms whereas there already exist the efficient quantum algorithms [27] for factoring integers and computing discrete logarithms. In addition, they require very simple computations, usually only modular addition, which makes them very efficient.

In 1997, Ajtai and Dwork [3] proposed the first lattice-based public-key cryptosystem. Its average-case security is based on the worst-case hardness of some lattice problem. By now, a lot of lattice-based cryptosystems, for example [10, 14, 6, 24, 25, 2, 11, 23], have been proposed. Although many of these cryptosystems have security proofs, we here focus on those without security proofs, such as GGH [10], the Cai-Cusick cryptosystem [6] and NTRU [14], which are usually thought as efficient cryptosystems.

GGH was proposed by Goldreich, Goldwasser and Halevi [10] in Crypto'97. Its security is related to the hardness of approximating the CVP in a lattice. Although it does not have a security proof, GGH has efficient encryption and decryption. Moreover, it has a natural signature scheme. However, Nguyen [21] showed there is a major flaw in it. So it can't provide sufficient security without being impractical.

Although the Ajtai-Dwork cryptosystem was thought to be secure if a particular lattice problem is difficult in the worst-case, Nguyen and Stern [20] gave a heuristic attack to show that in order to be secure, the implementations of the Ajtai-Dwork cryptosystem would require very large keys, making it impractical in a real-life environment. In 1998, Cai and Cusick [6] proposed an efficient lattice-based public-key cryptosystem with much less data expansion by mixing the Ajtai-Dwork cryptosystem with a knapsack. However, an efficient ciphertext-only attack presented by Pan and Deng [22] shows that it's not secure.

The NTRU cryptosystem proposed by Hoffstein, Pipher, Silverman [14] is the most practical lattice-based scheme known to date. It features reasonably short, easily created keys, high speed, and low memory requirements. By the results of Coppersmith and Shamir [8], the security of NTRU is related to the hardness of some lattice problems. To date, the chosen-ciphertext attacks against NTRU may be the most dangerous. Most of the ciphertext-only attacks [18, 13, 12] against NTRU rely on its underlying special cyclic structure.

Since NTRU is the most efficient lattice-based public-key cryptosystem known to date, many NTRU-based systems are presented [5, 7, 15, 17, 29]. These systems have nearly the same structure with NTRU, except using different algebraic objects instead of elements in $\mathbb{Z}_q[x]/(x^N - 1)$ as in NTRU. In this paper, we give a generalization of NTRU in a totally different way.

As we know, one of the most difficult points of constructing a new cryptosystem is to hide its trapdoor. So we study the idea how NTRU hides its trapdoor, and propose a general NTRU-like framework for constructing new lattice-based public-key cryptosystems. Under the framework, to construct a new lattice-based public-key cryptosystem, we can focus on finding some certain kinds of CVPs which can be solved efficiently, and leave the task of hiding the trapdoor to the framework.

Like GGH, the cryptosystem under the framework takes a matrix $H \in \mathbb{Z}^{m \times m}$ as its public key, and encrypts a message $\mathbf{m} \in \{0, 1\}^m$ by adding a small perturbation vector $\mathbf{r}$ to $H\mathbf{m}$. However, all the entries in our framework are over the ring $\mathbb{Z}_q$, where q is a small positive integer. So the public key size is usually smaller than that in GGH, and the computations are more efficient. What's more, when the attacker attempts to recover the encrypted message using direct lattice reduction, he needs to solve a CVP in a $2m$-dimensional lattice instead of an m-dimensional lattice which occurs in attacking GGH. Hence, smaller dimensional matrix may be used as public key to provide sufficient security.

Notice that the size of H is usually $O(m^2 \log m)$. It is bigger than the public key size in NTRU which is the most practical lattice-based public-key cryptosystem known to date. However, NTRU takes a cyclic matrix as its public key. A matrix with special structure can also improve the efficiency of the corresponding cryptosystem under our framework whereas a matrix without special structure makes the corresponding system resist some special attacks. For example, many attacks against NTRU are based on its special cyclic structure.

In addition, GGH and NTRU usually have decryption failure. The framework helps avoid decryption failure. We can also improve the new cryptosystem's efficiency and security by allowing a decryption failure as in GGH and NTRU.

We also give some examples to show how to use the framework, including

- reobtaining the NTRU cryptosystem;
- constructing a new lattice-based public-key cryptosystem.

Since we can reobtain the NTRU cryptosystem from the framework and there have not existed efficient successful attack against the structure of NTRU by now, it is reasonable to believe that there is no obvious weakness in the framework itself. However, it can't be concluded that the cryptosystems using the framework are as secure as NTRU. It is just shown that an attack utilizing only the structure of the framework may lead an attack against NTRU. We have to point out that the new cryptosystem does not have security proof.

The remainder of the paper is organized as follows. In Section 2, we give some preliminaries needed. In Section 3, we describe the general NTRU-like framework and discuss the security of the systems based on it. In Section 4, we show how to reobtain NTRU and present a new lattice-based public-key cryptosystem, both the basic and the enhanced system. Finally, we give a short conclusion in Section 5.

2   Preliminaries

We denote by $\mathbb{Z}$ the integer ring and by $\mathbb{Z}_q$ the residue class ring $\mathbb{Z}/q\mathbb{Z}$. We use bold letters to denote vectors, in column notation. If A is a matrix, then we denote by A_i the i-th column of A and if $\mathbf{v}$ is a vector, then we denote by $\mathbf{v}_i$ the i-th entry of $\mathbf{v}$.

2.1   Lattice

Let $\mathbf{b}_1, \mathbf{b}_2 \cdots, \mathbf{b}_d \in \mathbb{Z}^n$ be linearly independent vectors, the integer lattice $\mathcal{L}$ spanned by them is

$$\mathcal{L}(\mathbf{b}_1, \mathbf{b}_2, \cdots, \mathbf{b}_d) = \{\sum_{i=1}^{d} a_i \mathbf{b}_i | a_i \in \mathbb{Z}\}.$$

$B = [\mathbf{b}_1, \mathbf{b}_2, \cdots, \mathbf{b}_d]$ is called the basis of $\mathcal{L}$.

A lattice is full rank if $d = n$. If $\mathcal{L}$ is full rank, the determinant $\det(\mathcal{L})$ is equal to the absolute value of determinant of the basis B. If A is a matrix with d linearly independent columns, we denote by $\mathcal{L}(A)$ the lattice spanned by $A_1, A_2, \cdots, A_d$.

The shortest vector problem (SVP) refers the question to find the shortest non-zero vectors. It is known to be NP-hard under random reduction. Many exact algorithms and approximation algorithms are proposed to solve SVP. The celebrated LLL algorithm [16] among them approximates the shortest vector within a factor of $2^{n/2}$ in polynomial time. The closest vector problem (CVP) is to find a lattice vector which is closest to a given vector. An polynomial-time algorithm, the Nearest Plane Algorithm, proposed by Babai [4] approximates the closest vector by a factor of $(3/\sqrt{2})^n$.

Denote by $\|\mathbf{v}\|$ the Euclidean l_2-norm of a vector $\mathbf{v}$ and by $\lambda_1(\mathcal{L})$ the length of the shortest non-zero vector in the lattice $\mathcal{L}$. By the Gaussian Heuristic, $\lambda_1(\mathcal{L}) \approx \sqrt{\frac{n}{2\pi e}} \det(\mathcal{L})^{\frac{1}{n}}$ in an n-dimensional random lattice $\mathcal{L}$. Similarly, most closest vector problems for $\mathcal{L}$ have a solution whose size is approximately $\sqrt{\frac{n}{2\pi e}} \det(\mathcal{L})^{\frac{1}{n}}$. If we want to find a short vector $\mathbf{v}$ in $\mathcal{L}$, or a vector $\mathbf{v}$ such that $\mathbf{t} - \mathbf{v}$ is the vector in $\mathcal{L}$ close to the target vector $\mathbf{t}$, then experience tell us the smaller $\dfrac{\|v\|}{\sqrt{\frac{n}{2\pi e}} \det(\mathcal{L})^{\frac{1}{n}}}$ is, the more easily we will find $\mathbf{v}$ in practice.

2.2   NTRU

We give a simple description of the NTRU cryptosystem. For more details see [14].

The NTRU cryptosystem depends on three integer parameters (N, p, q) and four sets $\mathcal{L}_f, \mathcal{L}_g, \mathcal{L}_r, \mathcal{L}_m$ of polynomials of degree $N - 1$ with small integer coefficients. We choose p, q such that $gcd(p, q) = 1$ and p is much smaller than q.

Denote the ring $\mathbb{Z}[x]/(x^N - 1)$ by R and the multiplication in R by $*$ in this subsection. Every element in R can be represented as a polynomial or a vector. For example, for $f \in R$, we can represent f as

$$f = \sum_{i=0}^{N-1} f_i x^i$$

or the vector

$$\mathbf{f} = (f_0, f_1, \cdots, f_{N-1})^T.$$

We next work in the ring R.
Key Generation:

Step 1 Choose $f \in \mathcal{L}_f, g \in \mathcal{L}_g$ such that there exists $F_q, F_p \in R$ satisfying $f * F_q = 1 \mod q$ and $f * F_p = 1 \mod p$.
Step 2 Let $H = p * F_q * g \mod q$.

Public Key: H, p, q.
Private Key: f, F_p.
Encryption: To encrypt $m \in \mathcal{L}_m$, we first choose an $r \in \mathcal{L}_r$, then compute the ciphertext:

$$c = H * r + m \mod q.$$

Decryption: First we compute

$$
\begin{aligned}
a &= f * c &&\mod q, \\
&= pg * r + f * m &&\mod q.
\end{aligned}
$$

Then we choose the coefficients of a in the interval from $-\frac{q}{2}$ to $\frac{q}{2}$. By the fact that all the coefficients of $pg * r + f * m$ may be in the interval from $-\frac{q}{2}$ to $\frac{q}{2}$, we almost get

$$a = pg * r + f * m.$$

Then we can recover the message m by computing $m = F_p * a \mod p$.

3 The General NTRU-Like Framework

3.1 The General Framework

We denote the space of messages by $\mathcal{D}_{\mathbf{m}} \subset \mathbb{Z}^m$, the space of the random vectors by $\mathcal{D}_{\mathbf{r}} \subset \mathbb{Z}^m$.

Suppose we have already an efficient algorithm to recover $\mathbf{m}$ from $\mathbf{a}$, where $\mathbf{a} = F\mathbf{m} + G\mathbf{r}$, $F, G \in \mathbb{Z}^{m \times m}$, $\mathbf{m} \in \mathcal{D}_{\mathbf{m}}, \mathbf{r} \in \mathcal{D}_{\mathbf{r}}$, then we can let

$$
\begin{aligned}
s &= \min_{i=1,\cdots,m} (\min_{\mathbf{m},\mathbf{r}} \sum_{j=1}^{m} F_{i,j}\mathbf{m}_j + G_{i,j}\mathbf{r}_j) \\
t &= \max_{i=1,\cdots,m} (\max_{\mathbf{m},\mathbf{r}} \sum_{j=1}^{m} F_{i,j}\mathbf{m}_j + G_{i,j}\mathbf{r}_j) \\
q &= \text{the smallest prime larger than } t - s.
\end{aligned}
$$

Notice that s and t can be usually computed easily. If

- q **is small enough,**
- F **is invertible in** $\mathbb{Z}_q^{m \times m}$,

then we may use the following framework to construct a lattice-based public-key cryptosystem.

Key Generation:
   Let $H = F^{-1}G \bmod q$

Public Key: H, q.

Private Key: F, G, s, t.

Encryption: Choosing $\mathbf{m} \in D_{\mathbf{m}}$, $\mathbf{r} \in D_{\mathbf{r}}$, then we compute the ciphertext:

$$\mathbf{c} = H\mathbf{r} + \mathbf{m} \bmod q.$$

Decryption: First we compute

$$\begin{aligned} \mathbf{a} &= F\mathbf{c} \qquad\qquad \bmod q \\ &= F\mathbf{m} + G\mathbf{r} \ \bmod q. \end{aligned}$$

Notice that every entry of $F\mathbf{m} + G\mathbf{r}$ is in the interval from s to t. Since $q > t - s$, choosing the entries of $\mathbf{a}$ in the interval from s to t, we get $\mathbf{a} = F\mathbf{m} + G\mathbf{r}$. Finally, we can use the known algorithm to recover $\mathbf{m}$ from $\mathbf{a}$.

   We would like to point out that

- there are many other ways to generate q. For example, we can choose q first, then choose m depending on q. See the new system in Section 4 as an example. We can also store (s_i, t_i) for every row of $F\mathbf{m} + G\mathbf{r}$, namely, $s_i = \min\limits_{\mathbf{m},\mathbf{r}} \sum\limits_{j=1}^{m} F_{i,j}\mathbf{m}_j + G_{i,j}\mathbf{r}_j$, $t_i = \max\limits_{\mathbf{m},\mathbf{r}} \sum\limits_{j=1}^{m} F_{i,j}\mathbf{m}_j + G_{i,j}\mathbf{r}_j$ and let q be a prime greater than $\max\limits_{i=1,\cdots,m} (t_i - s_i)$.
- as we will see, the size of q affects the efficiency and security of the cryptosystem. So, we can choose q a little smaller than $t - s$ to improve the efficiency and security of the cryptosystem. However, it brings decryption failure. So we have to make the probability of decryption failure small enough.
- we can involve a permutation when $\mathcal{D}_{\mathbf{m}} = \mathcal{D}_{\mathbf{r}}$. See the new system in Section 4 as an example.
- if F, G are in a multiplicative subgroup of $\mathbb{Z}_q^{m \times m}$ and every element in the subgroup has a simple representation, then we will get a cryptosystem whose key size is smaller. For example, we may choose the subgroup of all the cyclic matrices, or the symmetric matrices or other special matrices. However, F and G must be complex enough to avoid being leaked from H easily.

3.2   Some Lattice-Based Attacks against the General Framework

As in [14], we give some lattice-based attacks against the general framework.

Key Security. The direct attack against the framework is to recover F and G from H. Since q is small enough, each row of F and G often has small norm. So we expect to recover F and G by finding m short vectors in the lattice spanned by

$$\left(\begin{array}{c|c} I & 0 \\ \hline H^T & qI \end{array} \right),$$

since every column of $[F|G]^T$ is in the lattice.

We denote by l the mean of $\|[F|G]_i^T\|$'s for $1 \le i \le m$. By the Gaussian Heuristic, the size of the solution of the shortest vector problems is approximately $\sqrt{\frac{n}{2\pi e}} \det(\mathcal{L}(B))^{\frac{1}{n}} = \sqrt{\frac{qm}{\pi e}}$. So we get the value of $c_{key} = \frac{l}{\sqrt{\frac{qm}{\pi e}}}$. The smaller c_{key} is, the more easily $[F|G]_i^T$'s may be found. As it gets closer to 1, to find $[F|G]_i^T$'s may be more difficult.

Obviously, we must reject specially simple matrices, like the identity matrix, as F or G, to resist the brute force attack. As we will see, if $\mathbf{m} \in \mathbb{Z}^m$, $\mathbf{r} \in \mathbb{Z}^m$ have the same distribution for their entries, we can involve a permutation to make F and G look not specially simple.

Message Security. The direct lattice attack to recover the message is to find a vector in the lattice spanned by

$$B = \left(\begin{array}{c|c} I & 0 \\ \hline H & qI \end{array} \right)$$

close to the target vector $\begin{pmatrix} 0 \\ \mathbf{c} \end{pmatrix}$, if $\left\| \begin{pmatrix} \mathbf{r} \\ -\mathbf{m} \end{pmatrix} \right\|$ is small, where $\mathbf{m} \in \mathcal{D}_{\mathbf{m}}, \mathbf{r} \in \mathcal{D}_{\mathbf{r}}$, because there exists a vector $\mathbf{u} \in \mathbb{Z}^m$, such that

$$\left(\begin{array}{c|c} I & 0 \\ \hline H & qI \end{array} \right) \begin{pmatrix} \mathbf{r} \\ \mathbf{u} \end{pmatrix} - \begin{pmatrix} 0 \\ \mathbf{c} \end{pmatrix} = \begin{pmatrix} \mathbf{r} \\ -\mathbf{m} \end{pmatrix}.$$

By the Gaussian Heuristic, the size of the solution of the closest vector problems is approximately $\sqrt{\frac{n}{2\pi e}} \det(\mathcal{L}(B))^{\frac{1}{n}} = \sqrt{\frac{qm}{\pi e}}$. For any message $\mathbf{m}$ and random vector $\mathbf{r}$, we get

$$c(\mathbf{m}, \mathbf{r}) = \frac{\sqrt{\|\mathbf{r}\|^2 + \|\mathbf{m}\|^2}}{\sqrt{\frac{qm}{\pi e}}} = \sqrt{\frac{(\|\mathbf{r}\|^2 + \|\mathbf{m}\|^2)\pi e}{qm}}.$$

$c(\mathbf{m}, \mathbf{r})$ gives a measure of the vulnerability of an individual message to a lattice attack. An encrypted message is most vulnerable if $c(\mathbf{m}, \mathbf{r})$ is small, and becomes less so as $c(\mathbf{m}, \mathbf{r})$ gets closer to 1.

Notice that the larger q is, the smaller $c(\mathbf{m}, \mathbf{r})$ is, then the more easily we can recover the message by the Gaussian Heuristic. So, we must ensure that q is small enough such that the new cryptosystem may resist the direct lattice attack and have reasonable key size.

4   Two Applications of the Framework

4.1   Reobtaining the NTRU Cryptosystem

We first show how to reobtain the NTRU cryptosystem by the general framework, which shows that there is no obvious successful attack against the framework itself since we have no efficient attack against NTRU. However, it can't be concluded that the cryptosystems using the framework are as secure as NTRU.

It is just shown that an attack utilizing only the structure of the framework may lead an attack against NTRU.

For NTRU, if we let

$$
F = \begin{pmatrix} f_0 & f_{N-1} & \cdots & f_1 \\ f_1 & f_0 & \cdots & f_2 \\ \vdots & \vdots & \ddots & \vdots \\ f_{N-1} & f_{N-2} & \cdots & f_0 \end{pmatrix}, \quad G = p \begin{pmatrix} g_0 & g_{N-1} & \cdots & g_1 \\ g_1 & g_0 & \cdots & g_2 \\ \vdots & \vdots & \ddots & \vdots \\ g_{N-1} & g_{N-2} & \cdots & g_0 \end{pmatrix},
$$

and the inverse of F in $\mathbb{Z}_p^{N \times N}$ be $\widetilde{F_p}$, it is obvious there is an efficient algorithm to recover $\mathbf{m}$ from $F\mathbf{m} + G\mathbf{r}$ by just computing $\widetilde{F_p}(F\mathbf{m} + G\mathbf{r}) \bmod p$. This fact allows us to reobtain NTRU by the general framework.

Note that q chosen in the original NTRU ensures its efficiency and security, but brings decryption failure. Choosing q as in the general framework, we can eliminate the decryption failure of NTRU. However, the efficiency and security decrease.

4.2 A New Lattice-Based Public-Key Cryptosystems Using the Framework

We next give the new lattice-based public-key cryptosystem using the framework.

The Basic Cryptosystem. We first give the basic system, which involves a diagonally dominant matrix.

Key Generation: Different from the general framework, we first choose a prime q and then let $m = q$, $D_{\mathbf{m}} = D_{\mathbf{r}} = \{0,1\}^m$. We randomly choose a matrix B such that

- the diagonal elements are $\lfloor \frac{q}{2} \rfloor$,
- every row has $\lfloor \frac{q}{4} \rfloor - 1$ elements equal 1,
- if $q = 1 \bmod 4$, every row has $\lfloor \frac{q}{4} \rfloor - 1$ elements equal -1, else if $q = 3 \bmod 4$, every row has $\lfloor \frac{q}{4} \rfloor$ elements equal -1,
- the rest elements are 0.

Then we can efficiently recover $\mathbf{m}$ from $\mathbf{a} = \mathbf{m} + B\mathbf{r}$ as below, where $\mathbf{m}, \mathbf{r} \in \{0,1\}^m$:

Algorithm R. Recovering $\mathbf{m}$ from $\mathbf{a}$

Input: a, B.

Output: m.

1. for i from 1 to m do
2.   if $\mathbf{a}_i \in (\frac{1}{4}q, \frac{3}{4}q)$, then $\mathbf{r}_i = 1$, else if $\mathbf{a}_i \in (-\frac{1}{4}q, \frac{1}{4}q)$, then $\mathbf{r}_i = 0$.
3. $\mathbf{a} = \mathbf{a} - \mathbf{r}_i B_i$
4. end for
5. $\mathbf{m} = \mathbf{a}$.
6. Output $\mathbf{m}$.

Denote $[I|B]$ by A. Then we uniformly randomly choose a permutation τ on n letters such that $F = [A_{\tau(1)}, A_{\tau(2)}, \cdots, A_{\tau(m)}]$ is invertible in $\mathbb{Z}_q^{m \times m}$. Let $G = [A_{\tau(m+1)}, A_{\tau(m+2)}, \cdots, A_{\tau(n)}]$. Obviously, we can recover $\mathbf{m}$ from

$$\mathbf{a} = F\mathbf{m} + G\mathbf{r}$$
$$= [F|G] \begin{pmatrix} \mathbf{m} \\ \mathbf{r} \end{pmatrix}$$
$$= [I|B]\mathbf{v}',$$

where $\mathbf{v}' = \begin{pmatrix} \mathbf{v}_{\tau^{-1}(1)} \\ \vdots \\ \mathbf{v}_{\tau^{-1}(n)} \end{pmatrix}$, $\mathbf{v} = \begin{pmatrix} \mathbf{m} \\ \mathbf{r} \end{pmatrix}$.

The Enhanced Cryptosystem. Next we describe the enhanced version of the new cryptosystem. We first choose a matrix $A \in \mathbb{Z}^{m \times n}$ as below:

- We let $A_{i,j} = 0$ for $i < j \leq m$.
- We randomly uniformly independently choose $A_{i,i} \in \{-1, 1\}$ and let $A_{i,m+i} = \lfloor \frac{1}{2}q \rfloor$.
- We choose $A_{i,j}$ from $\{-1, 0, 1\}$ for $j < i$ or $j > m + i$, such that every row of A' has totally $\lfloor \frac{1}{4}q \rfloor$ elements equal 1 and $\lfloor \frac{1}{4}q \rfloor - 1$ (resp. $\lfloor \frac{1}{4}q \rfloor$) elements equal -1 if $q = 1 \bmod 4$ (resp. $q = 3 \bmod 4$).
- We uniformly independently randomly choose $A_{i,j}$ from $\{0, 1, \cdots, q-1\}$ for $m < j < m + i$.

If we let $B = [A_1, A_2, \cdots, A_m]$ and $B' = [A_{m+1}, A_{m+2}, \cdots, A_n]$, then we also have an efficient algorithm to recover $\mathbf{m}$ from $\mathbf{a} = B\mathbf{m} + B'\mathbf{r}$ as below:

Algorithm EnR. Recovering $\mathbf{m}$ from $\mathbf{a}$
Input: $\mathbf{a}$, B, B'.
Output: $\mathbf{m}$.
1. for i from 1 to m do
2.   if $\mathbf{a}_i \in (\frac{1}{4}q, \frac{3}{4}q)$, then $\mathbf{r}_i = 1$, else if $\mathbf{a}_i \in (-\frac{1}{4}q, \frac{1}{4}q)$, then $\mathbf{r}_i = 0$.
3. $\mathbf{a} = \mathbf{a} - \mathbf{r}_i B'_i$
4. end for
5. $\mathbf{m} = B^{-1}\mathbf{a}$.
6. Output $\mathbf{m}$.

Then we uniformly randomly choose a permutation τ on n letters such that the new matrix $F = [A_{\tau(1)}, A_{\tau(2)}, \cdots, A_{\tau(m)}]$ is invertible in $\mathbb{Z}_q^{m \times m}$. Let $G = [A_{\tau(m+1)}, A_{\tau(m+2)}, \cdots, A_{\tau(n)}]$. Obviously, there is also an efficient algorithm to recover $\mathbf{m}$ from $\mathbf{a} = F\mathbf{m} + G\mathbf{r}$ with the known τ. By the general framework, we can have the enhanced cryptosystem easily.

Some Notes. We next give some basic information about the new systems in Table 1.

Table 1. Some Basic Information

System	Basic System	Enhanced System
Public Key Size	$O(m^2 \log m)$	$O(m^2 \log m)$
Private Key Size	$O(m^2)$	$O(m^2 \log m)$
Message Size	$O(m)$	$O(m)$
Ciphertext Size	$O(\log m)$	$O(\log m)$
Encryption Speed	$O(m^2 \log m)$	$O(m^2 \log m)$
Decryption Speed	$O(m^2 \log m)$	$O(m^2 \log^2 m)$

Since the basic system involves a diagonally dominant matrix, we try to recover every row of A by finding a vector close to a vector $\mathbf{t}^i$ whose i-th entry is $\lfloor \frac{q}{2} \rfloor$ and the rest are 0, for $i = 1, 2, \cdots, n$ in the lattice spanned by

$$\begin{pmatrix} I & 0 \\ H^T & qI \end{pmatrix}.$$

In the enhanced cryptosystem, we decrease this kind of threat by adding some random elements. However, the first row still has the diagonally dominant structure. For the first row, we compute the corresponding constant c_{key} by the attack above.

To compute the constant c_{msg}, we let $\|\mathbf{m}\| = \|\mathbf{r}\| = \sqrt{\frac{m}{2}}$. We give the constants of the enhanced cryptosystem for $q = 101, 211, 307, 401, 503$ in Table 2.

Table 2. The Constants of the Enhanced Cryptosystem

Constant	$q = 101$	$q = 211$	$q = 307$	$q = 401$	$q = 503$
c_{key}	0.203	0.141	0.117	0.102	0.092
c_{msg}	0.291	0.201	0.167	0.146	0.130

Remark 1. We would like to point out that

- as mentioned in Subsection 3.1, we can also use a smaller prime q' as the modulus, i.e. every computation is done over $\mathbb{Z}_{q'}$ instead of $\mathbb{Z}_q$, to improve the efficiency and the security. However, this brings the decryption failure.
- B is not necessarily a lower triangular matrix. We just need that it is invertible in $\mathbb{Z}^{m \times m}$.
- q is not necessarily a prime. To be a prime is to increase the probability of that F is invertible in $\mathbb{Z}_q^{m \times m}$. We tested the probability of that F is invertible in $\mathbb{Z}_q^{m \times m}$ for the enhanced cryptosystem on an AMD Athlon(tm) 64 Processor 2800+ 1.81 GHz PC using Shoup's NTL library version 5.4.1 [28]. For $q = 101, 211, 307, 401, 503$, we tested 10 instances respectively. In every instance, we uniformly randomly chose a permutation and found that F is always invertible in $\mathbb{Z}_q^{m \times m}$.

5   Conclusion

We propose a general NTRU-like framework for constructing new lattice-based public-key cryptosystems, which can help us hide the trapdoor. We also propose a new cryptosystem using the framework and involve some techniques to enhance the new system.

References

1. Ajtai, M.: Gennerating hard instances of lattice problems. In: The 28th STOC, pp. 99–108. ACM, New York (1996)
2. Ajtai, M.: Representing hard lattices with $O(n \log n)$ bits. In: The 37th STOC, pp. 94–103. ACM, New York (2005)
3. Ajtai, M., Dwork, C.: A public-key cryptosystem with worst-case/average-case equivalence. In: The 29th STOC, pp. 284–293. ACM, New York (1997)
4. Babai, L.: On Lovász lattice reduction and the nearest lattice point problem. Combinatorica 6, 1–13 (1986)
5. Banks, W.D., Shparlinski, I.E.: A Variant of NTRU with Non-Invertible Polynomials. In: Menezes, A., Sarkar, P. (eds.) INDOCRYPT 2002. LNCS, vol. 2551, pp. 62–70. Springer, Heidelberg (2002)
6. Cai, J.-Y., Cusick, T.W.: A Lattice-Based Public-Key Cryptosystem. In: Tavares, S., Meijer, H. (eds.) SAC 1998. LNCS, vol. 1556, pp. 219–233. Springer, Heidelberg (1999)
7. Coglianese, M., Goi, B.-M.: MaTRU: A New NTRU-Based Cryptosystem. In: Maitra, S., Veni Madhavan, C.E., Venkatesan, R. (eds.) INDOCRYPT 2005. LNCS, vol. 3797, pp. 232–243. Springer, Heidelberg (2005)
8. Coppersmith, D., Shamir, A.: Lattice Attacks on NTRU. In: Fumy, W. (ed.) EUROCRYPT 1997. LNCS, vol. 1233, pp. 52–61. Springer, Heidelberg (1997)
9. Diffie, W., Hellman, M.: New Directions in Cryptography. IEEE Transactions on Information Theory 22, 644–654 (1976)
10. Goldreich, O., Goldwasser, S., Halevi, S.: Public-Key Cryptosystems from Lattice Reduction Problems. In: Kaliski Jr., B.S. (ed.) CRYPTO 1997. LNCS, vol. 1294, pp. 112–131. Springer, Heidelberg (1997)
11. Gentry, C., Peikert, C., Vaikuntanathan, V.: Trapdoors for hard lattices and new cryptographic constructions. In: The 40th STOC, pp. 197–206. ACM, New York (2008)
12. Howgrave-Graham, N.: A Hybrid Lattice-Reduction and Meet-in-the-Middle Attack Against NTRU. In: Menezes, A. (ed.) CRYPTO 2007. LNCS, vol. 4622, pp. 150–169. Springer, Heidelberg (2007)
13. Howgrave-Graham, N., Silverman, J.H., Whyte, W.: A Meet-In-The-Meddle Attack on an NTRU Private Key. Technical report,
   http://www.ntru.com/cryptolab/technotes.htm#004
14. Hoffstein, J., Pipher, J., Silverman, J.H.: NTRU: A Ring-Based Public Key Cryptosystem. In: Buhler, J.P. (ed.) ANTS 1998. LNCS, vol. 1423, pp. 267–288. Springer, Heidelberg (1998)
15. Gaborit, P., Ohler, J., Sole, P.: CTRU, a polynomial analogue of NTRU. INRIA, Rapport de recherche 4621, INRIA (2002),
   ftp://ftp.inria.fr/INRIA/publication/publi-pdf/RR/RR-4621.pdf

16. Lenstra, A.K., Lenstra, H.W., Lovász, L.: Factoring polynomials with rational co-effcients. Math. Ann. 261, 515–534 (1982)
17. Malekian, E., Zakerolhosseini, A.: Ntru-like Public Key Cryptosystems beyond Dedekind Domain Up to Alternative Algebra, http://eprint.iacr.org/2009/446
18. May, A., Silverman, J.H.: Dimension Reduction Methods for Convolution Modular Lattices. In: Silverman, J.H. (ed.) CaLC 2001. LNCS, vol. 2146, pp. 110–125. Springer, Heidelberg (2001)
19. Merkle, R., Hellman, M.: Hiding Information and Signatures in Trapdoor Knapsacks. IEEE Transactions on Information Theory 24(5), 525–530 (1978)
20. Nguyen, P., Stern, J.: Cryptanalysis of the Ajtai-Dwork Cryptosystem. In: Krawczyk, H. (ed.) CRYPTO 1998. LNCS, vol. 1462, pp. 223–242. Springer, Heidelberg (1998)
21. Nguyen, P.: Cryptanalysis of the Goldreich-Goldwasser-Halevi Cryptosystem from Crypto'97. In: Wiener, M. (ed.) CRYPTO 1999. LNCS, vol. 1666, pp. 288–304. Springer, Heidelberg (1999)
22. Pan, Y., Deng, Y.: A Ciphertext-Only Attack Against the Cai-Cusick Lattice-Based Public-Key Cryptosystem. IEEE Transactions on Information Theory 57, 1780–1785 (2011)
23. Peikert, C.: Public-Key Cryptosystems from the Worst-Case Shortest Vector Problem. In: The 41th STOC, pp. 333–342. ACM, New York (2009)
24. Regev, O.: New lattice-based cryptographic constructions. Journal of the ACM 51, 899–942 (2004)
25. Regev, O.: On lattices, learning with errors, random linear codes, and cryptography. In: The 37th STOC, pp. 84–93. ACM, New York (2005)
26. Rivest, R., Shamir, A., Adleman, L.: A Method for Obtaining Digital Signatures and Public-Key Cryptosystems. Communications of the ACM, Mach. 21, 120–126 (1978)
27. Shor, P.: Algorithms for Quantum Computation: Discrete Logarithms and Factoring. In: The 35th Annual Symposium on Foundations of Computer Science, pp. 124–134. IEEE Computer Science Press, Santa Fe (1994)
28. Shoup, V.: NTL: A library for doing number theory, http://www.shoup.net/ntl/
29. Vats, N.: NNRU, a noncommutative analogue of NTRU, http://arxiv.org/abs/0902.1891

A Peer-to-Peer Content-Distribution Scheme Resilient to Key Leakage

Tatsuyuki Matsushita, Shinji Yamanaka, and Fangming Zhao

Corporate Research & Development Center, Toshiba Corporation
1, Komukai-Toshiba-cho, Saiwai-ku, Kawasaki, 212-8582, Japan
{tatsuyuki.matsushita,shinji1.yamanaka,fangming.zhao}@toshiba.co.jp

Abstract. We consider a problem of key leakage in peer-to-peer (P2P) content distribution. In content-distribution services, content is encrypted so that only legitimate users can access the content. Users (peers) cannot be fully trusted in a P2P network because malicious ones might leak their decryption keys. If the redistribution of decryption keys occurs, copyright holders may incur great losses caused by free riders who access content without purchasing it. Therefore, it is essential to solve this problem. In this paper, we propose a P2P content-distribution scheme resilient to the key leakage, and show its feasibility by conducting a large-scale experiment in a real network.

Keywords: Peer-to-Peer, Content Distribution, Key-Leakage Resilience, Individualization, Multiple Encryption.

1   Introduction

Although many content-distribution services are available to consumers, copyright holders are always concerned about the possibility of illegal access to content. They have actually suffered from it. For instance, the Motion Picture Association of America (MPAA) reported that the economic damage caused by Internet piracy in 2005 amounted to 2.3 billion U.S. dollars worldwide [13]. To give another example, Warner Bros., which was the last Hollywood studio to continue in business in South Korea, ceased distributing DVDs in the country because of Internet piracy in 2008 [21].

To protect content, a content provider encrypts the content in such a way that only legitimate users can access the content. This access control is realized by giving a decryption key only to each legitimate user in advance and encrypting the content with the corresponding encryption key. In a content-distribution service, legitimate but malicious users might redistribute their decryption keys to people who do not subscribe to the service. Because the leakage of decryption keys leads to serious damage by free riders, it is essential to solve this problem.

There are two measures against the key leakage. One is the revocation of decryption keys (e.g., [14]). This means that the content provider can make the decryption key(s) of a malicious user useless without confiscating it (them), and therefore prevent free riders from decrypting (i.e., playing back) other content.

S. Jung and M. Yung (Eds.): WISA 2011, LNCS 7115, pp. 121–135, 2012.

This functionality is very useful and indeed implemented for existing digital rights management (DRM) applications. In many cases, however, the revocation is not an effective measure since in reality the deadline when the revocation will be imposed is waived for some period of time (e.g., one month). Since free riders can keep using the leaked key during the grace period, local piracy can escalate into global piracy.

The other measure is the individualization of encrypted content. We mean by this terminology that a different (set of) decryption key(s) is required for each user to decrypt an encrypted version of the received content. The reason that the individualization of encrypted content is required is simple and clear: If a leaked decryption key of a malicious user cannot be used for the decryption of any encrypted content other than the one the malicious user received, the leaked key is useless except for the malicious user. This property is required when the content provider distributes premium content such as a high-definition movie, since it would pay malicious users to commit just small-scale piracy. In this paper, we seek an efficient content-distribution scheme that provides the individualization of encrypted content.

Regarding a content-distribution system, the focus of our interest is a peer-to-peer (P2P) content-distribution system, since the P2P network enables a large amount of data to be shared efficiently. In recent years, many P2P content-distribution schemes (e.g., [19,6,8]) have been proposed. The survey in [3] is helpful for grasping the literature of P2P content distribution. Content protection in a P2P network is studied in [9,18,16,15,11,7]. Key management is discussed in [16,11]. With regard to other properties, availability, file authenticity, and anonymity are extensively studied in the literature. This is the case also for a content delivery network (e.g., [2]). To the best of our knowledge, previous schemes except that of [23] in a P2P content-distribution system do not achieve the individualization of encrypted content.

The only previous scheme that achieves the individualization of encrypted content is that of [23], though the problem of the key leakage is dismissed as insoluble by making an unrealistic assumption. In [23], the implementation of players (software players, set-top boxes, etc.) is idealized and it is assumed that no decryption keys are leaked from any players. This assumption does not hold true in reality for software players. As implied in [1], not all of the players are implemented robustly enough to ensure protection from the key leakage in the real world. Therefore, we should make a realistic assumption that decryption keys might be leaked. Below, we show that the scheme of [23] has no key-leakage resilience to the realistic assumption.

The scheme of [23] is based on BitTorrent [19], which is one of the most popular P2P platforms. Let m_i ($1 \leq i \leq N$) be the i-th piece of content and g, p be parameters in the standard ElGamal encryption scheme. Calculations are done over $\mathbb{Z}_p^*$. Each user, P_j, generates a pair of secret and public keys, (s_j, g^{s_j}). A tracker, which is a server that keeps track of which users are online, generates secret random numbers, $r_{1,j}, \ldots, r_{N,j}$, for all of the users. At the initial stage of distribution, the tracker encrypts m_i with $r_{i,j}, g^{s_j}$ (in response to P_j's request) and sends the resulting ciphertext, $m_i g^{r_{i,j} s_j}$, to P_j. As users have encrypted pieces, they upload/download encrypted pieces to one another. Suppose that P_j wants to upload a ciphertext of m_i to another user, P_k. First, P_j makes a request for re-encryption to the tracker. Secondly, the tracker sends a re-encryption key, $RK_{j \to k}$, back to P_j, where $RK_{j \to k} = g^{r_{i,k} s_k - r_{i,j} s_j}$. Thirdly, P_j re-encrypts their ciphertext for P_k by calculating $(m_i g^{r_{i,j} s_j}) RK_{j \to k} = m_i g^{r_{i,k} s_k}$, and sends it to P_k. Lastly, P_k decrypts the received ciphertext with their decryption key, $(s_k, g^{r_{i,k}})$, where $g^{r_{i,k}}$ is given by the tracker after P_k pays for the content. Since the ciphertext for P_j and that for P_k are different (i.e., $m_i g^{r_{i,j} s_j} \neq m_i g^{r_{i,k} s_k}$), this scheme supports the individualization of encrypted content.

Unfortunately, the scheme is vulnerable to the leakage of decryption keys. Suppose that P_k is compromised and a set of their decryption keys, $(s_k, g^{r_{1,k}}, \ldots, g^{r_{i,k}}, \ldots, g^{r_{N,k}})$, is leaked. Because any user, P_ℓ, who just follows the above protocol and has their ciphertext, $m_i g^{r_{i,\ell} s_\ell}$, can obtain $RK_{\ell \to k}$ from the tracker, P_ℓ can get $m_i g^{r_{i,k} s_k} (= (m_i g^{r_{i,\ell} s_\ell}) g^{r_{i,k} s_k - r_{i,\ell} s_\ell})$ by re-encrypting their ciphertext. Therefore, P_ℓ can obtain m_i by decrypting the re-encrypted ciphertext with the leaked decryption key, $(s_k, g^{r_{i,k}})$. This means that anyone can play back the content without purchasing it and that just a single set of leaked decryption keys suffices for the free ride.

Based on the above analysis, we choose to take a simpler but more effective approach. To provide a P2P content-distribution scheme with both the individualization of encrypted content and the key-leakage resilience, we develop a mechanism in which each piece is multiply encrypted when transmitted via each user. In our scheme, sets of decryption keys for the same piece are designed to be different from one another. Therefore, the influence of the leakage of the decryption keys is minimized. In summary, our contributions are the following. (1) We point out the importance of the individualization of encrypted content. This property is necessary to suppress the damage caused by the key leakage. The previous scheme [23] achieves the individualization of encrypted content, but it has no key-leakage resilience. (2) We present a P2P content-distribution scheme that achieves both the individualization of encrypted content and the key-leakage resilience. In order to reduce the decryption cost for a user, we develop a piece-encryption scheme. (3) We implement the proposed scheme on BitTorrent, conduct a large-scale experiment in a real network, and show our scheme works well even for a large-scale network.

2   Overall System

As illustrated in Fig. 1, the entities participating in our scheme are:

A content provider provides content for a content server. For simplicity, we suppose that it also works as a content-distribution service provider.

A content server (a.k.a. an initial seeder) receives content from the content provider. It divides the content into multiple pieces and encrypts them. Then, it transmits the encrypted pieces to users. For simplicity, we suppose that it also works as a BitTorrent tracker.

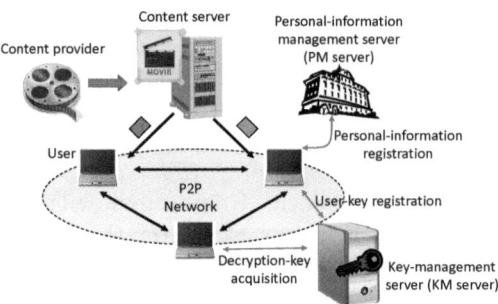

Fig. 1. Overall system

A personal-information management server (a PM server for short) receives and manages the personal information of all users. It issues a registration certificate stating that a user has registered his personal information with it, to the user. It is managed by e.g., the content provider, which is independent of a content-distribution system such as BitTorrent.

A key-Management server (a KM server for short) holds all keys assigned to the content server and users. It gives each user a unique key, which we call a user key. Each user uses its user key for generating an encryption key for a piece. In the decryption phase described below, it computes decryption keys for the encrypted pieces and gives them to users on request.

Users subscribe to the content-distribution service by registering them to the PM server and the KM server. The users upload/download encrypted pieces in a P2P network.

Our scheme involves the following five phases.

Personal-Information Registration. At first, for subscribing to the content-distribution service, a user registers his personal information with the PM server that includes his name, address, phone number, etc. Then, the PM server issues a registration certificate to the user after the confirmation process for the personal information. The composition of the registration certificate is similar to a public-key certificate. There is a pair of secret and public keys and a digital signature signed by the PM server in the registration certificate.

Metadata Acquisition. After obtaining the registration certificate, the user acquires the metadata for content from e.g., a shopping website. The metadata involves information of the P2P network, the ID and price of the content, the IP address of the content server, and the IP address of the KM server.

User-Key Registration. The user provides his registration certificate to the KM server for the user registration. If the verification of the registration certificate is successfully finished, the KM server generates and registers a unique user ID and a unique user key with which the user generates a symmetric key for encrypting a piece. The KM server also generates a signing key and a public-key certificate that includes a verification key corresponding to the signing key.

The public-key certificate is signed by the KM server. The signing key and the public-key certificate are used to verify the integrity of the encrypted piece. (Details will be described in 3.2.) Then, the KM server sends the user ID, the user key, the signing key, and the public-key certificate to the user.

Piece Downloading. Based on the information contained in the metadata, a user downloads encrypted pieces of content from the content server and other online users. (Details about how to encrypt a piece will be described in 3.1.)

Decryption. Users who want to access the content after all encrypted pieces are downloaded have to obtain their decryption keys from the KM server. (Details will be in 3.1.) For simplicity, we omit a billing process in this paper.

We assume that users are not trusted but the other entities are trusted. Regarding a threat model, we consider the following attacks in this paper: (1) A malicious user might leak his decryption keys, which are received from the KM server, to free riders. (2) A malicious user might alter a received encrypted piece and upload the altered piece to other users. This attack is called a pollution attack. If this attack happens, the quality of rendered content is degraded owing to altered pieces.

The requirements for secure P2P content distribution in our system are as follows: (1) Personal information, a user key, and decryption keys should be protected from eavesdroppers who intercept communications (i) between the PM server and a user and/or (ii) between the KM server and a user.[1] (2) Content should be protected from eavesdroppers who monitor communications among users. (3) Suppose that a malicious user leaks his decryption keys. In this case, the leaked decryption keys should not be able to be used for free riding. (4) Colluding users cannot compute any decryption keys other than those they have. (5) A user should be able to detect a pollution attack. We present our scheme that meets these requirements in the next section.

3   Proposed Scheme

3.1   Piece Encryption

We explain how an encrypted piece is multiply encrypted in the piece-downloading phase (see Fig. 2). We define k_A, k_B, k_C, k_I as the user keys of users, A, B, C, and a content server, I, respectively.

First, I generates a random number, r_I, and computes an encryption key, $W_I = H(k_I || r_I)$, where $H, ||$ denote a hash function and concatenation, respectively. In this paper, we suppose that (1) SHA-256 is used as H, (2) the length of W_i is 128 bits, and (3) the output of H is appropriately truncated, i.e., the lengths of k_i, r_i are 128 bits each, and W_i is the lower 128 bits of $H(k_i || r_i)$. Note that a different random number, r_i, is used each time an entity, i, (the content server or a user) encrypts a piece. Next, I encrypts a piece (plaintext), *piece*, and then sends a 3-tuple of data, (X_1, X_2, X_3), to A.

---

[1] We suppose that the communications are protected by e.g., TLS.

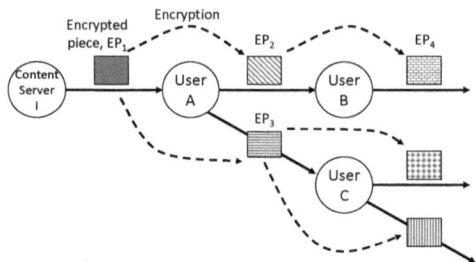

Fig. 2. Sketch of the flow of an encrypted piece

$$(EP_1 =)X_1 = Enc(W_I, Tr(= 1), piece), \ X_2 = ID_I, \ X_3 = r_I,$$

where ID_i, Tr denote ID of an entity, i, and the number of times of piece transfers, respectively. In other words, Tr means that the piece has traversed Tr nodes. A value of Tr can be computed by counting how many IDs are included in X_2. We explain Enc below. Note that I encrypts each of the pieces with a different encryption key.

When receiving (X_1, X_2, X_3), A increments Tr by one, generates a random number, r_A, and computes (X_1', X_2', X_3') as follows:

$$(EP_2 =)X_1' = Enc(W_A, 2, X_1), \ X_2' = X_2||ID_A = ID_I||ID_A,$$
$$X_3' = X_3||r_A = r_I||r_A, \ W_A = H(k_A||r_A).$$

Then, A sends (X_1', X_2', X_3') to B. As mentioned above, a distinct random number is generated each time A computes the encryption key, W_A. Therefore, EP_3, which is sent to C, is different from EP_2. To upload EP_3 to C, A generates a random number, r_A' ($\neq r_A$), then computes and sends (X_1'', X_2'', X_3'') to C.

$$(EP_3 =)X_1'' = Enc(W_A', 2, X_1), \ X_2'' = X_2||ID_A = ID_I||ID_A,$$
$$X_3'' = X_3||r_A' = r_I||r_A', \ W_A' = H(k_A||r_A'),$$

Now we describe one example of the algorithm, Enc. Suppose that a piece to be encrypted is $Y = Y_1||Y_2|| \cdots ||Y_t$ and the size of each sub-piece, Y_i, is the same. In our experiments, we set $t = 8$. First, the content server encrypts a piece in a conventional way (when $Tr = 1$). Secondly, a user encrypts Y_{Tr-1} and performs XOR of each subsequent sub-piece and Y_{Tr-1} when $Tr \leq t+1$. Thanks to the layered encryption, both the individualization of encrypted content and the key-leakage resilience are achieved. The reason for introducing the partial encryption for $Tr \geq 2$ is that we can reduce the decryption cost for a user. The rationale behind introducing the XOR operation is that, for example, we can prevent decrypting of EP_2 if the only leaked key is K_I. Lastly, a user just encrypts a sub-piece when $Tr \geq t + 2$, since the above concern is reduced.

Algorithm 1 (*Enc*)

Input: an encryption key, W, the number of times of piece transfers, Tr, a piece to be encrypted, Y, and the number of sub-pieces in Y, t.

Output: an encrypted data, Y'.

- If $Tr = 1$, then compute $Y' = E(W, Y)$, where E denotes that Y is encrypted with W. We suppose AES-CBC as E in this paper.
- Else if $2 \le Tr \le t + 1$, then compute Y' as follows, where $\oplus$ denotes XOR.

$$Y' = Y_1||Y_2||\cdots||Y_{Tr-2}||E(W, Y_{Tr-1})||Y_{Tr-1} \oplus Y_{Tr}||\cdots||Y_{Tr-1} \oplus Y_t.$$

- Else if $Tr \ge t + 2$, then compute Y' as follows:

$$Y' = Y_1||Y_2||\cdots||Y_{z-1}||E(W, Y_z)||Y_{z+1}||\cdots||Y_t,$$
$$z = \begin{cases} Tr - 1 \bmod t & (Tr \bmod t \ne 1) \\ t & (Tr \bmod t = 1) \end{cases}.$$

We explain what the KM server and a user do in the decryption phase. We define $\mathcal{K}_i$ as a set of the decryption keys of a user, i. The user sends the following information to the KM server as a key request: his user ID, a content ID, route information and random numbers. After receiving the key request from the user, the KM server authenticates the user and then checks if the total number of pieces is correct and also confirms the validity of the following items for each piece: $Tr \le Tr_{\max}$, user IDs included in route information, and the uniqueness of each user ID included in route information. After confirming all of these items, the KM server computes $\mathcal{K}_i$ for the key request, appends its digital signature to $\mathcal{K}_i$, and sends them to the user, i.

If B wants to get the decryption keys for EP_2, B sends (ID_B, CID, X_2', X_3') to the KM server, where CID denotes a content ID. When receiving (ID_B, CID, X_2', X_3'), the KM server computes the decryption keys, W_I, W_A, where the KM server knows all of the user keys. Likewise, B makes a request for a set of the decryption keys, $\mathcal{K}_B$, for all of the encrypted pieces of the content, and obtains $\mathcal{K}_B$. When receiving $\mathcal{K}_B$, B verifies the signature and decrypts the encrypted content with $\mathcal{K}_B$. It is obvious that a user can decrypt the encrypted pieces (and therefore play back the content) if all of the W_i's used in encrypting the pieces are obtained.

3.2 Integrity Verification

To detect a pollution attack, the integrity verification of (encrypted) pieces is necessary. We show how the integrity verification is integrated into the proposed piece-encryption scheme. Let $Sig(sk, M)$ denote a signature in which a message, M, is signed with a signing key, sk, using e.g., ECDSA. Let $sk_i, vk_i, cert_i$ be a signing key, a verification key corresponding to sk_i, and a public-key certificate of an entity, i, and ID_i, vk_i be included in $cert_i$. We reuse the same notations used in 3.1 and omit describing the same part of the protocol as in 3.1.

The content server, I, sends (X_1, X_2, X_3) to the user, A, where $X_2 = cert_I$, $X_3 = r_I||Sig(sk_I, X_1||X_2||r_I)$. When receiving (X_1, X_2, X_3), A verifies

(1) $cert_I$ with a (public) verification key of the KM server, vk_{KM}, and (2) $Sig(sk_I, X_1||X_2||r_I)$ with vk_I included in $cert_I$. If both verifications are successful, A transmits (X_1', X_2', X_3') to the user, B.

$$X_2' = X_2||cert_A = cert_I||cert_A, \ X_3' = X_3||r_A||Sig(sk_A, X_1'||X_2'||X_3||r_A).$$

Otherwise, A discards (X_1, X_2, X_3).

Likewise, when a user, U, receives a 3-tuple of data, (Z_1, Z_2, Z_3), U verifies both the public-key certificate and the signature that have been appended most recently. If both verifications are successful, U stores (Z_1, Z_2, Z_3). Otherwise, U discards it. If U transfers the encrypted piece to another user, V, then U encrypts Z_1 using Enc, appends $cert_U$ to Z_2, generates and appends a signature of the entire data to Z_3, and then sends the resulting data, (Z_1', Z_2', Z_3'), to V.

Since $cert_U$, which includes vk_U, is signed by the KM server (in the user-key registration phase), V can verify, using vk_{KM} and vk_U, that (1) the received data was generated by the legitimate user, U, and (2) it has not been altered since the time it was generated by U. Note that V does not need to know vk_U before he receives (Z_1', Z_2', Z_3'), since V does not have to verify that he is communicating with U but just needs to verify that (1) and (2) are satisfied. This is suitable for the P2P network, in which a user might not know in advance who will communicate with him.

The above method is sufficient to detect a pollution attack as long as U behaves honestly. But we should also consider a case in which U is malicious. Suppose that U is a legitimate but malicious user. The malicious user, U, can choose any data as Z_1' as long as U follows the above protocol in computing Z_2' and Z_3'. Such (Z_1', Z_2', Z_3') can pass the above verification for V. To cope with this attack, we adopt the following method in the decryption phase.

Suppose that a user, V, receives (1) an encrypted piece, c_i, and (2) a public-key certificate, $cert_{U_i}$, and a signature, Sig_{U_i}, that have been appended to c_i most recently. We denote by Sig_{U_i} a signature generated by a user, U_i, according to the above protocol. In conjunction with the above method used in the piece downloading phase, the following method is used in the decryption phase. After downloading $c_1, \ldots, c_N$, V executes the following procedures:

1. Receive a set of decryption keys, $\mathcal{K}_V$, for the content from the KM server.
2. Check if the received decryption keys are valid by verifying with vk_{KM} a signature appended to $\mathcal{K}_V$ by the KM server.
3. Repeat the following procedures for $1 \leq i \leq N$.
   3-1) Decrypt c_i with the corresponding keys in $\mathcal{K}_V$, and obtain a (potentially altered) piece, m_i'.
   3-2) (Let m_i denote a correct piece.) Compute $H(m_i')$ and check if $H(m_i')$ is equal to $H(m_i)$ obtained from the content server, in the same way as in the original BitTorrent system. If $H(m_i') = H(m_i)$, then determine that the piece is not altered. Otherwise, discard c_i.

In our scheme, a user has to decrypt an encrypted piece before the integrity verification. But this does not cause an efficiency problem, as analyzed in 4.2.

4   Performance Analysis

4.1   Large-Scale Data Distribution

Data-distribution experiments are conducted on StarBED [12,17], which is a popular large-scale network testbed in Japan. This experiment environment is a cluster-based testbed currently employing 1,070 PCs.

We use actual nodes (PCs) for our data-distribution experiments. Each node runs on the Intel Pentium 4 processor at 3.0 GHz with 2 GB of RAM. Each node also has two network devices. One network device is connected to a management network and the other network device is connected to an experiment network. Each node is controlled by a management node in the management network and data distribution is done in the experiment network. One node acts as a content server, which has all of the pieces of content. The other 150 nodes behave as clients. We also use LibTorrent C++ library [10] for implementing our client software. Regarding a tracker, we use the original BitTorrent tracker [20] and implement it to the content server.

First, we describe five parameters of the experiments. Then, we explain our experimental results from three viewpoints. All parameters and the results of the experiments are shown in Table 1.

The Number of Nodes. In our experiments, we run up to 150 nodes. The management node controls all of the nodes in the management network. Note that we run plural clients on one node in some experiments. Clients upload/download data pieces to/from one another.

Frequency of Re-entry to the Network. The frequency of re-entry to the network denotes the number of times one client node enters the experiment network in one experiment. If this parameter is set to 50, for instance, all clients do the following steps 50 times: (1) Generate a new client ID and a user key, (2) Enter the experiment network, (3) Upload/download pieces, (4) Finish downloading, (5) Escape from the experiment network, and (6) Save log data and clean up downloaded data. A re-entered client is assigned a new different ID, so this client acts as a newly joined client. In order to avoid a case in which most of the clients enter the network at the same time, we introduce a random delay, which is at most 10 [sec], between (1) and (2).

The Maximum Number of Times of Piece Transfers. As explained in 3.1, a piece is multiply encrypted as it is transferred through clients. The number of times of encryption of a piece increases as the number of times of piece transfers, Tr, grows. In case of the excessive increase in the number of times of encryption, we have the following three problems: (1) The KM server has to incur the heavier load of generating the decryption keys for the encrypted pieces. (2) The decryption cost for a client increases. (3) (Recall that (Z_1, Z_2, Z_3) denotes a 3-tuple of data transferred among users.) The size of $Z_2||Z_3$ increase as Tr grows, though the size of Z_1, which stays constant, is much larger than that of $Z_2||Z_3$ in most cases. In order to avoid these problems, $Tr_{\max}$, which is defined as the maximum number of Tr, needs to be set. At the same time, we should not set

Table 1. Parameters and results of StarBED experiments

Exp. no.	No. of nodes	Re-entry freq.	Max. no. of transfers (Tr_{max})	No. of clients per node	Size of data (MB)	Ratio of uploading to downloading (%)	Ave. no. of transfers	Ave. downloading time [sec]
1-1	10	10	254	1	195	46.7	1.8	8.2
1-2	50	10	254	1	195	89.8	10.0	8.8
1-3	100	10	254	1	195	94.5	21.3	9.5
1-4	150	10	254	1	195	96.2	26.2	9.7
1-5	10	50	20	1	195	52.5	1.8	8.2
1-6	50	50	20	1	195	89.6	8.2	9.3
1-7	100	50	20	1	195	93.4	11.0	10.7
2-1	10	50	254	1	195	45.6	1.7	8.1
2-2	150	50	254	1	195	96.5	55.7	9.6
2-3	10	500	254	1	195	45.8	1.7	8.1
2-4	150	500	254	1	195	97.1	60.7	9.6
2-5	150	50	15	1	195	94.2	9.4	12.1
3-1	150	50	5	1	195	78.2	3.1	47.9
3-2	150	50	10	1	195	91.3	6.3	16.3
3-3	150	50	20	1	195	95.1	12.0	11.1
3-4	150	50	30	1	195	95.8	16.4	10.4
4-1	30	50	254	5	195	96.7	38.0	27.8
4-2	150	50	254	5	195	99.4	89.6	28.9
4-3	30	50	20	5	195	95.7	11.9	27.5
4-4	150	50	20	5	195	98.9	14.9	30.9
5-1	50	50	254	1	1,954	93.1	11.0	77.0
5-2	150	50	20	1	1,954	97.2	11.9	90.6
5-3	150	50	20	5	1,954	100.2	13.1	616.0

Tr_{max} to a too small value. If a value of Tr_{max} is too small, most of the clients try to connect to the content server, and therefore the downloading time of the client that fails in connecting to the content server owing to congestion increases substantially.

The Number of Clients Per Node. Since a node is a PC, we can run one or more clients on it. In some experiments, we run five clients on one node.

The Size of Data. We generate two random data for our distribution experiment, 195-MB data and 1954-MB data. In most of the experiments, we use 195-MB data. Throughout the paper, we set the size of each piece to 1 MB.

Contribution Analysis. In a P2P system, data pieces are provided not only from the content server but also from participant nodes (clients). Therefore, a P2P system can distribute data more efficiently than a server-client system. We analyze the contribution of each client to our system, such as how many pieces are uploaded from clients. When the number of online clients is low (e.g., Exp. 1-1), half of the pieces are uploaded from clients. In Exp. 3-1, where Tr_{max} is set to 5, 78.2% of pieces are uploaded from clients. From these results, it follows that the number of online clients and a value of Tr_{max} should not be too small. In other experiments, about 90% or more pieces of data are uploaded from each client. Therefore, the cost of the content server is reduced in comparison. In other words, clients are provided with almost the same number of pieces they obtained from other clients (or the content server) in these experiments.

The Number of Times of Piece Transfers. In Exp. 1-1, 1-5, 2-1, and 2-3, where the number of online clients is very small, the average number of Tr is 1.7 or 1.8. This means that an encrypted piece is transferred 0.7 or 0.8 times among clients, since the encrypted piece is transferred at least once by the content server. So just over half of the transfers are performed by the content server and the load of the content server is very high like that of a server-client system. On the other hand, when the number of the online clients is relatively large (e.g., Exp. 1-2, 1-3, and 1-4), the average number of Tr increases. This means that the transmission burden of the content server is shifted to the users, as the number of the online clients grows.

In some experiments (Exp. 3-1, ..., 3-4, etc.), we set $Tr_{\max}$ to a different smaller value. In these experiments, the average number of Tr settles at around 60% of a value of $Tr_{\max}$. This trend is evident in experiments for both data sizes, 195 MB and 1954 MB. Recall that we set the number of sub-pieces in one piece, t, to 8. When $Tr_{\max} \leq 30$, i.e., the average number of Tr is less than 17, the decryption cost for a user is less than that of the straightforward double encryption on average. We will discuss the decryption cost in 4.2.

Downloading Time. As downloading time, we measure the time needed from the time the client process was started until the completion of downloading all of the encrypted pieces.[2] The downloading time is influenced by a value of $Tr_{\max}$. In Exp. 2-2, where $Tr_{\max}$ is set to 254, the average downloading time is 9.6 [sec] to obtain 195-MB data. As seen in the results of Exp. 2-5, Exp. 3-1,..., Exp. 3-4, the average downloading time increases as we set $Tr_{\max}$ to a smaller value. When a value of $Tr_{\max}$ is set to 20 or more, then extra downloading time is less than 16%. Considering the balance between the number of times of piece transfers, which influences the decryption cost for a user, and the downloading time, we find that it is appropriate to set $Tr_{\max} = 20$.

If we use a hybrid P2P network such as BitTorrent, our scheme works on a large-scale network since it is basically possible to accommodate more clients by grouping them into subsets.

4.2   Encryption and Decryption Costs

As described in 3.2, a user, U, performs two signature verifications, one piece encryption using Enc, and one signature generation in re-encrypting an encrypted piece. We estimate the time needed from the time U received (Z_1, Z_2, Z_3) until the completion of generating (Z_1', Z_2', Z_3'). We refer the following benchmarks on the Intel Core 2 processor at 1.83 GHz in [5]: 2.88 [msec] for a 256-bit ECDSA signing, 8.53 [msec] for a 256-bit ECDSA verification, and 109 [MB/sec] for a

---

[2] Owing to a contractual problem, in the client software, we have to substitute dummy programs for those of the piece encryption and the signature generation/verification shown in Sections 3.1 and 3.2.

128-bit AES-CBC. From these benchmarks, it follows that the estimated time is
21.1 ($= 8.53 \times 2 + (1/8)/0.109 + 2.88$) [msec], where U encrypts $1/t$ ($= 1/8$) of
the encrypted piece regardless of a value of Tr. Since the total downloading time
(shown in Table 1) overshadows the piece re-encrypting time, the computation
cost for a user in the piece downloading phase is acceptable.

One might be concerned about the computation cost for a user in the decryption phase, since it seems to explode as the number of times of piece transfers
increases. We numerically show that this is not true if we set $Tr_{\max}$ to an appropriate value. Suppose that (1) V has downloaded encrypted pieces, $c_1, \ldots, c_N$, of
content and (2) $Tr_{\max} = 20$. In the decryption phase, V executes the procedures
described in 3.2. We measured the time required for the repeated procedures (3-1
and 3-2) using our decryption software running on the Intel Pentium 4 processor
at 2.4 GHz with 1 GB of RAM. On average, it takes 174.2 [msec] per piece in the
worst case where each piece is encrypted 20 times using Enc. To give another
result, on the Intel Pentium D processor at 3.4 GHz with 2 GB of RAM, on
average, it takes 63.6 [msec] per piece in the worst case.

4.3   Performance of Key-Management Server

Since the computational burden is shifted to the KM server in the decryption
phase of our scheme, one might also worry about the computation and communication costs for the KM server to distribute decryption keys. We show that the
costs do not explode as the number of participating users increases by implementing our scheme to the KM server and evaluating the performance of distributing
decryption keys. We implement a key-management application, based on the
Java language. The application, which runs on the Intel Xeon processor X3320
at 2.50 GHz with 4 GB of RAM, performs the key-distribution service for users.
To simulate multiple virtual nodes that simultaneously access the KM server to
get their decryption keys, we use a load generator, which is based on WebLOAD
[22] and runs on the Intel Core 2 Duo processor P8400 at 2.26 GHz with 1 GB
of RAM.

We explain a key-distribution protocol in which users receive their decryption
keys from the KM server. A user sends a key request to the KM server. The key
request includes a ticket, a signature of the ticket, route information of pieces,
and random numbers used to encrypt the pieces. We use ECDSA as a signature
algorithm. The ticket includes the user's own user ID, a content ID, and payment
information of the content. When the KM server receives the key request, it first
authenticates the user using TLS 1.0 and therefore the communication between
the two is protected. Secondly, it verifies the signature of the ticket. If both the
user authentication and the ticket verification are successful, it generates a set
of decryption keys with the route information, the random numbers, and the
corresponding user keys. Finally, it sends the set of decryption keys to the user.

We choose three kinds of key requests for content whose sizes are 2,700, 4,700,
and 25,000 MB. These can be considered as MPEG-4 content (3 Mbps, 2 hours),
DVD content, and Blu-ray Disc [4] content, respectively. We suppose that each
1-MB piece is encrypted 20 times (i.e., $Tr = 20$). We measure processing time,

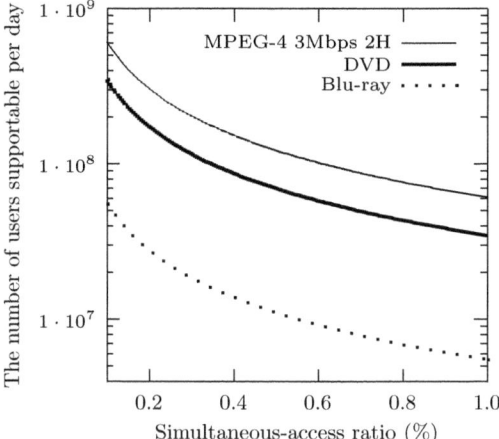

Fig. 3. Service capacity

t_{total}, for completing each key request. Note that t_{total} includes the overhead due to TLS. From the result that $t_{\text{total}} = 0.14$ [sec] for MPEG-4 content, it follows that the KM server can issue $t_{\text{total}}^{-1} = 7.1$ sets of decryption keys per second. To give other results, the KM server can issue 4.0 sets of decryption keys per second for DVD content, while it can do 0.64 sets of decryption keys per second for Blu-ray Disc content. Let S be the number of users that the KM server can support per day, i.e., service capacity of the KM server. Let R be the simultaneous-access ratio, which means R % of the users simultaneously access the KM server to receive their decryption keys. From the key-distribution capacity shown above, we can estimate $S = 24 \times 60^2 \times t_{\text{total}}^{-1}/(R/100)$ on the assumption that accesses from users are dispersed throughout a day. In Fig. 3, we show the service capacity when $0.1 \leq R \leq 1$.

4.4   Key-Leakage Resilience

We explain which user can get a free ride in our scheme. First, we consider a case in which there is one malicious user and focus on a single piece. Suppose that, in Fig. 2, B leaks a set of his decryption keys, $\mathcal{K}_B$. In this topology, A can decrypt EP_1 (and therefore obtain the plaintext piece) with the leaked key, W_I ($\subseteq \mathcal{K}_B$). A free rider (in this case, A) can decrypt an encrypted piece (EP_1) he received with leaked keys only if an encrypted piece (EP_2) a mailicious user (B) received has traversed the free rider. On the other hand, C cannot decrypt EP_3 with any leaked key because $W'_A \not\subseteq \mathcal{K}_B$.

Next, suppose that (1) k malicious users, $i_1, \ldots, i_k$, leak sets of their decryption keys, $\mathcal{K}_{i_1}, \ldots, \mathcal{K}_{i_k}$ and (2) a free rider, F, has downloaded N encrypted pieces, $c_1, \ldots, c_N$, of content where a set of decryption keys for each c_j is $\mathcal{K}_{F,j}$. If $\mathcal{K}_{F,j} \subseteq \cup_{\ell=1}^{k} \mathcal{K}_{i_\ell}$, F can decrypt c_j with the leaked keys. Therefore, F can obtain D % of the content if $|\{j \mid \mathcal{K}_{F,j} \subseteq \cup_{\ell=1}^{k} \mathcal{K}_{i_\ell}\}|/N = D/100$.

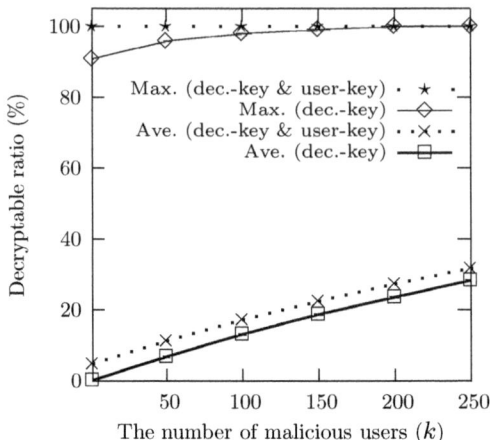

Fig. 4. Key-leakage resilience in Exp. 3-3

Fig. 4 shows the experimental results for the influence of the key leakage in Exp. 3-3. We mean by decryptable ratio what percentage of encrypted pieces of content can be decrypted by a free rider with leaked keys. The solid lines show the maximum and average decryptable ratios when k malicious users leak their decryption keys. In this case, the decryptable ratio is formulated as D.

Recall that a user has a user key, which is unique to each user. Malicious users might also give away their user keys to free riders, though the leaked user keys can immediately be traced back to them. The dotted lines show the maximum and average decryptable ratios when k malicious users leak their user keys in addition to their decryption keys. In this case, the decryptable ratio is formulated as $D' = 100 \times |\{j \mid \mathcal{K}_{F,j} \subseteq \cup_{\ell=1}^{k}(\mathcal{K}_{i_\ell} \cup \mathcal{K}'_{i_\ell})\}|/N$, where $\mathcal{K}'_{i_\ell}$ denotes a set of decryption keys that are derived from i_ℓ's user key.

In either case, a free rider can only decrypt a low percentage of the encrypted pieces on average, whereas only a few free riders can decrypt almost 100% of the encrypted pieces. Since the quality of rendered content is greatly degraded unless the decryptable ratio becomes high, these results verify that our scheme is resilient to the key leakage in the presence of hundreds of malicious users.

Acknowledgments. We would like to thank the National Institute of Information and Communications Technology for providing StarBED. We would also like to thank Satoshi Ito, Toru Kambayashi, Taku Kato, Ryuichi Koike, Hideki Matsumoto, Hideaki Sato, Haruhiko Toyama, and Kentaro Umesawa for illuminating discussion of the research.

References

1. Advanced Access Content System. Response to reports of attacks on aacs technology, http://www.aacsla.com/press
2. Akamai, http://www.akamai.com

3. Androutsellis-Theotokis, S., Spinellis, D.: A survey of peer-to-peer content distribution technologies. ACM Computing Surveys 36(4), 335–371 (2004)
4. Blu-ray Disc Association, `http://www.blu-raydisc.com`
5. Crypto++ 5.6.0 Benchmarks, `http://www.cryptopp.com/benchmarks.html`
6. eMule, `http://www.emule-project.net`
7. Garcia, L., Arnaiz, L., Álvarez, F., Menéndez, J.M., Grüneberg, K.: Protected seamless content delivery in P2P wireless and wired networks. IEEE Wireless Communications 16(5), 50–57 (2009)
8. Gnutella, `http://www.gnutella.com`
9. Iwata, T., Abe, T., Ueda, K., Sunaga, H.: A DRM system suitable for P2P content delivery and the study on its implementation. In: Proc. 9th Asia-Pacific Conference on Communications (APCC 2003), vol. 2, pp. 806–811 (2003)
10. LibTorrent, `http://libtorrent.rakshasa.no`
11. Liu, X., Yin, H., Lin, C., Du, C.: Efficient user authentication and key management for peer-to-peer live streaming systems. Tsinghua Science & Technology 14(2), 234–241 (2009)
12. Miyachi, T., Chinen, K., Shinoda, Y.: StarBED and SpringOS: Large-scale general purpose network testbed and supporting software. In: Proc. 1st International Conference on Performance Evaluation Methodologies and Tools (Valuetools 2006). ACM Press (2006)
13. Motion Picture Association of America. Internet piracy, `http://www.mpaa.org/piracy_internet.asp`
14. Naor, D., Naor, M., Lotspiech, J.: Revocation and Tracing Schemes for Stateless Receivers. In: Kilian, J. (ed.) CRYPTO 2001. LNCS, vol. 2139, pp. 41–62. Springer, Heidelberg (2001)
15. Palomar, E., Tapiador, J.M.E., Hernandez-Castro, J.C., Ribagorda, A.: Secure content access and replication in pure P2P networks. Computer Communications 31(2), 266–279 (2008)
16. Qiu, F., Lin, C., Yin, H.: EKM: An Efficient Key Management Scheme for Large-Scale Peer-to-Peer Media Streaming. In: Zhuang, Y.-t., Yang, S.-Q., Rui, Y., He, Q. (eds.) PCM 2006. LNCS, vol. 4261, pp. 395–404. Springer, Heidelberg (2006)
17. StarBED Project, `http://www.starbed.org`
18. Sung, J.Y., Jeong, J.Y., Yoon, K.S.: DRM enabled P2P architecture. In: Proc. 8th International Conference of Advanced Communication Technology (ICACT), vol. 1, pp. 487–490 (2006)
19. The BitTorrent Protocol Specification, `http://www.bittorrent.org/beps/bep_0003.html`
20. The BitTorrent Tracker Source Code, `http://download.bittorrent.com/dl/archive/BitTorrent-3.9.1.tar.gz`
21. THE WALL STREET JOURNAL. Warner Bros. to Pull Out of DVDs in South Korea, `http://online.wsj.com/article/SB122643080489917991.html`
22. WebLOAD, `http://www.webload.org`
23. Zhang, X., Liu, D., Chen, S., Zhang, Z., Sandhu, R.: Towards digital rights protection in BitTorrent-like P2P systems. In: Proc. 15th SPIE/ACM Multimedia Computing and Networking, MMCN 2008 (2008)

Rule Indexing for Efficient Intrusion Detection Systems

Boojoong Kang[1], Hye Seon Kim[1], Ji Su Yang[1], and Eul Gyu Im[2]

[1] Department of Electronics and Computer Engineering,
Hanyang University, Seoul, 133-791, Korea
[2] Division of Computer Science and Engineering,
Hanyang University, Seoul, 133-791, Korea
{deviri,danzun,yjisu,imeg}@hanyang.ac.kr

Abstract. As the use of the Internet has increased tremendously, the network traffic involved in malicious activities has also grown significantly. To detect and classify such malicious activities, Snort, the open-sourced network intrusion detection system, is widely used. Snort examines incoming packets with all Snort rules to detect potential malicious packets. Because the portion of malicious packets is usually small, it is not efficient to examine incoming packets with all Snort rules. In this paper, we apply two indexing methods to Snort rules, Prefix Indexing and Random Indexing, to reduce the number of rules to be examined. We also present experimental results with the indexing methods.

Keywords: Network security, indexing, pattern matching, intrusion detection system, Snort.

1   Introduction

The use of the Internet has increased tremendously in recent years and so has the volume of network traffic. Although most of the network traffic is generated for benign purpose such as web browsing, video streaming and peer-to-peer file sharing, a portion of the network traffic is malicious which might cause degradation of network performance or network based services. With the increased volume of general network traffic, intrusion detection systems based on network traffic analysis need to have very high performance to examine bypassing packets; moreover, the attacks are getting more sophisticated over time, making the detection of the attacks on the Internet difficult. Detecting the attacks on the Internet and blocking the attack traffic as fast as possible is very important to maintain a certain level of network quality of service, as these attacks can cause various problems.

Snort is an open-sourced network intrusion detection system that is widely used to detect malicious network activities. Snort provides various packet inspection methods such as signature-based detection, protocol-based detection and anomaly-based detection. The major components of Snort are: Packet Decode Engine, Detection Engine and Logging/Alert Engine. Snort contains thousands of rules that are to be examined with the contents of incoming network packets. Each Snort rule is

S. Jung and M. Yung (Eds.): WISA 2011, LNCS 7115, pp. 136–141, 2012.
© Springer-Verlag Berlin Heidelberg 2012

comprised of two fields, the header field and the option field. The header field contains information of packets such as source IP address/port number, destination IP address/port number, and so on. The option field includes Content, Message and others. The strings in the Content section are the signatures to be examined with input packets. A Snort rule can have one or more Contents.

The whole process of packet inspection with Snort is operated as follows: The packets captured by a packet sniffer are sent to the packet decode engine. The packets decoded are sent to the detection engine, to inspect the packet contents with thousands of rules stored in Snort. All Snort rules should be handled by the preprocessor before used in the detection engine. If there was a packet that has been matched with the signatures of some Snort rules, Snort considers the packet as an attack packet and handles the packet appropriately.

As described above, the detection engine in Snort basically examines incoming packets with all Snort rules; however, inspecting packet contents against every rule is a wasteful approach as the majority of packets would not contain signatures that are in the Snort rules [12]. The overall performance can be improved if the number of rules and/or the size of signatures to be examined decreases, rather than examining the whole Snort ruleset.

In this paper we suggest a technique to enhance the performance of network packet inspection with Snort. The technique includes a procedure that arranges a number of Snort rules into groups by indexing the Snort rules in an arbitrary way. With this technique, only a small portion of Snort rules are inspected and the processing time of each packet is reduced. We also present simulated results using our suggested method, which shows the efficiency of grouping Snort rules with our index selection algorithm. The rest of the paper is organized as follows: In Section 2, we explain our indexing method for grouping Snort rules. In Section 3, experimental results with the indexing method are shown. Section 4 summarizes the conclusions of the paper.

2   The Indexing Methods

In this section, we give an overview of indexing method, and explain the two indexing methods, Prefix Indexing and Random Indexing.

Chen et al. presented the relationship between the number of primary patterns and the number of Snort rules [10]. A primary pattern is a set of strings that appear repeatedly within Snort rule signatures. The result of their experiments shows that the number of primary patterns saturates at some points even though the number of Snort rules keeps increasing. This implies that classifying Snort rules with grouping methods can increase the efficiency and speed of packet inspection greatly because the size of primary patterns can be much smaller than that of entire Snort rules.

We focused on this idea and adopted the notion of grouping Snort rules by applying indexing method. Indexing is a method which is commonly used to find a certain item from a large set of data. An index is a substring which is part of a Snort rule signature. Each index points to a subset of Snort rules, which have signatures that include the index; therefore the Snort rules are arranged into several groups according to indices. Before the packet inspection stage, the rules are pre-processed to create indices and group the rules together.

One of the main issues on indexing is how to choose substrings from signatures of Snort rules when building indices. In the following paragraphs we describe the two indexing methods.

Sourdis et al. [9] proposed an index selection algorithm based on Prefix Indexing (PI). The indices for PI are determined by extracting first N bytes of strings from each Snort rule signature. To use the first N bytes as an index is efficient in cases that the beginning of rule signatures within a ruleset shares a number of common strings.

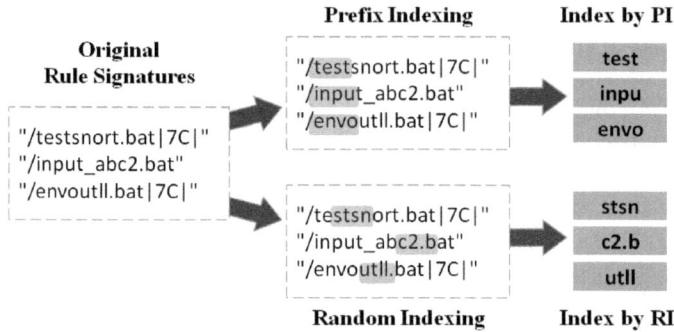

Fig. 1. Random Indexing and Prefix Indexing

While PI is the simplest way to group Snort rules with indices, grouping with other substrings that appear in the middle of Snort rule signatures could be more appropriate in some cases. Based on this intuition, we derived a naïve approach which selects indices randomly from signatures of the Snort rules. We called this naïve approach as Random Indexing (RI). RI extracts an N-byte substring from arbitrary point of Snort rule signatures. Figure 1 shows the difference between PI and RI, when applied to the same Snort ruleset.

3   Experiments

In this section, we present experimental results of the two indexing methods. We used Snort 2.9.0.0 to evaluate the effectiveness of our proposed method. Snort has a number of rule files which are divided into several categories by the types of attacks. We conducted the experiments with Web-cgi ruleset, by applying the two indexing methods. Web-cgi ruleset includes 371 rules to detect the attacks on CGI programs. The total length of signatures for the web-cgi ruleset is 4,686 bytes, with the average of 12.62 bytes per rule.

We introduce three statistical values for the performance estimation: the number of indices (NI), the average number of rules per index (ANPI) and the maximum number of rules per index (MNPI). NI refers to the size of the entire indices, which is related to the amount of strings to be examined with an input packet; therefore if NI decreases, it the packet inspection process can have better performance. ANPI is another important factor of performance as it has a close relationship with the amount of strings to be inspected; the fewer the strings, the less it takes for the deep packet inspection. We found that the appropriate value for ANPI is between 1.5 and 1.8, experimentally. MNPI has effects on the deep packet inspection time, especially for the worst case. If the size of MNPI, let's say M, is significantly large, the worst case time required for the deep packet inspection increases as the packet inspection involves at least M times of comparison to the input packet. To summarize, an indexing result with smaller MNPI, especially which has a close value to ANPI, shows the best performance in the packer inspection.

Table 1 shows the experimental results of the two indexing methods on web-cgi ruleset, where the length of each index is set to four bytes. The two methods, PI and RI show similar results in most cases. The best case of RI has the smallest MNPI, whose value is also close to ANPI; therefore the indexing with RI, in its best case, provides a fairly equally distributed result. Other results with bigger MNPI values mean that their rule groupings were biased to a certain index. If the biased index is matched, a large number of rules should be fully examined, causing longer deep packet inspection time. We will discuss the performance issues later in this section.

Table 1. Statistical values of web-cgi ruleset

Methods	PI	RI	
Values		Best	Worst
Length of Index	4	4	4
Number of Indices (NI)	209	175	133
Average Number of Rules per Index (ANPI)	1.77	2.12	2.78
Maximum Number of Rules per Index (MNPI)	13	13	53

To evaluate the performance of packet examination, we estimated the total amount of strings to be examined for an input packet, since the total number of bytes of strings is a critical factor of the performance in the attack detection process, regardless of the string matching approach being used. The smaller the total number of bytes of strings to be examined becomes, the shorter the packet examination time would be taken. We estimate the performance of the index selection algorithm, by calculating the total number of bytes of strings to be examined; we describe the calculation process of this value in the following paragraphs.

The total number of bytes of strings (TBS) is the sum of the number of bytes of all the indices (NBI) and the number of byes of signatures in the Snort rules of matched indices (NBR). NBI is the number of indices times the length of the index, as the whole indices should be examined during the inspection. NBR is the sum of the length of the rule signatures that are pointed to by matched indices. To calculate NBR, we need to know which index was matched, because only the rules that are linked to the index will be examined; however, every time the inspection proceeds, different indices will be matched according to incoming packets. There is no way to foresee the indices will be matched unless the packet inspection is actually conducted; therefore we formularized Equation 1 to estimate NBR.

$$\text{NBR} = \text{The Number of Matched Indices} \times \text{ANPI}$$

$$\times \text{The Average Length of Signatures.} \tag{1}$$

As mentioned above, it is hard to estimate the number of matched indices. To overcome this difficulty, we set the number of matched indices as a variable and conducted simulations. The simulations estimate TBS, assuming that $x\%$ of indices have been matched to an incoming packet. If we sort the indices by the number of rules per index, we can analyze the best case and the worst case. The best case is when $x\%$ of indices with the smallest number of rules were taken and the worst case is the opposite. We also calculated the average case by measuring the average of the best and worst cases. Equation (2) shows how these values are used for the simulation.

$$\text{TBS}(x) = \text{NI} \times \text{The Length of the Index} + \text{The Number of Rules for } x\% \text{ of}$$

$$\text{Indices} \times \text{The Average Length of Signatures per Rule.} \tag{2}$$

Figure 2 shows the results of the simulation for the web-cgi ruleset: Figure 2 (a) is for the average case and Figure 2 (b) is for the worst case. The Y axis represents TBS and the X axis represents the percentage of matched indices for an input packet. As can be seen in the graphs, the two index selection algorithms show better performance than the original Snort. RI shows unpredictable performance, showing two different aspects: in the best case, the performance of RI is almost equal to PI but, in the worst case, its performance is far worse than PI. This improvement is a result of having smaller MNPI. It can be said that the rules are well distributed into groups, which also implies that the amount of strings to be examined is normalized.

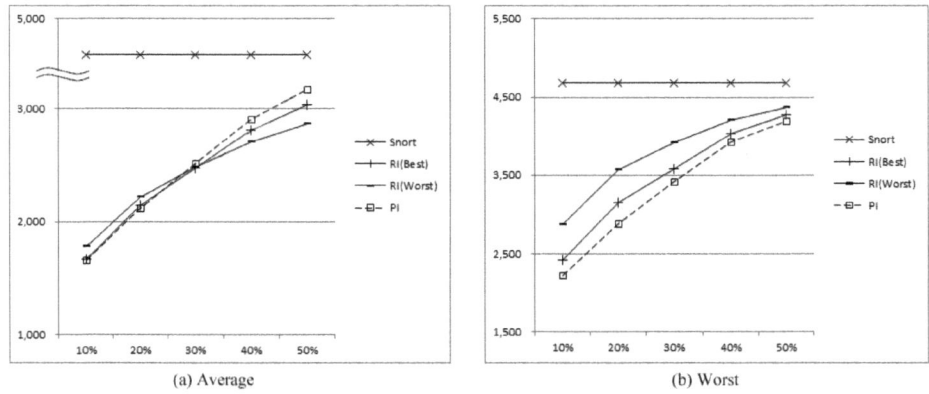

(a) Average   (b) Worst

Fig. 2. The estimation of the amount of strings to be examined for web-cgi ruleset

4   Conclusion

The importance of accurate network intrusion detection is growing over time. The common way of deep packet inspection is examining all signatures in signature-based intrusion detection systems (IDS). This approach, however, is inefficient because the majority of packets are benign. The overall performance of signature-based IDSs can be improved if the number of rules or the size of the signatures to be examined decreases. In this paper, we applied two indexing methods, Prefix Indexing and Random Indexing that extracts indices from Snort rule signatures, to reduce the number of rules to be examined. We conducted a number of experiments, which showed significant improvement to the packet inspection, reducing the number of strings to be matched to around 26% of the original Snort.

Acknowledgement. This work was supported by the Mid-career Researcher Program of the NRF grant funded by the MEST (NRF 2010-1179-000).

References

1. Tuck, N., Sherwood, T., Calder, B., Varghese, G.: Deterministic Memory-Efficient String Matching Algorithms for Intrusion Detection. In: IEEE INFOCOM (2004)
2. Peng, J., Chen, H., Shi, S.: The GPU-based string matching system in advanced AC algorithm. In: IEEE 10th International Conference on Computer and Information Technology (2010)
3. Tan, L., Sherwood, T.: A High Throughput String Matching Architecture for Intrusion Detection and Prevention. In: Proceedings of the 32nd Annual International Symposium on Computer Architecture (2005)
4. Song, T., Zhang, W., Wang, D., Xue, Y.: A Memory Efficient Multiple Pattern Matching Architecture for Network Security. In: IEEE INFOCOM (2008)
5. Yu, F., Chen, Z., Diao, Y., Lakshman, T.V., Katz, R.H.: Fast and Memory-Efficient Regular Expression Matching for Deep Packet Inspection. In: IEEE/ACM ANCS (2006)
6. Kastil, J., Korenek, J., Lengal, O.: Methodology for Fast Pattern Matching by Deterministic Finite Automaton with perfect Hashing. In: IEEE 12th Euromicro Conference on Digital System Design, Architectures, Methods and Tools (2009)
7. Bispo, J., Sourdis, I., Cardoso, J.M.P., Vassiliadis, S.: Regular Expression Matching for Reconfigurable Packet Inspection. In: IEEE International Conference on Field Programmable Technology (2006)
8. Baker, Z.K., Prasanna, V.K.: A Methodology for Synthesis of Efficient Intrusion Detection System on FPGAs. In: IEEE FCCM (2004)
9. Sourdis, I., Dimopoulos, V., Pnevmatikatos, D., Vassiliadis, S.: Packet pre-filtering for network intrusion detection. In: 2nd ACM/IEEE Symposium on Architectures for Networking and Communications Systems (ANCS), San Jose, pp. 183–192 (2006)
10. Chen, H., Summerville, D.H., Chen, Y.: Two-stage Decomposition of SNORT Rules towards Efficient Hardware Implementation. In: 7th International Workshop on Design of Reliable Communication Networks (DRCN), pp. 359–366 (2009)
11. Snort homepage, http://www.snort.org
12. Dharmapurikar, S., Lockwood, J.: Fast and Scalable Pattern Matching for Content Filtering. In: IEEE/ACM ANCS Symposium on Architectures for Networking and Communications Systems (ANCS), pp. 183–192 (2005)
13. Beale, J., Foster, J.C., Posluns, J., Caswell, B.: Snort 2.0 Intrusion Detection. Syngress Publishing, Inc. (2003)

Security Data Extraction from IEC 61850 ACSI Models for Network and System Management

Chung-Hyo Kim, Moon-Seok Choi, Seong-Ho Ju,
Yong-Hun Lim, and Jong-Mock Baek

KEPCO Research Institute, 105 Moonjiro, Yuseong-gu, Daejeon, 305-380 Korea
{ch2kim,cms96,shju1052,adsac,baekjmo}@kepco.co.kr

Abstract. The international standard IEC 62351 proposed the format of abstract data object for secure smart grid controls which is named as Network and System Management (NSM). It is devised to respond not only deliberate attacks such as cyber hacking and sabotage, but also inadvertent actions, such as operator carelessness and equipment failure. And it consists of three main parts, communication health, end system health, and intrusion detection, respectively However, the description of the abstract data object in the standard is so obscure that it is not enough to implement a complete system. Furthermore, to interact between devices and gather information for NSM in power systems, additional network protocols and devices (e.g. SNMP, IDS) should be needed, which makes the implementation more difficult. Nevertheless, mapping of three parts of NSM into detailed structure is indispensable for designing secure smart grid controls. This paper presents efficient NSM attributes extraction from data objects and logical nodes defined in IEC 61850 part 7-3 and 7-4, respectively by using Abstract Communication Service Interface (ACSI) in part 7-2. The proposed method extracts 21% of NSM from conventional protocol (IEC 61850) without any other network protocol or devices attachment. The 2nd edition was referenced for data extraction in IEC 61850 part 7-2 to 7-4.

Keywords: smart grid security, power grid security, IEC 61850, IEC 62351, network and system management.

1 Introduction

Recently the power systems are divided into two main parts, power system infrastructure and information infrastructure. As the latter automate and control the former, information infrastructure is becoming more and more a critical part in power systems. It is responsible not only for retrieving information from electrical equipment but also for putting out control commands. Furthermore, as the network of control systems in power industry are changing from the proprietary networks to public IP, information infrastructure can be mainly targeted by various ways of cyber attacks like DDoS, stuxnet. If the information infrastructure is exposed to these attacks, it is hard to prevent any type of outage.

There are several activities of important regulation and standardization relating to security in smartgrid systems. The North America Electric Reliability Corporation

S. Jung and M. Yung (Eds.): WISA 2011, LNCS 7115, pp. 142–150, 2012.

(NERC) develops and enforces reliability standards and monitors users, owners, and operators for preparedness. NERC Critical Infrastructure Protection (CIP) Cyber Security Standards CIP-002 through CIP-009 [1] provide a foundation of sound security practices across the bulk power system. The National Institute of Standards and Technology (NIST) publishes NISTIR 7628 originated from the Smart Grid Interoperability Panel (SGIP) and targets the development of a comprehensive set of cyber security requirements. The documents consists of three sub-part, Smart Grid Security Strategy, Architecture, and High-Level Requirements (Vol.1) [2], Privacy and Smart Grid (Vol.2) [3], and Supportive Analyses and References (Vol.3) [4].

However, the previous regulations or standards mainly deal with use case and policy. In respect of the implementation of secure power system (e.g. substation automation), detailed data architecture is not yet proposed except NSM in IEC 62351 part 7. To control and monitor the information infrastructure in secure, NSM like data object should be implemented in ES-ISAC[1] which totally manages the security situation and distributes security policies.

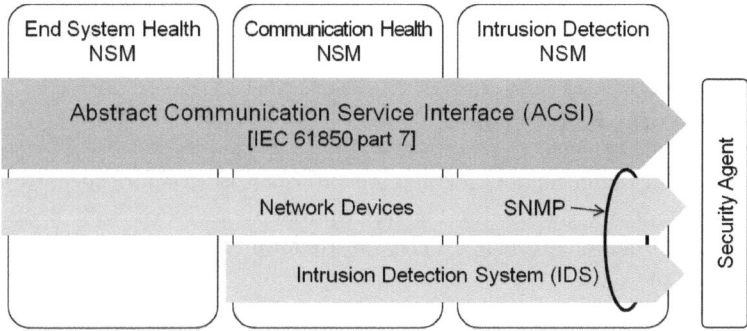

Fig. 1. NSM main components (3 boxes) and object mapping source (gray color) diagram

Fig. 1 shows NSM main components and their object mapping source. End systems may be intelligent electronic devices (IEDs), remote terminal units (RTUs), substation masters, and etc. Monitoring of these end systems consists of two detailed assessments. Internal assessments can be more precise in detecting anomalies, while external assessments can determine their state in situations in which the application or end system is not capable of assessing itself. Internal assessments can be performed by applications which directly handle the data being exchanged. External assessments must be performed by separate systems, such as gateways, proxy servers, and routers. That's why full NSM implementation needs additional network devices.

Typical network management monitors and controls the communication network configuration. Most vendors of network devices provide some degree of control. If these networks are used in power system operations, those control capabilities can be utilized. However, many communication networks used in power system operations are not configured as typical networks, and therefore do not include typical network

---

[1] ES-IAC; Electric Sector – Information Sharing and Analysis Center.

management control capabilities. Sometimes a few basic network management capabilities are included in SCADA systems, but are generally proprietary.

Intrusion detection NSM consists of six detecting parts, unauthorized access, resource exhaustion as DoS attack, buffer overflow DoS attack, tampered/malformed PDUs, physical access disruption, invalid network access, and coordinated attacks. By well formed combination of these detecting factors, NSM may deal with internal and external intrusion. [5, 6]

As described in the international standard IEC 62351 part 7, NSM are abstract data elements that need to be subsequently mapped to different protocols, including IEC 61850, IEC 60870-5, IEC 60870-6, and SNMP. To prepare in advance for secure implementation of substation automation (SA) system which will be built in Jeju Island in Korea, we mainly target the NSM mapping from IEC 61850. Of course, the information of communication and intrusion detection through SNMP from network device and IDS is also needed for full NSM mapping. However, if we extract more and more NSM factors from IEC 61850, we make the security system more easily. As the format of management information bases (MIB) should be designed for non-IEC 61850 data and more packets are transferred due to the MIBs. Therefore, the efficient extractions proposed in this paper contribute to reduce the implementation complexity.

2   NSM Data Extraction

IEC 61850 defines data models for making information structure of power systems. The model comprises classes for the description of a device with regard to data models and information exchange. The information modeling classes consist of 4 steps as shown in Fig. 2.

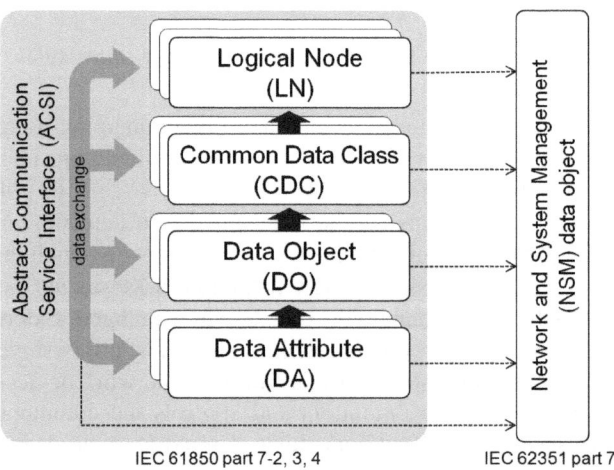

Fig. 2. Extraction (dotted line) from basic communication structure in IEC 61850 into NSM

Data Attribute (DA) is a basic element of information data which may be the lowest position of information hierarchy. Data Object (DO) provides means to define typed information, for example, position of a switch with quality information and timestamp, contained in logical nodes. Logical Node (LN) contains the information produced and consumed by a single domain-specific application function, for example, overvoltage protection or circuit breaker. Logical Device (LD) represents the information produced and consumed by a group of domain-specific application functions which is the top position of information hierarchy. [7, 8, 9]

ACSI provides two main functions, data modeling and information exchange. [10] Firstly, it defines the generic model of the utility information related DA, DO, LN, LD. Secondly, it also defines the information exchange services (SVC) between the information in the data models. To extract NSM data from IEC 61850 data models, it is of importance to understand the information hierarchy level and structure.

To extract security data, semantic relation between NSM and IEC 61850 data should be constructed. And then, related security data in IEDs are transferred to security agent in Fig. 1 by using ACSI. We analyzed them and tabulated the mappings as shown in Table 1~Table 3.

Table 1. Communication Health NSM data extraction

NSM Object	Extraction from	Description
EndLst	LPHD.PhyHealth, NumPwrUp, PwrUp, PwrDn (DO)	List of end systems connected in network
ACLLst	GSAL (LN)	Monitoring security violation regarding authorization, access control, inactive association
EndDct	LPHD.PwrUp, PwrDn (DO)	Detection of connect or disconnect of an end device
NodSet	GenDataObjectClass service (SVC)	Writing values of data object in a LN
NodRs	LLN0.LEDRs (DO)	Reset all LED, true causes reset to occur
PthLog	Log service (SVC)	Log of all path configuration changes
NodLog	Log service (SVC)	Log of all equipment status changes
TimSyncAlm	LTMS (LN)	Supervision of the time synchronization
BufOvrfAlm	LPHD.OutOv, InOv (DO)	Output and input communications buffer overflow

Table 1 depicts the mappings from IEC 61850 data models to NSM Communication Health data. The NSM object 'EndLst' has information about the list of end systems connected in network. As it manages the list, the data type has to be array. Therefore, the status, the number, and the variation of end systems are essential information to maintain 'EndLst'. By the way, Logical node LPHD in IEC 61850 part 7-4 has physical device information such as name plate, device health, in/out buffer overflow, number of power-ups/warm starts, power-up and down detections, external power supply alarm, etc. Of those values, we can extract necessary data for making 'EndLst' object. The information of device health, number of power-ups, power-up and down detections can be matched up with 'EndLst' object.

The NSM object 'ACLLst' set or update the access control list based on the list of object identifiers. It has to manage access control information with EndLst NSM described previously. As logical node GSAL (Generic Security Application) can provide the required access control data including authorization failure and inactive association information, combination of those would be a good source for making 'ACLLst' NSM. Therefore, all the information in GSAL should be transferred to security agent.

The rest five NSM Communication Health objects can be extracted as shown Table 1. Most of them get some information from data models, however, the NSM object 'NodSet' is used to set parameters and sequences for automated network actions. Therefore, the object has to employ SetDataValue service in GenDataObjectClass for IEC 61850 device or setting-value functions in SNMP for network devices.

Table 2 and Table 3 show end system health and intrusion detection NSM data extractions from IEC 61850 data models, respectively.

Table 2. End system Health NSM data extraction

NSM Object	Extraction from	Description
EndOI	LNReference (SVC)	Object Reference (identifier) of the LN
NetOILst	ITPC.EEHealth (DO)	The state of the communication channel
EndOILst	LCCH.ChLiv (DO)	Physical channel status; true if channel receives telegrams within a specified time interval
AppDatSt, DataInvAlm	Q (quality) (CDC)	Attribute Quality has validity information
CntInvAlm	opRcvd, (t)opOk (CDC)	Attribute opRcvd, (t)opOk has the information of control command validity.
NetSt, NetAlm	ITPC.LosSyn (DO)	Loss of Synchronism (No communication is possible)
AppSt	Common LN.Beh, Mod (DO)	Application behavior and mode controls
EndSt	EEHealth (DO)	Reflecting the state of external equipment
EndStrCnt	GSAL.NumCntRs (DO)	Number of counter resets
EndLog	Log service (SVC)	Log of all significant events in end system (implementation-dependent)

Table 3. Intrusion Detection NSM data extraction

NSM Object	Extraction from	Description
BufOvCnt, BufOvAlm	LPHD.OutOv & InOv (DO)	Output and input communications buffer overflow
PwrLosCnt, PwrLosAlm	LPHD.PwrSupAlm (DO)	External power supply alarm
PwrOnAlm	LPHD.PwrUp (DO)	Power-up detection
ComLosCnt	ITPC.LosSig (DO)	No signal alarm, indicate a channel problem
Syntmms, SynAlm	LTMS (LN)	Supervision of the time synchronization

3   Transferring of IEC 61850 Data to Security Agent

The previous section just shows the data mapping between NSM data object and IEC 61850 data models. To manage NSM in one system, mapped data models should be transferred to security agent with ACSI service. This section proposes the transferring methods categorized into 3 ways, single data transfer, multiple data transfer, and simple ACSI service.

3.1   Single Data Transfer through ACSI

ACSI data models have associated services to move specified data or data-set. Most of NSM data are extracted from DO as shown in Table 1~Table 3. The services to deliver DO are defined in GenDataObjectClass, and there are four services in the class, GetDataValues, SetDataValues, GetDataDirectory, and GetDataDefinition. A client, security agent in the below example, shall use GetDataValue service to retrieve value of data attribute of the referenced DO.

As shown in Fig. 3, the NSM object 'NetOILst' data are come from DO EEHealth in LN ITPC. As DO EEHealth include the communication channel states, security agent is able to manage 'NetOILst' based on the information.

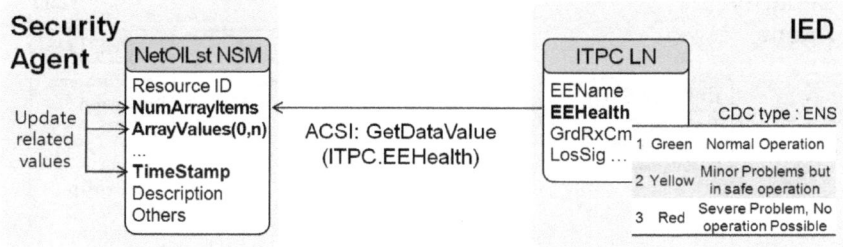

Fig. 3. Single data transfer example

Security agent, then, updates related value, number of array items (NumArrayItems), network object identifiers (ArrayValues), and recently updated time (TimeStamp).

3.2   Multiple Data Transfer through ACSI

In case that two or more DOs are necessary to build a NSM, continuous data transfer is needed for a NSM object. In ACSI, there is a data-set which is an ordered group of data object (DO, DA) references organized as a single collection for the convenience of the client. The references are called the members of the data-set. The membership and order of the object references in a data-set shall be known to both the client and the server, so that only the name of the data-set and the current values of the referenced DO and/or DA need to be transmitted. The capability thus permits more efficient use of the communication bandwidth.

As described in the Table 1, the NSM object 'EndLst' needs 4 DOs in LN LPHD. The four DOs can combine with one data-set and transmit the data with a single command service. Five services are defined in data-set class, GetDataSetValues, SetDataSetValues, CreateDataSet, DeleteDataSet, and GetDataSetDirectory. A client shall use GetDataSetValues service to retrieve the values of all referenced DOs and/or DAs. As shown in Fig. 4, the NSM object 'EndLst' data are come from a data-set having 4 DOs by GetDataSetValues service.

When a client needs some data from IED, network device, or IDS, it gets the demanded information with request-response based ACSI service. However, ACSI provides another efficient service based on event-driven report service. Buffered Report Control Block (BRCB) class supports the service that internal events (caused by trigger options data-change, quality-change, and data-update) issue immediate sending of reports or buffer the events for transmission. The data-set values are conceptually monitored by the event monitors. An event monitor determines, on the basis of the real data and the attributes of the class, when to generate a notification to the appropriate handlers. Then, the handler decides when and how to send a report to the subscribed client. By using this mechanism, clients can synchronize their databases with the current status of one or more DOs. The dotted line shows the event-driven report service.

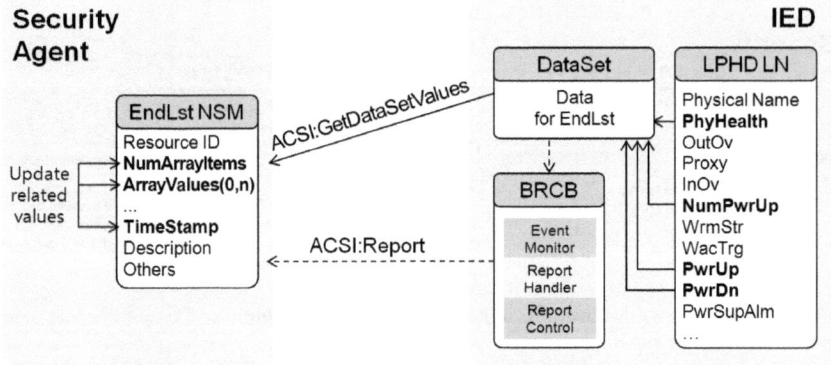

Fig. 4. Multiple data transfer example (event-driven report service is shown as dotted line)

The report service can be also applied to most ACSI class service including single data transfer. If Security Agent has to manage a data in real time, we may as well rely on event-driven services rather than request-response.

3.3   Simple ACSI

If we need complete data in LN or log service to make a NSM data, we just simply use one ACSI service, such as GetAllDataValues in GenLogicalNodeClass or log service in LogControlBlock (LCB) class.

The NSM object 'ACLLst' and 'TimSyncAlm' data should be gathered from LN GSAL and LTMS (Time Master Supervision). As the whole data in the LN have to be transferred, GetAllDataValues service of dedicated LN is enough. The NSM object 'PthLog', 'Nodlog', and 'Endlog' data can be made through log service which stores predefined data-set and retrieves them with QueryLog command in LCB.

Another services supported in ACSI can be used to organize NSM data such as Setting-Group-Control-Block, Control, and Time/Time-Synchronization class, etc. Its usages are implementation dependent.

4   Conclusions

Security by obscurity is no more valid policy nowadays. To monitor and control security factors in power system safely, it is of importance to make systematic data organization. Although abstract NSM data is the first security data frame proposed by IEC TC 57, the detail structure and format is not yet published.

In the view point of utility company, how to utilize the abstract data is the main issue. To cope with upcoming cyber attacks, we try to establish security data fundamentals in advance confirming to the standard and satisfying operational requirements. In this paper, we extracted NSM data from data models in IEC 61850 without any information in network devices. The more data extracted, the simpler the information structure is, because the same protocol usage enhances the efficiency of communication bandwidth in power grid.

Table 4. NSM Extracted rate from conventional standard

NSM part	# of NSM in IEC 62351 (A)	# of Extracted NSM from IEC 61850 (B)	Extracted Rate (A/B)
Communication Health	61	9	14.8%
End system Health	30	12	40.0%
Intrusion Detection	45	8	17.8%
Total	136	29	21.3%

Table 4 shows the result of extractions. Over 20 percent of NSM data can be mapped from IEC 61850 data models. Further works have to be done for full NSM mapping with SNMP and other protocols.

References

1. NERC, North American Reliability Corporation, Standards, Critical Infrastructure Protection (CIP), http://www.nerc.com/page.phpcid=2I20
2. NISTIR 7628, Guidelines for Smart Grid Cyber Security. Smart Grid Cyber Security Strategy, Architecture, and High-Level Requirement, vol. 1 (August 2010)
3. NISTIR 7628, Guidelines for Smart Grid Cyber Security. Privacy and the Smart Grid, vol. 2 (August 2010)

4. NISTIR 7628, Guidelines for Smart Grid Cyber Security. Supportive Analyses and References, vol. 3 (August 2010)
5. Cleveland, F.M.: IEC 62351-7: Communications and Information Management Technologies – Network and System Management in Power System Operations. In: Transmission and Distribution Conference and Exposition (2008)
6. International Electrotechnical Commission, Technical Specification, IEC/TS 62351-7 (July 2010)
7. Brunner, C.: IEC 61850 for Power System Communication, Transmission and Distribution Conference and Exposition (2008)
8. International Electrotechnical Commission, Technical Specification, IEC 61850-7-3 (December 2010)
9. International Electrotechnical Commission, Technical Specification, IEC 61850-7-4 (March 2010)
10. International Electrotechnical Commission, Technical Specification, IEC 61850-7-2 (October 2010)

Lightweight Middleware-Based ZigBee Security in Building Energy Management System[*]

Insung Hong, Jisung Byun, and Sehyun Park

School of Electrical and Electronics Engineering, Chung-Ang University,
151-756 Seoul, Korea
{axlrose11421,jinsung}@wm.cau.ac.kr,
shpark@cau.ac.kr

Abstract. Sensor networks have effects on various fields as usage of these increases. Building Energy Management System is one of the representative examples. Moreover, a variety of researches are added to the BEMS, and ZigBee is one of them. Various communication interfaces are used and tested but ZigBee security is relatively in an initial step. Furthermore, if heavyweight middleware is used in ZigBee networks, it could have influence on total system's performance. In this paper, we propose lightweight middleware to minimize load on the performance and provide security services.

Keywords: Building Energy Management System, ZigBee, Sensor Network.

1 Introduction

As the importance of energy management is increasing, the Building Energy Management System (BEMS) is also emphasized. The BEMS [1] performs not only to measure energy consumption in a building space but also collect necessary information which users need. A building space has more diverse variables compared with a home. Especially, for applying BEMS to the existing buildings, not new buildings, wireless communications are more preferred than the wired communications [2], and ZigBee is one of the wireless communications as an open global standard. Furthermore, the collected data are transferred to a central point through ZigBee, Ethernet, and PLC, and multiple network interfaces are mostly used in BEMS.

In this paper, we propose the ZigBee security in the BEMS which has compositive network interfaces. In particular, we compare normal ZigBee network security with

---

[*] This research was supported by the MKE(The Ministry of Knowledge Economy), Korea, under the HNRC(Home Network Research Center) –ITRC(Information Technology Research Center) support program supervised by the NIPA(National IT Industry Promotion Agency (NIPA-2010-C1090-1011–0010) and by the Human Resources Development of the Korea Institute of Energy Technology Evaluation and Planning (KETEP) grant funded by the Korea government Ministry of Knowledge Economy (20104010100570) and by the Ministry of Knowledge Economy(MKE) and Korea Institute for Advancement of Technology(KIAT) through the Research and Development for Regional Industry.

S. Jung and M. Yung (Eds.): WISA 2011, LNCS 7115, pp. 151–156, 2012.
© Springer-Verlag Berlin Heidelberg 2012

another in the BEMS, and analyze the difference between two networks. In the second section, the present ZigBee security protocol stack is simply described, and the properties of the BEMS and a security system in the BEMS is analyzed in the third section. We propose the lightweight middleware ZigBee security in the fourth section, and the last section is the conclusion of this paper.

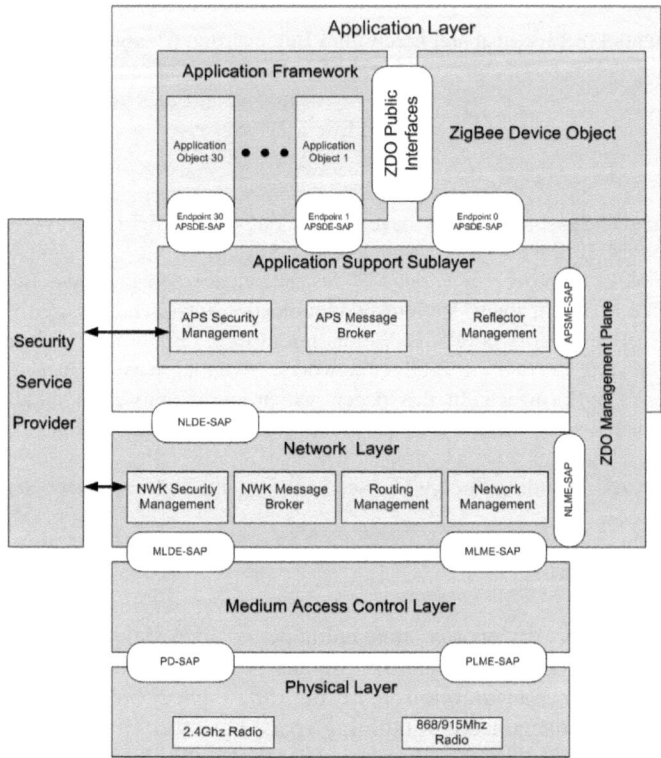

Fig. 1. ZigBee Security Protocol Stack

2   Related Work

In ZigBee network, security issues become significant in like manner to other wireless network [3]. Although ZigBee Alliance also includes a security layer, there are still problems in some cases such as over load of PAN coordinators and insecure master key in specific channels.

Fig. 1 shows the protocol stack given by the ZigBee Alliance. In Network layer and Application layer, security services are provided by the security service provider. The ZigBee security service uses symmetric key algorithm to perform a set of a secret key between two nodes and mutual certification. By using this key, it also gives security functions for data frames in MAC layer and Network layer. Although it is the most important to guarantee safety of the secret key in the symmetric key algorithm, ZigBee network has some structural disadvantages because it supposes that a trusted sensor and a node share the secret key, and the trusted sensor manage all secret keys of every node.

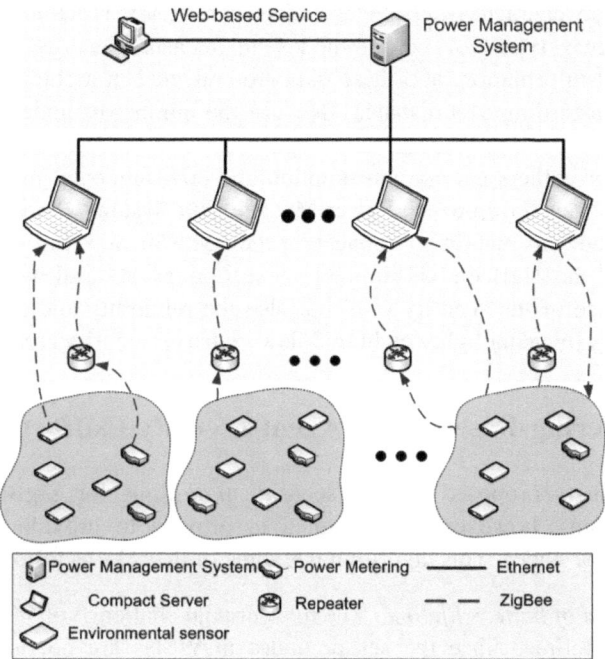

Fig. 2. Building Energy Management System Structure

3   Difference in Building Spaces

There are various required components in the BEMS. First, it includes to gather environmental information and energy measuring data, and these information and data become diverse according to a extent and types of an area [4]. Moreover, there are some closing spaces so that signal attenuation becomes serious according to the number of walls [5]. However, although there are many characteristics of a building, negative condition of wireless communications, the ZigBee communication is preferred because of suitability for sensor network.

In a building space, types of power supply in sensor nodes are various. For example, power supply of a node which provides urgent information such as fire and gas should be stable but it is permissible to use a battery for a node giving environmental information such as temperature and humidity. Furthermore, to extend battery life, low power sensor structure is preferred, and lightweight middleware is also used. The network response time according to coverage space of sensor network could be important in special cases, a fire alarm.

To summarize the described contents,

- Lightweight middleware architecture satisfying low power consumption
- Protocol structure to maximize reliability in a building space
- Optimal packet sizing for fast response time

Based on these characteristics, Fig.2 shows the BEMS structure. A gray section consists of two types of sensor nodes to measure energy consumption and environmental information, and these data are collected in a compact server directly or indirectly according to a distance. Because the number of nodes could be various depending on a coverage area, the compact server is located in each floor. Each compact server gathers energy consumption and environmental information, and the information is transferred to the Power Management System (PMS). Therefore, users can monitor the information by connecting the PMS on web. In this paper, we cover the security of the ZigBee nodes in the gray section. Most of all, we propose not only the performance of the security level but also the reliability and performance of the sensor network by using lightweight middleware based security architecture.

4   Clustering-Based Multi Agent Security Platform

Many researchers proposed various security algorithms for ZigBee based WSNs. These algorithms, however, are designed to provide to provide uniform security service to sensor nodes. This algorithm has some drawbacks as follows:

1) Reduction of battery lifetime: The most crucial challenge of WSNs is to increase the network lifetime, since the sensor nodes in WSNs are operated using a finite battery. The security algorithms which provide the same level of security service consume unnecessary battery power.

2) Low performance of security: The sensor node has limited processing, storage, and communication capabilities. So, uniform security algorithm in all sensor nodes is a waste of system resources.

In WSNs, each sensor node has a difference role such as data gathering, aggregating, routing, and processing. So, none of the sensor nodes have the necessity to provide the same level of security services. Therefore we propose multi agent security algorithms based on sensor's roles. The role of each sensor node can be defined and modified dynamically based on the application services. To enhance the efficiency, we utilize the clustering scheme. There is a cluster head and the role of sensor nodes is assigned by cluster head. The cluster head monitors status, location, sensed data, and battery capability of the sensor nodes. If the clustering scheme is employed, the cluster-head from the deployed sensor is selected, considering the node's power capability. We uses simply modified LEACH protocol for the cluster-head selection. The cluster head play a role as an agent for the security process.

Fig. 3 is the clustering-based multi agent security platform architecture.

Context Management Group (CMG) analyzes the context and generates the situational information through a reasoning process by the context analyzer (the inference engine) whose main role is to reason and decide when and which security services should be provided to a sensor node under a given situation.

Security and Authentication Management Group (SAMG) plays an important role in security service creation, security service decision, security service execution, security service configuration. Proper security services are selected by this group.

Sensor Node Management Group (SNMG) manages sensor nodes in the cluster. It transmits security algorithm bundles based on sensor's roles which are defined and modified dynamically based on the application services and sensor node situation.

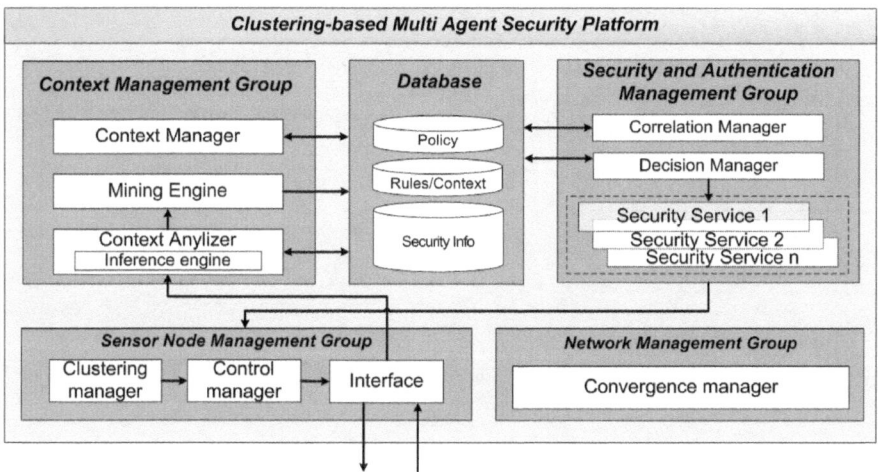

Fig. 3. Clustering-based multi agent security platform architecture

5   Conclusion

In this paper, we cover the ZigBee security in the BEMS. Actually, although researches of the BEMS have been studied, applications are few, and there is no certain standard. Moreover, it is difficult to use wired networks in the existing building, so wireless networks are preferred because of convenience of installation. Through these reasons, ZigBee is widely used in the BEMS. Therefore, we propose the ZigBee sensor network to gather environmental and energy consumption information in the BEMS, and design lightweight security middleware to have no effect on network performance.

References

1. Eastwell, A.S.: The status of BEMS. IEE Colloquium on Control in Building Energy Management Systems, 6/1–6/3 (1990)
2. Zheng, J., Lee, M.J., Anshel, M.: Toward Secure Low Rate Wireless Personal Area Networks. IEEE Transactions on Mobile Computing 5, 1361–1373 (2006)

3. Knight, M.: Wireless security – How safe is Z-wave? Computing & Control Engineering Journal 17, 18–23 (2006)
4. Virk, G.S., Cheung, J.M., Loveday, D.L.: The development of adaptive control techniques for BEMS. In: International Conference on Control 1991 (1991)
5. Nezami, M.: In-building wireless communication system design. In: Mosharaka International Conference on Communications, Computers and Applications, MICCCA, pp. ix–x (2008)

A Map-Layer-Based Access Control Model

Yingjun Zhang*, Yang Zhang, and Kai Chen

Institute of Software, Chinese Academy of Sciences,
Beijing 100190, China
{yjzhang,zhangyang,chenk}@is.iscas.ac.cn

Abstract. Access control is very important for database management systems. Although several access control models have been proposed for geographical maps, most of them are based on the concept of authorization window. If there are many complex authorizations, we have to define many windows and the processing of evaluation will be time-consuming. This paper presents a new access control model, which supports authorization on map layers. This model also supports both positive and negative authorizations, time constraint and so on. In order to compose a role's authorizations in several layers, Multicolor Combination Theory is defined here. Then we can overlay the authorization layers to map layers in authorization evaluation, which is more efficient. At last some propagation rules are defined to makes authorization simpler and more flexible. *abstract* environment.

Keywords: Access Control Model, Spatial database systems, Policy conflict, Authorization Evaluation.

1 Introduction

With the widespread development of spatial technology and geographical applications, people can observe spatial objects easily. For instance, if someone wants to find a nearest gas station from where he stays in an unfamiliar city, he can easily find it with the help of GPS, web services or other devices by putting the gas station layer onto the map. However, geographical information also discloses one's privacy. For example, the terrorists can make use of Google earth satellite images to find out sensitive position [1], which is very dangerous to states and individuals. Therefore, access control is very important for spatial database systems.

Map layers are important aspects for spatial data management, since geographical datasets in most of the databases are organized in layers. Each map is usually made up of several layers, and each layer is made up of many spatial objects. Fig.1 shows a map of 3 layers: road layer, garrison layer (which are secret) and public place layer. Using access control models of authorization window, only objects that appeared in blue rectangles will be authorized. Spatial object

---

* This work was supported by the National Natural Science Foundation of China(Grant No.60970028, No.61100226).

S. Jung and M. Yung (Eds.): WISA 2011, LNCS 7115, pp. 157–170, 2012.

can be accessed only if it is inside the window. But if the access of garrison layer is denied or there are some negative objects in the blue rectangle, we have to define more authorization windows. As a result, it costs a lot to evaluate the authorizations in all windows when processing the access request.

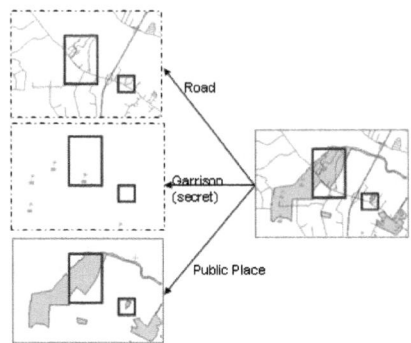

Fig. 1. Map-layer-based Authorization Model

In this paper, we present a Map-Layer-based Access control Model (MLAM). It is based on properties of layer, and the access control policies here are more flexible. Moreover, we will define some derivation rules in MLAM to simplify these policies. The main contributions of this paper are as follows: (1) giving the definition of the Map-Layer-based Access control Model, which supports positive/negative authorizations and time constraint; (2) composing all the authorizations in authorization layers for each role to make authorization evaluation easier, and coloring objects in the authorization layer differently based on Multicolor Combination Theory; (3) giving some propagation rules for authorization and evaluation, which makes authorization process flexible.

This paper is organized as follows. In Section 2, the related work is presented. In Section 3, we will introduce the basic theory. In Section 4, the MLAM model is specified. In Section 5, the derived rules are explained. In Section 6, authorization evaluation is given. In the last section conclusions and some future works are given.

2   Related Work

The traditional access control models can be classified to Discretionary Access Control (DAC), Mandatory Access Control (MAC) and Role Based Access Control (RBAC) [2]. The problem is that none of them concerns about the needs of spatial access control. Recently, several methods have been proposed to extend conventional access control models for dealing with spatial data types and models.

DAC system for geographical data has been proposed in [3,4], but it only works for raster maps (images). In this model, each spatial object is an image or part of an image. It does not support vector-based data or topological data in geographical maps. Several authorization methods of unified index are proposed later [5,6,7,8]. They are constructed using different index structures to distinct scenarios, including space, time or moving objects.

RBAC model is extended with some improvement to handle spatial and location-based information [9,10,11,12,13,14,15,16]. GEO-RBAC model proposed by Bertino et al. [10] is based on Open GIS Consortium, which handles spatial and location-based information. There are several papers about this model which extends GEO-RBAC with location-based services, mobile applications and time-based constraint [9,14,15,16]. These models concern more about location-based service and do not analyze vector data (map).

Access control models for geographical maps are mainly based on authorization window. The model proposed by Bertino [17] is an extension of discretionary access control models, and it handles vector data via Web service. In this model, the authorization will be limited inside a window, only the objects of certain features in this window will be visited. But it does not support negative authorizations. Bertino also presented an access control model for geographical maps [18], which is based on Layered Spatial Data Model (LSDM) [19]. According to various spatial representations, the object's dimensions and authorization windows, it allows a user to specify authorizations against map objects at a very fine granularity level. This model also supports both positive/negative authorization and strong/weak authorization. Another approach is based on geo-Web services [20], which are based on GeoXACML. This model gives access control restrictions in three categories, including class-based restrictions, object-based restrictions and spatial restrictions. This approach is similar to the concept of authorization window. Besides the notion of authorization window for geographical maps, in [21] a fine-grained authorization is implemented with dynamic spatial-temporal data by using the Truman Model. The model is designed as query modification on database level and supports the spatial and temporal authorization conditions.

3 Preliminaries

In order to put all authorizations of a role into several layers, we define Multicolor Combination Theory. The main idea is that giving each map layer a different color c. In authorization layer, the positive authorized regions are colored c^+ and the negative authorized regions are colored c^-. In this paper, we define $c = c^+$, which means the unauthorized regions can be seen.

Definition 1.(color combination operation $\oplus$) Giving a set $\mathbb{C}$ of colors, color combination operation $\oplus$ is to combine two colors to a new color:
$$\exists c_1, c_2, c_3 \in \mathbb{C}, c_1 \oplus c_2 = c_3$$

Each layer is given a color to differentiate the same regions in other layers. When composing a portion of space in different layers, the layer colors will be combined to a new color, which will be decomposed uniquely: $c_3 = c_1 \oplus c_2, c_1, c_2, c_3 \neq \tau \wedge c_3 \neq \zeta$.($\tau, \zeta$ are special colors, which are defined as follows.)

Definition2.(opaque color ζ) When a opaque color $\zeta \in \mathbb{C}$ is added to some regions on the map, the regions will not be seen. And opaque color can not be decomposed.
$\forall c \in \mathbb{C}, c \oplus \zeta = \zeta$

If a region is colored as opaque, nothing will be seen in this region. It means the region in all the layers is defined as negative authorization when composing. This is useful for map-based negative authorization and time constraint.

Definition3.(transparent color τ) When a transparent color $\tau \in \mathbb{C}$ is added to another layer colored c, the composed color of the layer will not change. And transparent color can not be decomposed.
$\forall c \in \mathbb{C} \wedge c \neq \zeta, c \oplus \tau = c$

Transparent color is very important for negative authorization. In addition, we define the authorization conflicts as follows: $\forall c \in \mathbb{C} \wedge c \neq \zeta, c \oplus c^- = c^+ \oplus c^- = \tau$. For example, if the access of garrison layer in figure 1 is denied, we color the authorization layer to be c_g^-. When overlaying the authorization layer onto the garrison layer, the composed color will be transparent. So the garrison layer is denied without impacting other layers. We can use Multicolor Combination Theory to define the relationship, as in Fig.2.

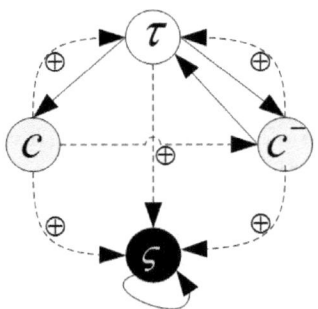

Fig. 2. Multicolor Combination Theory

Definition4.(Gcolor) The function is to get the colors of an object.
$Gcolor(o : O) \rightarrow \mathbb{C}$

Definition5.(color) The color function is to give the object o a new color c.
$color(o : O, c : \mathbb{C}) \rightarrow \mathbb{C}$.

Definition6.(super color θ) It means regions in all the map layers are positively authorized.
$\theta = \sum c_i, c_i = Gcolor(ml_i), mli \in ML.$
$\theta \oplus \zeta = \zeta$

4   Authorization Model for Geographic Data

An authorization $a \in A$ is defined as: $a =< u, o, p, < ml, c >, pt, t, al >$, where u is the authorized subject, o is the authorized object, p is the operation that can be performed by the subject on the given object, ml is the map layer which is organized base on the features of objects, c is the color of the layer, pt is authorization type(positive/negative), t is the time to constrain users' privilege, al is the authorization layer.

4.1   Subjects, Objects and Privileges

Subjects are all users that interact with the system, and users can be classified by the roles they play in the organization. One or more roles can be assigned to a user, such as administrator at work time and a user at other time etc. And each role has several privileges. In addition, there are some partial orders on R, which is called role hierarchy [2].

Definition7.(role hierarchy) Given two roles r_1 and r_2, if r_2 inherits all the privileges of r_1, it is represented as $r_2 \succeq_R r_1$.

Objects are defined as oid, $features$, or $region$. Oid is the specific spatial object. For example we want to view "Yosemite National Park" on the map. Spatial features are objects having the same properties. The region is the authorized area. The object is defined as $o \in O$, $O = \{oid, feature, region\}$. Here O means all kinds of objects, $o = *$ means all the objects; $o = \times$ indicates no object.

Definition8.(contain function) The function is defined as follows:

$$contain(a:O, b:O) \rightarrow \begin{cases} 0, a \cap b = NULL \\ 1, (a \cap b = a) \cap (a \neq b) \\ 2, a = b \\ -1, else \end{cases}$$

In MLAM, if a user is allowed to access o in one layer, he/she is allowed to access any object contained in o at this layer.

Various privileges are defined corresponding to various operations, including traditional and spatial operations. Spatial operations are important in spatial databases, like zoom-in, zoom-out, overlay, etc. Let $p \in P$, where P stands for a set of all privileges. A definition of privilege hierarchy is defined as follows:

Definition9.(privilege hierarchy) If p_1 ,$p_2 \in P$ are privileges, the privilege p_2 contains privilege p_1. Then it will be presented as $p_2 \succeq_P p_1$.

In MLAM, we support three kinds of privilege modes in authorization: viewing, modifying and downloading. The viewing mode includes viewing, zooming-in, zooming-out. The modifying mode includes inserting, deleting, updating, overlaying and so on. The downloading mode includes downloading. There are partial order relations among privileges, which means that one privilege can be derived from others. For example, if David can download a map, obviously, he can view all objects on the map. So the partial order is $download \succeq_P view$.

4.2   Map Layers

Geographical maps are often made up by layers. Each layer often presents a special property, like road, soil, etc. Images are also allowed to be added to the map, and each image is a layer. Furthermore, in order to explain it clearly, multi-resolution presentation is not considered here.

Definition10.(map layer function) In order to find out the relationship between a spatial object and its layer, we define the function as follows:
$F(o : O) \to ML$

In MLAM, when $ml = *$, it means all the layers in a map, $ml = \perp$ means it is in authorization layers, which is not in map layers. So the authorization is easy to grant.

Definition11.(map layer mapping function) In order to give each map layer one color, we define the color function as follows:
$M(ml : ML) \to \mathbb{C}$
$M^{-1}(c : \mathbb{C}) \to ML$

When users request to access some objects, first we will map the objects onto the layers, then using the mapping functions to get colors. After composing the colors with the authorized colors, the result will be given.

4.3   Authorization Layers

In addition to traditional map layers, we add authorization layers to MLAM. Each role has several authorization layers according to privilege modes. In this paper, each role has 3 authorization layers. But a user's request can be mapped to the only one authorization layer. After overlaying the authorization layer onto the map layers, the result will be the objects that are allowed to be accessed in the map.

Definition12.(authorization layer mapping function) The   relationship between roles and authorization layers are defined as follows:
$MA(r : R) \to al : AL$
$MA^{-1}(al : AL) \to r : R$

Definition 12 defines the relationship of users and authorization layers. When processing the requests, we should first find out the corresponding authorization layers.

When we compose the authorization layer, we have to color different objects differently according to their authorizations. For example in Fig.3, we give the

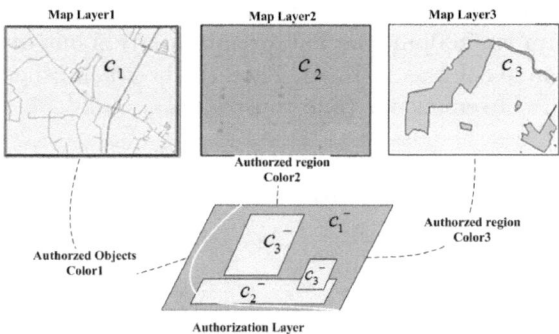

Fig. 3. The Processing of Authorized Layer

three map layers colors c_1, c_2, c_3 and the corresponding colors c_1^+, c_2^-, c_3^+ as the authorization colors. According to Definition 1, when doing authorization evaluation, c_1^+, c_2^-, c_3^+ will not impact each other.

In conclusion, with the help of authorization layers, MLAM could be more flexible and efficient, because overlaying the authorization layer to the map is more effective than comparing each object in the map with the authorizations.

4.4   Authorization Type and Time

Authorization type is used for positive and negative authorization. And time is used to constrain when a user can operate the objects.

Definition13.(authorization type pt) pt is defined as $pt \in \{+, -\}$, where $'+'$ means positive authorization and $'-'$ means negative authorization. We give precedence to negative authorization. For example, if a user has both positive and negative authorization on one object, he is still denied to access it.

In an authorization layer, if a user has a positive authorization on objects colored c, the authorization layer will be colored as c^+ for the same area. If a user has a negative one, it will be colored as c^- instead.

In MLAM, time is added, it is used to describe time periods that users are allowed to access objects. It is very useful. For example, administrators are constrained to modify map objects at work time, such as from $7:00am$ to $5:00pm$. So we can use time to constrain users.

Definition14.(time-containing function) The function of time-containing is to compare two times.

$$Tcontain(t_1, t_2) = \begin{cases} ture(if\ t_1\ is\ contained\ in\ t_2) \\ false(else) \end{cases}$$

Time is used for constraining objects. For example, if users are allowed to access maps from 7:00am to 5:00pm, the authorization layers out of this time period will be set to opaque color as in Fig.4. Then the layers in other time will not be impact. It is very convenient for time constraint.

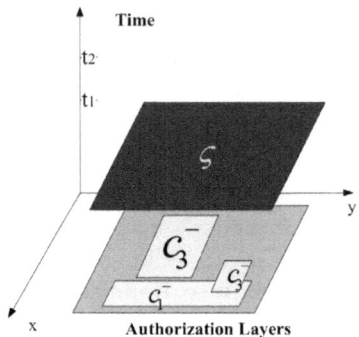

Fig. 4. Authorized Layers in Time Dimension

In conclusion, the authorization rules are defined as above. Here we will give some examples.

Example 1

$$a_1 = \langle user, *, Overlay, \langle L_R, c_R \rangle, +, t_1, al_{uM} \rangle$$
$$a_2 = \langle Admin, *, Modify, \langle *, \theta \rangle, +, \langle 7 : 00am \sim 5 : 00pm \rangle, al_{AM} \rangle$$
$$a_3 = \langle user, *, View, \langle *, \theta \rangle, +, *, al_{uV} \rangle$$
$$a_4 = \langle user, ZhongzeRoad, View, \langle L_R, c_R \rangle, -, t_3, al_{uV} \rangle$$
$$a_5 = \langle user, *, View, \langle L_M, c_M \rangle, -, *, al_{uV} \rangle$$

We give out above 5 authorization policies. The first one allows a user to overlay all the objects on road layer L_R at t_1; the second one defines that admin is allowed to modify the map from $7 : 00am$ to $5 : 00pm$; the third one defines a user is allowed to view the map at any time; a_4 is a negative one, it blocks a user to view the $ZhongzeRoad$ in rode layer L_R at t_3; the last one a_5 defines that a user is blocked to view all the data in the layer of military sites L_M at t_4. These examples show that MLAM is very flexible. Next we will define some derivation rules in order to simplify the policies.

5   Derivation Rules

We define Authorization Base (AB), so other authorizations can be derived from it. The authorization layers are composed by all authorizations when the system is initialized. Derivation among the authorizations can be derived from rules.

Definition15.(derivation relation) If authorization a_2 can be derived from a_1, we denote it as $a_1 \rightarrow a_2$. According to definitions as Section 4, there are some rules as follows:

Rule1. Let $p_2 \succeq_P p_1$, then
$$a_1 = \langle r, o, p_2, \langle ml, c_{ml} \rangle, pt, t, al_{rp_2} \rangle \rightarrow a_2 = \langle r, o, p_1, \langle ml, c_{ml} \rangle, pt, t, al_{rp_1} \rangle \rightarrow$$

$$a_2 = \begin{cases} \langle r, o, p_1, \langle \perp, c_{ml}^+ \rangle, +, t, al_{rp_1} \rangle \\ \langle r, o, p_1, \langle \perp, c_{ml}^- \rangle, -, t, al_{rp_1} \rangle \end{cases}$$

According to Definition 9, if there is partial order between p_2 and p_1, a_2 can be derived from a_1. For example, if u can download the object o, u can view o too.

Rule2. Let $r_2 \succeq_R r_1$, then
$$a_1 = \langle r_1, o_1, p_1, \langle ml_1, c_{ml_1} \rangle, pt_1, t_1, al_{r_1 p_1} \rangle \rightarrow a_2 = \langle r_2, o_2, p_2, \langle ml_2, c_{ml_2} \rangle, pt_2, t_2, al_{r_2 p_2} \rangle$$

According to Definition 7, if there are two roles r_1 and r_2, r_2 inherits all the privileges of r_1. But if there are conflicts among authorizations, we adopt some rules to solve them, like larger principle for the same privilege or negative priority principle for different privileges. For example, if r_1 is allowed to view the World map at any time and r_2 is allowed to modify the same map from 7:00am to 5:00pm, we can derive that r_2 is allowed to view the map from 7:00am to 5:00pm according to Rule1. Besides, if $r_2 \succeq_R r_1$, r_2 inherits r_1's privileges. As a result, there is a conflict that r_2 is allowed to view the map of China from 7:00am 5:00pm or at any time. In larger principle for the same privilege, we adopt that r_2 can view the map at any time. And negative priority is similar.

Rule3. Let $a_1 = \langle r, *, p, \langle ml, c_{ml} \rangle, pt, t, al_{rp} \rangle, o \in region \rightarrow$

$$a_2 = \begin{cases} \sum_{o_i \in ml} \langle r, o_i, p, \langle \perp, c_{ml}^+ \rangle, +, t, al_{rp} \rangle \\ \sum_{o_i \in ml} \langle r, o_i, p, \langle \perp, c_{ml}^- \rangle, -, t, al_{rp} \rangle \end{cases}$$

From Rule3, if a role is allowed to access one map layer, he/she can see all objects on it. It is the same for negative authorization. If r is allowed/denied to access all objects in ml, he is allowed/denied to access all objects colored c_{ml}^+ (c_{ml}^-) in the authorization layer at time t.

Rule4. Let $a_1 = \langle r, o, p, \langle *, \theta \rangle, pt, t, al_{rp} \rangle, o \in region \rightarrow a_2 = \sum_{ml_i \in ML} \langle r, o, p, \langle ml_i, c_i \rangle, pt, t, al_{rp} \rangle$

$$\rightarrow a_3 = \begin{cases} \sum_{ml_i \in ML} \langle r, o, p, \langle \perp, c_i^+ \rangle, +, t, al_{rp} \rangle \\ \sum_{ml_i \in ML} \langle r, o, p, \langle \perp, c_i^- \rangle, -, t, al_{rp} \rangle \end{cases}$$

In Rule4, based on the relationship between map and layers as Fig.1, we can easily find out that if a role is allowed to access the map, he is allowed to access all the layers of the map. So if a privilege is granted to objects in a map, it means this privilege is propagated to objects in each layer of the map. Then we color the authorization layer at that time as their match colors $< ml_i, c_i^+ >$.

Rule5. Let $obj \in O$ be all objects in a region, b_1, b_2 are two authorizations. If all objects in this region are not accessed $b_i = \sum_{obj \in O} \langle r, obj, p, \langle ml_i, c_i \rangle, -, t, al_{rp} \rangle$, then $b_i \rightarrow NULL$

$$\begin{cases} b_1 = \langle r, o_1, p, \langle ml, c \rangle, +, t, al_{rp} \rangle \\ b_2 = \langle r, o_2, p, \langle ml, c \rangle, -, t, al_{rp} \rangle \end{cases} \xrightarrow{contain(o_1, o_2) > 0}$$

$$b_2 = \langle r, o_2, p, \langle \bot, c^- \rangle, -, t, al_{rp} \rangle$$

Rule5 specifies optimization of each map layer. For instance, when there is no spatial object or there are all negative objects in the region of a specific layer, we should simply get rid of the positive authorizations in this layer. For example in Fig.1, the blue rectangles in garrison layer should be removed for more efficiency.

Rule6. Let $a_1 = \langle r, o, p, \langle ml, c \rangle, pt, t, al_{rp} \rangle \rightarrow$

$$a_2 = \begin{cases} \langle r, o, p, \langle \bot, c^+ \rangle, pt, t', al_{rp} \rangle \wedge (Tcontain(t', t) = ture) \\ \langle r, o, p, \langle \bot, \zeta \rangle, pt, t', al_{rp} \rangle \wedge (Tcontain(t', t) = false) \end{cases}$$

Rule 6 defines the relationship of time. If t' is contained in t, the authorization is effective as the map will be seen. If t' is not contained in t, the map will colored as opaque.

According to these rules, we can simplify the definition of the authorization policies and privileges, here are some examples:

Example 2

$a_1 \rightarrow a_6, a_6 = \langle user, *, view, \langle \bot, c_R^+ \rangle, +, t_1, al_{uV} \rangle$

$a_2, a_3 \rightarrow a_7, a_7 = \langle Admin, *, View, \langle *, \theta \rangle, +, *, al_{AV} \rangle$

$a_1 \rightarrow a_8, a_8 = \langle user, ZhongzeRoad, View, \langle \bot, c_R^+ \rangle, +, t_1, al_{uV} \rangle$

$a_3 \rightarrow a_9, a_9 = \langle user, *, View, \langle \bot, c_M^+ \rangle, +, *, al_{uV} \rangle$

$a_3 \rightarrow a_{10}, a_{10} = \langle user, *, View, \langle *, \theta \rangle, +, \langle 9:00am \sim 12:00am \rangle, al_{uV} \rangle$

$a_5, a_9 \rightarrow a_5$

Base on a_1 and Rule1, we can tell that a user can view all objects on L_R at t_1. From a_2, a_3 and Rule2, admin is allowed to view the map at any time. From a_1 and Rule3, a user is allowed to view all objects (eg.ZhongzeRoad) on L_R at t_1. According to a_3 and Rule4 a user is allowed to access all the layers on the map, like L_M. In a_3 and Rule6, a user is allowed to view the map at any time, including $\langle 9:00am \sim 12:00am \rangle$.The last one is conflicts between a_5 and a_9. We adopt the negative priority principle.

According to the definitions and rules above, the authorizations in MLAM are more flexible and efficient. Moreover, the authorization layers make authorization evaluation easily, and it can be extended to spatial databases easily.

6   Authorization Evaluation

When a user requests to access geographical objects in geographical maps, the access control mechanism must evaluate whether such request is granted.

We define the access request by a user: $rq = \langle u, ob, pr, t_n \rangle$, where $u \in U$ is a subject, $o \in O$ is an object which can be one of the following: a set of objects *oids*; or *features* of objects with the same properties; or a *region*; and $p \in P$ is a privilege mode, t_n is the time to send request.

According to Definition 1, the composed color can only be decomposed in one way. So the colors on authorization layer can be separated when doing authorization evaluation, and do not impact other layers. Fig.5 is the architecture of the system, which shows the process of access control. Firstly, a user sends an access request to visit geographical objects in a map, then the access control module verifies it. This verification is implemented by Authorization Evaluation Model. In Authorization Evaluation Model, authorization layers contain all the authorized information, which is based on authorization base and its derived rules. Authorization Evaluation Model verifies the request by composing authorized layers onto the map layers. If there is no relevant authorization, the request is allowed, or else it is denied.

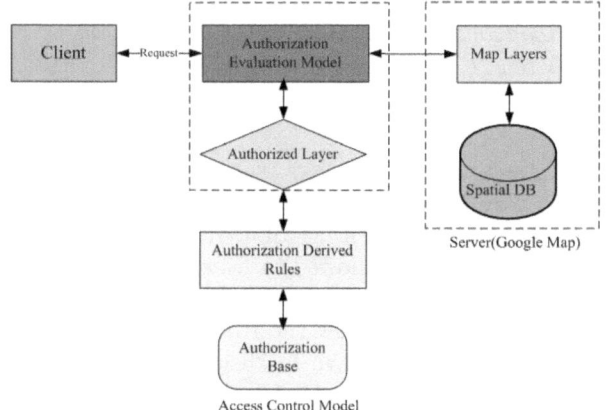

Fig. 5. The System Architecture

In order to verify the request according to authorizations and to add the time constraints, we have to introduce algorithms in detail. ALGORITHM 1 is used to make up the authorization layer. According to Multicolor Combination Theory, we can color each map layer differently. Then we add each layer's authorizations to the authorization layers. When we combine it to the map, it will show the allowed area in the map. When the requesting time is out of allowed time, we will combine opaque color to the authorization layer.

ALGORITHM2 is the evaluation processing. When a user gives his request, the authorization evaluation model will check it using the authorization layers. After checking all the colors of the request's area in authorization layers, the request will be allowed or denied. We will give some example of authorization evaluation as follows.

ALGORITHM 1	ALGORITHM 2
$Input: A, \mathbb{C}, ML$ $al = MA(rq.u)$ $for\ each\ a_j \in A$ $\quad ml_j = F(a_j.o);\quad c_j = M(ml_j)$ $\quad if\,(contain(al.o, a_j.o) > 0)\{$ $\qquad if\,(a_j.pt == -)\{color(al.o, Gcolor(al.o) \oplus c_j^-);\ break;\}$ $\qquad else\ if\,(a_j.pt == +)\{$ $\qquad\quad color(al.o, Gcolor(al.o) \oplus c_j^+);\ break;\}\}$ $for\ each\ time\ layer\ tl_k$ $\quad if\,(tcontain(t, a.time) == 0)$ $\qquad color(tl_k, \varsigma)$ $return$	$judge(rq)$ $Input: rq$ $al = MA(rq.u)$ $ml = F(rq.ob)$ $c = M(ml)$ $overlay(ml, al)$ $//overlay\ the\ al\ to\ ml$ $\mathbb{C}_n = Gcolor(rq.ob\ in\ al\,)$ $//find\ all\ colors\ in\ al$ $for\ each\ c_n \in \mathbb{C}_n$ $//check\ each\ authorization$ $\quad if\,(c_n \oplus c == \tau)$ $\qquad color(rq.ob, \tau)$ $return$

Example 3

$$rq_1 = (Alice, Road, overlay, T_{na})$$
$$rq_2 = (Bob, *, View, T_{nb})$$
$$rq_3 = (Cathy, L_R, view, T_{nc})$$
$$Alice, Bob \in user, Cathy \in Admin$$

Suppose that *Alice* wants to overlay *Road* in the map. According to a_1 and Rule6, if $Tcontain(T_{na}, t_1) = 1$, it is allowed; we can find out that except *ZhongzeRoad*, the whole map is allowed to be viewed according to a_3, but *Bob* is refused to view the military layer L_M and *ZhongzeRoad*, because of a_3 and a_5 ; *Cathy* is admin, and she can view the road layer L_R except *ZhongzeRoad* based on a_4 and a_7. We do not have to discuss how to handle the comparison of geographical objects in maps in this paper, it is handled by Spatial Database.

7   Conclusion and Future Work

This paper proposes a Map-Layer-based Access control Model for geographical maps, which is based on map layers and supports positive and negative authorization, time constraint and so on. In addition, authorization layers are defined, which are composed by authorized objects based on Multicolor Combination Theory. The authorization process simplified as overlaying the authorization layers onto the map, which is much more efficient than traditional methods. We also define some rules to derivate authorizations, which can make the policies more flexible and simple.

Our future plan is to develop some efficient techniques for authorization administration, and to extend MLAM to multi-resolution geographical data.

References

1. Google Earth accused of aiding terrorists (December 2008),
   http://www.cnbeta.com/articles/71154.htm
2. Sandhu, R.S., Coyne, E.J., Feinstein, H.L., Youman, C.E.: Role-based access control models. Computer 29, 38–47 (1996)
3. Chun, S.A., Atluri, V.: Protecting privacy from continuous high-resolution satellite surveillance. In: Proceedings of the IFIP TC11/ WG11.3 Fourteenth Annual Working Conference on Database Security: Data and Application Security, Development and Directions (2000)
4. Atluri, V., Chun, S.A.: An authorization model for geospatial data. IEEE Transactions on Dependable and Secure Computing 1, 238–254 (2004)
5. Atluri, V., Mazzoleni, P.: A uniform indexing scheme for geo-spatial data and authorizations. In: Proceedings of the 16th IFIP WG 11.3 Conference on Data and Application Security, pp. 207–218 (2002)
6. Atluri, V., Guo, Q.: STAR-Tree: An index structure for efficient evaluation of spatiotemporal authorizations. IFIP, vol. 144, pp. 31–47 (2004)
7. Atluri, V., Guo, Q.: Unified Index for Mobile Object Data and Authorizations. In: de Capitani di Vimercati, S., Syverson, P.F., Gollmann, D. (eds.) ESORICS 2005. LNCS, vol. 3679, pp. 80–97. Springer, Heidelberg (2005)
8. Atluri, V., Shin, H., Vaidya, J.: Efficient security policy enforcement for the mobile environment. Journal of Computer Security 16(4), 439–475 (2008)
9. Chandran, S.M., Joshi, J.B.D.: loT-RBAC: A location and time-based RBAC model. In: Ngu, A.H.H., Kitsuregawa, M., Neuhold, E.J., Chung, J.-Y., Sheng, Q.Z. (eds.) WISE 2005. LNCS, vol. 3806, pp. 361–375. Springer, Heidelberg (2005)
10. Damiani, M.L., Bertino, E., Catania, B., Perlasca, P.: GEO-RBAC: a spatially aware RBAC. ACM Transactions on Information and System Security 10 (2007)
11. Kumar, M., Newman, R.E.: STRBAC-An approach towards spatio-temporal role-based access control. Communication, Network, and Information Security, 150–155 (2006)
12. Aich, S., Sural, S., Majumdar, A.K.: STARBAC: Spatiotemporal Role Based Access Control. In: OTM Conferences (2007)
13. Atluri, V., Chun, S.A.: A geotemporal role-based authorisation system. International Journal of Information and Computer Security 1, 143–168 (2007)
14. Damiani, M.L., Bertino, E., Perlasca, P.: Data security in location-aware applications: an approach based on RBAC. International Journal of Information and Computer Security 1, 5–38 (2007)
15. Ray, I., Toahchoodee, M.: A Spatio-Temporal Role-Based Access Control Model. In: Barker, S., Ahn, G.-J. (eds.) Data and Applications Security 2007. LNCS, vol. 4602, pp. 211–226. Springer, Heidelberg (2007)
16. Damiani, M.L., Silvestri, C.: Towards movement-aware access control. In: Proceedings of the SIGSPATIAL ACM GIS 2008 International Workshop on Security and Privacy in GIS and LBS (2008)
17. Bertino, E., Damiani, M.L., Momini, D.: An access control system for a web map management service. In: RIDE 2004 Proceedings of the 14th International Workshop on Research Issues on Data Engineering: Web Services for E-Commerce and E-Government Applications (2004)
18. Belussi, A., Bertino, E., Catania, B., Damiani, M.L., Nucita, A.: An authorization model for geographical maps. In: GIS 2004 Proceedings of the 12th Annual ACM International Workshop on Geographic Information Systems (2004)

19. Belussi, A., Catania, B., Bertino, E.: A reference framework for integrating multiple representations of geographical maps. In: GIS 2003 Proceedings of the 11th ACM International Symposium on Advances in Geographic Information Systems (2003)
20. Matheus, A.: Declaration and enforcement of fine-grained access restrictions for a service-based geospatial data infrastructure. In: SACMAT 2005 Proceedings of the Tenth ACM Symposium on Access Control Models and Technologies (2005)
21. van Velden, B.J., Voorbij, J.B., Breure, L.: Authorized access to dynamic spatial-temporal data using the Truman Model. Department of Information and Computing Sciences. Utrecht University, Utrecht (2007)

Application Authentication for Hybrid Services of Broadcasting and Communications Networks

Go Ohtake and Kazuto Ogawa

Japan Broadcasting Corporation
1-10-11 Kinuta, Setagaya-ku, Tokyo 157-8510, Japan
{ohtake.g-fw,ogawa.k-cm}@nhk.or.jp

Abstract. Broadcasting and communications networks can be used together to offer hybrid broadcasting services that incorporate a variety of personalized information from communications networks in TV programs. To enable these services, many different applications have to be run on a user terminal, and it is necessary to establish an environment where any service provider can create applications and distribute them to users. The danger is that malicious service providers might distribute applications which may cause user terminals to take undesirable actions. To prevent such applications from being distributed, we propose an application authentication protocol for hybrid broadcasting and communications services. Concretely, we modify a key-insulated signature scheme and apply it to this protocol. In the protocol, a broadcaster distributes a signing key to a service provider that the broadcaster trusts. As a result, users can verify that an application is reliable. If a signed application causes an undesirable action, a broadcaster can revoke the privileges and permissions of the service provider. In addition, it can update the signing key. That is, our protocol is secure against leakage of the signing key by the broadcaster. Moreover, a user terminal uses only one verification key for verifying a signature, so the memory needed for storing the verification key in the user terminal's is very small. With our protocol, users can securely receive hybrid services from broadcasting and communications networks.

Keywords: hybrid services of broadcasting and communications networks, application authentication, ID-based signature, key-insulated signature.

1 Introduction

1.1 Background

Several hybrid services combining the functionalities and resources of broadcasting and communications networks have been developed. Hulu[TM] [12] in the US is an online video service that offers TV programs and movies through the Internet. All content is provided by broadcasters, such as NBC, FOX, and ABC, and movie companies. HbbTV[®] [11] is a pan-European initiative aimed at harmonizing broadcast and broadband delivery of entertainment through digital

S. Jung and M. Yung (Eds.): WISA 2011, LNCS 7115, pp. 171–186, 2012.

TVs and set-top boxes. Its services include video on demand (VoD) as well as program-related services such as digital text and electronic program guides (EPGs). The founding members of the HbbTV consortium consist of European television broadcasters and consumer electronics companies. YouView [13] in the UK is a hybrid service that offers high-definition TV, catch-up TV, and Internet services such as YouTube and Facebook through digital TVs and set-top boxes. YouView is jointly being developed by broadcasters (BBC, ITV, Channel 4, and Channel 5) and information and communication companies (TalkTalk, BT, and Arqiva). Korean broadcasters (KBS, MBC, SBS, and EBS) are in the midst of preparing Open Hybrid TV (OHTV) [6], a service which combines terrestrial digital TV and Internet. They are cooperating with TV manufacturers, such as Samsung Electronics, LG Electronics, and Net&TV, and academia in standardization of OHTV. In OHTV, broadcasters provide users with services such as advanced EPGs, VoD, video bookmarking, advertising, etc. In Japan, NHK is developing Hybridcast ^{TM} [7], which will leverage communications networks to enhance existing digital broadcasting services in various aspects such as customization, social networking, related program recommendations, and collaboration with portable devices.

Hybrid services have to run many applications on a user terminal. Moreover, to offer more attractive services to users, it is necessary to establish an environment in which any service provider can create applications and distribute them to users. However, malicious service providers might distribute applications that cause the user terminal to take undesirable actions. To thwart such malicious service providers and assure users that they can use an application securely, *application authentication* can be used to verify that an application originated from a trusted service provider and has not been modified in any way.

Generally, a digital signature scheme is used for application authentication purposes. That is, a service provider signs an application by using its signing key and distributes it to user terminals. The user terminals receive it and verify the signature by using the corresponding verification key. The trouble is that if the signing key is leaked to an adversary, he or she can easily impersonate the service provider. To prevent this from happening, it must be easy to update the signing key. If malicious service providers give user terminals signed applications that cause undesirable actions to occur, the service provider's privileges and permissions must be revoked by using the Certificate Revocation List (CRL). Since hybrid services will likely have a large number of service providers, a countermeasure must take into account the ease of signing key updates, the need for efficient transmission of the huge CRL, and the huge memory taken up by storing the verification key in a user terminal.

1.2   Our Contribution

We propose an application authentication protocol for hybrid services of broadcasting and communications networks. For this purpose, we modified the key-insulated signature (KIS) scheme [3,5,8] and applied it to this protocol. Concretely, the temporal identity for a service provider is calculated with a time period that denotes the valid time for a single signing key and the provider's real identity. We consider the temporal identity to be a time period in the key insulated signature scheme and construct a modified key-insulated signature scheme. The integrity of two dimensions, i.e., the time period and provider identity, enables us to simplify the structure of the CRL. That is, we make it so that the size of the CRL is not in proportion with the number of revoked providers. A broadcaster distributes the provider's signing keys to the providers whom the broadcaster trusts. Through the protocol, users can verify that an application is reliable. A user terminal uses only one verification key for verifying signatures, so the memory needed for storing the verification key in a user terminal is very small. If a signed application causes some undesirable action, a broadcaster can easily revoke the privileges and permissions of the service provider by setting the service provider's identity in the CRL. When a broadcaster updates a signing key for a service provider, it transmits a partial key used for signing key updates to the service provider. This means our protocol enables broadcasters to update signing keys online. In hybrid services, a broadcaster can use broadcast channels, such as the airwaves, as secure channels for distributing a large amounts of data to users simultaneously. Our protocol is more suitable for hybrid services than for Internet services since a broadcaster can distribute the verification key and a CRL to users through the secure and efficient broadcast channels. By using our application authentication protocol, users can securely receive hybrid broadcasting and communications services.

2 Model

Generally, there are two models for authentication using a digital signature scheme: one model is where a signer generates a pair of signing and verification keys and distributes the verification key to a verifier, and the other model is where a certain authority (manager) generates the key pair and distributes the signing key to a signer and the verification key to a verifier. Figures 1 and 2 show these two application authentication models for hybrid services. In each model, a service provider transmits an application to a user terminal through the Internet in answer to a user request. The service provider adds its signature to the applications and transmits them to the user. The user can verify the signature with the corresponding verification key in the user terminal and make sure that the application originated from the service provider and has not been modified in any way.

Figure 1 shows the model where the service provider generates signing and verification keys. For example, the model can use the Public Key Infrastructure (PKI). The service provider generates a pair of keys and gets a certificate corresponding to the verification key from a Certificate Authority (CA), which is a trusted third party. Service providers A and B get certificates corresponding to their verification keys from the CA. On the other hand, service provider C does not have a certificate. Service providers A and B can add their signature to applications with their signing key, so the user terminal can verify the

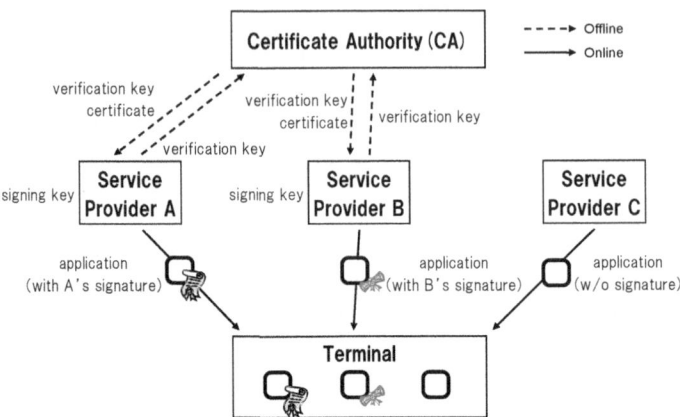

Fig. 1. Application authentication model in hybrid services of broadcasting and communications networks (service provider generates keys)

signatures by using their verification keys with the certificates and make sure that the service provider certified by the CA has made a signed application.

Figure 2 shows the model where the broadcaster generates a pair of signing and verification keys. The broadcaster distributes the signing key to only a trusted service provider in advance. The difference from Fig. 1 is that only one entity generates the key pair. The broadcaster distributes signing keys to service providers A and B, which are trusted, but it does not distribute one to service provider C, which is not trusted. The subsequent processes of service providers A, B, and C are the same as those of Fig. 1. The service providers certified by the broadcaster make signed applications.

3   Requirements

To perform application authentication securely and efficiently in hybrid services, the following requirements should be satisfied.

(1) *Verify a signature with only one verification key*
A verification key must be stored in a user terminal to verify a signature. However, in the general signature scheme used in PKI (e.g. RSA signature), all of the verification keys of the service provider must be stored in the user terminal. If the number of service providers were to grow in the future, the memory needed for storing verification keys may be huge. Therefore, a signature should be able to be verified with only one verification key.

(2) *Revoke a service provider efficiently*
If a malicious service provider posts an application which causes a user terminal to take an undesirable action, the broadcaster must revoke the service provider's privileges and do so efficiently.

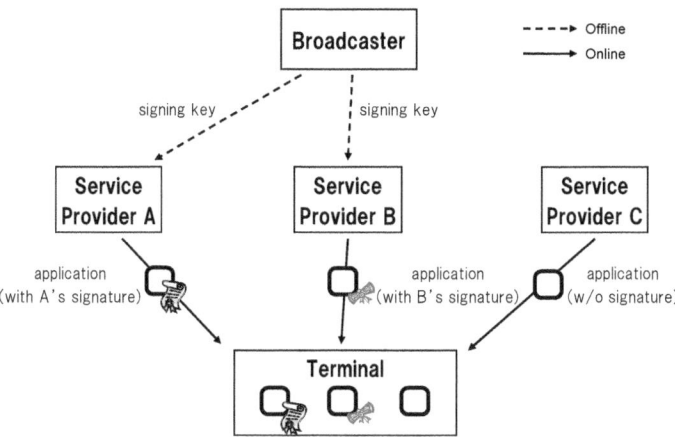

Fig. 2. Application authentication model in hybrid services of broadcasting and communications networks (broadcaster generates keys)

(3) *Update a signing key easily*

Although a service provider must manage its signing key securely, the signing key might nonetheless be leaked to an adversary as the result of a server attack. Therefore, the signing key must be easy to be updated.

In the model shown in Fig. 1, the CA certifies the relation between a service provider and its verification key, which means that a verification key is assigned to each service provider. Thus, the model shown in Fig. 1 does not satisfy requirement (1) since a user terminal must hold all of the verification keys for the service providers. We thus will consider only the model shown in Fig. 2 in the following.

4   Generic Construction of Application Authentication from IBS and KIS

In the model shown in Fig. 2, the broadcaster distributes a different signing key to each service provider. Moreover, it has to distribute only one verification key to users, as per requirement (1) in Sect. 3. The ID-based signature (IBS) scheme [9,2,1,10,4] and key-insulated signature scheme [3,5,8] can satisfy the above requirement. That is, these two schemes have one verification key for many signing keys. Therefore, we applied these schemes to application authentication. We first review the above signature schemes and then describe two generic constructions of the application authentication protocol applying each signature scheme to the model of Fig. 2.

4.1 ID-Based Signature Scheme

ID-based signature scheme [9,2,1,10,4] consists of the following four polynomial-time algorithms (Setup, Extract, Sign, Vrfy).

Setup: This is a probabilistic algorithm that takes as input a security parameter 1^k. It returns a verification key vk and a master key msk.

Extract: This is a probabilistic algorithm that takes as inputs msk, vk, and a user identity ID. It returns the corresponding signing key sk_{ID}.

Sign: This is a probabilistic algorithm that takes as inputs sk_{ID} and a message M. It returns a signature σ.

Vrfy: This is a deterministic algorithm that takes as inputs vk, ID, M, and σ. It returns a bit b, where $b = 1$ means that a signature is accepted.

In this scheme, a trusted authority issues a signing key corresponding to a user identity and only one verification key for the system. The verification key vk can be a common system parameter. A user identity is used for verifying a signature.

4.2 Key-Insulated Signature Scheme

Key-insulated signature scheme [3,5,8] consists of the following five polynomial-time algorithms (Gen, Upd*, Upd, Sign, Vrfy).

Gen: This is a probabilistic algorithm that takes as inputs a security parameter 1^k and the total number of time periods N. It returns a verification key vk, a master key SK^*, and an initial signing key SK_0.

Upd*: This is a probabilistic algorithm that takes as inputs SK^* and indices i and j for time periods (we assume that $1 \leq i, j \leq N$). It returns a partial key $SK'_{i,j}$.

Upd: This is a deterministic algorithm that takes as inputs indices i and j, a signing key SK_i for time period i and $SK'_{i,j}$. It returns a signing key SK_j for time period j.

Sign: This is a probabilistic algorithm that takes as inputs a index j, a message M, and SK_j. It returns a signature $\langle j, s \rangle$ consisting of an index j for a time period and a signature s.

Vrfy: This is a deterministic algorithm that takes as inputs M, $\langle j, s \rangle$, and vk. It returns a bit b, where $b = 1$ means that the signature is accepted.

In this scheme, a signer updates his or her signing key by using a time period. Therefore, a signing key has an expiration time and the damage caused by signing key leakage can be limited to being within a particular time period. Moreover, the corresponding verification key does not need to be updated even if the signing key is updated.

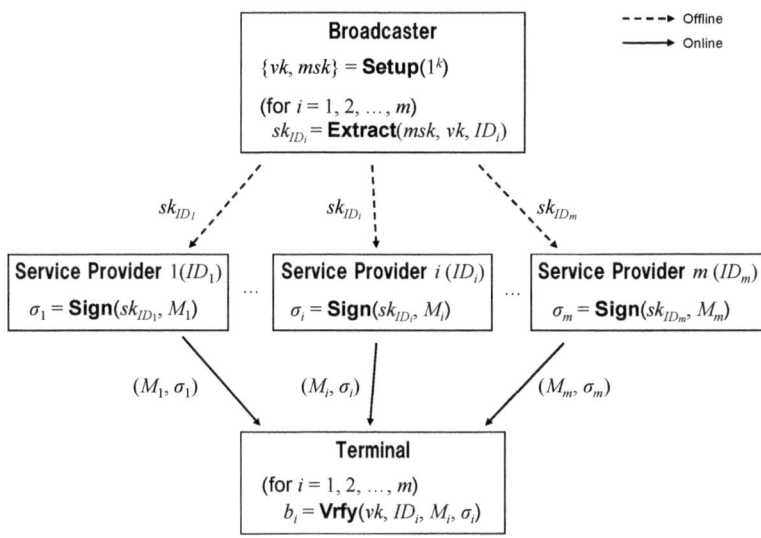

Fig. 3. Application authentication protocol using ID-based signature

4.3 Generic Construction from ID-Based Signature Scheme

Figure 3 shows a generic construction of an application authentication protocol using an ID-based signature scheme in the model of Fig. 2. A broadcaster runs Setup and generates a verification key vk and a master key msk. The verification key vk is published. The broadcaster runs Extract(msk, vk, ID_i) and distributes a signing key sk_{ID_i} for a trusted service provider i offline (ID_i, $i = 1, 2, ..., m$). The service provider i runs Sign(sk_{ID_i}, M_i) for an application M_i and transmits the signed application (M_i, σ_i) to user terminals. The user terminals receive it and run Vrfy(vk, ID_i, M_i, σ_i).

In Fig. 3, a user terminal needs only one verification key vk for application authentication. Therefore, requirement (1) is satisfied. When revoking the privileges of service providers, a broadcaster creates a CRL including identities for the service providers whose privileges a broadcaster wants to revoke and then distributes the CRL to all user terminals. A user terminal checks the CRL before it verifies the received signature. If the signature is created by a service provider in the CRL, the terminal can determine that the signature is invalid. Thus, requirement (2) is satisfied. However, when updating a signing key, a broadcaster must assign a new identity to each service provider, run Extract to generate the corresponding signing key, and distribute it to each service provider offline. This process incurs a heavy load. Therefore, requirement (3) is not necessarily satisfied.

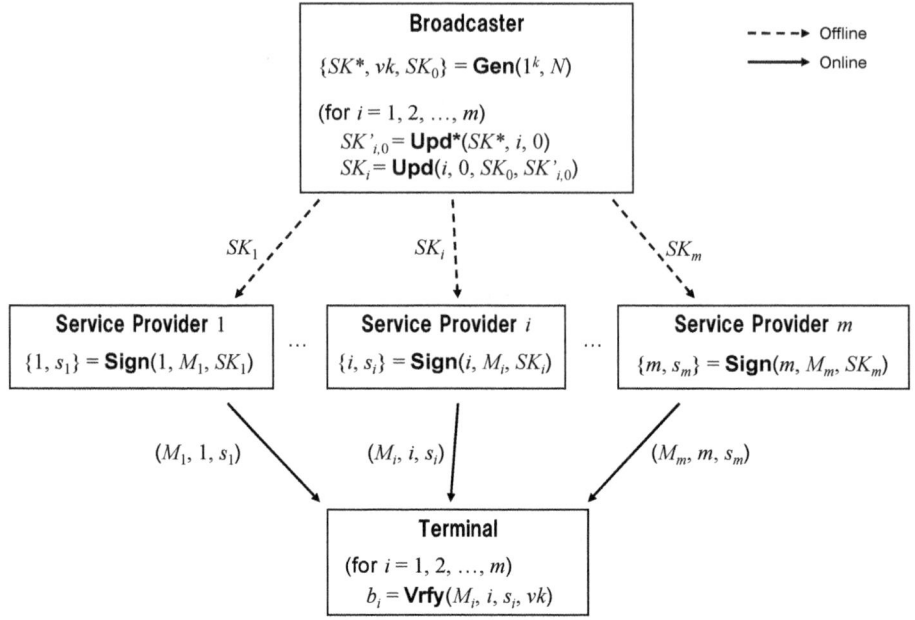

Fig. 4. Application authentication protocol using key-insulated signature

4.4 Generic Construction from Key-Insulated Signature Scheme

Figures 4 and 5 show a generic construction of an application authentication protocol using a key-insulated signature scheme in the model of Fig. 2. The time period i in a key-insulated signature scheme is used as a temporal identity for a service provider. A broadcaster runs Gen and generates a master key SK^*, a verification key vk, and an initial signing key SK_0. The verification key vk is published. Then, the broadcaster runs $\mathsf{Upd}^*(SK^*, i, 0)$ to create a partial key $SK'_{i,0}$ and $\mathsf{Upd}(i, 0, SK_0, SK'_{i,0})$ to create a signing key SK_i, and it distributes the signing key to a trusted service provider i offline, where $i = 1, 2, ..., m$ and $m \leq n$ (m is the number of current service providers and n is the maximum number of service providers). When adding a trusted service provider i ($m < i \leq n$), the broadcaster runs $SK'_{i,0} = \mathsf{Upd}^*(SK^*, i, 0)$ and $SK_i = \mathsf{Upd}(i, 0, SK_0, SK'_{i,0})$ to create a signing key SK_i, and it distributes the signing key to the service provider offline. When a service provider i distributes an application M_i to users, it runs $\mathsf{Sign}(i, M_i, SK_i)$ to create a signature $\langle i, s_i \rangle$ and transmits the signed application (M_i, i, s_i) to the user terminals. The user terminals receive it and run $\mathsf{Vrfy}(M_i, i, s_i, vk)$.

To update a service provider's signing key, the broadcaster generates the temporal identity for the service provider by using two-dimensional elements of the

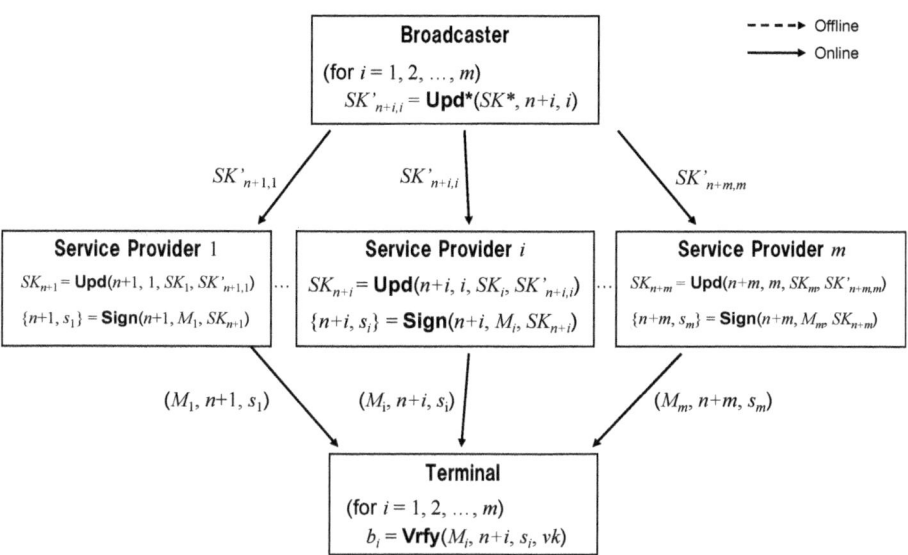

Fig. 5. Application authentication protocol using key-insulated signature (signing key update)

time period and the real identity. That is, the temporal identity for a service provider is

$$i_t = t \times n + i$$

where $t = 1, 2, \ldots$ is the time period and i is the real identity of a service provider. Figure 5 shows the flow of updating a signing key SK_i for a service provider i ($i = 1, 2, \ldots, m$) to a new signing key SK_{n+i} (in the case of $t = 1$). Signing key updates are performed for all service providers. The broadcaster runs $\mathsf{Upd}^*(SK^*, n + i, i)$ to create a partial key $SK'_{n+i,i}$ ($i = 1, 2, \ldots, m$) and transmits it to a service provider i. The service provider i then runs $\mathsf{Upd}(n + i, i, SK_i, SK'_{n+i,i})$ to create a new signing key SK_{n+i}. When distributing an application M_i to a user, the service provider i runs $\mathsf{Sign}(n + i, M_i, SK_{n+i})$ to create a signature $\langle n+i, s_i \rangle$ and transmits the signed application $(M_i, n + i, s_i)$ to a user terminal. The user terminal receives it and runs $\mathsf{Vrfy}(M_i, n + i, s_i, vk)$.

In Figs. 4 and 5, a user terminal needs only one verification key vk for application authentication. Therefore, requirement (1) is satisfied. When revoking service providers, a broadcaster creates a CRL including the identities of the service providers whose privileges a broadcaster wants to revoke. The broadcaster then distributes the CRL to all user terminals. For example, to update signing keys $SK_1, SK_2, \ldots, SK_m$ to $SK_{n+1}, SK_{n+2}, \ldots, SK_{n+m}$ as shown in Fig. 5, the broadcaster sets

$$CRL = \{n\}$$

so that the old signing keys SK_1, SK_2, ..., SK_m cannot be used[1]. Here, the first element, n, of the CRL means that the privileges of all service providers i ($i \leq n$) are revoked. When revoking the privileges of particular service providers, the broadcaster sets the identities of the service providers as the subsequent elements of the CRL. For example, to revoke the privileges of service providers k and l ($1 < k < l < m$), the broadcaster sets

$$CRL = \{0, k, l\}.$$

and does not transmit a partial key to them during the next signing key update so that they cannot update their signing keys. Therefore, requirement (2) is satisfied. Moreover, as shown in Fig. 5, a signing key can easily be updated since the broadcaster only has to distribute a partial key to a service provider online and does not have to distribute a new signing key to a service provider offline. Thus, requirement (3) is satisfied.

Remark 1. In the above generic construction, the broadcaster runs $\mathsf{Upd}^*(SK^*, i, 0)$ to create a partial key $SK'_{i,0}$ and $\mathsf{Upd}(i, 0, SK_0, SK'_{i,0})$ to create a signing key SK_i. If the key-insulated signature scheme can deal with only sequential signing key updates, the broadcaster runs $\mathsf{Upd}^*(SK^*, i, i-1)$ to create a partial key $SK'_{i,i-1}$ and $\mathsf{Upd}(i, i-1, SK_{i-1}, SK'_{i,i-1})$ to create a signing key SK_i.

Remark 2. In both of the generic constructions in Sect. 4.3 and 4.4, the broadcaster can distribute the verification key and the CRL to users through broadcast channels, which are secure, in order to prevent them from being modified by an adversary. Therefore, these generic constructions are suitable for hybrid services of broadcasting and communications networks.

5   Concrete and Practical Protocol

As shown in Sect. 4, the generic construction of an application authentication protocol from a key-insulated signature scheme satisfies all of the requirements (1)–(3) in Sect. 3. We propose a concrete and practical application authentication protocol for hybrid services of broadcasting and communications networks. Our protocol applies the key-insulated signature scheme proposed by Ohtake et al. [8] for application authentication.

5.1   Algorithms of Key-Insulated Signature Scheme [8]

The key-insulated signature scheme proposed by Ohtake et al. [8] is efficient in terms of the key size, signature size, and computational cost. The algorithms of the scheme are as follows:

---

[1] A broadcaster may set $CRL = \{m\}$ so that the old signing keys SK_1, SK_2, ..., SK_m cannot be used.

Gen: Let $\mathbb{G}_q$ be a cyclic group of prime order q. Randomly select $g \in \mathbb{G}_q$, where g is a generator of $\mathbb{G}_q$. Then, randomly select x and $x' \in Z_q$. The master key $x_0 = x - x'$ is stored in a secure device, and x' is managed by a signer. Calculate $y_0 = g^{x_0}$ and $y' = g^{x'}$, and publish the verification key $vk = \langle q, g, y_0, y', G(\cdot, \cdot), H(\cdot, \cdot, \cdot, \cdot)\rangle$. Here, G and H are hash functions, where $G : \mathbb{G}_q \times \{0,1\}^* \to Z_q$ and $H : \mathbb{G}_q \times \mathbb{G}_q \times \{0,1\}^* \times \{0,1\}^* \to Z_q$.

Upd*: Randomly select $r_1 \in Z_q$ from a secure device, and calculate $v_1 = g^{r_1}$. Then, calculate $c_1 = G(v_1, T)$ using the inputted time period T, and obtain a partial key $x_1 = c_1 r_1 + x_0 \bmod q$ using the inputted master key x_0. x_1, v_1, and T are transmitted to the signer.

Upd: The signer obtains the signing key $SK_T = x_1 + x' \bmod q$ for a time period T by using x_1 and the inputted x'.

Sign: The signer randomly selects $r_s \in Z_q$ and calculates $v_s = g^{r_s}$. Then, the signer calculates $c_s = H(v_1, v_s, T, M)$ and $\sigma_s = c_s r_s + SK_T \bmod q$ by using the inputted message M, T, the signing key SK_T, and v_1. Finally, the signer transmits M, (σ_s, c_s, v_1), and T to a verifier.

Vrfy: Using the inputted y_0, y' M, (σ_s, c_s, v_1), and T, the verifier calculates $c_1 = G(v_1, T)$. If the following equation holds, it returns $b = 1$; otherwise, it returns $b = 0$.

$$c_s = H(v_1, (g^{\sigma_s}(v_1^{c_1} y_0 y')^{-1})^{1/c_s}, T, M)$$

The above scheme is a *strong* key-insulated signature scheme, which is secure against either signing key leakage or master key leakage. That is, an adversary cannot create a new signing key unless both the master key x_0 and the key x' (or a signing key SK_T) are leaked.

5.2   Proposed Protocol

We propose an application authentication protocol by using the algorithms of the key-insulated signature scheme in Sect. 5.1.

Signing key issue. Figure 6 shows the flow of issuing the signing key for a service provider T ($T = 1, 2, ..., m$ is an identity for service provider). The broadcaster has two servers. Broadcaster server 1 securely manages the master key x_0, and broadcaster server 2 securely manages the key x'. Broadcaster server 1 randomly selects $r_1 \in Z_q$ and calculates $v_1 = g^{r_1}$. Then, it obtains $c_1 = G(v_1, T)$ by using T and obtains a partial key $x_1 = c_1 r_1 + x_0 \bmod q$ by using the master key x_0. Broadcaster server 1 stores x_1 for the service provider and transmits x_1, v_1, and T to broadcaster server 2. Broadcaster server 2 calculates the signing key $SK_T = x_1 + x' \bmod q$ by using x' and transmits SK_T, v_1, and T to a service provider T. Service provider T stores them.

Application authentication. Figure 7 shows the flow of application authentication when service provider T distributes an application to a user terminal. Service provider T randomly selects $r_s \in Z_q$ and calculates $v_s = g^{r_s}$. Then, it obtains $c_s = H(v_1, v_s, T, M)$ and $\sigma_s = c_s r_s + SK_T \bmod q$ by using an application M, T,

Broadcaster server 1		Broadcaster server 2		Service provider T
(x_0)		(x')		
$r_1 \in_U Z_q$				
$v_1 = g^{r_1}$				
$c_1 = G(v_1, T)$				
$x_1 = c_1 r_1 + x_0 \bmod q$				
Store x_1				
	$\xrightarrow{x_1, v_1, T}$			
		$SK_T = x_1 + x' \bmod q$		
			$\xrightarrow{SK_T, v_1, T}$	
				Store (SK_T, v_1, T)

Fig. 6. Proposed scheme (issue signing key)

Service provider T		User terminal
(SK_T, v_1, T)		(y_0, y', CRL)
$r_s \in_U Z_q$		
$v_s = g^{r_s}$		
$c_s = H(v_1, v_s, T, M)$		
$\sigma_s = c_s r_s + SK_T \bmod q$		
	$\xrightarrow{M, (\sigma_s, c_s, v_1), T}$	
		Output error message if T is included in CRL
		$c_1 = G(v_1, T)$
		$c_s \stackrel{?}{=} H(v_1, (g^{\sigma_s}(v_1^{c_1} y_0 y')^{-1})^{1/c_s}, T, M)$

Fig. 7. Proposed scheme (authenticate application)

SK_T, and v_1 and it transmits M, (σ_s, c_s, v_1), and T to the user terminal. The user terminal gets CRL from broadcaster server 1. If T is included in CRL, the user terminal outputs an error message. Otherwise, the user terminal calculates $c_1 = G(v_1, T)$. If the following equation holds, the authentication is successful.

$$c_s = H(v_1, (g^{\sigma_s}(v_1^{c_1} y_0 y')^{-1})^{1/c_s}, T, M)$$

Signing key update. Figure 8 shows the flow of the signing key update for a service provider T ($T = 1, 2, ..., m$: an identity for service provider). Signing key update is performed for all of the service providers. Broadcaster server 1 randomly selects $r_2 \in Z_q$ and calculates $v_2 = g^{r_2}$. Then, it obtains $c_2 = G(v_2, T + n)$ by using $T + n$ (identity for service provider after signing key update) and obtains $x_2 = c_2 r_2 + x_0 \bmod q$ by using the master key x_0. Broadcaster server 1 calculates a partial key $\Delta x_2 = x_2 - x_1 \bmod q$ and stores x_2 by overwriting x_1. It then transmits Δx_2, v_2, and $T + n$ to the service provider T. Service provider T obtains a new signing key $SK_{T+n} = SK_T + \Delta x_2 \bmod q$ by using the current signing key SK_T and stores $(SK_{T+n}, v_2, T + n)$. The above process enables the

Broadcaster server 1		Service provider T
(x_0, x_1)		(SK_T)
$r_2 \in_U Z_q$		
$v_2 = g^{r_2}$		
$c_2 = G(v_2, T+n)$		
$x_2 = c_2 r_2 + x_0 \bmod q$		
$\Delta x_2 = x_2 - x_1 \bmod q$		
Store x_2 overwriting x_1		
	$\xrightarrow{\Delta x_2, v_2, T+n}$	
		$SK_{T+n} = SK_T + \Delta x_2 \bmod q$
		Store $(SK_{T+n}, v_2, T+n)$

Fig. 8. Proposed scheme (update signing key)

signing key for service provider T to be updated as follows: $SK_T \rightarrow SK_{T+n} \rightarrow SK_{T+2n} \rightarrow \cdots$

Add service provider. To add a trusted service provider, the broadcaster assigns T ($m < T \leq n$) to the identity of the new service provider and then issues its signing key through the *signing key issue* in Fig. 6

Revoke privileges of service provider. Broadcaster server 1 distributes a CRL including the identities of the service providers whose privileges the broadcaster wants to revoke to all user terminals. The way of setting the CRL is as follows:

- *Revoke privileges of all service providers*
  If the broadcaster wants to revoke the privileges of all service providers at once, it sets the maximum number of the identities to the first element of the CRL. For example, for all of the identities $1, 2, ..., n$, the broadcaster may set
  $$CRL = \{n\}.$$

- *Revoke privileges of a particular provider*
  To revoke the privileges of a particular provider, the broadcaster sets the identities to the subsequent elements of the CRL. For example, to revoke the privileges of service providers k and l ($1 < k < l < m$), the broadcaster may set
  $$CRL = \{0, k, l\}.$$

Remark 3. In the *signing key update* process, the broadcaster updates the signing key for a service provider T as follows: $SK_T \rightarrow SK_{T+n} \rightarrow SK_{T+2n} \rightarrow \cdots$. This is because the broadcaster uses a temporal identity $i_t = T+n, T+2n, ...$, which is constructed from two-dimensional elements: the time period $t = 1, 2, ...$ and the real identity $i = T$.

Remark 4. In the proposed protocol, the number of service providers is limited by the parameter n. However, this is not a fatal weak point since the broadcaster can set n to a sufficiently large number in case of growing the number of service providers in the future.

5.3   Security of Proposed Protocol

Our protocol is based on the key-insulated signature scheme proposed by Ohtake et al. [8], which is provably secure under the discrete logarithm assumption (See [8]). Therefore, we only discuss the security of the proposed protocol against key leakages in the system.

Our protocol is secure because the broadcaster uses two servers. Let us consider the case in which the master key x_0 is leaked from broadcaster server 1. In this case, x_1, managed by the same server, may be leaked. However, key x' is managed by broadcaster server 2, so an adversary cannot create a signing key $SK_T = x_1 + x'$ unless x' is leaked simultaneously. An adversary can create x_1, x_2, and their difference Δx_2. However, since the signing key SK_T is managed by the service provider T, the adversary cannot create a signing key $SK_{T+n} = SK_T + \Delta x_2$ unless SK_T is leaked as well.

Now let's consider the case in which key x' is leaked from broadcaster server 2. In this case, an adversary cannot create x_1 unless x_0 is leaked from broadcaster server 1 at the same time. Therefore, the adversary cannot create a signing key $SK_T = x_1 + x'$.

Finally, let us consider the case in which the signing key SK_T is leaked from service provider T. In this case, the broadcaster revokes the signing key SK_T by using the CRL as described in Sect. 5.2.

In Fig. 6, broadcaster server 2 must offline issue a signing key SK_T to service provider T. However, in Fig. 8, broadcaster server 1 can online transmit a partial key Δx_2 for the signing key update to the service provider, since Δx_2 has no information about the signing key. The strong point is that the signing key update can be performed online (See Fig. 5). In contrast, in an application authentication protocol using an ID-based signature (Fig. 3), the broadcaster must transmit the new signing key to the service provider when updating the signing key. Therefore, it is inconvenient that its signing key update is performed offline.

5.4   Performance Evaluation

Table 1 compares application authentication protocols in terms of their verification key size, revocation efficiency, and ease of signing key update. 'Revocation efficiency' means that the number of elements in the CRL can be smaller than that of the revoked service providers. 'Ease of signing key update' means that the broadcaster can update the signing keys of the service providers online. In this table, "PKI" denotes an application authentication

Table 1. Comparison of application authentication protocols (n: number of service providers)

	PKI	IBS	OURS
Verification key size	$O(n)$	$O(1)$	$O(1)$
Revocation efficiency	-	-	$\checkmark$
Ease of signing key update	-	-	$\checkmark$

protocol by using the digital signature schemes in PKI, "IBS" denotes an application authentication protocol by using an ID-based signature scheme, and "OURS" denotes the application authentication protocol in Sect. 5.2. PKI can be applied to the model in Fig. 1, whereas IBS and OURS can be applied to the model in Fig. 2.

In PKI, a user terminal requires all of the verification keys and certificates for service providers to verify a signature. Therefore, the verification key size is dependent on the number of service providers. If the broadcaster wants to revoke the privileges of a service provider whose applications caused an undesirable action to occur, it requests the CA to issue a CRL including the certificates of the service providers. The number of elements in the CRL equals the number of revoked service providers. To update the signing key of a service provider, the broadcaster requests the CA to reissue a certificate. This process must be performed offline.

In IBS, a user terminal uses only one verification key for verifying a signature. Therefore, the verification key size is independent on the number of service providers. If a broadcaster wants to revoke the privileges of certain service providers, it sets the identities of the service providers to a CRL. The number of elements in the CRL equals the number of revoked service providers. To update the signing key of a service provider, the broadcaster reissues a signing key corresponding to the new identity offline.

In our protocol, a user terminal uses only one verification key for verifying a signature. Therefore, the verification key size is independent of the number of service providers. If the broadcaster wants to revoke the privileges of service providers, it puts the identities of the service providers in a CRL. Moreover, the identity of a service provider is always sequential number. Therefore, the broadcaster can revoke identities all at once and the description of the CRL is simpler than in PKI or IBS, as described in Sects. 4.4 and 5.2. To update the signing key for a service provider, the broadcaster transmits the partial key used for the signing key update to the service provider. The partial key has no information about the signing key. That is, the broadcaster can transmit the partial key online without using a secret channel and hence can update the signing key easily.

The above discussion clearly shows that our protocol is the most practical.

6 Conclusion

We proposed an application authentication protocol for hybrid services of broadcasting and communications networks. We modified a key-insulated signature scheme and applied it to this protocol. Concretely, we considered a time period in a key-insulated signature scheme to be a temporal identity for a service provider, which is generated by two-dimensional elements: the time period and the real identity. We showed that our protocol is secure and practical. Using our protocol, users can securely receive hybrid services of broadcasting and communications networks.

References

1. Boneh, D., Boyen, X.: Efficient Selective-ID Secure Identity-Based Encryption Without Random Oracles. In: Cachin, C., Camenisch, J.L. (eds.) EUROCRYPT 2004. LNCS, vol. 3027, pp. 223–238. Springer, Heidelberg (2004)
2. Boneh, D., Franklin, M.: Identity-Based Encryption from the Weil Pairing. In: Kilian, J. (ed.) CRYPTO 2001. LNCS, vol. 2139, pp. 213–229. Springer, Heidelberg (2001)
3. Dodis, Y., Katz, J., Xu, S., Yung, M.: Strong Key-Insulated Signature Schemes. In: Desmedt, Y.G. (ed.) PKC 2003. LNCS, vol. 2567, pp. 130–144. Springer, Heidelberg (2002)
4. Gentry, C.: Practical Identity-Based Encryption Without Random Oracles. In: Vaudenay, S. (ed.) EUROCRYPT 2006. LNCS, vol. 4004, pp. 445–464. Springer, Heidelberg (2006)
5. González-Deleito, N., Markowitch, O., Dall'Olio, E.: A New Key-Insulated Signature Scheme. In: López, J., Qing, S., Okamoto, E. (eds.) ICICS 2004. LNCS, vol. 3269, pp. 465–479. Springer, Heidelberg (2004)
6. Lee, D., Lee, M., Kang, D.: OHTV(open hybrid TV) service platform based on terrestrial DTV. In: Proc. of ICACT 2010, pp. 399–402. IEEE Press (2010)
7. Matsumura, K., Kanatsugu, Y., Kato, H.: Toward the Construction of Hybridcast ^{TM}. In: ATSC Symposium on Next Generation Broadcast Television (2010)
8. Ohtake, G., Hanaoka, G., Ogawa, K.: Efficient Provider Authentication for Bidirectional Broadcasting Service. IEICE Trans. Fundamentals E93-A(6), 1039–1051 (2010)
9. Shamir, A.: Identity-Based Cryptosystems and Signature Schemes. In: Blakely, G.R., Chaum, D. (eds.) CRYPTO 1984. LNCS, vol. 196, pp. 47–53. Springer, Heidelberg (1985)
10. Waters, B.: Efficient Identity-Based Encryption Without Random Oracles. In: Cramer, R. (ed.) EUROCRYPT 2005. LNCS, vol. 3494, pp. 114–127. Springer, Heidelberg (2005)
11. http://www.hbbtv.org/
12. http://www.hulu.com/
13. http://www.youview.com/

Accelerating Multiparty Computation by Efficient Random Number Bitwise-Sharing Protocols

Naoto Kiribuchi[1], Ryo Kato[1], Takashi Nishide[2],
Tsukasa Endo[3], and Hiroshi Yoshiura[1]

[1] The University of Electro-Communications, 1-5-1 Chofugaoka,
Chofu-shi, Tokyo, 182-8585, Japan
[2] Kyushu University, 744 Motooka Nishi-ku, Fukuoka, 819-0395, Japan
[3] Toshiba Corporation, 1 Komukai-Toshiba-cho, Saiwai-ku, Kawasaki,
212-8582, Japan

Abstract. It is becoming more and more important to make use of personal or classified information while keeping it confidential. A promising tool for meeting this challenge is multiparty computation (MPC), which enables multiple parties, each given a snippet of a secret s, to compute a function $f(s)$ by communicating with each other without revealing s. However, one of the biggest problems with MPC is that it requires a vast amount of communication and thus a vast amount of processing time. We analyzed existing MPC protocols and found that the random number bitwise-sharing protocol used by many of them is notably inefficient. We proposed efficient random number bitwise-sharing protocols, dubbed "Extended-Range I and II," by devising a representation of the truth values that reduces the communication complexity to approximately 1/6th that of the best of the existing such protocol. We reduced the communication complexity to approximately 1/26th by reducing the abort probability, thereby making previously necessary backup computation unnecessary. Using our improved protocols, "Lightweight Extended-Range II," we reduced the communication complexities of equality testing, comparison, interval testing, and bit-decomposition, all of which use the random number bitwise-sharing protocol, by approximately 91, 79, 67, and 23% (for 32-bit data) respectively. Our protocols are fundamental to sharing random number $r \in \mathbb{Z}_p$ in binary form and can be applicable to other higher level protocols.

1 Introduction

Although gathering personal information (e.g., age, address, and buying history) and using it directly or via data mining enable the provision of higher quality services, leakage of such information has become a serious problem. Utilizing sensor logs also makes a profit, but their leakage becomes a problem. Moreover, in cloud computing, personal or classified information is remotely located while its confidentiality must be guaranteed. It has thus become more important to balance data availability against information confidentiality.

S. Jung and M. Yung (Eds.): WISA 2011, LNCS 7115, pp. 187–202, 2012.
© Springer-Verlag Berlin Heidelberg 2012

A promising tool for meeting this challenge is multiparty computation(MPC). Here we focus on MPC based on Shamir's (k, n) threshold secret sharing [10] in which a "share," or snippet, of secret information is distributed to n parties, and the parties can reconstruct the secret by gathering k shares.

MPC based on Shamir's scheme enables multiple parties to obtain the function value for secrets without revealing them. Various existing protocols (e.g., addition, multiplication, equality testing, and comparison) [2,5,6,7,8,11] enable the construction of the function for using personal or classified information, thus can be used to balance the data availability against information confidentiality.

However, one of the biggest problem with MPC is that it requires a vast amount of communication and thus a vast amount of processing time. The multiplication protocol, which obtains the product of secrets $a, b \in \mathbb{Z}_p$, requires $n(n-1)$ times of communication since n parties communicate with each other. The complexity of MPC for protocols other than for multiplication, such as for comparison and equality testing, is evaluated in terms of the number of times the multiplication protocol is used. Much research has gone into making these other protocols more efficient by reducing the number of multiplications and parallelizing them [5,7,8,11]. For example, the comparison of two 32-bit secrets among five parties using the protocol [5] requires $36,640$ multiplications and 44 rounds (number of parallel multiplications), resulting in approximately 2.8MB of information being communicated. Nishide and Ohta [8] improved this protocol so that only 8933 multiplications and 15 rounds are required, resulting in approximately 698KB of information being communicated. However, the protocols still require a vast amount of communication and parallelization of multiplications does not reduce the amount of communicated information. Hence it is required to make the protocols more efficient.

In this work, we analyzed the existing protocols and found that the random number bitwise-sharing protocol used by many of them is notably inefficient. For the comparison above, the random number bitwise-sharing protocol accounts for 7296 of the 8933 multiplications. Though Toft improved this protocol [11] so that only 5424 multiplications are required, it is still dominant. On the basis of our finding, we constructed several more efficient protocols for random number bitwise-sharing and used them to improve the efficiency of higher level protocols (such as comparison and equality testing) that use the random number bitwise-sharing protocol.

Our Contributions. In this work, we constructed efficient random number bitwise-sharing protocols on the basis of two novel ideas.

The first idea is to use a new representation of the truth values. The random number bitwise-sharing protocol first generates candidates for ℓ-bit random number r in binary form. This random number must be less than the prime p used in the underlying secret sharing scheme. While existing protocols represent the result of the $r < p$ comparison as either 1 or 0, we remove inefficient bit operations by replacing these values with 0 and a non-zero value. On the basis of this idea, we constructed two protocols, dubbed "Extended-Range I and II."

Table 1. Complexities of existing and proposed protocols

Protocol		Random number sharing		Equality testing		Comparison	
		Comm.	Rounds	Comm.	Rounds	Comm.	Rounds
Nishide and Ohta [8]		76ℓ	7	81ℓ	8	$279\ell + 5$	15
Toft [11]		$52\ell + 24\sqrt{\ell}$	7	-	-	-	-
Extended-Range	I	$8\ell + 8$	4	$13\ell + 8$	5	$75\ell + 29$	12
	II	$8\ell + 12$	4	$13\ell + 12$	5	$75\ell + 41$	12
Lightweight	I	$2\ell + 4$	3	$7\ell + 4$	4	$57\ell + 17$	11
Extended-Range	II	$2\ell + 5$	4	$7\ell + 5$	5	$57\ell + 20$	12

The second idea is to reduce the probability that the protocol aborts. If random number candidate r is not less than p, the protocol aborts and the parties retry. The abort probability for existing protocols is approximately $1/2$ in the worst case. To reduce this probability to less than $1/2^\kappa$, where κ is a predefined parameter, the existing protocols generate alternative candidates. We thus propose using protocols that have an inherent abort probability of less than $1/2^\kappa$, making the generation of alternative candidates unnecessary. On the basis of this idea, we constructed two protocols dubbed "Lightweight Extended-Range I and II." The complexities of these protocols along with those of two existing protocols are shown in Table 1.

All four of the proposed protocols reduce the communication complexity and the rounds complexity, i.e., the number of parallel multiplications, for equality testing, comparison, interval testing, and bit-decomposition, which use random number bitwise-sharing. The Lightweight Extended-Range II protocol, for example, reduced the communication complexities by respectively about 91, 79, 67, and 23%(for 32-bit data). Our protocols are fundamental to sharing random number $r \in \mathbb{Z}_p$ in binary form and can be applicable to other higher level protocols. We describe our protocols as they are applied to the "honest-but-curious" model. Application of standard techniques will make them more robust.

The constitution of this paper is as follows. In Section 2 we analyze existing MPC protocols. In Section 3 we introduce our Extended-Range protocols and discuss their complexity, correctness, and security. In Section 4 we introduce our improved Lightweight Extended-Range protocols and discuss their complexity, correctness, and security. In Section 5 we describe the application of these protocols to higher level protocols and discuss their complexities. We conclude in Section 6 with a summary of the key points.

Notation

- p: an ℓ-bit prime number
- $\mathbb{Z}_p$: a set of integer x where $0 \leq x < p$
- $[a]$: a set of shares of secret $a \in \mathbb{Z}_p$
- $[a] + [b]$: shares of addition $[a + b \pmod{p}]$ where secrets $a, b \in \mathbb{Z}_p$
- $[a] \times [b]$: shares of multiplication $[a \times b \pmod{p}]$ where secrets $a, b \in \mathbb{Z}_p$

- $[a = b]$: shares of result of equality testing $a = b$ where secrets $a, b \in \mathbb{Z}_p$
- $[a < b]$: shares of result of comparison $a < b$ where secrets $a, b \in \mathbb{Z}_p$
- $[a_i]_B$: i'th bit shares of $a \in \mathbb{Z}_p$
- $[a]_B$: set of all bit shares of $a \in \mathbb{Z}_p$; i.e., $[a]_B = \{[a_i]_B | 0 \le i < \ell\}$

2   Related Work

Shamir's (k, n) Threshold Secret Sharing. Given a secret $s \in \mathbb{Z}_p$, Shamir's (k, n) threshold secret sharing scheme generates a polynomial,

$$f(x) = s + r_1 x + r_2 x^2 + \cdots + r_{k-1} x^{k-1} \pmod{p}, \tag{1}$$

where $r_i \in \mathbb{Z}_p$ is a random number ($1 \le i \le k - 1$). Each of n parties P_d is given a share, $f(d)$ ($1 \le d \le n$). To reconstruct the secret, the parties must gather k shares [10] .

Multiparty Computation Based on Secret Sharing Scheme. Because communication complexity is more dominant than local computational complexity, complexity for MPC is evaluated in terms of the communication complexity. Basic protocols for MPC are addition and multiplication. Given secrets $a, b \in \mathbb{Z}_p$, the addition protocol obtains $[c] = [a + b \pmod{p}]$ without revealing a, b. To compute $[c]$, each party simply adds $[a]$ and $[b]$ on $\mathbb{Z}_p$ independently. The complexity of the addition protocol is negligible since communication is unnecessary.

Given secrets $a, b \in \mathbb{Z}_p$, the multiplication protocol obtains $[c] = [a \times b \pmod{p}]$ without revealing a, b. The details are reported elsewhere [2,6]. The communication complexity of the multiplication protocol is evaluated on the basis of the number of times the parties communicate with each other. As mentioned above, one invocation of the multiplication protocol requires $n(n - 1)$ communications since n parties communicate with each other. However, if secret $a \in \mathbb{Z}_p$ and public value $e \in \mathbb{Z}_p$ are given, the computation of $[c] = [a \times e]$ requires no communication. Moreover, the complexity of computing any second-order polynomial, such as $[c] = [a^2 + b^2]$, is one multiplication operation.

Most existing MPC protocols use addition and multiplication, so their communication complexity is evaluated in terms of the number of multiplications required. The round complexity is also important in these protocols. We call protocols that use addition and multiplication "higher level protocols."

Problem of Multiparty Computation. One of the biggest problem with MPC is that it requires a vast amount of communication. The multiplication protocol requires $n(n - 1)$ communications and higher level protocols require many more communications.

Proposals have been made for improving each protocol. Damgård et al. [5] proposed bit-decomposition, which requires $94\ell \log_2 \ell + 93\ell$ multiplications and 38 rounds as well as several protocols based on his improved bit-decomposition. Nishide et al. [8] improved several protocols by eliminating bit-decomposition, but they also reduced the complexity of bit-decomposition to $47\ell \log_2 \ell + 93\ell$

Table 2. Complexities of higher level protocols and Joint Random Number Bitwise-Sharing protocols used in them

Protocol	Overall		Random number sharing	
	Comm.	Rounds	Comm.	Rounds
Equality testing [8]	81ℓ	8	76ℓ	7
Comparison [8]	$279\ell + 5$	15	228ℓ	7
Interval testing [8]	$110\ell + 1$	13	76ℓ	7
Bit-Decomposition [11]	$31\ell \log_2 \ell + 71\ell + 30\sqrt{\ell}$	23	$54\ell + 24\sqrt{\ell}$	7

multiplications and 25 rounds. Recently, Toft [11] focused on and improved bit-decomposition so that it requires $31\ell \log_2 \ell + 71\ell + 30\sqrt{\ell}$ multiplications and 23 rounds. However, the protocols still require a vast amount of communication. For example, comparing two 32-bit secrets using the Nishide's protocol [8] requires 8933 multiplications.

The complexities of random number sharing account for a substantial portion of the complexity of the higher level protocols. The Joint Random Number Bitwise-Sharing protocol is particularly dominant. For example, it accounts for 76ℓ multiplications and 7 rounds out of a total 81ℓ multiplications and 8 rounds for equality testing. Even with Toft's improvement [11], the complexity is still $54\ell + 24\sqrt{\ell}$ multiplications and 7 rounds, and it is still dominant, as shown in Table 2. Cramer et al. proposed a protocol for pseudo-random secret sharing [4], but this protocol does not generate bitwise shares. Though most of the higher level protocols require both a random bitwise number and a random non-bitwise number, Cramer's protocol only cannot effectively reduce their complexity since the random bitwise number protocol is much more inefficient than the non-bitwise one.

Protocols for Random Number Sharing

Joint Random Number Sharing. This protocol generates shares $[r]$ where $r \in \mathbb{Z}_p$ is a uniformly random number [1]. Though this protocol contains no multiplication, the complexity is evaluated as 1 multiplication and 1 round since communication is necessary.

Joint Random Non-zero Sharing. This protocol generates shares $[r^*]$ where r^* is a uniformly non-zero random value. The complexity of this protocol is 3 multiplications and 2 rounds. The procedure of this protocol is as follows. First, the parties generate two sets of shares of uniformly random numbers $r_1, r_2 \in \mathbb{Z}_p$. Next, obtain $[s] = [r_1] \times [r_2]$ and reveal s. If $s = 0$, the parties retry. If $s \neq 0$, the parties outputs $[r_1]$.

Joint Random Bit Sharing. This protocol generates shares of a uniformly random bit $[r]$ where $r \in \{0, 1\}$. The complexity is 2 multiplications and 2 rounds [5].

Joint Random Number Bitwise-Sharing. This protocol generates bitwise shares of a uniformly random number $[r]_B$ where $r \in \mathbb{Z}_p$. Though required for various higher level protocols, this protocol is quite inefficient. The complexity is 76ℓ multiplications and 7 rounds [8].

The general procedure of this protocol is as follows. First, generate bitwise shares $[r]_B$ by applying Joint Random Bit Sharing ℓ times. Next, using the Bitwise Less-Than protocol, obtain the result of $r < p$ without revealing r, and then output $[r]_B$ if $r < p$. Otherwise, the parties retry.

The Bitwise Less-Than protocol accounts for 68ℓ multiplications and 7 rounds out of the total 76ℓ multiplications and 7 rounds of Joint Random Number Bitwise-Sharing.

The procedure of the Bitwise Less-Than protocol is as follows [5]. Let p_i be the i'th bit of ℓ-bit prime p.

1. For $0 \leq i < \ell$, compute $[c_i] = [r_i \oplus p_i] = [r_i] + p_i - 2p_i[r_i]$.
2. For each i, compute $[d_i] = \vee_{j=i}^{\ell-1}[c_i]$ using the Prefix-Or protocol [5,8].
3. For each i, compute $[e_i] = [d_i - d_{i+1}]$ where $[e_{\ell-1}] = [d_{\ell-1}]$.
4. Compute $[r < p] = \sum_{i=0}^{\ell-1}(p_i \times [e_i])$.

Toft improved Joint Random Number Bitwise-Sharing and reduced its complexity to $52\ell + 24\sqrt{\ell}$ multiplications. However, the round complexity is still 7. In this work, we reduced the complexity further by making the Bitwise Less-Than protocol more efficient.

3   Extended-Range Protocols

Our proposed Joint Random Number Bitwise-Sharing protocols, "Extended-Range I and II," generate bitwise shares $[r]_B$ where r is a uniformly random number $r \in \mathbb{Z}_p$.

Key Ideas of Extended-Range Protocols. As shown in Fig. 1, the main procedure of the Extended-Range protocols is as follows.

1. Generate bitwise shares $[r]_B$ by applying Joint Random Bit Sharing ℓ times.
2. Obtain the result of $[z] = [r < p]$ by applying the Bitwise Less-Than protocol.
3. Reveal z. If $z = 0$, output $[r]_B$. If z is a non-zero value, the parties retry.

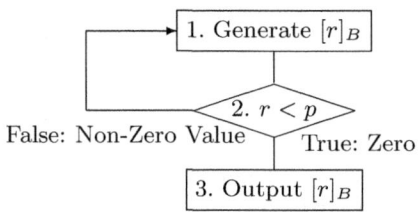

Fig. 1. Main procedure of Extended-Range protocols

The existing Bitwise Less-Than protocol outputs $[1]$ if $r < p$, otherwise $[0]$. A key idea of the Extended-Range protocols is to replace the values output by the Bitwise Less-Than protocol with $[0]$ and a non-zero value. Another is that to assume that prime p satisfies some requirements as long as the requirements keep its use practical.

We focused on the second step (i.e., the Bitwise Less-Than protocol) since the other protocols used in the Extended-Range protocols are the same as in the existing protocols. Given ℓ bitwise shares $[r]_B$ and a public prime p, our Bitwise Less-Than protocol outputs $[0]$ if $r < p$ and shares of a non-zero value otherwise without revealing r.

Extended-Range I. We use an ℓ-bit prime p that includes three 1s in its binary form. Since p is an ℓ-bit odd prime, the binary representation of p is as follows.

$$p : \underbrace{10\cdots010\cdots01}_{\ell \text{ bits}} \tag{2}$$

We use $p_0, p_{\ell-1}$, and p_m to denote LSB, MSB, and the remaining 1 bits between LSB and MSB. The output of the Bitwise Less-Than protocol is used in the Extended-Range I protocol as follows.

$$[r_{\ell-1}]_B \times \left\{ \left(\sum_{i=m+1}^{\ell-2} [r_i]_B \right) + [r_m]_B \times \left(\sum_{i=0}^{m-1} [r_i]_B \right) \right\} \tag{3}$$

The complexity of this formula is 2 multiplications and 2 rounds.

Correctness of Extended-Range I. The Bitwise Less-Than protocol used in the Extended-Range I protocol outputs $[0]$ if $r < p$ and a share of a non-zero value if $r \not< p$. Let A and B designate ranges of bits in p.

$$p : 1 \underbrace{0 \cdots 0}_{A} 1 \underbrace{0 \cdots 0}_{B} 1 \tag{4}$$

If $r \not< p$, r is in at least one of the two following states in binary form.

$$p : 1 \quad 0 \quad \cdots \quad 0 \; 1 \; 0 \cdots \cdots 0 \; 1 \tag{5}$$

$$1. \quad r : 1 \quad \underbrace{\# \cdots \#}_{includes \; 1} \quad \underbrace{* \cdots \cdots \cdots *}_{arbitrary} \tag{6}$$

$$2. \quad r : 1 \quad \underbrace{* \cdots \cdots *}_{arbitrary} \; 1 \underbrace{\# \cdots \cdots \#}_{includes \; 1} \tag{7}$$

We can translate these states into the following respective conditionals.

1. $r_{\ell-1} = 1$ and A includes 1.
2. $r_{\ell-1} = r_m = 1$ and B includes 1.

For each conditional, we can construct the following formulas that output a non-zero value if the condition is true and 0 if the condition is false.

1. $r_{\ell-1} \times \sum_{i=m+1}^{\ell-2} r_i$
2. $r_{\ell-1} \times r_m \times \sum_{i=0}^{m-1} r_i$

If $r < p$, these formulas output 0. If $r \not< p$, at least one formula outputs a non-zero value. Thus, by adding these formulas, we can obtain formula (8), which outputs 0 if $r < p$ and a non-zero value if $r \not< p$.

$$r_{\ell-1} \times \left\{ \left(\sum_{i=m+1}^{\ell-2} r_i \right) + r_m \times \left(\sum_{i=0}^{m-1} r_i \right) \right\} \tag{8}$$

The maximum output of formula (8) is $\ell - 2$ and less than p. Hence we can translate formula (8) into formula (3), which is computed over $GF(p)$. And we can see that formula (3) outputs $[0]$ if $r < p$ and shares of a non-zero value if $r \not< p$ and that the output is correct.

Extended-Range II. The value of prime p that satisfies the assumption of the Extended-Range I protocol is mostly $p \equiv 1 \pmod 4$. However, there are protocols that require $p \equiv 3 \pmod 4$, such as some of the Nishide's protocol [8]. Thus, we developed the Extended-Range II protocol for $p \equiv 3 \pmod 4$. Here we use a prime p that includes four 1s in its binary form and $p_{\ell-1} = p_m = p_1 = p_0 = 1$ where $1 < m < \ell - 1$. The binary representation of p is as follows.

$$p : \underbrace{10 \cdots 010 \cdots 011}_{\ell \text{ bits}} \tag{9}$$

The output of the Bitwise Less-Than protocol used in Extended-Range II is as follows.

$$[r_{\ell-1}]_B \left(\sum_{i=m+1}^{\ell-2} [r_i]_B \right) + ([r_{\ell-1}]_B \times [r_m]_B) \left\{ \left(\sum_{i=2}^{m-1} [r_i]_B \right) + [r_1]_B \times [r_0]_B \right\} \tag{10}$$

To obtain the output, the parties compute $[r_{\ell-1}]_B \times [r_m]_B$ and $[r_1]_B \times [r_0]_B$ in parallel. This makes the formula second-order, so its complexity is 1 multiplication and 1 round. Hence the total complexity of formula (10) is 3 multiplications and 2 rounds.

Correctness of Extended-Range II. The Bitwise Less-Than protocol used in Extended-Range II outputs $[0]$ if $r < p$ and shares of a non-zero value if $r \not< p$. If $r \not< p$, r is in at least one of the three following states in binary form.

$$p : 1 \ \ 0 \ \ \cdots \ \ 0 \ 1 \ 0 \cdots\cdots 0 \ 11 \tag{11}$$

1. $r : 1 \ \underbrace{\# \cdots \#}_{includes\ 1} \ \underbrace{* \ \cdots\cdots\cdots\ *}_{arbitrary}$ (12)

2. $r : 1 \ \underbrace{* \cdots\cdots *}_{arbitrary} \ 1 \underbrace{\# \cdots\cdots \#}_{includes\ 1} * \ *$ (13)

3. $r : 1 \ \underbrace{* \cdots\cdots * }_{arbitrary} \ 1 \ \underbrace{* \cdots\cdots\ *}_{arbitrary} \ 11$ (14)

For each state, we can construct a formula that outputs a non-zero value if r is in the state and 0 if r is not in the state.

1. $r_{\ell-1} \times \sum_{i=m+1}^{\ell-2} r_i$
2. $r_{\ell-1} \times r_m \times \sum_{i=2}^{m-1} r_i$
3. $r_{\ell-1} \times r_m \times r_1 \times r_0$

If $r < p$, these formulas output 0. If $r \not< p$, at least one formula output a non-zero value. Thus, by adding these formulas, we can obtain formula (15), which outputs 0 if $r < p$, and a non-zero value if $r \not< p$.

$$r_{\ell-1} \times \left(\sum_{i=m+1}^{\ell-2} r_i \right) + (r_{\ell-1} \times r_m) \times \left\{ \left(\sum_{i=2}^{m-1} r_i \right) + r_1 \times r_0 \right\} \tag{15}$$

The maximum output of formula (15) is $\ell - 3$ and less than p. Hence we can translate formula (15) into formula (10), which is computed over $GF(p)$. And we can see that formula (10) outputs $[0]$ if $r < p$ and shares of a non-zero value if $r \not< p$ and that the output is correct.

Complexity of Extended-Range Protocols. The Extended-Range protocols generate ℓ sets of bitwise shares $[r_i]_B$ in parallel through Joint Random Bit Sharing. The complexity of this step is 2ℓ multiplications and 2 rounds. Then the parties obtain the result of $r < p$ from the Bitwise Less-Than protocol. The complexity of this step is 2 multiplications and 2 rounds for Extended-Range I and 3 multiplications and 2 rounds for Extended-Range II. Thus, the complexity to generate one random number candidate and obtain the result of $r < p$ is $2\ell+2$ multiplications and 4 rounds for Extended-Range I and $2\ell + 3$ multiplications and 4 rounds for Extended-Range II.

Since the abort probability for existing protocols is approximately $1/2$ in the worst case, these protocols generate four random number candidates [5,8,11]. Because the abort probability for the Extended-Range protocols is the same as that of the existing protocols, we evaluate the complexities for Extended-Range in the case of generating four candidates in parallel. The complexity is $8\ell + 8$ multiplications and 4 rounds for Extended-Range I and $8\ell + 12$ multiplications and 4 rounds for Extended-Range II (Table 3).

Security of Extended-Range Protocols. The Extended-Range protocols consist of two steps. The first step, which generates a candidate, is the same as in the existing protocols, and thus its security can be reduced to a (k, n) threshold secret sharing scheme. The second step reveals the result of $r < p$. If $r < p$, the output is 0, and no information about r is leaked. If $r \not< p$, the output is a non-zero value and information about r is apparently leaked. However, since r is abandoned, the output causes no problem. Therefore, the security of the Extended-Range protocols can be reduced to a (k, n) threshold secret sharing scheme. Note that p can be public without compromising the security, so the condition of p used in our scheme cannot affect the security of the secret.

Practicality of Extended-Range Protocols. Though the Extended-Range protocols use an ℓ-bit prime p that satisfies some requirements, there are a sufficient number of prime p. For $\ell = 32$, there are 6 primes in Extended-Range I and 2 in Extended-Range II. Hence Extended-Range protocols are sufficiently practical.

4   Improvement of Extended-Range Protocols

Although the Extended-Range protocols are efficient compared to existing protocols [8,11], the abort probability is still $1/2$ in the worst case. In this section, we introduce our more efficient protocols "Lightweight Extended-Range" protocols, which make the abort probability negligible.

The Lightweight Extended-Range I protocol uses a Mersenne prime. It is efficient but not practical since a Mersenne prime is sparse. The Lightweight Extended-Range II protocol uses a modified Mersenne prime, a "semi-Mersenne prime," which is sufficiently abundant. This protocol is thus practical as well as efficient.

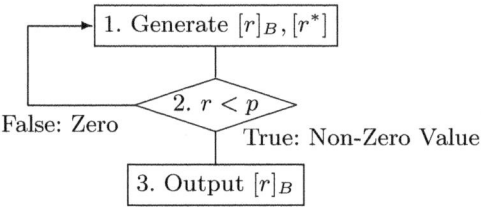

Fig. 2. Main procedure of Lightweight Extended-Range protocols

Key Idea of Lightweight Extended-Range Protocols. The Lightweight Extended-Range protocols use a Mersenne or semi-Mersenne prime to make the abort probability negligible. However, the straightforward use of these primes would increase the protocol's complexity. The key idea of Lightweight Extended-Range is making the abort probability negligible without increasing the complexity by exchanging the truth values. These protocols use a non-zero value if $r < p$ and 0 if $r \not< p$ whereas the Extended-Range protocols use 0 if $r < p$ and a non-zero value if $r \not< p$. As shown in Fig. 2, the main procedure of the Lightweight Extended-Range protocols is as follows.

1. Generate bitwise shares $[r]_B$ by applying Joint Random Bit Sharing protocol ℓ times and generate a share of a non-zero value $[r^*]$ by applying Joint Random Non-zero Sharing protocol in parallel.
2. Obtain $[s] = [r < p]$ without by applying Bitwise Less-Than protocol and reveal $[s \times r^*]$.
3. If $s \times r^*$ is non-zero (i.e., $r < p$), output $[r]_B$. If $s \times r^* = 0$ (i.e., $r \not< p$), the parties retry.

Again we focused on the Bitwise Less-Than protocol used in the second step since the other protocols used in the Lightweight Extended-Range protocols are the same as in the existing protocols. Given bitwise shares of an ℓ-bit random number $[r]_B$ and a public prime p, our Bitwise Less-Than protocol outputs shares of a non-zero value if $r < p$ and $[0]$ otherwise without revealing r.

Lightweight Extended-Range I. A Mersenne prime is a prime p such that $p = 2^\ell - 1$; i.e., the binary representation of an ℓ-bit Mersenne prime is as follows.

$$p = (\underbrace{1\ldots1}_{\ell \text{ bits}})_2 \tag{16}$$

The output of the Bitwise Less-Than protocol used in Lightweight Extended-Range I is as follows.

$$[r^*]([r_0] + [r_1] + \cdots + [r_{\ell-2}] + [r_{\ell-1}] - \ell) \tag{17}$$

The complexity of formula (17) is 1 multiplication and 1 round.

Correctness of Lightweight Extended-Range I. If $r \not< p$, all r_is are 1 since p is a Mersenne prime $(0 \le i < \ell)$. Thus, formula (17) obviously outputs $[0]$. If $r < p$, the output is shares of a non-zero value since $(r_0 + \cdots + r_{\ell-1} - \ell)$ is non-zero. Thus we can see that the output is correct.

Lightweight Extended-Range II. Using a Mersenne prime is hardly practical since it is sparse, as noted above. Thus, we define a semi-Mersenne prime, which is sufficiently abundant.

Definition 1. *A semi-Mersenne prime is an ℓ-bit prime such that*

$$p = 2^\ell - 1 - 2^c \tag{18}$$

where $0 < c < \ell - 1$.

The binary representation of a semi-Mersenne prime is

$$p = (1\ldots101\ldots1)_2 \tag{19}$$

and $p_c = 0$.

The output of the Bitwise Less-Than protocol used in Lightweight Extended-Range II is as follows.

$$[r^*]\left\{\sum_{i=c}^{\ell-1}[\overline{r_i}]\right\}\left\{\left(\sum_{i=c+1}^{\ell-1}[\overline{r_i}]\right) + [r_c] + \left(\sum_{i=0}^{c-1}[\overline{r_i}]\right)\right\} \tag{20}$$

Note that a bitwise NOT can be computed as $[\overline{r_i}] = 1 - [r_i]$. The complexity of formula (20) is 2 multiplications and 2 rounds.

Correctness of Lightweight Extended-Range II. If $r \not< p$, r is in either one of the two following states in binary form.

$$p : 1 \cdots 1\ 0\ 1 \cdots\cdots 1 \qquad (21)$$

$$1. \quad r : 1 \cdots\ 1 \underbrace{* \cdots\cdots *}_{arbitrary} \qquad (22)$$

$$2. \quad r : 1 \cdots 1\ 0\ 1 \cdots\cdots 1 \qquad (23)$$

We can translate these states into the following respective conditionals.

1. $r_{\ell-1}, \ldots, r_c = 1$.
2. $r_{\ell-1}, \ldots, r_{c+1} = 1$ and $r_c = 0$ and $r_{c-1}, \ldots, r_0 = 1$.

For each conditional, we can construct a formula that outputs a non-zero value if the condition is true and 0 if the condition is false.

1. $\sum_{i=c}^{\ell-1} \overline{r_i}$
2. $(\sum_{i=c+1}^{\ell-1} \overline{r_i}) + r_c + (\sum_{i=0}^{c-1} \overline{r_i})$

Both of these formulas output a non-zero value if $r < p$. If $r \not< p$, one of them outputs 0. By multiplying these formulas, we can obtain formula (20), which outputs shares of a non-zero value if $r < p$ and $[0]$ if $r \not< p$.

Complexity of Lightweight Extended-Range Protocols. The Lightweight Extended-Range protocols generate ℓ sets of bitwise shares $[r_i]_B$ and non-zero shares $[r^*]$ in parallel by Joint Random Bit Sharing and Joint Random Non-zero Sharing, respectively. The complexity of this step is $2\ell + 3$ multiplications and 2 rounds. The parties obtain the result of $r < p$ from the Bitwise Less-Than protocol. The complexity of this step is 1 multiplication and 1 round for Lightweight Extended-Range I and 2 multiplications and 2 rounds for Lightweight Extended-Range II. Thus, the complexity to generate one random number candidate and obtain the result of $r < p$ is $2\ell + 4$ multiplications and 3 rounds for Lightweight Extended-Range I and $2\ell + 5$ multiplications and 4 rounds for Lightweight Extended-Range II.

As mentioned, the abort probability for the previous protocols is approximately $1/2$ in the worst case. To reduce this to $1/2^\kappa$, they generate four random number candidates where κ is a predefined parameter [5,8,11].[1] Meanwhile, the inherent abort probability of the Lightweight Extended-Range protocols is $1/2^\kappa$. In the case of Lightweight Extended-Range I, which uses a Mersenne prime $p = 2^\ell - 1$, $\kappa = \ell$. For example, Mersenne prime $p = 2^{31} - 1$ gives an abort probability of $1/2^{31}$. In the case of Lightweight Extended-Range II, which uses a semi-Mersenne prime $p = 2^\ell - 1 - 2^c$, $\kappa > \ell - c - 1$. For example, semi-Mersenne prime $p = 2^{32} - 1 - 2^2$ gives an abort probability of less than $1/2^{29}$. Thus, the Lightweight Extended-Range protocols do not need to generate four candidates, which means that we can evaluate their complexities using only one candidate. The complexities of the Random Number Bitwise-Sharing protocols are summarized in Table 3.

---

[1] The generation of four candidates is further discussed elsewhere [5].

Table 3. Complexities of Random Number Bitwise-Sharing protocols

Protocol	Comm.	Rounds
Nishide and Ohta [8]	76ℓ	7
Toft [11]	$52\ell + 24\sqrt{\ell}$	7
Extended-Range I	$8\ell + 8$	4
Extended-Range II	$8\ell + 12$	4
Lightweight Extended-Range I	$2\ell + 4$	3
Lightweight Extended-Range II	$2\ell + 5$	4

Security of Lightweight Extended-Range Protocols. The Lightweight Extended-Range protocols consist of two steps. The first step, which generates a candidate, is the same as in the existing protocols and thus its security can be reduced to a (k, n) threshold secret sharing scheme. The second step reveals the result of $r < p$. If $r < p$, the output is a non-zero value and information about r is apparently leaked. However, since shares of a random non-zero number $[r^*]$ mask r, no information about r is leaked.

Practicality of Lightweight Extended-Range Protocols. Although the Lightweight Extended-Range protocols use an ℓ-bit prime p that satisfies some requirements, there are sufficient number of primes p for Lightweight Extended-Range II. For $\ell = 32$, there are 7 primes in Lightweight Extended-Range II while there is no prime in Lightweight Extended-Range I since a Mersenne prime is sparse. Hence Lightweight Extended-Range II is sufficiently practical while I is somewhat restricted.

5   Application to Higher Level Protocols

We applied our four proposed protocols to equality testing [8], comparison [8], interval testing [8], and bit-decomposition [11]. Table 4 summarizes their complexities along with those of existing such protocols. The proposed protocols can be applied to higher level protocols simply by replacing the existing Joint Random Number Bitwise-Sharing protocol with a proposed protocol.

We briefly explain each of these higher level protocols. They are described in more detail elsewhere [8,11]. Given sets of shares $[a], [b]$ where $a, b \in \mathbb{Z}_p$, the equality testing protocol [8] and the comparison protocol [8] obtains a set of shares $[a = b]$ and $[a < b]$ without revealing $a = b$ and $a < b$, respectively. Given a set of shares $[a]$ where $a \in \mathbb{Z}_p$ and public values $c_1, c_2 \in \mathbb{Z}_p$, the interval testing protocol [8] obtains a set of shares $[c_1 < a < c_2]$ without revealing $c_1 < a < c_2$. Given a set of shares $[a]$ where $a \in \mathbb{Z}_p$, the bit-decomposition protocol [11] obtains sets of bitwise shares $[a]_B$ without revealing any a_i.

Table 4. Complexities of higher level protocols

Protocol			Comm.	Rounds
Equality testing	Cramer and Damgård [3]		ℓ	ℓ
	Damgård et al. [5]		$94\ell \log_2 \ell + 98\ell$	39
	Nishide and Ohta [8]		81ℓ	8
	Extended-Range	I	$13\ell + 8$	5
		II	$13\ell + 12$	5
	Lightweight	I	$7\ell + 4$	4
	Extended-Range	II	$7\ell + 5$	5
Comparison	Damgård et al. [5]		$188\ell \log_2 \ell + 205\ell$	44
	Nishide and Ohta [8]		$279\ell + 5$	15
	Extended-Range	I	$75\ell + 29$	12
		II	$75\ell + 41$	12
	Lightweight	I	$57\ell + 17$	11
	Extended-Range	II	$57\ell + 20$	12
Interval testing	Damgård et al. [5]		$94\ell \log_2 \ell + 127\ell + 1$	44
	Nishide and Ohta [8]		$110\ell + 1$	13
	Extended-Range	I	$42\ell + 9$	10
		II	$42\ell + 13$	10
	Lightweight	I	$36\ell + 5$	9
	Extended-Range	II	$36\ell + 6$	10
Bit-Decomposition	Damgård et al. [5]		$94\ell \log_2 \ell + 93\ell$	38
	Nishide and Ohta [8]		$47\ell \log_2 \ell + 93\ell$	25
	Toft[11]		$31\ell \log_2 \ell + 71\ell + 30\sqrt{\ell}$	23
	Extended-Range	I	$31\ell \log_2 \ell + 27\ell + 6\sqrt{\ell} + 8$	20
		II	$31\ell \log_2 \ell + 27\ell + 6\sqrt{\ell} + 12$	20
	Lightweight	I	$31\ell \log_2 \ell + 21\ell + 6\sqrt{\ell} + 4$	19
	Extended-Range	II	$31\ell \log_2 \ell + 21\ell + 6\sqrt{\ell} + 5$	20

6   Conclusion

Multiparty computation (MPC) is a promising tool for making use of personal or classified information while keeping it confidential, but one of the biggest problem with MPC is that it requires a vast amount of communication and thus a vast amount of processing time. Our analysis of existing MPC protocols revealed that the random number sharing protocol used by many of them is notably inefficient. The Joint Random Bitwise-Sharing protocol, which is used to generate random numbers in binary form, is particularly inefficient. By replacing truth values 1 and 0 used in this protocol by 0 and a non-zero value, we constructed more efficient protocols, commonly dubbed "Extended-Range I and II." Compared with the best of the existing Joint Random Bitwise-Sharing protocol, which requires $52\ell + 24\sqrt{\ell}$ multiplications and 7 rounds (number of parallel multiplications), the complexity is $8\ell + 8$ multiplications and 4 rounds for Extended-Range I and $8\ell + 12$ multiplications and 4 rounds for Extended-Range II. Furthermore, by reducing the abort probability and thus making the previously necessary backup computation unnecessary, we constructed improved protocols, commonly dubbed "Lightweight Extended-Range I and II." The complexity is $2\ell + 4$ multiplications and 3 rounds for Lightweight Extended-Range I and $2\ell + 5$ multiplications and 4 rounds for Lightweight Extended-Range II. Using Lightweight Extended-Range II reduced the communication complexity for equality testing, comparison, interval testing, and bit-decomposition, all of which use a random number sharing protocol, by approximately 91, 79, 67, and 23%, respectively (for 32-bit data). Our protocols are fundamental to sharing random number $r \in \mathbb{Z}_p$ in binary form and can be applicable to other higher level protocols.

References

1. Bar-Ilan, J., Beaver, D.: Non-Cryptographic Fault-Tolerant Computing in a Constant Number of Rounds of Interaction. In: 8th Annual ACM Symposium on Principles of Distributed Computing, pp. 201–209. ACM Press, New York (1989)
2. Ben-Or, M., Goldwasser, S., Wigderson, A.: Completeness Theorems for Non-Cryptographic Fault-Tolerant Distributed Computation. In: 20th Annual ACM Symposium on Theory of Computing, pp. 1–10. ACM Press, New York (1988)
3. Cramer, R., Damgård, I.: Secure Distributed Linear Algebra in a Constant Number of Rounds. In: Kilian, J. (ed.) CRYPTO 2001. LNCS, vol. 2139, pp. 119–136. Springer, Heidelberg (2001)
4. Cramer, R., Damgård, I., Ishai, Y.: Share Conversion, Pseudorandom Secret-Sharing and Applications to Secure Computation. In: Kilian, J. (ed.) TCC 2005. LNCS, vol. 3378, pp. 342–362. Springer, Heidelberg (2005)
5. Damgård, I., Fitzi, M., Kiltz, E., Nielsen, J.B., Toft, T.: Unconditionally Secure Constant-Rounds Multi-party Computation for Equality, Comparison, Bits and Exponentiation. In: Halevi, S., Rabin, T. (eds.) TCC 2006. LNCS, vol. 3876, pp. 285–304. Springer, Heidelberg (2006)
6. Gennaro, R., Rabin, M.O., Rabin, T.: Simplified VSS and Fast-track Multiparty Computations with Applications to Threshold Cryptography. In: 17th Annual ACM Symposium on Principles of Distributed Computing, pp. 101–111. ACM Press, New York (1998)
7. Ning, C., Xu, Q.: Multiparty Computation for Modulo Reduction without Bit-Decomposition and a Generalization to Bit-Decomposition. In: Abe, M. (ed.) ASIACRYPT 2010. LNCS, vol. 6477, pp. 483–500. Springer, Heidelberg (2010)
8. Nishide, T., Ohta, K.: Multiparty Computation for Interval, Equality, and Comparison Without Bit-Decomposition Protocol. In: Okamoto, T., Wang, X. (eds.) PKC 2007. LNCS, vol. 4450, pp. 343–360. Springer, Heidelberg (2007)
9. SecureSCM. Security Analysis. Technical Report D9.2, SecureSCM (July 2009), http://www.securescm.org
10. Shamir, A.: How to Share a Secret. Communications of the ACM 22(11), 612–613 (1979)
11. Toft, T.: Constant-Rounds, Almost-Linear Bit-Decomposition of Secret Shared Values. In: Fischlin, M. (ed.) CT-RSA 2009. LNCS, vol. 5473, pp. 357–371. Springer, Heidelberg (2009)

A   Variations of Proposed Protocols

We can easily construct a series of protocols based on the idea of the proposed ones. We show two types of variations of our protocols. The first type is variations of the Extended-Range protocol for $p = (10\ldots01\ldots10\ldots01)_2$. Let $p = (10\ldots0110\ldots01)_2$ and $p_{\ell-1} = p_{m+1} = p_m = p_0 = 1$ for simplicity. The output of $r < p$ is computed as follows, and its complexity is 3 multiplications and 3 rounds.

$$[r_{\ell-1}] \times \left\{ \left(\sum_{i=m+2}^{\ell-2} [r_i] \right) + [r_{m+1}] \times [r_m] \times \left(\sum_{i=1}^{m-1} [r_i] \right) \right\}$$

The second type is variations of the Lightweight Extended-Range protocol for $p = (1\ldots10\ldots01\ldots1)_2$. Let $p = (1\ldots1001\ldots1)_2$ and $p_{c+1} = p_c = 0$ for simplicity. The output of $r < p$ is computed as follows, and its complexity is 3 multiplications and 2 rounds.

$$[r^*] \times \left\{ \left(\sum_{i=c+2}^{\ell-1} [\overline{r_i}] \right) + [\overline{r_{c+1}}] \times [\overline{r_c}] \right\} \left\{ \left(\sum_{i=c+2}^{\ell-1} [\overline{r_i}] \right) + [r_{c+1}] + [r_c] + \left(\sum_{i=0}^{c-1} [\overline{r_i}] \right) \right\}$$

These variations increase the number of applicable primes for our protocols and help in the selection of a suitable prime in practical use.

Biometric Based Secure Communications without Pre-deployed Key for Biosensor Implanted in Body Sensor Networks

Kwantae Cho and Dong Hoon Lee

The Graduate School of Information Security, Korea University
{ckt27,donghlee}@korea.ac.kr

Abstract. Key establishment is a fundamental service for secure communications between a central device and each biosensor implanted in the human body. It provides and manages the cryptographic keys to enable security services such as confidentiality, integrity and authentication. There exist several schemes to provide secure communications; however, some existing schemes employ unsuitable cryptography mechanisms or share a pre-deployed key in body sensor networks(BSNs). Due to stringent constraints of power, memory and computation capability, it is inadequate to apply asymmetric cryptography mechanisms to biosensors. Besides, it is also inappropriate to store the pre-deployed key in the implanted biosensor because, if the key is exposed, a person will have transplantation surgery for the secret to be redistributed. In this paper, we proposed the secure communication scheme only using symmetric cryptosystem without a pre-deployed key between a central device and each biosensor in BSNs.

Keywords: secure communication, security, body sensor network, biometric, biosensor, sensor network.

1 Introduction

Health care system is a very important phase of our life. Hence it is imperative that pervasive computing be extended to health care applications. BSNs, which are one of pervasive computing, are essential to the health care system. Pervasive computing has the potential to provide low cost, high performance for health care and monitoring. Current advanced technologies have made it possible to implant biosensor inside the human body for observing his health status [11]. In such a biosensor arrangement scenario, a certain device will be located on the body. It acts as a wireless relay between the implanted biosensors and a base station distant from the body. The device calls a central device [21]. The central device collects biometrics received from the implanted biosensor and forwards them to the base station using secure channel. Most existing schemes [16,19,21,22] describe a distance between central device and each biosensor as one hop; i.e. each biosensor can directly connect with central device without any intermediate node. Biometrics which biosensors measure are sensitive data from an angle of

S. Jung and M. Yung (Eds.): WISA 2011, LNCS 7115, pp. 203–218, 2012.

personal privacy. The biometrics periodically report to a doctor and is used for diagnosis. Anybody do not hope that his biometrics are revealed to others. It is well known that the individual physiological data should be kept in privacy legally. If an malicious person who intends to do harm to certain patient modify the revealed biometrics and forward them to his central device, the central device will transmit the modified biometrics to a doctor. The doctor would make an incorrect diagnosis, which can leads the patient to get into danger. Therefore, secure communication between a central device and is one of the most important things that engineers should be concerned about while implementing the whole health care system.

Key establishment between central device and each biosensor for secure communication is inevitable. The key enabling the secure communication in BSNs appears to be biometrics. That is why a biosensor are severely limited in resources, making traditional security mechanisms [1,23] impractical. Instead, by incorporating the body itself and the various physiological pathways as biometrics, secure communication can be feasibly implemented for BSNs [5,20]. On the other hand, biometrics differ rather significantly from conventional signals, being more noisy and variant. Therefore, in order to solve the noise and errors, fuzzy signal processing is typically required [5,12]. The extent of variations in biometrics is such that two keys derived from the physiological traits do not match perfectly. And, the derived keys are not employed in conventional schemes, which by design do not tolerate even single-bit error [3,23]. For BSNs, it has been found that the heart rate variations can especially be a sufficient source of randomness to cryptographic keys [4,17,18]. The heart rate can be measured using several methods such as electrocardiogram(ECG)signals or photoplethysmogram(PPG) [14]

Considering stringent constraints of biosensor, we employed symmetric cryptosystem. A symmetric cryptosystem refers to an encryption system in which the sender and receiver share a single and common key that is used to encrypt and decrypt the message. Symmetric cryptosystem are simpler and faster compared with asymmetric one; however, their main defect is the difficulty of establishing a session key between both parties. Establishing a session key in BSNs is totally different from conventional schemes. Although biometrics are measured from different parts of the same body at the same time, they are not completely identical. A cryptosystem employed in BSNs necessarily require error-correcting code [12] to correct the error bits.

A secret key in symmetric cryptosystem must not be exposed; however, the secret key could be revealed by reason of unpredicted accidents or an compromise attack by an adversary. In such a case, the secret key has to be renewed in order to prevent more serious damage such as an impersonation attack or message forgery. If each biosensor implanted inside the body has pre-deployed key as a secret and the key is revealed, the patient should undergo a operation to reassign new pre-deployed key to each biosensor. For that reason, most patients do not desire that biosensors implanted for their health care system employ symmetric cryptosystem using pre-deployed key. Therefore, symmetric cyptosystem to be applied to the implanted biosensors do not deploy any secret in advance.

In our scheme, we amend the existing fuzzy scheme [12] to correct error bits and hide biometrics regared as a secret. our scheme transmits the biometrics through several steps so that an adversary can not easily guess it. And, any secret is not stored in biosensors before biosensor deployment; besides, our scheme makes it easy to reestablish and revoke a session key. Although additional communication overhead is needed against the existing scheme [5,7] in the initial phase, the entire communication overhead gradually reduces. Because we do not figure MAC for message verification in our scheme.

In this paper, our contributions can be largely summarized into three items as follows.

- No pre-deployed secrets : Our scheme does not store any secret in advance; namely, the security of our scheme does not depend on a pre-deployed secret. Because depending on a certain secret would be very dangerous if it is uncovered.
- High efficiency : Memory overhead is sufficiently trivial, although it is needed more than [5]. And, computation overhead is also tiny for securely transmitting an payload because we does not compute MAC to authenticate a payload. Instead, we check the sequence number of decrypted payload for message authentication. Communication overhead of our scheme is low in the long run. It requires extra transmission to share a key between a central device and each implanted biosensor in the initial phase; however, after that phase, the size of a payload is smaller than [5] because it does not contain MAC.
- Simple key renewal and key revocation : Key renewal and key revocation are very easy in our scheme. That is why we does not perform an additional task for key renewal and key revocation. It just demands to start the session again. Because it does not need to renew any secrets such as an master key.

Organization. The remainder of this paper is organized as follows. In Section 2, we give a description of related works. We take preliminaries of BSNs as our application environments in Section 3. Later on we focus on our scheme in Section 4, and we analyze our scheme in Section 5. Lastly, Section 6 concludes this paper and points out future lines of work.

2   Related Works

Several researches have been done in this area security for BSNs. The most researches have not given a serious consideration for the implanted biosensor environments inside human's body with extremely stringent constraints as in case of biosensors.

Sriram et al. [5] propose the method that obviated the need for expensive computation and avoided unnecessary communication using their novel scheme in the implanted biosensors. They suggest a scheme based on biometrics derived from the human body itself for securing the keying material used for accomplishing security of the implanted biosensors. Their idea is a novel one; however, before implanting biosensors inside human's body for randomizing biometrics, they store a secret in biosensor. The secret is used in order to compute the commit key K_{commit}. As above-mentioned, it could be mortal for a life of human if the secret is exposed.

Francis et al. [7] have proposed multi-point key management and novel data scrambling method, which is based interpolation and random sampling. They employ IPI(Inter-Pulse Interval) as a random source for key generation as our scheme, which selects IPI from ECG for the same object. Francis et al. apply BCH code to biosensor for error correcting. The BCH code causes the communication overhead to increase more than the existing schemes [5,20,21]. And, their key management also has the same problem, which is to distributes a secret in advance. It is a fatal defect as stated above.

Oscar et al. [16] have used the Deterministic Pairwise Key Pre-distribution Scheme(DKPS) for key management of BSNs. It exhibits excellent energy and memory properties on resource-restricted BSNs; however, it has the same problem like [5].

There have proposed several researches for the security of BSNs. Though Krishna et al. [13] presented a means of using biometrics from the wearer's body to secure implanted biosensor communications, it is not suitable for our object. Because each biosensor shares pre-deployed pairwise master key K_m with base station. Fei et al. [6] designed practical TSN hardware/software platform with a medical security scheme to achieve confidential IPI data transmission in wireless medium; however, if an adversary compromises the gateway and acquires a SK, anybody cannot guarantee the privacy of patients.

Our scheme has applied fuzzy commitment scheme proposed by Juels and Wattenberg [12]. Juels et al. present a fuzzy commitment scheme which tolerates some error bits. Their scheme is very useful for BSNs. This is due to the fact that any two readings of a biometric are hardly identical as it depends heavily on the way the human body generates them, which is not the same at every time. We slightly modify the fuzzy commitment scheme in order to provide the secure key establishment between a central device and each biosensor.

3   Preliminary of BSNs (Body Sensor Networks)

In this section, we describe the concept and the features of BSNs. We explain why IPI is used as a secret. At last, we simply introduce a fuzzy commitment scheme [12] we refer to.

3.1   Concept of BSNs

Fig. 1 shows a concept of BSNs. BSNs consist of an external device(a central device), several implanted biosensors and a base station. BSNs are formed by the biosensors between themselves and the central device. The central device is

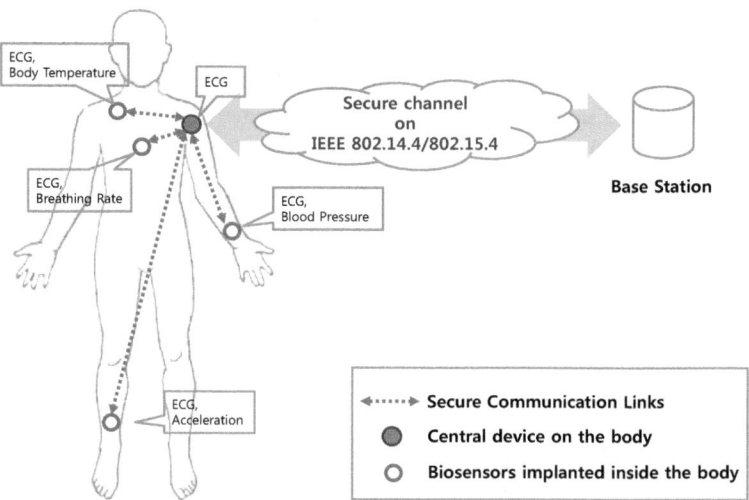

Fig. 1. The Concept of BSNs

connected to an remote base station. Each biosensor contains a process. memory, transceiver, sensors and a power unit. The biosensors conduct operation such as measuring biometrics, processing it and delivering it to the central device, external signals to trigger action inside the body. The central device periodically carries out data aggregation and sends the collected data to the base station, where it is accumulated for next operation such as monitoring a patient's health status.

In our scheme, a central device and implanted biosensors all together can measure IPI, one of biometrics. Central device located on the human body and measures IPI, which can be also found in/on the human body [4]. The implanted biosensors measure biometrics more than two kinds of biometrics. The implanted biosensors measure IPI for sharing a session key with the central device and measure other biometrics which the central device requires. After encrypting the required biometrics using a session key with the central device, the implanted biosensors transmit it to the central device.

3.2 Threat Models

The ultimate goal of an adversary is divided into the following. The first is to know who possess the biometrics even though an adversary does not have a secret which is shared between a central device and each biosensor and used in process of authentication. The second is to produce a correct response to a challenge even though she is not a legitimate biosensor. In other words, she wants to be authenticated by a central device(ultimately database), whether she impersonates a legitimate biosensor to the central device and participates in authentication protocol or not. Below, we can commonly classify attack models achieving such goals.

Passive Attack. It is classified into a passive attack if an adversary can just eavesdrop and collect the exchanged messages between a central device and each biosensor but cannot inject and modify an payload to the central device(a biosensor) and have no ability to make a physical attack to a biosenor. For example, tracing through eavesdropping is included in this passive attack.

Active Attack. We define an active attack as injecting/ modifying/blocking payload as well as eavesdropping. In this attack it is possible to impersonate a biosensor. Still an active attack does not include a physical access to a biosensor. Physically accessing to an implanted biosensor is impossible. DoS attack or spoofing attack belongs to this attack.

3.3   Features of BSNs

Wireless communication technologies have developed for wireless personal area networks(WPANs). They have been studied to interconnect biosensors within the human's body. The BSNs have its own characteristics compared to general WPANs and wireless sensor networks(WSNs) as follows.

Except for the central device, all implanted biosensors are exceedingly limited in their power, memory, computation and commutation capability, especially for those implanted biosensor networks. Power management is the most challengeable. It is almost impossible to change the battery in the implanted biosensor unless surgery is operated.

BSNs are a network with small scale structure and ultra-short range of communications. It consists of a central device and some biosensors.

The same kind of biometric can be found from diverse parts of the body. A biometric is physiological data that is detected, gathered, processed and forwarded to a base station. Although the same kind of biometrics are detected, the location where they are detected could be not all the same. For example, a certain biometric such as IPI can be measured from several part of the body, not one part of one.

Biometrics in BSNs compared to it in conventional biometric systems is that the biometrics to be used in BSNs should be random in nature [4]. This is contrary to the requirement of a biometric for a conventional biometric system, where templates of the biometric are stored in the system as a reference to compare against a copy of the biometric captured in real time for user authentication. Unlike the conventional biometric systems, the biometric in BSNs is captured independently but coincidentally. This property makes it very difficult for an adversary to guess the biometric, which can be the authentication or a secret to encrypt the data.

Biometrics in BSNs is distinctive. The feature should be sufficiently different on any two individuals when copies of it are captured coincidentally, although the copies are captured by the same types of biosensors and at the same positions of the body.

Biometrics in BSNs is time-variant but invulnerable. The feature should change with time and have a high class of randomness so that biometrics captured at different times would not match although they are acquired from the same individual. This guarantees higher class of security.

Two types of error, FRR and FAR, are considered in BSNs. FRR means that the rate of which two biometrics measured from the same body during the same period of time are unmatched. And, FAR means that the rate of which two biometrics measured from the different body or at a different time are matched. That is why hamming distance is used to verify the body where the biometric belongs to in the most papers related to BSNs.

3.4 IPI(Inter-Pulse Interval) as a Biometric

This section explains why IPI among many kinds of biometrics is selected as a secret.

Cherukuri et al. [5] proposed using physiological parameters with higher levels of entropy such as blood glucose, blood pressure, temperature, hemoglobin and blood flow. According to them, heart rate is not a good choice because of insufficient randomness. On the other hand, using the timing information of heart beats can be actually an excellent biometric feature. A biometric pattern generated from a sequence of IPI provides a high class of randomness [4].

IPI can be gained using different types of biosensors and from different physiological signals such as ECG, PPG, and blood pressure wave. IPI also has the advantage that the variation of it is always acceptable although it is detected at different body parts; besides, IPI can be measured without much variation using biosensors implanted in the body or placed on the body unlike body temperature, which varies in the body or on the body.

Carmen et al. [4] have presented that the biometric system accomplished a minimum half total error rate of 2.58 percent by using IPI as the biometric when the IPIs measured from signals, which were sampled at 1000Hz, were coded into 128-bit binary sequences. In other words, in case of using IPI as a biometric, the sum of false rejection rate(FRR) and false acceptance rate(FAR) are small. Such a result surely supports the reason why IPI is chosen as a biometric.

In our scheme, the combination of IPIs is used as a key for data encryption. As mentioned before, IPI guarantees sufficient randomness.

3.5 Fuzzy Commitment Scheme for Error-Correcting

Ideally, two biometrics should be matched only if they were measured from the same body during the same period of time; however, mostly, the result of measurement is not complete. The difference could be the extent of a hamming distance of 10%. It causes FRR and FAR. Error correction would facilitate to alleviate the problems.

Our scheme use a fuzzy commitment scheme [12] to correct the errors. We commonly declare the fuzzy commitment scheme as a (N, K, D) code, where N

is the size of the code, K is the size of real biometric, and D is the minimum distance of the element in the code. The merit of the fuzzy commitment scheme does not require an additional payload to correct the errors; however, there is the demerit of it. It can correct error bits to the extent of $T(= \lfloor \frac{D-1}{2} \rfloor)$. The number of errors can be reduced by taking multiple readings independently.

The fuzzy commitment scheme, there are two phases, namely commit phase and decommit phase. $F_{com}(c, x) = (h(c)||\delta)$ is the fuzzy commitment function to commit c. δ means $x \oplus c$ and $h()$ is a one-way hash function. The receiver receives $(h(c)||\delta)$ from the sender and decommits c using $F_{dec}(h(c)||\delta, x\prime)$. It computes $c\prime = f(x\prime \oplus \delta)$, where $x\prime$ is variant version of proof x available to the receiver. f is an error correcting function. Finally, the receiver checks if $h(c\prime) = h(c)$. If the check passes, the receiver use $c\prime$ instead of c.

For example, we define an error correcting code with code set $C = \{000, 111\}^3$, and f is a major decoding function which decodes three bits at one time. Hence error up to one bit can be corrected. Now select $c = \{000\ \ 111\ \ 111\}$ from C. Assume that the proof for committing $c, x = \{101\ \ 001\ \ 010\}$. A sender computes $\delta = x \oplus c = 101\ \ 110\ \ 101$ and $F_{com}(c, x) = (h(000\ \ 111\ \ 111), \ \ 101\ \ 110\ \ 101)$ and transmits F_{com} to the receiver. On another side, it supposes that a receiver detects $x\prime = 111\ \ 101\ \ 010$ corrupted in one bit. As $c\prime = x \oplus c \oplus x\prime$, now the receiver decommits $f(x\prime \oplus \delta) = f(010\ \ 011\ \ 111) = f(c\prime) = c$ in order to compute $c\prime$, which is available to find c. Therefore, the receiver can get $c = 000\ \ 111\ \ 111$ from $c\prime$. After checking $h(c\prime) = h(c)$, if passing it, the receiver can believe $x\prime$.

4   Our Scheme

In this section, we introduce our scheme for secure communication between a central device and each biosensor by stages. The ultimate goal of our scheme is to securely communicate without any pre-deployed secret.

4.1   Background of Our Scheme

Before explaining our scheme, we state some backgrounds to readily understand our scheme. The following backgrounds was already explained in details above.

- An extent of errors at any certain time should be corrected within limits bearable by fuzzy commitment scheme [5].
- IPI, one of biometrics, should have high randomness so that it can not be easily guessed by anybody. The details of it are described in [4] and quoted by [5,7,20,21].
- IPIs can be measured at several parts of the body with various types of biosensor. This background can be also confirmed by [4].
- IPI can be found inside the body or on the body surface. IPI can be measured by a intra-arterial catheter with biosensors implanted inside the body [4]. And, it can be obtained on the body face with using electrodes to collect ECG such as [15].

4.2   Notations

For concreteness and simpler presentation, we use notations as below.

$m_{i,j}$ is the jth biometric measured from a biosensor in the jth session.

f is an error correcting function.

C is an set of commitments for correcting error bits.

$c_{i,j}$ is the jth commitment to correct error bits of biometrics in the jth session. $(c \in C)$.

$h(\cdot)$ is one-way hash function.

$H(\cdot)$ is the starting or ending 128-bit segment of the output of $h(\cdot)$.

$\oplus$ is a XOR operator.

$|y|$ is the bits length of y.

$a||b$ is the concatenation of a and b.

seq is an sequence number of each payload.

$Data$ is an biometric information for observing patient's health status. It is separated from $m_{i,j}$.

$eData$ is an encrypted data.

$E_x(Data)$ is a symmetric cryptosystem to encrypt $Data$ with key x.

$D_x(eData)$ is a symmetric cryptosystem to decrypt $eData$ with key x.

key^i_{AB} is a session key shared between node A and node B at ith session.

There are an code set $C = \{0^l, 1^l\}^k$ to correct error bits. l is the length of a commitment $c_{i,j}$ from C and k is the number of c for committing one secret. The secret is IPI for generating a session key. Consider the distribution of a 128-bit cryptographic key in BSNs, it should be $l \times k = 128$ to commit biometrics. Considering a typical heart rate of 70 beats per minute [2] and 8 bits obtained from each IPI value at a time, we need to sufficiently collect several IPIs for generating 128-bit secret.

4.3   Single Commitment Scheme Applying Original Fuzzy Scheme

In Table 1, we introduce single commitment scheme applying an original fuzzy scheme.

The fuzzy commitment scheme [12] is applied to BSNs without any modification. We use seq instead of MAC to verify $eData$. If payload loss or data fabrication occur during delivering $eData$ from node A to node B, node B can not derive seq by decrypting $eData$. If seq does not extracted, node B requests node A to transmit the payload again. Otherwise, node B accepts $eData$ and waits for next $eData$. However, Table 1 includes a vital problem. An adversary can collect $m_i \oplus c_i$ through eavesdropping the communication between node A and node B at the ith session. c_i is selected from C and everybody know its code set, C. Thus the adversary can exactly guess c_i with the probability $\frac{1}{2^k}$. Considering $l \times k = 128$, the probability is $\frac{1}{2^{\frac{128}{l}}}$. If we consider that a cryptographic key consists of 128 bits [5,7] commonly in BSNs, l should be 1 because the probability must be smaller than $\frac{1}{2^{128}}$ for an adversary not to easily guess the key. However, in case of that, the extent of error bits to be corrected is

Table 1. Single commitment protocol using an original fuzzy scheme

Biosensor(node A)		Central device(node B)
measure m_i, choose c_i		measure $m\prime_i$
$\delta_i = m_i \oplus c_i$		
$(\delta_i, h(c_i))$	$\rightarrow$	
		$c\prime_i = \delta_i \oplus m\prime_i$
		$c_i = f(c\prime_i)$
		check if $h(c_i) = h(c\prime_i)$
		else, restart a session
		$m_i = \delta_i \oplus c_i$
eData $= \mathbf{E}_{\mathbf{m_i}}(\mathbf{seq}\|\mathbf{Data})$	$\rightarrow$	
		$\mathbf{seq}\|\mathbf{Data} = \mathbf{D}_{\mathbf{m_i}}(\mathbf{eData})$

$0(= |\frac{1-1}{2}|)$ bits. It is useless under BSNs, which is an environment that error bits often occur. That is why we need alternative.

4.4 Multiple Commitments Scheme Applying an Original Fuzzy Scheme

The alternative describes in Table 2. As you can see, the alternative is that node A sends node B several biometrics in Table 2. As the length of $m_{i,j}$ consists of 8 bits [7], it is suitable that the length of l is 8. k is computed as $16(= \frac{128}{8})$. Because l is 8, the extent of error bits to be corrected is $3(= |\frac{8-1}{2}|)$ bits per 8 bits. In order to create a 128-bit key, the number of biometrics is $8(= \frac{128}{16} = n)$. In other words, if $n = 8$, it is possible to generate a session key with high security, $\frac{1}{2^{128}}$. And, a session key between node A and node B is generated like (1) using biometrics collected during the session. H uses the first 128 bits of $H(m_1\| \cdots \|m_n)$.

$$key^i_{AB} = H(m_1\| \cdots \|m_n) \tag{1}$$

However, the scheme of Table 2 has a problem as mentioned above. It is available for an adversary to predict each $c_{i,j}$ by computing $h(c_{i,j})$. Because $h_{c_{i,j}}$ enables the adversary to find the exact $c_{i,j}$ by checking if $c_{i,j}$ arbitrarily chosen by her is dependable. Assuming that l be 8, the adversary can exactly guess each $c_{i,j}$ with the probability $\frac{1}{2^{16}}(= \frac{1}{2^k} = \frac{1}{2^{\frac{128}{8}}})$ through checking whether $h(c_{i,j})$ is equal to $h(c^{adv}_{i,j})$; $c^{adv}_{i,j}$ is voluntarily chosen from C by the adversary.

4.5 Multiple Commitments Scheme Applying a Modified Fuzzy Scheme

Table 3 displays the final scheme. To eliminate the reliable source for confirming c, node A does not transmit each $h_{c_{i,j}}$ in the final scheme. Instead, node A transmits γ_i to node B after terminating the transmission of all $\delta_{i,j}$ in the ith

Table 2. Multiple commitments scheme using an original fuzzy scheme

Biosensor(node A)	Central device(node B)
measure $m_{i,1}$, choose $c_{i,1}$	measure $m\prime_{i,1}$
$\delta_1 = m_{i,1} \oplus c_{i,1}$	
$(\delta_{i,1}, H(c_{i,1}))$ $\rightarrow$	
	$c\prime_{i,1} = \delta_{i,1} \oplus m\prime_{i,1}$
	$c_{i,1} = f(c\prime_{i,1})$
	check if $H(c_{i,1}) = H(c\prime_{i,1})$
	else, ask new $\delta_{i,1}$ to node A
	$m_{i,1} = \delta_{i,1} \oplus c_{i,1}$
$\bullet\ \bullet\ \bullet$	$\bullet\ \bullet\ \bullet$
measure $\mathbf{m_{i,n}}$, choose $\mathbf{c_{i,n}}$	measure $m\prime_{i,n}$
$\delta_{i,n} = \mathbf{m_{i,n}} \oplus \mathbf{c_{i,n}}$	
$(\delta_{ni,}, \mathbf{H(c_{i,n})})$ $\rightarrow$	
	$c\prime_{i,n} = \delta_{i,n} \oplus \mathbf{m\prime_{i,n}}$
	$\mathbf{c_{i,n}} = \mathbf{f(c\prime_{i,n})}$
	check if $\mathbf{H(c_{i,n})} = \mathbf{H(c\prime_{i,n})}$
	else, ask new $\delta_{i,n}$ to node A
	$m_{i,n} = \delta_{i,n} \oplus c_{i,n}$
$\mathbf{key^i_{AB}} = \mathbf{H(m_{i,1}||\cdots||m_{i,n})}$	$\mathbf{key^i_{BA}} = \mathbf{H(m_{i,1}||\cdots||m_{i,n})}$
$eData = E_{key^i_{AB}}(seq||Data)$ $\rightarrow$	
	$seq||Data = D_{key^i_{BA}}(eData)$

session. γ_i is computed as (2). And, node B also computes $\gamma\prime$ in order to check if $\gamma_i = \gamma_i\prime$. If the check is satisfied, node B believes that it correctly predicts all $c_{i,j}$. It means that node B leads to the same ith session key, key^i_{AB}, with node A.

$$\gamma_i = H(c_1||\cdots||c_n) \qquad (2)$$

Due to delivering the hash value only once, the probability that an adversary precisely guesses all $c_{i,j}$ can be close to 0. Namely, an adversary can not compute each $c_{i,j}$ from γ_i because of the property of one-way hash function [8]. Supposing that l be 8, k would be $16(= \frac{128}{8})$. We define the probability that the adversary guesses $c_{i,j}$ as $p^{adv}_{i,j}$. Now, each $p^{adv}_{i,j}$ is determined as $\frac{1}{2^{16}} = (\frac{1}{2^k})$. That is to say, the adversary has no bases in order to verify $c^{adv}_{i,j}$. To decrease $p^{adv}_{i,total}$ as mentioned in (3), we have to expand n, which is the number of flows. Each $p^{adv}_{i,j}$ is $\frac{1}{2^k}$ so that $p^{adv}_{i,total}$ is decided on $\frac{1}{2^{k \times n}}$.

$$p^{adv}_{i,total} = p^{adv}_{i,1} \times \cdots \times p^{adv}_{i,n} \qquad (3)$$

In case of that k is 16, n must be at least $8(\because \frac{1}{2^{16 \times n}} \leq \frac{1}{2^{128}})$. For that reason, the adversary can not get any information to compromise a session key in the

Table 3. Multiple commitments scheme using modified fuzzy scheme

Biosensor(node A)	**Central device(node B)**
measure $m_{i,1}$, choose $c_{i,1}$ $\delta_{i,1} = m_{i,1} \oplus c_{i,1}$ $\delta_{i,1} \quad\quad \rightarrow$	measure $m\prime_{i,1}$
	$c\prime_{i,1} = \delta_{i,1} \oplus m\prime_{i,1}$ $c_{i,1} = f(c\prime_{i,1})$ $m_{i,1} = \delta_{i,1} \oplus c_{i,1}$
$\bullet\ \ \bullet\ \ \bullet$	$\bullet\ \ \bullet\ \ \bullet$
measure $m_{i,n}$, choose $c_{i,n}$ $\delta_{i,n} = m_{i,n} \oplus c_{i,n}$ $\delta_{i,n} \quad\quad \rightarrow$	measure $m\prime_{i,n}$
	$c\prime_{i,n} = \delta_{i,n} \oplus m\prime_{i,n}$ $c_{i,n} = f(c\prime_{i,n})$ $m_{i,n} = \delta_{i,n} \oplus c_{i,n}$
	$\gamma\prime_i = \mathbf{H(c_{i,1}||\cdots||c_{i,n})}$
$\gamma_i = \mathbf{H(c_{i,1}||\cdots||c_{i,n})} \quad \rightarrow$	**check if** $\gamma_i = \gamma\prime_i$ **else, restart a session**
$key^i_{AB} = H(m_{i,1}||\cdots||m_{i,n})$ $eData = E_{key^i_{AB}}(seq||Data) \quad \rightarrow$	$key^i_{BA} = H(m_{i,1}||\cdots||m_{i,n})$ $seq||Data = D_{key^i_{BA}}(eData)$

final scheme. And, the extent of error bits to be corrected is also 3 bits each one IPI like as Table 2.

5 Analysis

5.1 Security Analysis

We discuss security of our final scheme in Table 3. Assume that an adversary can launch passive attack and active attack as explained in Section 3.2. Furthermore, an adversary tries to know a secret and/or want a central device to regard her as a legitimate biosensor. Therefore, authentication scheme in BSNs should be able to protect an adversary from achieving the goal of attacks. Below, we summarize security briefly due to limited pages.

Secure against Passive Attack. An adversary launching passive attack such as eavesdropping cannot succeed in both goals since the proposed scheme supports biometrics as randomness and any information about a secret is never disclosed through eavesdropping.

Secure against Active Attack. Even though an adversary under active attack tries such as spoofing to be illegally authenticated, she succeeds with a negligible probability($\leq \frac{1}{2^{128}}$) which is about as much as she guesses biometrics or collision occurs. To achieve it, she must compromise an implanted biosensor or correctly guess the inputs of γ_i to share the secret with a central device. Compromising the implanted biosensors inside the body is physically infeasible. And, it is impossible to correctly presume each $c_{i,j}$, which is the input of γ_i. The advantage she can get is negligible because there is the property of one-way hash function [8].

5.2   Efficiency Analysis

We analyze efficiency in terms of memory space, operation, and communication overhead each session in BSNs.

Memory Cost. Table 4 shows the required memory overhead to share a key between a central device and each biosensor. In our scheme, memory cost is tiny. Each biosensor implanted in body stores only n biometrics, which consist of 128 bits, to establish a session key with a central device; besides, the old n biometrics are deleted at new session and are newly measured. Considering that n is 4, the required memory overhead is remarkably tiny considering the measurement flash memory of MICA2 is 4,194,304 bits($=$ 512K bytes) [24].

Table 4. The memory overhead to establish a pairwise key between a central device and each biosensor(unit : *bits*)

Scheme	Memory Overhead
[5]	128
Single - Original fuzzy commit.	0
Multiple - Original fuzzy commit.	$128 \times n$
Multiple - Modified fuzzy commit.	$256 \times n$

Computation Cost. Authentication can be divided into user authentication and message authentication. BSNs do not need to carry out user authentication because the acceptable biometric can not be produced if it is not measured inside the same body. And, our scheme does not compute MAC for message authentication. Instead, sequence number to authenticate the payload is included. An original message, *Data*, can be recovered from the encryption data, *eData*, without a key. Therefore, if *eData* has no problem, a sequence number can be obtained from the *eData*. Otherwise, an irregular message may be generated. XOR operation is not displayed in Table 5 because it is negligible.

Communication Cost. We analyze communication overhead of the existing scheme [5] and our schemes in this section. Table 6 indicates communication overhead of each scheme. Table 3 is entirely composed of two phases, initial phase and transmission phase. Key establishment is executed in initial phase and encrypted payloads is delivered in transmission phase. In [5] sharing a pre-deployed key,

Table 5. The computation overhead to generate each payload

Scheme	Hash	Encryption	MAC
[5]	1	1	1
Single - Original fuzzy commit.	1	1	0
Multiple - Original fuzzy commit.	$n+1$	1	0
Multiple - Modified fuzzy commit.	2	1	0

the length of payload is 312 bits, which contains 64 bits for encrypted data, 128 bits for MAC and 128 bits for commitments. Because it has to compute MAC and commitments each payload, a payload is made of 312 bits. Communication overhead of Table 1 is low. Instead, the probability exposing a secret is high. Communication overhead of Table 3 is less than one of Table 2. On the other side, communication overhead of our schemes may be increased more than one of Table 1 at the beginning; however, communication overhead of our schemes is lower than one of Table 1 in the long terms. We compare communication overhead of each scheme in Table 6. N_i stands for the number of $eData$ transmitted at ith session. The length of $eData$ is defined as 64 bits like [5].

Table 6. The communication overhead to securely transmit data(unit : $bits$)

Scheme	Initial Phase	Transmission Phase
[5]	0	$312 \times S_i$
Single - Original fuzzy commit.	256×1	$64 \times N_i$
Multiple - Original fuzzy commit.	$256 \times n$	$64 \times N_i$
Multiple - Modified fuzzy commit.	$128 \times (n+1)$	$64 \times N_i$

6   Conclusion

In this paper, we have proposed and described secure communication scheme in BSNs. We apply the features of biometrics to our scheme for secure key establishment. At the same time, our scheme can be utilized in the medical application environments, which employ the implanted biosensors to monitor patients' health care system. In our scheme, any secrets do not be stored before biosensor deployment. If a secret is exposed, it should be renewed;however, in case of the implanted biosensors, a patient should be operated on to renew the secret. It is absurd. For that reason, our scheme does not deploy any secret beforehand. And, key renewal and key revocation are also very simple. It only requires to restart a session. Our scheme is of good performance. Although communication overhead is additionally required in the initial phase for key establishment, total communication overhead is on the decrease because of small data packet size in comparison with the existing scheme. In the future, we would like to analyze our scheme in details and consider different kinds of error correcting code, which is admissible in BSNs.

Acknowledgments. This work was supported by the IT R&D program of MKE/KEIT [KI002113, Development of Security Technology for Car-Healthcare].

References

1. Alfred, J.M., Paul, C.O., Scott, A.V.: Handbook of Applied Cryptography. CRC Press (1997)
2. Bruce Foster, D.: Twelve-lead Electrocardiography: Theory and Interpretation, 2nd edn. Springer, Heidelberg (2007)
3. Cavoukian, A., Stoianov, A.: Biometric Encryption:A Positive-Sum Technology that Achieves Strong Authentication. In: Security and Privacy (2007)
4. Carmen, C.Y.P., Yuan-Ting, Z., Shu-di, B.: A Novel Biometrics Method to Secure Wireless Body Area Sensor Networks for Telemedicine and M-Health. IEEE Communications Magazine, 73–81 (2006)
5. Cherukuri, S., Venkatasubramaniam, K.K., Gupta, S.K.S.: Biosec: A biometric based approach for securing communication in wireless netwokrs of biosensors implanted in the human body. In: Proceeding IEEE Conference Parllel Processing Workshop, pp. 432–439 (2003)
6. Fei, H., Meng, J., Mark, W.: Privacy-Preserving Telecardiology Sensor Networks: Toward a Low-Cost Portable Wireless Hardware/Software Codesign. IEEE Transactions on Information Technology in Biomedicine, 619–627 (2007)
7. Francis, M.B., Dimitrios, H.: Biometric Methods for Secure Communications in Body Sensor Networks: Resource-Efficient Key Management and Signal-Level Data Scrambling. EURASIP Journal on Advances in Signal Processing (2008)
8. Goldreich, O.: Foundations of Cryptography: Basic Tools. Cambridge Unversity Press (2001)
9. Huang, Q., Kobayashi, H., Liu, D., Zhang, J.: Energy/Security Scalable Mobile Crytosystem. Mitsubishi ElectricResearch Laboratories, Inc. (2004)
10. Hoi-Jun, Y., Seong-Jun, S., Namjun, C., Hye-Jeong, K.: Low Energy On-Body Communication for BSN. Springer, Heidelberg (2007)
11. Ineke, M.: Biomedical Applications of Nanotechnology. American Institute of Physics (2002)
12. Juel, A., Wattenberg, M.: A fuzzy commitment scheme. In: Proceeding 6th ACM Conference on Computer and Communication Security, pp. 28–36 (1999)
13. Krishna, K.V., Sandeep, K.S.G.: Security for Pervasive Health Monitoring Sensor Applications. In: Intelligent Sensing and Information Processing, ICISIP, pp. 197–202 (2006)
14. Malmivuo, J., Plonsey, R.: Bioelectromagnetism:Principles and Applications of Bioelectric and Biomagnetic Fields. Oxford University Press, New York (1995)
15. MacLeod, R.: Birchler,B.: ECG Measurement and Analysis (2008)
16. Oscar, G.M., Heribert, B., David, S.S.: Resource-Efficient Security for Medical Body Sensor Networks. In: BSN (2006)
17. Shu-Di, B., Yuan-Ting, Z., Lian-Feng, S.: A new symmetric cryptosystem of body area sensor networks for telemedicine. In: Proceeding of the 6th Asian-Pacific Conference on Medical and Biological Engineering (2005)
18. Shu-Di, B., Yuan-Ting, Z., Lian-Feng, S.: Physiological signal based entity authentication for body area sensor networks and mobile healthcare systems. In: Proceedings of the 27th Annual International Conference of the IEEE Engineering in Medicine and Biology Society (2005)

19. Shu-Di, B., Yuan-Ting, Z., Lian-Feng, S.: A Design Proposal of Security Architecture for Medical Body Sensor Networks. In: BSN (2006)
20. Shu-Di, B., Lian-Feng, S., Yuan-Ting, Z.: A Novel Key Distribution of Body Area Networks for Telemedicine. In: Proceeding of IEEE Workshop on Biomedical Circuits and System (2004)
21. Stefan, D.: Tutorial on Body Area Networks. Philips (2006)
22. Thomas, F., Heribert, B., Javier, E., Karin, K.: Plug 'n Play Simplicity for Wireless Medical Body Sensors. Springer Science+ Business Media, LLC (2007)
23. Willliam, S.: Cryptography and Network Security:Principles and Practice. Prenticall Hall, New Jersey (2006)
24. http://www.xbow.com/products/Product_pdf_files/Wireless_pdf/MICA2_Datasheet.pdf

Mutual Private Set Intersection
with Linear Complexity*

Myungsun Kim, Hyung Tae Lee, and Jung Hee Cheon

ISaC & Dept. of Mathematical Sciences, Seoul National University,
599 Gwanangno, Gwangak-gu, Seoul 151-747, Korea
{msunkim,htsm1138,jhcheon}@snu.ac.kr

Abstract. A private set intersection (PSI) protocol allows players to obtain the intersection of their inputs. While in its unilateral version only the client can obtain the intersection, the mutual PSI protocol enables all players to get the desired result. In this work, we construct a mutual PSI protocol that is significantly more efficient than the state-of-the-art in the computation overhead. To the best of our knowledge, our construction is the *first* result with linear computational complexity in the semi-honest model. For that, we come up with an efficient data representation technique, called *prime representation*.

Keywords: Mutual Private Set Intersection, Prime Representation.

1 Introduction

The *mutual* Private Set Intersection (PSI) problem is the following: both of two players with private sets learn the intersection of their sets without releasing any other information to each other. Roughly speaking, a mutual PSI (mPSI) protocol is a secure computation protocol for the ideal functionality $\mathcal{F}_{\mathsf{mPSI}}$: $(\mathsf{X}_A, \mathsf{X}_B) \to (\mathsf{X}_A \cap \mathsf{X}_B, \mathsf{X}_A \cap \mathsf{X}_B)$ where X_A (resp., X_B) is a private set of the player A (resp., B). This paper's main goal is to construct a secure mPSI protocol that is more efficient than existing work.

There has been much research on the PSI problem. Examples include [2, 14, 19, 16, 5, 18, 17, 10, 9, 11, 7]. In contrast to our work, however, most of prior work except for [19, 5, 11, 7] is focused on solving the *unilateral* PSI problem.[1] In this problem, two players – a server and a client – are allowed to interact on their private sets such that the client only learns the intersection of their input sets, while the server learns nothing.

According to De Cristofaro and Tsudik [10], a mutual PSI protocol can be easily obtained by two instantiations of a unilateral PSI protocol. This argument works fairly well under the semi-honest model. Given a secure mPSI protocol designed by the above approach, consider a way to transform it to one secure

---

* This work was supported by the National Institute for Mathematical Sciences (NIMS) grant funded by the Korea government (No. A21101).
[1] In [10], the authors call this problem a one-way version of the PSI problem.

S. Jung and M. Yung (Eds.): WISA 2011, LNCS 7115, pp. 219–231, 2012.
© Springer-Verlag Berlin Heidelberg 2012

in the malicious model. In general, we enforce a malicious player to behavior as a semi-honest player using zero-knowledge proof techniques. In this model, however, since there is no way to prevent a player from prematurely suspending the execution one of users always can abort when he obtains the intersection and before his counterpart obtains the intersection [15]. Therefore, this approach has a principal limitation to get an mPSI protocol with better security. This is the main reason why we choose not to pursue the direction.

This work may find applications in real-life business requiring enhanced privacy. For example, our work is useful in the relationship-graph example in social networks of Mezzour et al. [21]. A social relationship can correspond to a private personal real-world relationship. Further, the relationship paths are often used for access control mechanisms: nearby people deserve a higher level of trust. Thus, the discovery of relationship paths may be maliciously used in the large-scale targeting and monitoring of multiple individuals in real life based on exposed relationship paths. Mezzour et al. [21] present techniques to protect the privacy of relationship paths in a social network by means of private set intersection.

1.1   Our Contributions

We begin with the novel work by Kissner and Song [19]. Their set-intersection protocol incurs $\mathcal{O}(k^2)$ computation but linear communication overhead where k is the cardinality of each private set. Recall that our goal is to construct a secure and efficient mPSI scheme, more specifically, an mPSI scheme with *linear* computational complexity in the semi-honest model.

Contributions of our work include:

- We present a new representation technique. We call it *Prime Representation*. In contrast to prior work, we represent each element in a private set as a prime number in $\mathbb{Z}^+$. This technique enables to significantly improve the computation complexity.
- We construct an mPSI protocol more efficient than prior work in the computation overhead. To the best of our knowledge, our mPSI protocol is the *first* result with linear computational complexity in the semi-honest model.

1.2   Related Work

Mutual PSI Protocols. Kissner and Song [19] propose an mPSI protocol using oblivious polynomial evaluation (OPE) technique [22]. This protocol is secure in the semi-honest and also malicious model with quadratic computation complexity in the cardinality of set. As mentioned before, they use zero-knowledge proofs (ZKP) to prevent players from deviating the protocol. Later, Dachman-Soled et al. [11] propose an improved construction using Shamir's secret sharing instead of ZKPs. Complexity of their work amounts to $\mathcal{O}(k^2 \log k + k \log^2 k)$ in computation. Camenisch and Zaverucha [5] propose an mPSI protocol for certified sets.

Their protocol also builds on OPE and achieves quadratic computation overhead. Finally, Cheon et al. [7] improve efficiency of Kissner and Song's protocol using the fast Fourier transformation. Complexity of this protocol amounts to sub-quadratic ($\mathcal{O}(k \log^2 k)$) in computation, which is not still linear.

Unilateral PSI Protocols. Freedman et al. [14] introduce the PSI problem and first present protocols based on OPE. The construction in the semi-honest model incurs quadratic computational complexity. But, the number of modular exponentiations can be reduced to $\mathcal{O}(k \log \log k)$ exponentiations for server and $\mathcal{O}(k)$ exponentiations for client. Later, Hazay and Lindell [16] propose one solution using oblivious pseudorandom functions (OPRF). This protocol has been later improved by Jarecki and Liu [18]. The latter incurs the linear computational complexity for each server and client. More recently, Hazay and Nissm [17] improve Freedman et al.'s construction by combining with OPRF. Another family of unilateral PSI protocols utilize blind-RSA signatures [6]. De Cristofaro and Tsudik [10] present unilateral PSI protocols with linear complexity. De Cristofaro et al. [9] provide a unilateral PSI protocol secure in malicious setting with the same complexity.

Organization. The remainder of this paper is organized as follows. In the next section, we briefly introduce the security model and the cryptographic tool. Section 3 provides a full explanation of our representation technique. We present our construction in Section 4 along with analysis. Finally, in Section 5 we discuss how to convert our semi-honest protocol to a malicious one.

2 Preliminaries

In this section, we present our cryptographic tools and security model.

2.1 Additive Homomorphic Encryption

Our construction requires a semantically-secure public-key encryption scheme that holds the group homomorphism of addition and multiplication by a constant. Let $\mathcal{E}_{pk}(\cdot)$ denote the encryption with a key pair (pk, sk). Precisely speaking, an additive homomorphic encryption scheme $\mathcal{E}_{pk}$ supports the following operations that can be performed without knowledge of the private key: (1) Given two encryptions $\mathcal{E}_{pk}(m_1)$ and $\mathcal{E}_{pk}(m_2)$, we can efficiently compute the encryption of $(m_1 + m_2)$, denoted by $\mathcal{E}_{pk}(m_1 + m_2) = \mathcal{E}_{pk}(m_1) +_h \mathcal{E}_{pk}(m_2)$, (2) Given some constant c and an encryption $\mathcal{E}_{pk}(m)$, we can also efficiently obtain $\mathcal{E}_{pk}(cm) = c *_h \mathcal{E}_{pk}(m)$. This property is satisfied by the Paillier encryption [23] or the ElGamal encryption [13], but our protocol utilizes the Paillier encryption.

Remark 1. *One can say the ElGamal encryption [13] can be applied to get the same property. In fact, when an encoding to an individual element a in a set is defined as $a \mapsto g^a$ where g is a generator of a cyclic group, one can* *use the ElGamal encryption and can enjoy the homomorphic properties under addition as well. However, one can easily see that the ElGamal encryption does not provide the efficient decryption.*

Threshold Decryption. Working from Shoup's threshold version of RSA in [24], Damgård and Jurik propose in [12] a threshold version of Paillier's encryption scheme. Threshold encryption requires a pre-determined number of players to collaborate on fully decrypting a message. Any collaboration between fewer than the specified number of contributors does not result in a complete decryption.

2.2 Security Model

We mainly consider the semi-honest model rather than the malicious model. Of course, our final goal is to construct an mPSI secure against malicious adversaries; but sometimes it is not easy to directly obtain the desired result and so we first construct an mPSI protocol secure in the semi-honest model. We then convert this to an construction secure in the malicious model using ZKPs.

In the semi-honest model, all players behavior according to the protocol specification. Security in this model is straightforward: (1) Correctness. an mPSI protocol is *correct* if at the conclusion of execution all of two players output the exact intersection (possible empty) of their respective sets. (2) Privacy. an mPSI protocol is *private* if no players learn information about the subset elements on each player that are not in the intersection of their respective sets.

3   Prime Representation

In this section, we describe the basic intuition of our data representation technique, which is called *prime representation*.

We begin with explaining the rationale behind prime representation. Roughly speaking, our idea is to represent the individual elements of a set as prime numbers. As mentioned above, in Freedman et al.'s protocol [14] a set is represented as a polynomial and the elements of the set is as its roots. That is, a player represents elements in his private set, $X = \{a_1, \ldots, a_k\}$, as the roots of a k-degree polynomial on a ring $\mathbf{R}$, $f(x) = \prod_{i=1}^{k}(x - a_i) \in \mathbf{R}[x]$. Most of mPSI protocols [19, 5, 7] follow this idea.

Our basic observations are:

- Each linear term of the polynomial $f(x)$ is irreducible in the ring of polynomials.
- The fundamental reason that existing mPSI schemes are not practically efficient is that polynomial multiplication and evaluation over encrypted data are too expensive.

Accelerating these operations needs a well-known method called the fast Fourier transformation, or simply FFT. Then polynomial multiplication incurs linear complexity in multiplications on $\mathbf{R}$. However, this technique requires a polynomial to be written by point-value pairs instead of its coefficients. Thus when there are required to evaluate at the product of polynomials, we again have to rewrite the polynomial by its coefficients. In fact, all prior work based on OPE should do polynomial evaluation in the last step. This last step for polynomial evaluation over encrypted data requires at least $\mathcal{O}(k \log^2 k)$ exponentiations. This is the direction that Cheon et al. pursue in [7].

The essence of our idea is simple. While OPE-based mPSIs view each element $a_i \in \mathsf{X}$ as an irreducible element $(x - a_i) \in \mathbf{R}[x]$, we view each element a_i as an *irreducible* element in $\mathbf{R}$ where $i \in [1, k]$. Here we should use $\mathbf{R}$ that has non-trivial irreducible elements, for example, the integers.

3.1 Map-To-Prime

The trivial algorithm for prime representation is as follows. Let $\mathbf{R} = \mathbb{Z}$. Given as input an element $a \in \mathsf{X}$, using a hash function $H : \{0, 1\}^* \to \mathbb{Z}$ it first computes $\alpha = H(a)$. The algorithm then determines whether α is prime or composite. If α is prime, the algorithm outputs α and terminates; otherwise it increments α and checks if $\alpha + 1$ is prime or not. The algorithm repeats this process until obtaining prime.

The above algorithm appears to be suitable for our purpose. However, this solution may be still problematic: if a probabilistic algorithm (e.g., Miller-Rabin algorithm) is employed to determine whether a given value is prime, some composite numbers could be declared "probably prime" with some probability. This may make our protocol work incorrectly. Therefore, we have to use a deterministic algorithm for primality test such as the Agrawal-Kayal-Saxana (AKS) algorithm [1]. In turn, we face to the problem that the AKS algorithm is not efficient enough to be used in practice.

In order to address both non-determinism and inefficiency, we utilize the prime number table $\mathcal{P}_\eta$ that contains η-bit primes. Then we only have to define a random hash function to an index of the table. More specifically, denote by $\wp$ a function to a prime table $\wp : \{0, 1\}^* \to \mathcal{P}_\eta$ and denote by H a hash function $H : \{0, 1\}^* \to \{1, \ldots, \ell\}$ where ℓ is a constant. However, we can see that the function $\wp$ is not collision-free and must be accommodated in some way. For that, we define a process that throws prime numbers into ℓ buckets, such that each bucket contains at most m elements. We will briefly analyze the collision probability later in this section. Our simple algorithm is as follows:

1. Access to a prime table $\mathcal{P}_\eta$ consisting of η-bit primes.
2. For each $a_i \in \mathsf{X}$
   - $\alpha_i = \wp(a_i)$
   - Add α_i to a bucket $\mathcal{B}_j$ where $j = H(\alpha_i)$ for some $j \in \{1, \ldots, \ell\}$.
3. Return $\{\mathcal{B}_j\}_{j=1}^{\ell}$.

Brief Analysis. When it is assumed that the function $\wp$ is uniformly random, the probability that collision does not occur in m results of $\wp$ from distinct elements is

$$\left(1 - \frac{1}{|\mathcal{P}_\eta|}\right) \times \cdots \times \left(1 - \frac{m}{|\mathcal{P}_\eta|}\right) \geq \left(1 - \frac{m}{|\mathcal{P}_\eta|}\right)^m.$$

In our protocol, because we do not need to take care of collision between data elements in different buckets and the average number of elements in each bucket is small (e.g., $m \approx 10$), the probability that collision by $\wp$ occurs in a given bucket is negligible if the size of $\mathcal{P}_\eta$ is sufficiently large (e.g., $|\mathcal{P}_\eta| = 2^{20}$). Moreover, the size of $\mathcal{P}_\eta$ does not depend on the cardinality of datasets since the problem of large datasets can be addressed by adding to the number of buckets. The set of all 20-bit primes is a good example of $\mathcal{P}_\eta$.

4   Our mPSI Protocol

In this section, we provide our mPSI protocol secure against a semi-honest adversaries and analyze the security of the proposed mPSI protocol. Then we compare the complexities with previous mPSI protocols.

Notation. We denote the map-to-prime function by $\wp : \{0,1\}^* \to \mathcal{P}_\eta$ and a uniform random hash function by $H : \{0,1\}^* \to \{1, \ldots, \ell\}$ where ℓ is the number of buckets. $\mathcal{E}_{pk}(\cdot)$ denotes a threshold additive homomorphic encryption scheme. In particular, in this paper we use a threshold version [12] of Paillier's cryptosystem [23] with 2048-bit Paillier modulus N^2, whose message space is $\mathbb{Z}_N^*$.

4.1   Protocol Description

Now, we are ready to describe our mPSI. Each player A, B participates in the protocol with own private input $\mathsf{X}_A = \{a_1, \ldots, a_k\}$ and $\mathsf{X}_B = \{b_1, \ldots, b_k\}$, respectively. For each private element, each player first calculates its bucket index and then maps to a prime using $\wp$. Then, for each bucket index j, the player A (resp. the player B) computes $A_j = \prod_{j=H(a_i)} \wp(a_i)$ (resp., $B_j = \prod_{j=H(b_i)} \wp(b_i)$). In addition, the player A (resp., the player B) chooses random elements r_1, r_2 (resp., s_1, s_2) in $\mathbb{Z}_{\lfloor \sqrt{N}/4 \rfloor}$ for each bucket. Then for each bucket, players A and B do the following:

1. The player A (resp., the player B) computes $\mathcal{E}_{pk}(r_2), \mathcal{E}_{pk}(A_j^2), \mathcal{E}_{pk}(r_1 A_j^2)$ (resp., $\mathcal{E}_{pk}(s_1), \mathcal{E}_{pk}(B_j^2), \mathcal{E}_{pk}(s_2 B_j^2)$) and sends them to his counterpart.
2. Each player computes $\mathcal{E}_{pk}((r_1 + s_1)A_j^2 + (r_2 + s_2)B_j^2)$ using additive homomorphic property.
3. Players A and B perform a threshold decryption to obtain $(r_1 + s_1)A_j^2 + (r_2 + s_2)B_j^2$.
4. Each player checks whether $\wp(a)^2 \mid (r_1 + s_1)A_j^2 + (r_2 + s_2)B_j^2$ or not for all own private input a whose bucket index is j. If $\wp(a)^2$ divides $(r_1 + s_1)A_j^2 + (r_2 + s_2)B_j^2$, then a is included in the intersection.

Common Input: $(\mathcal{E}_{pk}(\cdot),\, H,\, \wp)$

Player A's private input: Player B's private input:
$\mathbf{X}_A = \{a_1, \ldots, a_k\}$ $\mathbf{X}_B = \{b_1, \ldots, b_k\}$

For all $i = 1, \ldots, k,$ For all $i = 1, \ldots, k,$
$\quad A_{H(a_i)} \leftarrow A_{H(a_i)} \cdot \wp(a_i)$ $\quad B_{H(b_i)} \leftarrow B_{H(b_i)} \cdot \wp(b_i)$

For each $j = 1, \ldots, \ell$

$r_1 \leftarrow_R \mathbb{Z}_{\lfloor \sqrt{N}/4 \rfloor},$ $s_1 \leftarrow_R \mathbb{Z}_{\lfloor \sqrt{N}/4 \rfloor},$
$r_2 \leftarrow_R \mathbb{Z}_{\lfloor \sqrt{N}/4 \rfloor},$ $s_2 \leftarrow_R \mathbb{Z}_{\lfloor \sqrt{N}/4 \rfloor},$
computes   computes
$\mathcal{E}_{pk}(r_2), \mathcal{E}_{pk}(A_j^2), \mathcal{E}_{pk}(r_1 A_j^2)$ $\mathcal{E}_{pk}(s_1), \mathcal{E}_{pk}(B_j^2), \mathcal{E}_{pk}(s_2 B_j^2)$

$\xrightarrow{\quad \mathcal{E}_{pk}(r_2), \mathcal{E}_{pk}(A_j^2), \mathcal{E}_{pk}(r_1 A_j^2) \quad}$

$\xleftarrow{\quad \mathcal{E}_{pk}(s_1), \mathcal{E}_{pk}(B_j^2), \mathcal{E}_{pk}(s_2 B_j^2) \quad}$

computes   computes
$\mathcal{E}_{pk}((r_1 + s_1)A_j^2 + (r_2 + s_2)B_j^2)$ $\mathcal{E}_{pk}((r_1 + s_1)A_j^2 + (r_2 + s_2)B_j^2)$
$= (A_j^2 *_h \mathcal{E}_{pk}(s_1))$ $= (B_j^2 *_h \mathcal{E}_{pk}(r_2))$
$+_h (r_2 *_h \mathcal{E}_{pk}(B_j^2)) +_h \mathcal{E}_{pk}(r_1 A_j^2)$ $+_h (s_1 *_h \mathcal{E}_{pk}(A_j^2)) +_h \mathcal{E}_{pk}(s_2 B_j^2)$
$+_h \mathcal{E}_{pk}(s_2 B_j^2)$ $+_h \mathcal{E}_{pk}(r_1 A_j^2)$

Players A and B perform a threshold decryption to obtain $(r_1 + s_1)A_j^2 + (r_2 + s_2)B_j^2$. Then each player checks whether $\wp(a)^2$ divides $(r_1+s_1)A_j^2+(r_2+s_2)B_j^2$ or not for all a in his private set, satisfying $j = H(a)$. If $\wp(a)^2 \mid (r_1 + s_1)A_j^2 + (r_2 + s_2)B_j^2$, a belongs to $\mathbf{X}_A \cap \mathbf{X}_B$.

Fig. 1. Our mPSI for Semi-Honest Model (mPSI-SH)

4.2   Security Analysis

Correctness. Players participating in the protocol correctly obtain the intersection of participating players' private inputs. The following lemma shows that our protocol gives the correctness with overwhelming property.

Lemma 1 (Correctness). *Protocol mPSI-SH correctly computes for the function $\mathcal{F}_{\mathsf{mPSI}}$ with overwhelming property.*

Proof. When a is an element in the intersection $\mathbf{X}_A \cap \mathbf{X}_B$, $\wp(a)$ divides A_j and B_j for the bucket $j = H(a)$. Hence $\wp(a)^2$ divides A_j^2, B_j^2, and $(r_1 + s_1)A_j^2 + (r_2 + s_2)B_j^2$. Therefore, each player learns that a is an element in the intersection.

Assume that a is not an element in the intersection $\mathbf{X}_A \cap \mathbf{X}_B$. We do not consider a is not in $\mathbf{X}_A$ and not in $\mathbf{X}_B$, since no players try to check the divisibility of $\wp(a)^2$. Without loss of generality, suppose a is in $\mathbf{X}_A$, but not in $\mathbf{X}_B$. Then, $\wp(a)$ divides A_j, but does not divide B_j. Hence $\wp(a)^2$ divides A_j^2, but does not divide B_j^2.

In order that $\wp(a)^2$ does not divide $(r_1+s_1)A_j^2+(r_2+s_2)B_j^2$, $\wp(a)^2$ should not divide $r_2 + s_2$. Since r_2 and s_2 are chosen randomly in $\mathbb{Z}_{\lfloor \sqrt{N}/4 \rfloor}$, the probability that $\wp(a)^2$ divides $r_2 + s_2$ is $\dfrac{1}{\wp(a)^2}$. It is the probability that the player A misunderstands that a belongs to the intersection. When the bit size of primes in $\mathcal{P}_\eta$ is 20-bit, the probability becomes about $\dfrac{1}{2^{40}}$. $\qquad\square$

Remark 2. *One may object that the message* $(r_1 + s_1)A_j^2 + (r_2 + s_2)B_j^2$ *may be wrap-rounded by the modular exponentiation of the encryption scheme. Although it is assumed that H is a uniform random hash function, it occurs that some buckets have more than m elements where m is a pre-fixed value such as 10. When players are faced with this situation, they select another uniform random hash function and increase the number of buckets.*

In general, players set m to 10 and use $\mathcal{P}_{20}$ *in the protocol. Then since* r_i's *and* s_i's ($i = \{1,2\}$) *are chosen at random in* $\mathbb{Z}_{\lfloor \sqrt{N}/4 \rfloor}$, A_j *and* B_j *are about 20m-bit,* $(r_1 + s_1)A_j^2 + (r_2 + s_2)B_j^2$ *does not exceed N where N is an 1024-bit integer.*

Privacy. During participating in our mPSI-SH protocol, an adversary can only obtain inputs of a player who is manipulated by himself, encrypted values, and the last value $(r_1 + s_1)A_j + (r_2 + s_2)B_j$. Suppose that a utilized additive homomorphic threshold encryption $\mathcal{E}_{pk}(\cdot)$ is semantically secure. Without loss of generality, it is assumed that the player B is manipulated by the adversary. In order that the adversary learns any information of the player A, he has to find the factor of A_j in the equation

$$(r_1 + s_1)A_j + (r_2 + s_2)B_j = d.$$

Since s_1, s_2, d and B_j are known values to the adversary, it is equivalent to find the factor of an appropriate value of x in the equation

$$xy + c_1 x + c_2 z = c_3, \tag{1}$$

for variables x, y and z and constant c_1, c_2 and c_3, where x can be a product of m primes in table $\mathcal{P}_\eta$. Equation (1) can be substituted by the equation

$$xy + c_1 z = c_2. \tag{2}$$

As far as we know, Equation (2) has finitely many positive integer solutions but there is no efficient algorithm to find solutions. Hence we believe the following conjecture is true.

Conjecture 1. *For variables* x, y, z *and given constant* c_1, c_2, *there is no efficient algorithm to find all solutions for Equation (2).*

Moreover, since z is chosen at random in $\mathbb{Z}_{\lfloor \sqrt{N}/4 \rfloor}$, the number of possible values of z is about 2^{510}. Hence one has to factor about 2^{510} $(c_2 - c_1 z)$'s to solve Equation (2).

The following lemma guarantees the security of our mPSI-SH assuming Conjecture 1 is true and an additive homomorphic threshold encryption is semantically secure.

Lemma 2 (Privacy). *Assume that an additive homomorphic threshold encryption* $\mathcal{E}_{pk}(\cdot)$ *is semantically secure and Conjecture 1 is true, with overwhelming probability, any adversary learns no more information than would be obtained by using the same private inputs in the ideal model with a trusted third party.*

Proof. Since we know that an instance of additively homomorphic encryption is semantically secure, a corrupted player (say B) obtains no information from ciphertexts received from his counterpart.

After engaging in a threshold decryption, the corrupted player learns

$$I = (r_1 + s_1)A_j^2 + (r_2 + s_2)B_j^2.$$

Since only one of players can be controlled over by the adversary, r_i's ($i = \{1, 2\}$) look to be random and are unknown to the adversary.

Hence, by Conjecture 1, $I = (r_1 + s_1)A_j^2 + (r_2 + s_2)B_j^2 = xy + c_1z + c_2$ for some variables x, y and z and constants c_1 and c_2, reveals no information about the private inputs of the honest player (say A), with overwhelming probability, except for that given by computing the intersection of their private sets.   □

4.3   Efficiency Analysis

In this subsection, we analyze the computational and communicational complexity of our mPSI protocol. Also we compare the complexities with those of previous mPSI protocols.

In our protocol, we utilize integer multiplications, modular exponentiations (ME) and integer divisions. Among these operations, ME is the most expensive operations. Hence, we analyze and compare the computational complexity based on the number of MEs.

Complexity of Our mPSI-SH. In our protocol, each player sends three ciphertexts per each bucket. Also each player sends one element to perform a threshold decryption per each bucket. Hence the total communication complexity of mPSI-SH is $8\ell \approx 8k/m$ ciphertexts when ℓ is the number of buckets, k is the cardinality of private input sets, and m is a pre-fixed number which is the bound of the number of elements in a bucket. Therefore, the communication complexity of mPSI-SH is $\mathcal{O}(k)$.

In case of the computational complexity, it is assumed that the threshold Paillier encryption [12] is utilized, which requires 2 MEs for one encryption and 3 MEs (1 ME for share decryption and 2 MEs for share combining) for a threshold decryption per each player. Hence, per each bucket, each player requires 6 MEs for encryptions, 2 MEs for $\mathcal{E}_{pk}((r_1 + s_1)A_j^2 + (r_2 + s_2)B_j^2)$ computation using additive homomorphic property and 3 MEs for a threshold decryption. Therefore, the total computational complexity is $22\ell \approx 22k/m$ MEs and hence it is $\mathcal{O}(k)$.

Comparison with Previous Works. As mentioned before, Kissner and Song [19], Dachman-Soled et al. [11], Camenisch and Zaverucha [5], and Cheon et al. [7] proposed mPSI protocols. Referred to previous analyses, their work has linear communication complexity and more than quasi-linear computational complexity. Table 1 compares our mPSI protocol with the complexity of previous mPSI protocols when two players participate in the protocol.

Table 1. Complexity Comparison

Protocol	Computation	Communication
[19]	$\mathcal{O}(k^2)$	$\mathcal{O}(k)$
[11]	$\mathcal{O}(k^2 \log k + k \log^2 k)$	$\mathcal{O}(k \log^2 k)$
[5]	$\mathcal{O}(k^2)$	$\mathcal{O}(k)$
[7]	$\mathcal{O}(k \log^2 k)$	$\mathcal{O}(k)$
OURS	$\mathcal{O}(k)$	$\mathcal{O}(k)$

Remark 3 (ElGamal Encryption vs. Paillier Encryption). *While our* mPSI-SH *can not utilize the threshold ElGamal encryption scheme, previous* mPSI's *[19, 5, 7] can utilize the ElGamal encryption or a threshold ElGamal encryption. In case of the ElGamal or a threshold ElGamal encryption over elliptic curves, the ciphertext size is 320-bit, but that of the threshold Paillier encryption is 2048-bit. We would like to note that since our protocol requires $7k/m$ ciphertexts, the total transmitted bits are similar to those of other protocols. When $m = 10$, our protocol transmits 1433.6k $(= 2048 \cdot 7k/10)$ bits. However, protocols in [19, 5, 7] transmit $3480k$, $960k$ and $3480k$ bits, respectively.[2]*

In case of ME, 160-bit ME over 1024-bit modulus is about 30 times faster than 1024-bit ME over 2048-bit modulus. Hence, ME in the ElGamal encryption is 30 times faster than that in the Paillier encryption. However the factor m can cancel out the effect of the use of the ElGamal encryption. Since the constant term of the computational complexity of other mPSI protocols are similar with that of ours, the relation between the computational complexities still holds.

5   Transformation to a Malicious Protocol

In this section, we discuss modifications of the protocol mPSI-SH so as to be secure in the malicious model. We add zero-knowledge proofs to mPSI-SH in order to ensure the correctness of all computation. Note that we just provide a sketch for a way to construct a malicious protocol instead of detailed descriptions. Moreover, it should be pointed out that in general generic zero-knowledge proofs are not efficient – especially range proof used in our protocol, and so although our malicious protocol still has the asymptotically linear complexity it may work inefficiently.

We take a look at deviating activities by a malicious player (let say B). The following malicious activities should be taken care:

1. A malicious player uses a random s_i such that $s_i \geq \lfloor \frac{\sqrt{N}}{4} \rfloor$ for $i = 1, 2$.
2. A malicious player makes a product B_j for $j \in [1, \ell]$ that is multiplied by more than m primes.

---

[2] The communication complexity of protocols in [19, 5, 7] are $12k$, $3k$ and $12k$, respectively.

Recall that any other correctness can be detected at the beginning of a threshold decryption. For example, one may think that as a verifier the player A should check the player B has correctly multiplied $\mathcal{E}_{pk}(A_j^2)$ by s_1. However, if the corrupted player B participates in the threshold decryption with different values committed to in encryptions, the honest player can detect his counterpart has a different value and so he can abort the protocol.

Zero-Knowledge Proofs. We use $PK\{(a)|\phi(a)\}$ to denote a zero-knowledge proof of knowledge of the value a that satisfies a publicly computable relation ϕ. For the Paillier encryption, we can efficiently construct zero-knowledge proofs using well-known constructions [3, 8, 4]. Let $\mathcal{C} = (\mathsf{G}, \mathsf{C}, \mathsf{O})$ be the generation, the commit and the open algorithm of a trapdoor commitment scheme [20].

- $PK\{(\alpha_1, \alpha_2)|u = \mathsf{C}(\alpha_1) \wedge v = \mathcal{E}_{pk}(\alpha_2) \wedge w = \alpha_1 *_{\mathsf{h}} v\}$: a zero-knowledge proof of knowledge that C encrypts $\alpha_1 \alpha_2 \pmod{N}$ [8, Sec. 8.1.2].
- $PK\left\{(r)|C = \mathcal{E}_{pk}(r) \wedge r \in \left[0, \lfloor \frac{\sqrt{N}}{4} \rfloor \right]\right\}$: a zero-knowledge proof of knowledge that r lies in $r \in \left[0, \lfloor \frac{\sqrt{N}}{4} \rfloor \right]$ [4].
- $PK\{(\alpha_1, \ldots, \alpha_m)| \wedge_{i=1}^{m} (u_i = \mathsf{C}(\alpha_i)) \wedge_{i=1}^{m-1} (v_i = \mathcal{E}_{pk}(\alpha_{i+1})) \wedge_{i=1}^{m-1} (w_i = w_{i-1} *_{\mathsf{h}} v_i)\}$ where $w_0 = \alpha_1$: the generalized proof of $PK\{(\alpha_1, \alpha_2)|u = \mathsf{C}(\alpha_1) \wedge v = \mathcal{E}_{pk}(\alpha_2) \wedge w = \alpha_1 *_{\mathsf{h}} v\}$ for m tuples $\{\alpha_1, \ldots, \alpha_m\}$ [3, 8].

Transformation. Recall that the primary purpose of this section is to show that using generic zero-knowledge techniques we can convert our mPSI-SH to one that is secure in the malicious model. To do so, when the player A sends $\mathcal{E}_{pk}(r_2)$ to the player B, he sends it along with a zero-knowledge proof of range proof (the second PK in the above list). The player A sends $\mathcal{E}_{pk}(r_1 A_j^2)$ along with a zero-knowledge proof of the correct multiplication, i.e., the first PK. Further, he sends $\mathcal{E}_{pk}(A_j^2)$ along with the third PK, which is the generalization of a zero-knowledge proof of the correct multiplication.

6 Conclusion

In this work, primarily we present a mutual private set intersection protocol with linear complexity. Further we compare our construction with existing work and show it is secure in the semi-honest model. However, there is still remaining work as follows: (1) present a detailed description for the malicious mPSI protocol, (2) show that this construction is secure in the malicious model in the simulation paradigm, and (3) finally extend it to the multiparty setting.

References

1. Agrawal, M., Kayal, N., Saxena, N.: PRIMES is in P. Annals of Mathematics 160(2), 781–793 (2004)
2. Agrawal, R., Evfimievski, A., Srikant, R.: Information sharing across private database. In: Halevy, A., Ives, Z., Doan, A. (eds.) SIGMOD, pp. 86–97 (2003)

3. Camenisch, J.: Proof systems for general statements about discrete logarithms. Technical Report TR 260, Dept. of Computer Science, ETH Zurich (1997)
4. Camenisch, J.L., Chaabouni, R., shelat, a.: Efficient Protocols for Set Membership and Range Proofs. In: Pieprzyk, J. (ed.) ASIACRYPT 2008. LNCS, vol. 5350, pp. 234–252. Springer, Heidelberg (2008)
5. Camenisch, J., Zaverucha, G.M.: Private Intersection of Certified Sets. In: Dingledine, R., Golle, P. (eds.) FC 2009. LNCS, vol. 5628, pp. 108–127. Springer, Heidelberg (2009)
6. Chaum, D.: Blind signatures for untraceable payments. In: Chaum, D., Rivest, R., Sherman, A. (eds.) Advances in Cryptology-Crypto, pp. 199–203 (1982)
7. Cheon, J.H., Jarecki, S., Seo, J.H.: Multi-party privacy-preserving set intersection with quasi-linear complexity. Cryptology ePrint Archive, 2010/512 (2010)
8. Cramer, R., Damgård, I., Nielsen, J.B.: Multiparty Computation from Threshold Homomorphic Encryption. In: Pfitzmann, B. (ed.) EUROCRYPT 2001. LNCS, vol. 2045, pp. 280–299. Springer, Heidelberg (2001)
9. De Cristofaro, E., Kim, J., Tsudik, G.: Linear-Complexity Private Set Intersection Protocols Secure in Malicious Model. In: Abe, M. (ed.) ASIACRYPT 2010. LNCS, vol. 6477, pp. 213–231. Springer, Heidelberg (2010)
10. De Cristofaro, E., Tsudik, G.: Practical Private Set Intersection Protocols with Linear Computational and Bandwidth Complexity. In: Sion, R. (ed.) FC 2010. LNCS, vol. 6052, pp. 143–159. Springer, Heidelberg (2010)
11. Dachman-Soled, D., Malkin, T., Raykova, M., Yung, M.: Efficient Robust Private Set Intersection. In: Abdalla, M., Pointcheval, D., Fouque, P.-A., Vergnaud, D. (eds.) ACNS 2009. LNCS, vol. 5536, pp. 125–142. Springer, Heidelberg (2009)
12. Damgård, I., Jurik, M.: A Generalisation, a Simplification and some Applications of Paillier's Probabilistic Public-Key System. In: Kim, K. (ed.) PKC 2001. LNCS, vol. 1992, pp. 119–136. Springer, Heidelberg (2001)
13. El Gamal, T.: A Public Key Cryptosystem and a Signature Scheme Based on Discrete Logarithms. In: Blakely, G.R., Chaum, D. (eds.) CRYPTO 1984. LNCS, vol. 196, pp. 10–18. Springer, Heidelberg (1985)
14. Freedman, M.J., Nissim, K., Pinkas, B.: Efficient Private Matching and Set-Intersection. In: Cachin, C., Camenisch, J.L. (eds.) EUROCRYPT 2004. LNCS, vol. 3027, pp. 1–19. Springer, Heidelberg (2004)
15. Goldreich, O.: The foundations of cryptography, vol. 2. Cambridge University Press (2004)
16. Hazay, C., Lindell, Y.: Efficient Protocols for Set Intersection and Pattern Matching with Security Against Mailicious and Covert Adversaries. In: Canetti, R. (ed.) TCC 2008. LNCS, vol. 4948, pp. 155–175. Springer, Heidelberg (2008)
17. Hazay, C., Nissim, K.: Efficient Set Operations in the Presence of Malicious Adversaries. In: Nguyen, P.Q., Pointcheval, D. (eds.) PKC 2010. LNCS, vol. 6056, pp. 312–331. Springer, Heidelberg (2010)
18. Jarecki, S., Liu, X.: Efficient Oblivious Pseudorandom Function with Applications to Adaptive ot And secure Computation of Set Intersection. In: Reingold, O. (ed.) TCC 2009. LNCS, vol. 5444, pp. 577–594. Springer, Heidelberg (2009)
19. Kissner, L., Song, D.: Privacy-Preserving Set Operations. In: Shoup, V. (ed.) CRYPTO 2005. LNCS, vol. 3621, pp. 241–257. Springer, Heidelberg (2005)
20. MacKenzie, P.D., Yang, K.: On Simulation-Sound Trapdoor Commitments. In: Cachin, C., Camenisch, J.L. (eds.) EUROCRYPT 2004. LNCS, vol. 3027, pp. 382–400. Springer, Heidelberg (2004)

21. Mezzour, G., Perrig, A., Gligor, V., Papadimitratos, P.: Privacy-Preserving Relationship Path Discovery in Social Networks. In: Garay, J.A., Miyaji, A., Otsuka, A. (eds.) CANS 2009. LNCS, vol. 5888, pp. 189–208. Springer, Heidelberg (2009)
22. Naor, M., Pinkas, B.: Oblivious transfer and polynomial evaluation. In: STOC, pp. 245–254 (1999)
23. Paillier, P.: Public-Key Cryptosystems Based on Composite Degree Residuosity Classes. In: Stern, J. (ed.) EUROCRYPT 1999. LNCS, vol. 1592, pp. 223–238. Springer, Heidelberg (1999)
24. Shoup, V.: Practical Threshold Signatures. In: Preneel, B. (ed.) EUROCRYPT 2000. LNCS, vol. 1807, pp. 207–220. Springer, Heidelberg (2000)

Advanced Path Selection Method for Detection of False Reports in Statistical Filtering Based WSNs

Chung Il Sun and Tae Ho Cho

School of Information and Communication Engineering, Sungkyunkwan University,
Suwon, Korea
{cisun,taecho}@ece.skku.ac.kr

Abstract. Sensor nodes communicate with each other via wireless channels, which are not particularly secure. Accordingly, sensor nodes are vulnerable to physical attacks, potentially compromising the node's keys. An adversary can capture deployed nodes and inject the false reports using captured nodes. False reports attacks can lead not only false alarms, but also the depletion of energy resource of nodes. Yet *et al.* proposed statistical en-route filtering scheme to filter out such false report in en-route process. Several research efforts to improve the detection power of SEF have been made. Sun *et al.* proposed a path selection method (PSM) for improving the detection power of SEF using a control message contained the key information of visited nodes. However, the key information does not be updated or reset in the flooding process. Consequently, nodes which are located far from the sink cannot evaluate accurate quality of the incoming path and choose the secure paths. In this paper, we proposed an advanced path selection method for improving the detection power of PSM using two partition arrays and information of downstream nodes of forwarding node. By using this information, each node evaluates and chooses the most secure paths. To show the effectiveness, we have compared the proposed method with the two existing methods, SEF and PSM, in terms of filtering ratio of false reports and energy consumption for detection by providing simulation results.

Keywords: wireless sensor networks, false data injection attack, false reports, statistical filtering, security, secure routing.

1   Introduction

A wireless sensor network (WSN) is a collection of sensor nodes which monitor various changes of environment in a collaborative manner without any underlying infrastructure support [1]. Recent advances in wireless communications and low-power highly integrated electronics have enabled the development of low-cost and multi-functional sensors with sensing, computation and wireless communications capabilities [2]. Moreover, research efforts of MEMS (micro-electro-mechanical-systems) have been made to develop the sensor hardware and network architecture in order to deploy sensor network in various applications effectively. In many

S. Jung and M. Yung (Eds.): WISA 2011, LNCS 7115, pp. 232–241, 2012.

applications, sensor networks consist of a number of small sensor nodes which is deployed in open, wide, and unmanned environments to collect sensing data and forward it to the base station via wireless communication [3]. Sensor nodes communicate with each other via wireless channels, which are not particularly secure [4]. Accordingly, sensor nodes are vulnerable to physical attacks, potentially compromising the node's cryptographic keys [5]. An adversary having the hostility can easily capture and compromise the deployed nodes due to environmental characteristic of sensor nodes. An adversary's goal is to case false alarms, or to deplete the limited energy resource of nodes by injecting the false data through the compromised nodes. The injected false reports should be dropped en-route as early as possible to minimize the grave damage. The few elusive one should be further filtered out at the sink node [6].

Several symmetric cryptography-based security solutions [6, 7, 8] have recently been proposed to filter out such false reports. Typical one is the statistical en-route filtering (SEF) scheme proposed by Ye et al [6]. This method can filter out false reports during the forwarding process. In this scheme, sensing nodes sensed an identical event collaboratively create an event report which contains multiple message authentication codes (MAC). Each MAC is generated by a sensing node using one of own symmetric keys, and represented its agreement on the report [6]. The event report is forwarded towards the base station over multi hops. In the forwarding process, each forwarding node verifies the MACs attached in the event report and checks those MACs if it has any of keys used to generate in the report. If it does not have any of those keys, the report will be transmitted to the next node without verification process.

The path selection method (PSM) [9] was proposed to improve the detection power of SEF. In this scheme, deployed sensor nodes evaluate the incoming paths from the base station and select the most secure paths against false report attack. Each message to establish the routing paths attaches a partition array which contains the additional information about the partition index of the visited nodes. However, the partition array is fixed and does not be updated or reset if all the bits in the partition array are set in the flooding process. Consequently, nodes which are located far from the base station cannot evaluate accurate quality of the incoming path and choose the secure paths.

In this paper, we proposed an advanced path selection method for improving the detection power of PSM using additional partition array and neighbor information of node. The size of both partition arrays are fixed by the threshold which is determined by user before the deployment of nodes. The first partition array contains the key information about the current visited nodes and the second one is copy of former partition array in which all bits are set. By using this information, each node evaluates and chooses the most secure paths. To show the effectiveness, we have compared the proposed method with the two existing methods, SEF and PSM, in terms of filtering ratio of false reports and energy consumption for detection by providing simulation results.

The remainder of the paper is organized as follows: Section 2 briefly explains the related works and the motivation. Section 3 describes the new proposed method.

Simulation results are given in Section 4. Finally, the conclusions and future works are discussed in Section 5.

2   Related Works and Motivation

In this section, we brief the two existing methods [6, 9] and explain the motivation of purpose.

2.1   Statistical En-route Filtering (SEF)

SEF is the first solution that address false data injection attacks in presence of captured nodes and it focus on the detection of false reports [6]. In this scheme, the base station maintains a global key pool which is divided into multiple partitions by user. Every node pre-loads a small number of keys from a randomly selected partition in global key pool.

If real events occur in sensor field, each of the sensing nodes reports its sensed data and one of them is elected as the center-of-stimulus (CoS) node to generate a sensing report. The detecting nodes, which sense the same event, generate the report with MACs for the event using their stored keys. The CoS collects all the received sensing data, and produces a sensing report using the collected MACs. The choice of parameter T, which is the number of distinct MACs needed to produce the legitimate report, trades off between detection power and overhead [6]. The set of multiple MACs in the sensing report acts as the proof that a sensing report is legitimate [6]. The sensing report is forwarded toward the base station over multi hops. In forwarding process, when a node receives a report it verifies the correctness of the MACs attached in the report by using it stored keys. If an attached MAC in the repot differs from the one locally produced by a forwarding node, the report is generated an adversary with incorrect keys through a compromised node. Such a MAC is forged and the report will be dropped. If a forwarding node does not have any of the keys indicated by the key indices, it passes the report to the next hop. When a repot arrives at a base station, it can be verified by base station because it has complete knowledge of the global key pool [6].

2.2   Path Selection Method

A path selection method for improving the detection power of the SEF scheme is presented. In PSM, routing paths are established by flooding with a control message. The control message contains information about the partition IDs of visited nodes and hop count. By using the partition ID arrays received from the incoming paths, each node can choose the safest path against false data injection attacks. A simple function to evaluate the qualification of the paths can be provided. A routing path is chosen by the node, using a qualification evaluation function, which considers the distance travelled and the security level [9].

2.3   Motivation

In SEF, the filtering power of false reports is affected by the selection of the routing paths largely. In the worst case, forwarding nodes cannot verify any false reports because these forwarding nodes may not have any of the keys used in report. Also, the larger number of verifying the false reports in the forwarding process increases the probability that forwarding nodes drop the false reports as early as possible. If false reports cannot be detected and dropped by forwarding nodes, it can be rejected by base station. However, transmitting the false reports drains the finite energy resource of the forwarding nodes so that it results in reducing the life time of network. To provide the detection power of path, PSM is proposed. In PSM, a partition ID array in a control message is fixed and does not be initialized when all bit of array are set. Consequently, nodes located in far from the BS cannot insert its own key information into the control message and updated it so that they cannot evaluate the incoming paths. It can evaluate the incoming path using only hop count in a control message. Therefore, they cannot select the secure path for detecting the false report.

In this paper, we propose an advanced path selection method (APSM). In our method, two partition arrays are in a control message and are used to gain the key information of visited nodes. One of them loads the key information and resets periodically, when all bit of array is set. The other saves the filled partition array while the previous partition array is initialized. The control message includes the number of downstream nodes of visited node. It reflects the energy consumption of nodes. If a node has many downstream nodes, it will consume more energy than others that has small number of downstream nodes. Each node evaluates incoming paths using a qualification evaluation function, which considers the security level, the distance travelled, and energy consumption aspect. The detailed description is presented in section 3.

3   Proposed Method

3.1   Assumption

A sensor network is considered, composed of a large number of small sensor nodes. The network is static (i.e., the topology of the network does not change), and it is assumed that the routing paths are established by flooding with a control message [10]. It is also assumed that the network uses a single-path routing protocol. To simplify the problem, it is further assumed that each node chooses a routing path based on the distance from the BS in the hop count, and the security level against false data injection attacks. After suitable paths have been established, every node forwards packets sent by its downstream (toward source nodes) nodes along the paths and packets sent by others are discarded immediately. An adversary can launch false positive attacks using compromised nodes but it is assumed that the adversary cannot compromise while the routing paths are being set up. The issues of other security attacks, such as false negative attacks, are out of the scope of this paper.

3.2   Overview

In the proposed method, every control message contains additional two partition ID arrays. They include key information about the partition IDs of visited nodes. The information is used to evaluate the security level of a path. As a control message is flooded through the network over multiple hops, each forwarding node updates the partition ID information of the message. Also, the control message includes the number of downstream nodes of visited nodes to evaluate the aspect energy consumption of path. A routing path is chosen by the node, using a qualification evaluation function, which considers the distance travelled, the security level, and energy consumption of nodes. By varying a given security weighting factor, the user can give more priority to the security aspects or to saving energy.

3.3   Advanced Path Selection Method

Similar to the existing PSM, this proposed method evaluates the quality of the paths at early stage of routing paths. Each node pre-loads a few keys from randomly selected partition in global key pool before it is deployed in sensor field. A routing path is established through the flooding of control message transmitted from BS. This fashion is commonly used in most routing protocols. The control message is formed and transmitted in a similar manner with PSM. The following figure 1 shows the format of control message used by the proposed method.

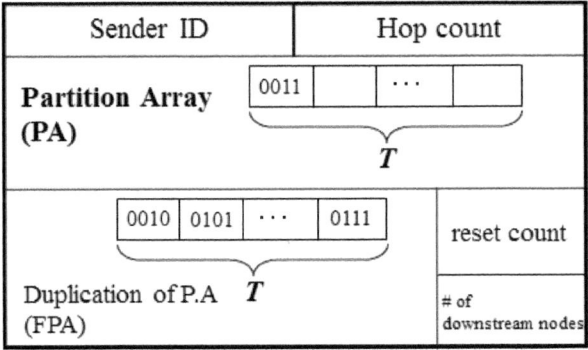

Fig. 1. The control message

Similar to PSM, a control message contains the sender's ID and the number of hops that have taken place from BS. Two arrays of bits are additionally attached into each control message. These arrays are used to mark the partition IDs of the visited nodes. In the control message, the size of partition array is equal to the threshold (T) previously defined by user. The threshold (T) means the number of individual MAC necessary to generate the report. In a case where the partition array is filled, a copy of partition array (FPA) is saved within the control message while the previous partition array is initialized. The number of times the partition array is initialized is separately stored. Figure 2 shows that how a partition array can be updated when a global key pool is divided into ten partitions.

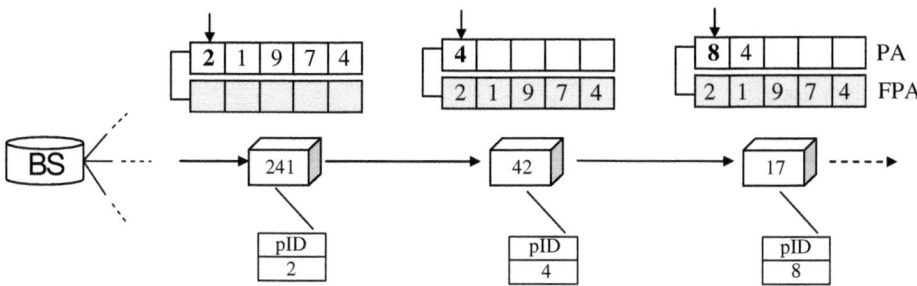

Fig. 2. Flooding the control message

As shown in the figure 2 above, the control message transmitted from BS is delivered to nodes bypassing multi hops. When a node receives a control message, it stores the sender's ID, the hop count from the base station, and the partition array attached in the message. After then it checks whether partition array is filled or not, if all bits are set in the partition array then it saves the partition array into the FPA.

For example, node 241, 42, and 17 have some keys pre-loaded from partition 2, 4, and 8 respectively. When node 241 receives the first control message, it inserts the key information into the first bit of the array. After inserting the key information, it checks whether or not the PA is filled. If PA is filled, it duplicates a PA into the FPA and reset the PA. Then node 241 transmits a control message to the next nodes (i.e., node 42) after updating the number of hop and ID of the node being sent. Similar to the preceding nodes, node 42 and 17 also receives the control message, update the key information and forwards updated message if necessary.

Table 1. Updating the control message

```
Node Nrcv;
SenderID is Nrcv.ID;
HopCount = HopCount +1;

If PA in CM is FULL
      then Nrcv copies PA into FPA;
              Reset the PA;
              ResetCount++;
              Nrcv sets PID to PA;
      else
              Nrcv sets PID to PA;

Nrcv COUNTS duplicated PIDs;
Nrcv FLOODS the CM to neighbor Nodes;
Nrcv COUNTS the number of transmitting the CM to the downstream;
```

Table 1 show the process of updating the control message when a node receives the control message. In the table, CM and PID are control message and the partition ID loaded in a node.

When the flooding of the control message is completed, all nodes evaluate the quality of the incoming paths. A path is chosen by an evaluation function that decides the qualification regarding the path that is both most secure and yet energy conserving, based on the detection power, hop count, and the number of candidates for child node. Each nodes use the following equation (1) in evaluating the qualification of each paths.

$$Q(p) = D(p) + \alpha \cdot S(p) + (1 - \alpha) \cdot N(p) \tag{1}$$

Three factors are considered for evaluation, $Q(p)$, $D(p)$, and $S(p)$. Where p is a path, $Q(p)$ represents the qualification of p. α is a security weight factor determined by the user. The security weighting factor, α, can be between 0 and 1, as that as α increases, each node would choose a more secure but less energy-efficient, path. On the other hand, the network does not consider the detection power if α is 0; each node would select the shortest path. Note that a smaller $Q(p)$ is more qualifialbe than a larger one. $D(p)$ represents the number of hop count within each path. $N(p)$ represents the number of control message being transmitted downstream (i.e., opposite direction of BS). It is clear that energy consumption is affected by hops and the number of downstream nodes (opposite direction the base station). If a node that has many downstream nodes will consume the more energy than others that have small number of downstream nodes. $S(p)$ represents the detection power in accordance with partition array within the a control message. $S(p)$ can also be represented as the following equation (2).

$$S(p) = \frac{DP(p) + 1}{P(p)} \tag{2}$$

$P(p)$ represents the number of unset bits in the partition array received from p. $DP(p)$ represents the number of duplicated partition information among PA and FPA. After receiving the control message, a node evaluates the qualification of each path by using the equation (1) and selects a path with the highest secure path.

4   Simulation Results

To show the effectiveness, the proposed method scheme is compared with the SEF and PSM through simulation studies. The sensor network in the simulation environment consists of 1,000 nodes over a field size is 110 x 110m^2. The nodes are assumed to be randomly distributed in the field and the base station is located at the end of the field. Each node takes 16.56 µJ/12.5µJ to transmit/receive a byte, and each MAC generation consumes 15µJ [6]. The size of a MAC is 1 byte, and the report size is 12 bytes. There are 1,000 keys in the global key pool, which is divided into 10 partitions. Every node evaluates the qualification of a path using equation (1).

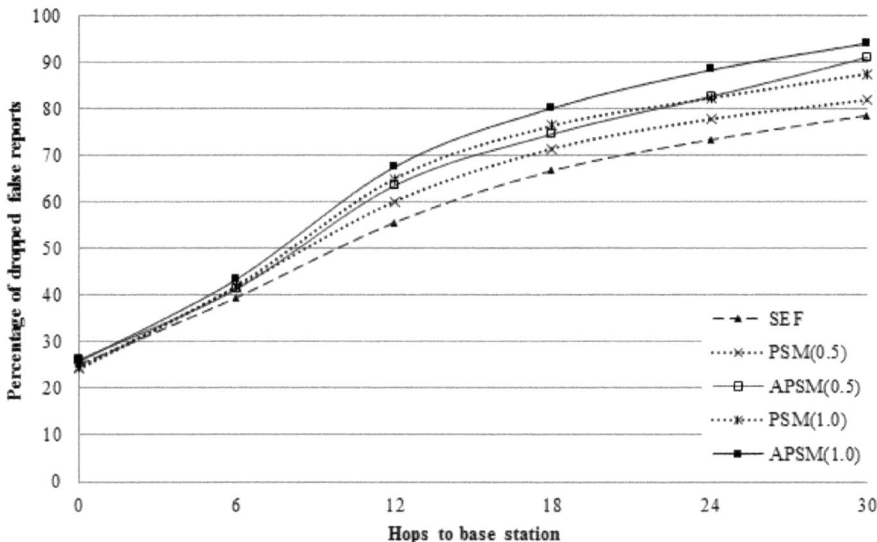

Fig. 3. Percentage of dropped false reports

In Fig. 3 compares the percentage of the dropped false reports of SEF, PSM, and APSM, according to α value, when the hops to base station are 6, 12, 18, 24 and 30. As shown in the figure, the proposed method (α = 0.50 and 1.00), which means the average of α, can filter out a larger number of false reports, during the forwarding process, than PSM (α = 0.50 and 1.00). The figure illustrates a similar performance for APSM and PSM within 12 hops to base station. On the other hand, when the hops between the report generation CoS to the BS are over 12, the performance of the proposed method is a more efficient than PSM and SEF.

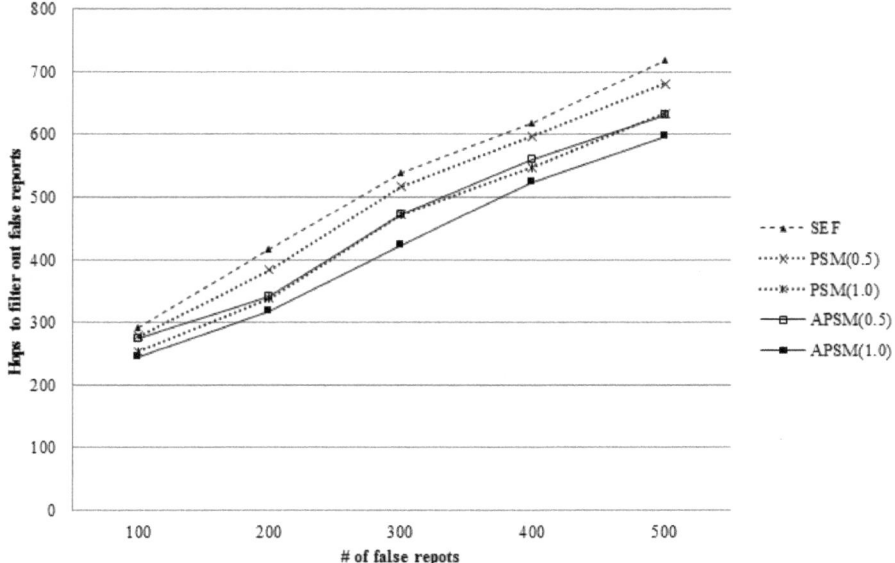

Fig. 4. Hops to filter out false reports

Fig. 4 illustrates the number of traveled nodes to filter out false reports. The number of traveled nodes in the original SEF approach is the highest since routing paths are chosen with consideration of only hop counts ($\alpha = 0$). As shown in above figure, the proposed method detects the false reports earlier than PSM and SEF.

Fig. 5 shows the average energy consumption per legitimate report. The proposed method is less efficient than the original SEF ($\alpha = 0.00$). However, the difference between them is very small. Also, average energy consumption of the proposed method is very similar to PSM. For a legitimate report, the choice of α does not greatly affect the energy consumption characteristics. On the other hand, as α increase, more energy can be saved from false data injection. That is, the proposed method can conserve energy better than the original SEF scheme ($\alpha = 0.00$).

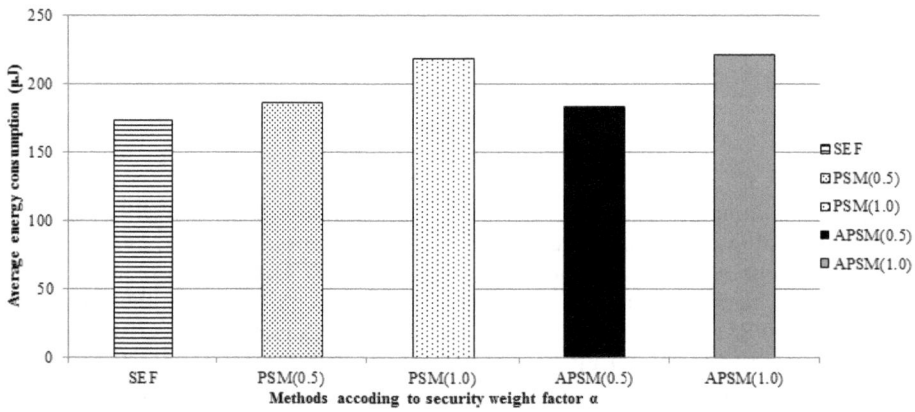

Fig. 5. Average energy consumption per legitimate reports

5   Conclusions

An advanced path selection method for improving the filtering power of PSM is presented. In this method, two partition ID arrays received from the control messages, each node can evaluate security level of incoming paths and select the safest path against false reports attacks. Also, the proposed method improves problem of PSM that the partition ID array does not completely reflect the possession of forwarding nodes located in far from the base station. An improved function to evaluate the qualification of path can be provided. The effectiveness of the proposed method is shown with simulation results. As future works, some AI algorithms will be applied in order to find further optimal solutions.

Acknowledgements. This research was supported by Basic Science Research Program through the National Research Foundation of Korea (NRF) funded by the Ministry of Education, Science and Technology (No. 2011-0004955).

References

1. Akyldiz, I.F., et al.: A Survey on Sensor Networks. IEEE Wireless Communication Magazine 40(8), 102–116 (2002)
2. Arampatzis, T., Lygeros, J., Manesis, S.: A survey of applications of wireless sensor and wireless sensor networks. In: Proceedings of IEEE International Symposium on, Mediterrean Conference on Control and Automation, Limassol, Cyprus, June 27-29, pp. 719–724 (2005)
3. Culler, D., Estrin, D., Srivastava, M.: Overview of sensor networks. IEEE Comput. 8, 41–49 (2004)
4. Wang, Y., et al.: Intrusion Detection in Homogeneous and Heterogeneous Wireless Sensor Networks. IEEE Transaction on Mobile Computing 7(6), 698–711 (2008)
5. Karlof, C., Wagner, D.: Secure routing in wireless sensor networks: attacks and countermeasures. Ad Hoc Netw. 1, 293–315 (2003)
6. Ye, F., Luo, H., Lu, S.: Statistical en-route filtering of injected false data in sensor networks. IEEE J. Sel. Area. Commun. 23, 839–850 (2005)
7. Li, F., Wu, J.: A probabilistic voting-based filtering scheme in wireless sensor networks. In: Proceedings of International Conference on Wireless Communications and Mobile Computing, vol. 3-6, pp. 27–32 (2006)
8. Yu, Z., Guan, Y.: A Dynamic En-route Scheme for Filtering False Data in Wireless Sensor Networks. In: Proceedings of the 3rd International Conference on Embedded Networked Sensor Systems, pp. 294–295 (2006)
9. Sun, C.I., Lee, H.Y., Cho, T.H.: A path selection method for improving the detection power of statistical filtering in sensor networks. J. Inf. Sci. Eng. 25, 1163–1175 (2009)
10. Lee, H.Y., Cho, T.H.: Fuzzy-based path selection method for improving the detection of false reports in sensor networks. IEICE Trans. Inf. Syst. E92-D, 1574–1576 (2009)

Evaluating the Security and Privacy of Near Field Communication – Case: Public Transportation

Jarno Salonen

VTT Technical Research Centre of Finland,
P.O. Box 1300, FI-33101 Tampere, Finland
Jarno.Salonen@vtt.fi

Abstract. Public transportation has been the killer application of Radio Frequency Identification (RFID) technology in recent years. However, RFID-based Near Field Communication (NFC) is gaining the advantage by challenging RFID technology in its own environment. NFC enables the enhanced use of value-adding features, such as obtaining a ticket over-the-air, by using the already existing Internet channel of the mobile device. Smart posters on the other hand provide an improved service initialization method for the mobile device that enhances the functionalities of the existing user interface. This article describes security and privacy challenges related to NFC. We describe the use of NFC in smart posters within services related to public transportation and discuss about further NFC research activities. By providing information to consumers about the security and privacy issues related to NFC, it is possible to increase their awareness and perhaps prevent some potential current or future threats facing the technology.

Keywords: Near Field Communication, NFC, RFID, public transportation, security, privacy.

1   Introduction

Public transportation can be considered as the killer application of radio-frequency identification (later referred to as RFID). RFID technology was invented in the beginning of the twentieth century and since then it has been used in various application areas, for instance in World War II for identifying allied airplanes, these days in retail stores to detect shoplifting and in companies for physical access control. Despite the use in different areas, the actual advantage of the technology was discovered within the mass market; product (and animal) tracking and mass transportation ticketing, being perhaps the largest target applications currently in the global scale.

The drawbacks of RFID technology in public transportation have related mainly on the technical security of the contactless cards and privacy issues related to their information content, but also to the fact that RFID provides merely a basic level of service to the customers. For example adding value to a RFID transportation card generally requires a visit to a ticket office or an automatic ticket vending machine. Also the verification of the card validity or balance requires the same kind of

S. Jung and M. Yung (Eds.): WISA 2011, LNCS 7115, pp. 242–255, 2012.
© Springer-Verlag Berlin Heidelberg 2012

activities from the card holders, i.e. the management of the card and its contents are often considered as fraught in the customer's perspective.

Near Field Communication (later referred to as NFC) is an emerging wireless communication technology that provides the mobile devices, generally mobile phones, with RFID capabilities. In addition to emulating a smart card or working as a reader device, one of the advantages of NFC is the possibility to make use of the existing network connections (mobile network, Internet) of the mobile device in order to add value to the services provided to the customer. In other words NFC enables the possibility to check the validity of the smart card (though now a virtual version stored within the mobile device) over the network as well as add value to the card (e.g. a bus ticket or virtual money) when needed. NFC technology enables also other kind of services for the users, for example information services that can be initiated by touching a tag or launching an application within the mobile device. In other words, NFC technology can be said to enhance the usability of mobile commerce applications and services.

The development of novel NFC based applications and services have increased during the last few years. Mobile phone manufacturers, telecom and service operators have noticed the potential of NFC and put some effort in it in order to be among the first exploiters of this end-user technology. The number of companies taking part in the development process is still growing while, according to a forecast made by ABI Research in April 2007, the number of shipped NFC-enabled handsets in 2012 will be almost 300 million units or 20% of all handsets [1]. This is supported by another forecast made by Frost & Sullivan in December 2010 with the estimated number of shipped NFC-enabled mobile devices increasing from 128 million units or 10% of all handsets in 2011 to over 800 million units or over 50% of all handsets in 2015 [2].

One of the largest user groups of future NFC based applications are going to be the ordinary consumers, who will use the technology in their daily activities. According to ABI Research, electronic paying and mass transport are going to be among the primary applications, and therefore available to a broad range of subscribers right from the beginning. [3] These applications can consist of e.g. accessing one's home using the mobile device as a key, viewing images stored to the digital camera from the television or even operating different home peripherals. Outside home, the technology can be used for acquiring various information items from RFID-based tags, such as public transport timetables, hyperlinks and multimedia advertisements. In addition, NFC technology enables the exchange of, for example contact information between people, payment transactions between shops and their customers or perhaps even between individual people.

This article describes a case of using NFC technology and especially so called "smart posters" in public transportation. Smart posters are used for providing information (timetables and other information), opening an e-ticketing application in the mobile device for obtaining a ticket, and finally using the ticket in the bus or other public transportation. The service process in the first two cases is initialized by touching a tag that is embedded in a so called smart poster, attached to a physical object or acts as an advertisement by itself (e.g. the logo has been printed directly on the tag). Since the third case (using the ticket) is more related to the eTicketing application than the smart poster, it is not covered in this article. The article answers to the following research questions:

1.   What are the main security threats related to NFC in the described use cases?
2.   How to deal with the previously mentioned threats?
3.   What kind of privacy issues can be identified from the use cases?

The results are based on research results and current research work from two European research projects in 2006-2011. The first project had an objective of developing and demonstrating novel and innovative mobile services, which are as easy and intuitive to use as touch and the second project has the objective of developing tools and mechanisms for role and identity management within organisations, taking into account also mobile devices and the possibility to use them for innovative role functionalities.

The article is structured as follows. We begin by determining the basics of NFC and smart posters. Next, we describe two case-examples within the public transportation service area along with their details. In the results chapter we identify the security and privacy challenges of the previously described case-examples. In the discussion chapter we discuss about the difference in NFC and traditional RFID approach and also provide some solutions to dealing with the security issues. Finally we describe some further research activities in the field before concluding the article.

2   Theoretical Perspective to NFC

Near Field Communication (NFC) is an emerging wireless communication technology that is based on already existing RFID (Radio Frequency Identification) technologies. NFC, consisting of two ISO/IEC standards (18092 - NFC Interface and Protocol 1 and 21481 - NFC Interface and Protocol 2), has its background on the ISO14333 (Mifare / Felica) standard [4,5,6] and it provides a short-range communication channel between mobile phones and other devices. The working distance of NFC ranges from only a few centimeters up to 20 centimeters. Therefore the transactions are initialized by practically touching a device to another and the range of services vary from simple information exchange to multimedia or other data transfer. Even though NFC data transfer speed can be up to 424 Kbit/s, the short communication range results into NFC often being used for configuring and initializing other wireless network connections such as Bluetooth or even Wireless LAN.

NFC technology supports two communication modes; in passive mode the initiator device provides an electromagnetic (carrier) field to which the target device, called "transponder" or simply a tag, answers by modulating the existing field and, if required, drawing its operating power from the initiator-powered field. In active mode, both of the devices communicate by generating their own electromagnetic fields which typically requires a power supply from both of the devices. [4]

NFC compliant devices, generally mobile phones, can support three different operation modes:

- Reader mode
- Card emulation mode
- Peer to peer mode

In reader mode, the mobile device functions as a standard contactless reader that performs an action that is initiated by a touch to a tag. The tag then provides information to the device consisting of an action and content. The action can be for example:

- Send (a SMS), call (a number), launch (an application, e.g. the browser)
- Save for later (store a SMS, a telephone number, a bookmark, etc.)
- Open for editing (SMS, telephone number, bookmark, etc.)

The action refers to the content, i.e. the content is the SMS message, the telephone number, the bookmark etc. that is to be used (sent, saved or edited) while performing the action [6].

In card emulation mode, the mobile device functions as a ISO14443 (Mifare / Felica) compliant smart card that can be used for instance in access control and electronic ticketing [6].

In peer-to-peer mode, two devices function as readers and by touching them to each other, the users can initialize a communication channel between them. Peer-to-peer mode can be used for exchanging information between the devices, e.g. business card, individual files or other pieces of data [6].

3   Methodology

In this chapter, we present the methodology used in the research. We begin by introducing smart posters and how they work as a service initiator. Then we present two case-examples in the public transportation area that are partly the results of a European public research project executed in 2006-2008.

3.1   Smart Poster as a Service Initiator

In addition to public transportation, smart posters can be used as advertising elements such as signs or billboards. They incorporate a passive NFC tag that contains data, for example URI (Uniform Resource Identifier), picture or other kind of useful information depending on the service provider and the data memory size. The data can be extracted by touching the tag with a NFC-enabled handset that initiates the data exchange between the tag and the device. Other targets of application for a smart poster can comprise of:

- storage & logistics (tag contains information about products),
- retail store advertisements (coupons, location and other information),
- movie advertisements (movie information, screening times, eTicketing services)
- other services related to the previous

These previously mentioned applications are similar to the public transportation case-example and therefore not discussed in further detail within this article.

Figure 1 shows the general outline of a smart poster transaction. The transaction begins when the user touches the Smart Poster tag with a mobile NFC device (displayed with number 1 in Figure 1). As a response, the tag provides the mobile device with information consisting of action and content (2). The functionalities of the mobile device, for instance the capability of accessing the Internet using mobile data, GPRS, Bluetooth or even WLAN connection, provide the user with added value services. This makes it possible to acquire information from an external source, for example the Internet (3). It is also possible to store information to an external location (4) that can be either a public web server or a private database within the internal company network.

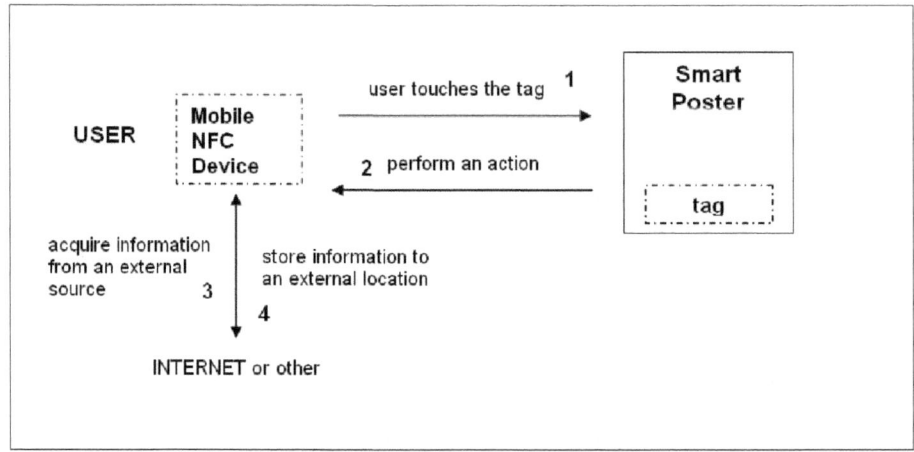

Fig. 1. General outline of a smart poster transaction

The public transportation use case, described in this article, features a mobile eTicketing application that is initialized by touching a NFC tag located at a public transportation station or stop. The primary task of the tag is to launch the application and provide the mobile device information about the location of the user for buying a suitable ticket.

In the following two chapters, we describe two NFC based service concepts within the public transportation area. The examples are a part of a European public research project called SmartTouch in the field of NFC technology that was executed in 2006-2008. The project was funded by the Information Technology for European Advancement (ITEA) strategic programme and had an objective of demonstrating NFC-based services and applications in the European level. The three year project began in 2006 and had 23 partners from 8 European countries that represented mobile device manufacturers, telecommunications service providers, research organisations and SME companies with a common objective of promoting the use of NFC technology among the consumers.

3.2   eTicketing Service

The eTicketing use case described in this article features a method for selecting and purchasing a ticket for public transportation by using the smart poster. The service process is illustrated in Figure 2.

The service process begins as the user touches a tag with his mobile device at a certain public transportation station (displayed with the number 1 in Figure 2). The tag can be located in a smart poster or embedded in a plastic housing that provides better protection for the tag from malicious damage (this can still be considered a smart poster as the casing itself may consist of an advertisement). After the connection establishment, the tag sends the mobile device a command to launch the eTicketing application (2). Next the user is required to select a ticket type, e.g. single ticket, return ticket or other (3). Then the user selects a travel destination point (4). This information is based on the location information provided by the tag, i.e. the application displays only the stations that can be reached from the current location. Finally the user is shown the ticket together with its price and asked for a confirmation in order to purchase the ticket (5). In the last phase, the user consumes the ticket in a public transportation vehicle by touching the mobile device to a reader located in the vehicle. This part is however not covered in this article, because we are focusing only on the smart poster topic.

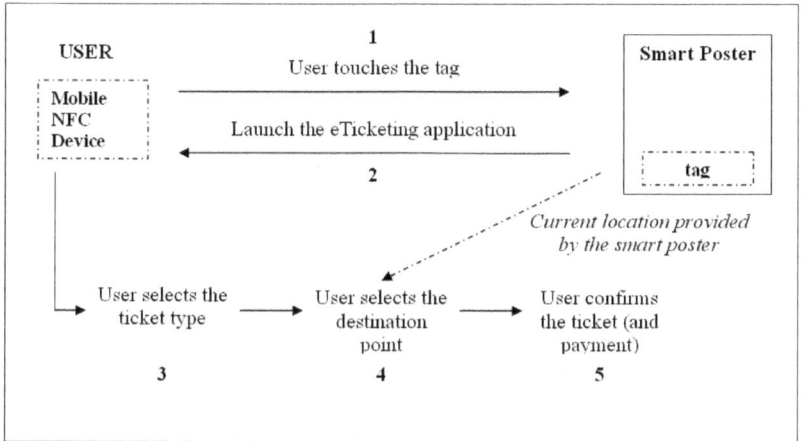

Fig. 2. eTicketing service process

As a prerequisite, the users have to register themselves to the service in order to use the eTicketing application for buying tickets. Registration is done at the service provider's office and requires information about the user (contact information), mobile device (serial number of the NFC interface) and payment information (e.g. credit card number). The eTicketing application can be downloaded to the device during registration or it can be obtained afterwards from a specific web site that can be included in the smart poster tag information content within the public transportation station.

3.3   Timetable Service

The timetable use case described in this article features a method for obtaining timetable information via the smart poster. The service process is illustrated in Figure 3.

The service process in this case is similar to the previous. However, instead of the eTicketing application, the tag provides the mobile device an Internet hyperlink and therefore initiates the launch of the browser application (displayed with the number 2 in Figure 3). The browser is directed to a specific web site that is capable of providing the user with an interface that has been designed for the mobile device. In case the current location information cannot be obtained from the tag, the user has to first select the starting point (3) followed by the destination point (4) after which the service provides the user with the personalized timetable information (5).

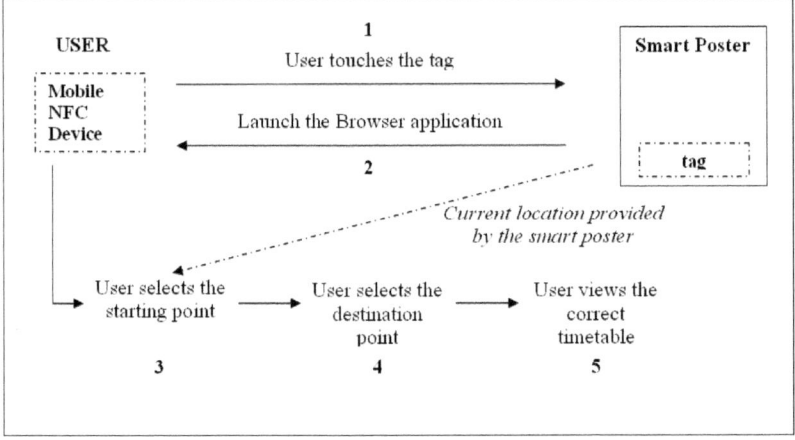

Fig. 3. Timetable service process

This case example differs from the previous case by the fact that there is no specific application for providing the timetable information. Instead, the information is provided through a standard browser and a mobile Internet connection. With the user not required to download any specific application, but instead using the browser already existent in his mobile device, the usability of the service can be considered to be better than using a specific application for this purpose.

3.4   Security Evaluation of the Case-Examples

The security of the previous applications was evaluated by using the "Expression of Needs and Identification of Security Objectives" (EBIOS)-method [7]. EBIOS consists of a variety of tools that can be used for discovering, training and employing methods related to the security of information systems (ISS) and risk management within that area. The conducted security analysis consists of the following four parts:

1. Security design
2. Vulnerability and risk analysis
3. Risk mitigation and security policies
4. Security deployment and monitoring

The *security design* section determines the basic information for the security analysis, i.e. the necessary organisation and other background description as well as the scope of the analysis. This is performed by defining the target functionalities, components and architectures as well as determining the security objectives of the case-example. Finally we define the assets and security requirements that are partially derived from the previously described sections.

The second section of the analysis consists of *vulnerability and risk analysis*. The analysis is performed by evaluating the potential vulnerabilities and risks (threats) using e.g. the following questions:

- **Who** is going to conduct the attack? (beneficiary)
- **What** are the objectives of the attack/attacker?
- **When** will the attack happen?
- **Where** will the attack take place in?
- **How** will the attack realize?

In addition to the previous, the attack potential is measured by using a three-point scale consisting of different threat elements and affected security criteria. Also the scale of vulnerabilities is evaluated for each threat. This is done by using a five-point scale that is used for identifying the key threats.

The third section of the analysis deals with *risk mitigation* (i.e. management) and *security policies*. This is performed by determining the actual risks that have an effect within the target system. Based on the mitigation, we propose a security policy for the target environment in order to counter some of the retained threats.

The final section of the security analysis deals with *security deployment and monitoring*. This means encountering the remaining threats and providing an expression of assurance requirements according to the strength level of the security objectives defined earlier in the risk mitigation paragraph. The security objectives form the grounds for a confidence that a system is protected by mechanisms that are resistant enough against the identified threats.

The results shown in chapter four are based on the overall results of the conducted security analysis as well as explorative research on issues related to privacy. The latter is based on the fact that EBIOS focuses on the security of information systems and has very little tools to deal with privacy, which is more related to individual people and their concerns.

4   Results

In this chapter, we present the main identified security challenges that relate to NFC and services based on the technology with a focus on the smart poster. In addition, we determine some main challenges of NFC technology related to privacy and use of personal information. The challenges are based on the two public transportation case-examples described earlier in this article.

4.1   Security Challenges

Based on the results of the security analysis as well as exploratory research performed within this area, we can categorize the main security challenges of the smart poster case examples in three areas:

1. Physical security
2. Technical security
3. Content security

In the context of this article, the term physical security refers to the physical means of securing the tag by, for example guarding or monitoring its surroundings. The term technical security refers to disabling or aggravating any attacks against the tag by technical means, i.e. locking the tag contents in order to prevent any change to them. The third term, content security, focuses on securing the content instead of the store (i.e. tag). This can be done for instance by using digital signing or other methods for verifying the content within the tag.

A major threat in the eTicketing and timetable case-examples lies in the integrity of a tag located in a public transportation station or stop. The tag content can be for example changed, the whole tag can be tampered physically by disabling it or it can even be replaced by a malicious tag that forwards the users to download an identical version of the ticketing application to their mobile devices. The application might contain a virus or some other unwanted feature that might transfer the tickets or money to another location. The malicious application might also perform some other action that would perhaps raise distrust towards NFC technology and services. As an example, a call to a location that the user has not intended or unnecessary GPRS data transfers might easily result into unexpected transaction costs that would require settling thus wasting both the user's and service provider's time and other resources.

In order to improve the physical security dimension, the service provider should disable or at least complicate the possibilities for tag tampering within the smart posters. This can be done for instance by placing the tag inside a protective shell or attaching it behind a plexiglass. This is however considered to be against the initial idea of smart posters as the have been thought to be a cheap and easily replaceable marketing tool. Other methods for improving the physical security of smart posters are locating them into public areas, guarding and camera surveillance that make it impossible or at least difficult for the malicious party to tamper the tag.

Another threat in the eTicketing and timetable case-examples exists in the technical security of the tags. The NFC Data Exchange Format (NDEF) used in the tags, doesn't restrict the addition of new data records to the NDEF message, which in the case of a malicious third party would mean the possibility of having an unwanted feature within the tag without the user noticing it. In this case, disabling the write-mode function in the tag, could be used for preventing tag tampering and provide an additional barrier alongside the previously mentioned physical measures.

Digital signing of NDEF data can be used as another way of preventing tag tampering, or actually preventing any change of content despite the tag. By implementing a digital signature to the tag, it is possible to provide authenticity and integrity of data, but at the same time enable easy copying and therefore distribution of content. Digital signing does not depend on the tag like technical security, but instead focuses on the content and therefore has perhaps more value to the end user who can be informed automatically if the integrity or authenticity of a certain piece of data has been broken.

4.2   Privacy Challenges

One of the biggest challenges of NFC related to privacy is, without doubt, ensuring the anonymity of the users during the transaction process. NFC, together with wireless Internet connection, provides customers with services that can acquire information over the Internet in order to make the service more value-adding. However, the added value requires personalization of the service in order to be of use to the consumers and therefore constitutes a threat on the privacy issues. Based on the previous case-examples, we can identify three main areas that might constitute a threat on privacy.

1.   collecting personal information provided by users without their consent
2.   collecting location-based information about users during transactions
3.   combination of personal information from different sources

In the next chapters, the previously mentioned areas are described in more detail.

4.2.1   Collecting Personal Information Provided by Users without Their Consent
Since NFC is based on already existing RFID technology, the identification of the mobile device during transactions is generally based on the serial number of the NFC interface. In addition, also other information such as the International Mobile Equipment Identity number (IMEI), i.e. the serial number of the mobile device could be obtained over the NFC interface. Both of the serial numbers in this case are considered as personal information and therefore not to be used in anything else, but the actual service transaction. The use of personal information in other service areas is possible in case the user (in this case, the owner of the information) provides a permit for other service usage. Even after acquiring this kind of permission from the user, the information can be used for only the specific purpose that the permission covers.

4.2.2   Collecting Location-Based Information about Users during Transactions
In the previously described ticketing case, the tag already consists of information related to the current location. This is because the ticketing application uses this information to enable better usability of the service, when it provides the users with the destinations that they are able to travel to from that station. Can this information be considered anonymous enough, as one station might comprise tens of tags that are used on a daily basis? In terms of better usability, the tags on a specific location (e.g. one side of the tracks, a certain bus stop etc.) may, however, provide information about the direction of vehicles from that location, in which case even more detailed location information could be acquired by the service provider from the users that are touching the tags.

   The previous case might not result into any privacy issues in the case of existing public transportation company customers, since they are already registered within the system and therefore have agreed on their personal information usage. However, as the same tag that might launch the ticketing application, might also provide the non-registered users with public transport timetable information, in which case user consent is not necessarily given. When acquiring timetable information from the Internet, the tag serial number could be easily transmitted over to the application server providing the timetable information. Also, since the information acquired from the application server is in any case based on the user's location, this already provides it a threat to the privacy of the individual user.

4.2.3 Combination of Personal Information from Different Sources

One of the future threats of NFC as well as information systems in common, is how to prevent the possibility of combining the personal or for example location-based information of an individual customer in different back-office databases. Until now, this has been constricted by legislation as well as consumer protection policies. However, as more and more information is being collected from different sources and the amount of detail is also increasing, it is important to perceive also the possibility of such issue. Following the privacy protection acts as well as co-operating with consumer advocates, a set of basic principles defining the privacy guidelines of NFC can be produced. This requires also consciousness from the consumers in terms of understanding the service providers' intentions and avoiding optimism when granting access rights to their personal data.

5   Discussion

In this chapter, we discuss about the overall security and privacy challenges of NFC technology and also present an idea for adding value to the technology in the perspective of service providers. In addition, we discuss about the on-going and potential future research activities related to NFC.

5.1   The Challenges and Added-Value of NFC Technology

The security and privacy challenges of NFC are in most cases far more complicated, compared to traditional RFID. Even though mobile devices can handle security functions, the added-value features, such as the possibility to access the mobile Internet, makes it also an interesting target of abuse for some people. Also the increased use of mobile devices in our everyday lives has attracted some malicious parties to disturb the "harmony" of the mobile service environment. In the future, both the security and privacy issues will surely increase, but by providing information to the users on the previously mentioned issues, it is possible to also increase their awareness and by doing that perhaps prevent any major threats to the security and privacy of the technology.

One feature of NFC-based services that is of interest to the service providers, is keeping track of the tags, thus enabling various optimization and maintenance tasks. Currently, keeping track of different tags in each public transport station is rather difficult as it has to be done manually by the maintenance personnel. This means testing all of the tags periodically by touching them with a NFC capable mobile device and making sure that each tag works. This could be done much easier by simply adding a unique ID to each tag that would be transmitted over the air to the application server each time that the tag is touched. This wouldn't increase the data transfer from the user to the server almost at all, but in the service providers' viewpoint, this would provide them with data from each transaction initiated by that certain tag. The data could be then used for monitoring the tag usage for example in the following ways:

- tag is or isn't functioning properly
- tag is being overused or used only seldom

The first option would enable the maintenance personnel to locate the tags that don't provide any information to the server and fix them. The second option would enable the service provider to identify the requirement on whether the number of tags should be increased in crowded places and seldom used tags could be moved to a better location. This kind of personal information usage is somewhat questionable, as there is only a thin line between the previously described anonymous use of location information and individual user tracking.

5.2   Further Research Activities

Despite many different NFC-based services have already been published, some potential killer applications using NFC technology are yet to be discovered. Most of the services, like public transportation, paying and information acquirement are targeted towards ordinary customers, but the technology can also be used efficiently in the corporate world. A European public research project called Role-centric Identity (role-ID, 2009-2012), funded by the Information Technology for European Advancement (ITEA2) strategic programme, currently develops mechanisms and tools for identity management purposes that could make use of NFC technology for e.g. the exchange of roles between different actors or for access control purposes. The following three case-examples describe the usage of NFC in different situations related to the project focus area, which is the public safety and healthcare sector.

1. In the public safety sector the emergency response center (ERC, the operator of the emergency number 112 in a specific area) could provide a specific fire rescue unit electronic access to an office building that has sent an automatic fire alarm. The credentials could be sent over-the-air from the ERC to a NFC-enabled mobile handset and they could be used for faster access to the building just like any RFID-based access control card or tag. Especially in the case of a false alarm, this would save time, because no time would be spent on obtaining the master key located in one part of the building, but instead the fire rescue personnel could access the building from any accessible door.

2. In the healthcare sector the personnel of a hospital (doctors, nurses) could "log on" to a patient and acquire patient information via NFC enabled handset that would be touched to a tag attached either directly to a patient (e.g. in a wristband) or in the hospital bed. Touching the tag would inform the hospital system about a specific nurse or doctor taking care of the patient and the tag could also consist of important information regarding the patient, i.e. allergies to specific medication or other vital information, which is normally read from a (paper) patient file. The advantage of NFC in this case is to enable better tracking of hospital personnel (in terms of administration

and better service) and also help patients in case of emergency by providing the most important information electronically and at a glance.

3. In both the public safety and emergency sector NFC technology could be used for exchanging responsibility at a specific field location. For example in the case of a traffic accident, the first available emergency unit (either police, fire rescue or ambulance) at the location receives responsibility for that operation. In some cases, especially in the case of casualties, the unit responsible for overall operation changes from police to fire rescue and from fire rescue to ambulance during the rescue process. The process of changing roles and responsibilities is verbal and is based on training and long-term co-operation between these units, but it also makes the process vulnerable to communication errors or misinterpretation. In some cases NFC technology could be used to document this responsibility change in the information systems and also to disseminate the change to other units yet to arrive to the scene or that are otherwise related to the process. In practice this would mean that the responsibility "credentials" for that operation would be transferred from one mobile device to another by touching them with each other and corresponding information would then be automatically sent out to other nearby devices.

The security and/or privacy of these previously mentioned case-examples have not been studied since it is not a part of the ongoing project. However, especially the privacy aspect can be considered not as important an issue in the public safety sector as it is in the consumer market. This is due to the fact that the personnel dealing with private information in these cases are working in public administration, which makes it easier to manage than if they were in the private sector. In any case the security of these case-examples would be interesting to study as well as the usability of the services in terms of the focus group, i.e. public safety and healthcare.

Regarding further research within the overall NFC security and privacy field, a questionnaire survey targeted to NFC technology users, should be performed. By doing such a survey, we could determine the consumers' perceptions towards the technology and the services available to the public. Based on the analysis of the survey results, we could form a common insight into the consumers' minds and in the future perhaps focus on issues that are of importance to them.

6   Conclusion

This article focuses on Near Field Communication (NFC), an emerging wireless communication technology that provides mobile devices with RFID capabilities. The article describes two cases of using NFC technology in public transportation with smart posters as the primary service initialization method.

The main security threats related to NFC in the described use cases can be categorized into physical (the physical means of securing the tag by, for example guarding or monitoring its surroundings), technical (disabling or aggravating any attacks against the tag by technical means) and content (securing the content for example by using digital signing or other methods for securing verifying the integrity and authenticity of content) security.

Physical security can be improved by placing the tag inside a protective shell, or locating the tag in a public place. Also guarding and camera surveillance can be utilized as means of physical security. Technical security issues on the other hand can be managed for instance by disabling the write-mode from the tag. Also digital signing of content can be used, though it does not prevent the users from copying the data.

The primary identified privacy issues within the use cases are

1. collecting of personal information,
2. collecting location-based information about users during transactions, and
3. combination of personal information from different sources.

By providing information to the users on the previously mentioned issues, it is possible to increase their awareness and perhaps prevent any future potential threats to security and privacy.

References

1. ABI Research. Twenty Percent of Mobile Handsets Will Include Near Field Communication by 2012. ABI Research press release (April 11, 2007),
   http://www.abiresearch.com/abiprdisplay.jsp?pressid=838
2. Frost & Sullivan. Real start for NFC (December 2010)
3. ABI Research. Near Field Communication Handsets Are Not Just for Big Spenders. ABI Research press release (September 7, 2007),
   http://www.abiresearch.com/abiprdisplay.jsp?pressid=930
4. ISO, ISO/IEC 18092:2004 Near Field Communication Interface and Protocol 1 (NFCIP-1) standard (2004), International Organization for Standardization (2011),
   http://www.iso.org
5. NFC Forum, NFC Forum Tag Type Technical Specifications, NFC Forum (2011),
   http://www.nfc-forum.org/specs/
6. ECMA. ECMA-352 Near Field Communication Interface and Protocol 2 (NFCIP-2) standard (2010),
   http://www.ecma-international.org/publications/
   files/ECMA-ST/ECMA-352.pdf
7. EBIOS. Expression of Needs and Identification ofSecurity Objectives (EBIOS) description (2011),
   http://www.ssi.gouv.fr/en/the-anssi/publications-109/
   methods-to-achieve-iss/ebios-2010-expression-of-needs-and-
   identification-of-security-objectives.html

Exploiting Routing Tree Construction in CTP

Islam Hegazy, Reihaneh Safavi-Naini, and Carey Williamson

Department of Computer Science, University of Calgary, Canada
{islam.hegazy,rei,carey}@ucalgary.ca

Abstract. Sensor nodes in a Wireless Sensor Network (WSN) are scattered in an environment to collect data. These nodes are limited in resources and cannot process the collected data or store it for long periods of time. Thus, the sensor nodes rely on routing protocols to relay the collected data wirelessly to a central controller for analysis and storage. However, the routing protocols are not immune against malicious nodes because they sacrifice the security aspect to meet the limited resources of the sensor nodes. In this paper, we demonstrate how a malicious node can exploit the computation of link qualities in the Collection Tree routing Protocol (CTP) to disrupt the construction of routing trees. We propose a lightweight detection system to detect this malicious node. The proposed detection system is implemented and evaluated using the network simulator *ns-2*. The simulation results show that the detection system provides a robust detection.

Keywords: Wireless sensor networks, Link quality routing protocols, Collection Tree Protocol, Intrusion Detection.

1 Introduction

A WSN is a special type of wireless networks composed of tiny sensors that collect data from their surrounding environments. These sensors send the collected data to a central collector (base station) for further processing and decision making. The base station connects the WSN to an existing infrastructure where the user can access the collected data [2]. The sensor nodes are highly constrained devices: they operate on batteries; and they have limited computational and storage capabilities. WSNs are designed to be left unattended in inaccessible environments. As a result of the aforementioned characteristics, software applications of WSNs should conserve as much memory space and battery power as possible to prolong the lifetime of the network. Despite their limited capabilities, WSNs are gaining more attention in several application fields. WSNs can be used in: military applications, such as battlefield surveillance; in environmental applications, such as fire detection; health application, such as patient tracking; home applications, such as home automation; and other applications, such as interactive museums, managing inventory control, and [1].

Sensor nodes play a dual role of collecting data and relaying data from other sensor nodes using wireless communication until the data reaches the base station. A WSN may be deployed in a vast area such that not all the sensor nodes

S. Jung and M. Yung (Eds.): WISA 2011, LNCS 7115, pp. 256–270, 2012.

can communicate directly with the base station. To overcome this limitation, the sensor nodes use a wireless routing protocol to deliver data to the base station. Since the sensor nodes use wireless radio frequency (RF) for communication, they are susceptible to different types of attacks that target the routing protocol. These attacks are different from the attacks against wired networks because they exploit the wireless nature of communication in the WSN.

Routing attacks in WSNs take advantage of the wireless communication It is difficult to guarantee physical security for the vast areas where WSNs are deployed; this enables adversaries to insert devices such as malicious nodes or repeaters into the environment to disrupt the routing protocol. Because of the scarcity of the resources of sensor nodes, WSN routing protocols rarely incorporate trust or security mechanisms. An non-trusted protocol is itself a threat.

Security mechanisms that depend on cryptography cannot defend against all types of attacks against WSNs. An insider malicious node will have all the cryptographic credentials that allow it to participate in any implemented cryptography mechanism. For example, in this paper, we show how a malicious node can manipulate the parameters of CTP [7] to disrupt the construction of the routing tree to its favour. Hence, another security mechanisms should be implemented in the WSN to detect such types of attack.

This paper has three main contributions. First, it shows how a single malicious node can exploit CTP to disrupt the construction of the routing tree to its favour. Second, it proposes a lightweight intrusion detection system (IDS) to detect this malicious node. In this IDS, each sensor node reaches a decision about a neighbouring sensor node by monitoring its advertised routing cost and its frequency of broadcasting beacons. This IDS does not require the sensor nodes to share their detection information nor send network information to the base station. Thus, it does not generate any extra communication in the WSN. Third, it presents the simulation results of implementing the IDS using ns-2 [12].

The paper is organized as follows. Section 2 gives a survey of related work. Section 3 discusses the vulnerabilities of CTP. Section 4 proposes the IDS. Section 5 explains the setup of the simulation environment. Section 6 presents and discusses the simulation results. Finally, Section 7 concludes the paper.

2   Related Work

Detection mechanisms for routing attacks in WSNs have gained attention in literature due to the severity of these attacks, such as the works in [4], [9], [11], and [14]. However, to the best of our knowledge, most of these detection mechanisms focus on detecting the activities of malicious nodes, rather than on the vulnerabilities of the routing protocols.

Krontiris et al. [10] present an IDS that detects malicious nodes that manipulate link qualities in MintRoute routing protocol [15]. In their IDS, sensor nodes broadcast their neighbour lists in response to a suspicious activity. Then the sensor nodes do an intersection of all neighbour lists and if a node remains, they will detect it as malicious.

Hegazy *et al.* [8] introduce the sequence number gap trick to detect malicious nodes that exaggerate their link qualities in MintRoute. This IDS makes use of the cooperation of sensor nodes in MintRoute to compute link qualities to introduce a gap in their sequence numbers. This trick allows the sensor nodes to compute an upper bound for the link qualities computed by their neighbours. If a neighouring sensor node does not meet its expected link quality, the tricking sensor nodes will flag it as malicious.

3   Problem Statement

This section begins be explaining CTP and how it constructs a routing tree to the base station. Next, it explains the vulnerabilities in CTP and how a malicious node can exploit them.

3.1   Primitives of CTP

CTP is a link quality routing protocol that computes anycast routes to a single or a small number of base stations in a WSN. It is a best-effort protocol that implements several mechanisms to improve data delivery but it does not guarantee 100% delivery [7]. It is a data collection protocol that fulfills the primitives of data collection that are set in TEP 119 [6]: estimate link quality of 1-hop links, detect and repair routing loops, and detect and suppress duplicate packets.

CTP uses the expected transmission count (ETX) metric [3] to construct routing trees that minimize the expected number of transmissions and retransmissions required to deliver data to the base station. In CTP, sensor nodes compute unidirectional link qualities for their inbound links and bidirectional link qualities for their outbound links. An inbound link is a link that a sensor node receives packets on and an outbound link is a link that a sensor node sends data on.

Figure 1 depicts the types of links that a CTP sensor node, S, shares with its neighbouring sensor nodes, N_1, N_2, and N_3. Sensor node S has chosen N_1 as its parent. Sensor node S computes unidirectional inbound link qualities for all its neighbours since it hears beacons broadcast from them. On the other hand, it computes another link quality for its outbound link with its parent only because it relays its data through this parent. Then sensor node S computes a bidirectional link quality combining the inbound and outbound link qualities of its parent N_1.

The computation of unidirectional link qualities depends on the number of beacons a sensor node receives from each neighbour. A sensor node requires the transmission of three beacons from a neighbour to update its inbound link quality. Although the name bidirectional link quality may imply some cooperation between the sensor nodes, each sensor node computes it independently as follows. For every five data packets sent to a parent, the child sensor node computes an outbound link quality according to the number of acknowledgements received from the parent. Then the child sensor node computes a bidirectional

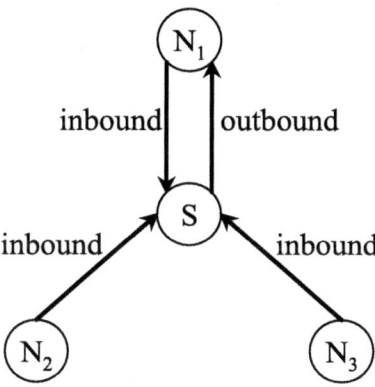

Fig. 1. Types of links in CTP

link quality using the values of the inbound and outbound link qualities with its parent sensor node.

CTP constructs a routing tree rooted at the base station where the routes have the minimum bidirectional link qualities along them. Thus, it constructs routes that have the minimum number of transmissions and retransmissions. A path cost or routing cost is the summation of all the values of bidirectional link qualities of the links that constitute that path.

CTP applies an adaptive beaconing strategy to achieve both fast recovery and low bandwidth and energy usage. In brief, CTP begins with a minimum beacon transmission interval where it sends a beacon at random. Then with every eligible beacon, CTP doubles the beacon transmission interval until it reaches the maximum. Then it keeps using the maximum interval afterwards. The minimum beacon transmission interval is set to 128 and the maximum is set to 512,000. However, CTP resets the beacon transmission interval to the minimum in three cases:

- When a data packet is received to forward with a lower path cost, CTP assumes the existence of topology inconsistency or a possible routing loop. A beacon is scheduled for broadcast as soon as possible to fix the topology.
- When a new route that has a significantly lower path cost than the current value is found, CTP shrinks its beacon transmission interval to the minimum. Thus, a beacon is sent as soon as possible to update the neighbouring sensor nodes of the new value. A significant drop in the path cost may mean that this sensor node has a better route to the base station. Resetting the beacon transmission interval propagates this information to the neighbouring sensor nodes quickly. Significant means having a path cost value that is 20 points lower than the current value.
- When a new sensor node joins the WSN or a sensor node loses its route, it requests topology information to populate its routing table. CTP cancels the current beacon transmission interval and schedules a new minimum interval to send the updates as soon as possible.

3.2   Vulnerabilities in CTP

In this subsection, we explain how a malicious node can exploit CTP to disrupt the construction of the routing tree.

CTP does not require the sensor nodes to cooperate to compute link qualities. Each sensor node computes its link qualities independent of the other sensor nodes. Knowing that each sensor node computes its link qualities independently, a malicious node cannot influence the computation of link qualities by sharing false information with its neighbours. However, the malicious node can manipulate its protocol parameters to convince its neighbours of its route to the base station. For example, it can advertise fake path cost, or it can manipulate its beacon transmission intervals to send frequent beacons. Advertising a low path cost makes the route of the malicious node appealing whereas, sending frequent beacons gives advantage to the malicious node by having its neighbours compute their link qualities to it quickly.

A malicious node that sends frequent beacons takes advantage of the count-based property of the computations and the adaptive beacon transmission intervals of CTP. A sensor node computes its inbound link quality for a neighbouring sensor node for every three beacons received from this neighbour. These beacons should be received in adaptive intervals, which means that the time difference between any two beacons should increase over time. A malicious node may compromise the beacon transmission interval by always using the minimum beacon transmission interval. Thus, the neighbouring sensor nodes will receive more frequent beacons from the malicious node than the other good sensor nodes.

For example, Figure 2 compares between the beacon transmission intervals of a good sensor node versus a malicious node. We can see that if a malicious node uses the minimum beacon transmission interval, 128 time units, it will send seven beacons for every three beacons sent by a good sensor node. This means that the inbound link qualities for the malicious node will be computed twice versus once for the other sensor nodes. This helps the malicious node to reinforce the inbound link qualities of its children sensor nodes and attract other neighbouring sensor nodes. This behaviour does not look suspicious because, in CTP, sensor nodes use the minimum beacon transmission interval if they do not have routes to the base station and for the reasons explained in Section 3.1.

A more vicious node would combine the transmission of frequent beacons with advertising a low path cost to the base station. If a malicious node broadcasts low path cost in frequent beacons, then it will be more convincing to its neighbouring sensor nodes to route their sensed data through it. Moreover, these neighbouring sensor nodes will be offering low path costs as well and thus, more sensor nodes will join the subtree of the malicious node.

4   Proposed Detection System

The proposed detection system is composed of two detection modules to detect a malicious node that advertises a low path cost and violates the adaptive behaviour of beacons transmission.

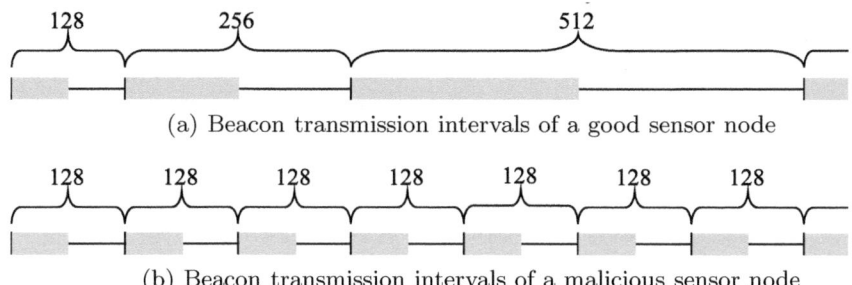

(a) Beacon transmission intervals of a good sensor node

(b) Beacon transmission intervals of a malicious sensor node

Fig. 2. Behaviour of malicious node in Scenario 3

The first module implements the watchdog concept to detect sensor nodes that broadcast a low path cost than their parents. The second detection module implements a state machine to test the arrivals of beacons. Every sensor node in the WSN has a local copy of the detection system to reach a decision about the suspected sensor node independently. Also, every sensor node runs a separate image of the detection system for each neighbouring sensor node.

4.1   System Model

We make the following assumptions about the sensor nodes and the malicious node:

- Sensor nodes are deployed uniformly at random in a planar square region.
- All sensor nodes have the same wireless communication range, following the unit disk model.
- All sensor nodes run the CTP routing protocol, and have loosely synchronized clocks.
- A single malicious node is present when the WSN is first deployed. The malicious node may be a compromised node or an implanted node. It has the same basic capabilities as good sensor nodes.
- The malicious node participates in the CTP routing protocol, but manipulates its parameters to affect the construction of the routing tree.
- The malicious node may also drop, modify, or divert the network traffic.

4.2   Detection Module 1

Detection module 1 takes advantage of the common neighbouring sensor nodes between a parent sensor node and its child sensor node to detect malicious nodes that fake their path costs. To detect malicious nodes, the sensor nodes work as watchdogs for the advertised path cost values of every parent-child pair. They take advantage of the following property: every child sensor node should add its link quality to its parent to the path cost of the parent to compute its path cost. Thus, the path cost of a child sensor node must be greater than the path cost of its parent. Accordingly, if the path cost of the malicious node is equal to or less than the path cost of its parent, then the common neighbours will detect it.

4.3 Detection Module 2

Detection module 2 takes advantage of the adaptive transmission of beacons. However, the detection is not straightforward due to the reasons of resetting beacon transmission interval as explained in Section 3.1

Figure 3 shows a state machine that implements detection module 2, where *cost* is the path cost of the received beacon, *EB* is an expected beacon that arrives in an adaptive fashion, *UEB* is an unexpected beacon, and *alert* is a counter of beacon violations. This state machine considers the following factors in CTP:

- At least three beacons are required to compute a link quality.
- Sensor nodes will use the minimum beacon transmission interval if they do not have routes to the base station.
- After establishing routes to the base station, sensor nodes should adapt their beacon transmission intervals.

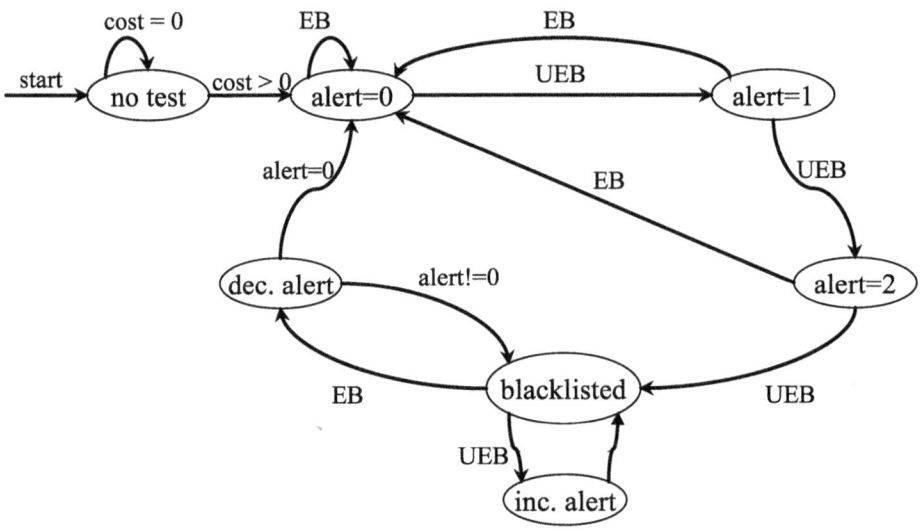

Fig. 3. Detection Module 2

The state machine tests only beacons from sensor nodes that have routes to the base station, *cost* > 0. After starting to monitor the arrival of beacons, the state machine requires three consecutive beacon violations from the same neighbouring sensor node to blacklist this neighbour. This threshold is important to ensure that malicious nodes are not considered for parent choice after computing the link qualities. To punish malicious nodes and to prevent the isolation of good sensor nodes by blacklisting, the state machine decreases the value of the *alert* variable for every conformant beacon. On the other hand, it will increase the value if the beacon is suspicious. A blacklisted sensor node that has its *alert* reaches 0 is removed from the blacklist.

5   Setup of Simulation Environment

We have built a *ns-2* simulator to evaluate the proposed detection system. Firstly, we have implemented CTP in *ns-2* with the help of its source code in TinyOS [13] and the papers [5] and [6]. Secondly, we have extended the source code of CTP to support the proposed detection system. To measure the success of the detection system, we have configured the malicious node to drop traffic that traverses it. Thus, we are able to measure the percentage of data delivered to the base station before and after detecting the malicious node.

We have simulated WSNs of different sizes namely, 25, 50, and 100 sensor nodes, to evaluate the proposed IDS. The wireless range of the sensor nodes differs in each size to have at least 95% of the sensor nodes connected. Table 1 shows the different wireless ranges of the sensor nodes in the different sizes of WSNs. We have simulated 100 different WSN for each network size.

Table 1. Wireless ranges of sensor nodes in CTP simulations

Size of WSN	Range of sensor nodes
25 nodes	45 units
50 nodes	35 units
100 nodes	25 units

The malicious node has been placed at different locations in the simulation area along the diagonal from the base station. The locations of the malicious node depend on its wireless range as shown in Table 2. The malicious node has the same wireless range of the sensor nodes in the WSN it is compromising. Figure 4 shows the locations of the malicious node relative to the base station.

Table 2. Physical locations of the malicious node vs. its wireless range

Range	Physical locations
45 units	(45, 45), (55, 55), (65, 65)
35 units	(35, 35), (45, 45), (55, 55), (65, 65), (75, 75)
25 units	(25, 25), (35, 35), (45, 45), (55, 55), (65, 65), (75, 75), (85, 85)

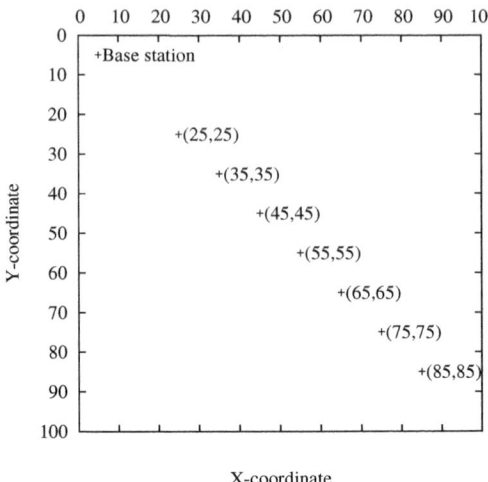

Fig. 4. Locations of the malicious node relative to the base station

6   Simulation Results

This section presents the simulation results of the malicious node before and after the detection. First, its presents the performance of the malicious node when the IDS is not running. Next, it discusses how a running IDS affects the performance of the malicious node after detection.

6.1   Simulation Results of Manipulating CTP

Figure 5 depicts the simulation results of the different approaches that a malicious node may follow to disrupt the routing tree construction in CTP. In Scenario 0, the malicious node follows the routing protocol without any manipulations. However, the malicious node is configured to drop traffic that passes through it. Scenario 0 acts as a reference for the other approaches.

A malicious node that fakes its path cost will be most effective in locations where this path cost is lower than the other path costs in the vicinity. See Scenario 1 in Figure 5. The malicious node is configured to advertise a path cost of value 20. In locations far from the base station, the malicious node is offering a low path cost value that looks appealing to its neighbours. Moreover, when these neighbours join the subtree of the malicious node, they will offer low path costs in return, which in turns attracts more sensor nodes to the subtree of the malicious node.

Another approach for the malicious node is to advertise its real path cost but does not adapt its beacon transmission interval after sending a beacon. Scenario 2 in Figure 5 shows the simulation results of a malicious node that is configured to use the minimum beacon transmission interval, 128 time units, for each beacon transmission. The frequent beacons help the neighbouring sensor nodes to reach

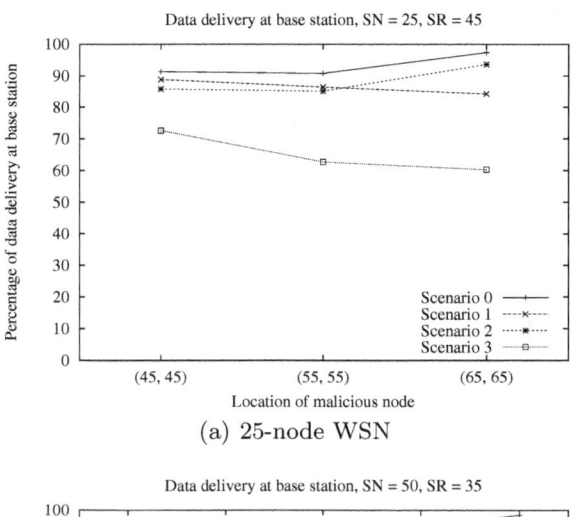

(a) 25-node WSN

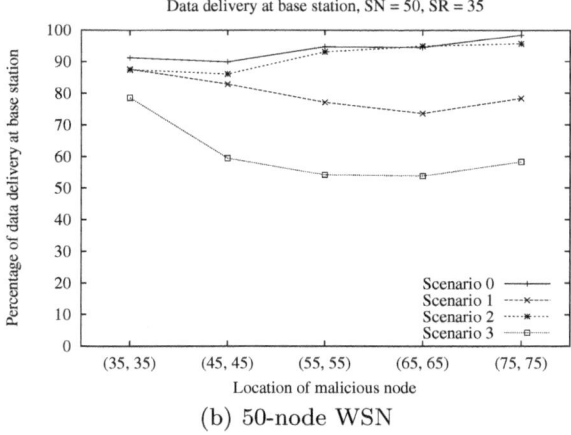

(b) 50-node WSN

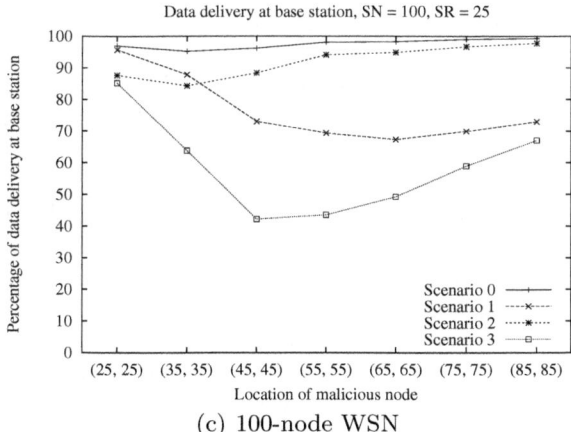

(c) 100-node WSN

Fig. 5. Simulation results of manipulating CTP

the minimum link quality value to the malicious node quickly. However, their choice of the malicious node as the next hop depends on the value of its path cost, which depends on how far the malicious node is from the base station. Near the base station, the malicious node has a low path cost value. Consequently, the route through the malicious node encourages the neighbouring sensor nodes to join the subtree of the malicious node. Far from the base station, the routing cost of the malicious node gets higher. As a result, the low link quality values of the neighbouring sensor nodes are not incentive enough to lure them to join the subtree of the malicious node.

A more vicious node combines the previous two approaches of advertising a low path cost value and frequent beacons. Thus, it aims to quickly convince its neighbours of its fake good path to the base station. The simulation results depicted by Scenario 3 in Figure 5 show that the malicious node succeeds to attract more sensor nodes to its subtree by following this behaviour. The malicious node reaches the highest success around the centre of the WSN. Close to the base station other sensor nodes will have low path costs so the malicious node may not be the only choice. Near the edges far from the base station, the malicious node does not have a large number of sensor nodes to lure. Around the centre, the malicious node will lure almost half of the sensor nodes in the WSN. Any sensor node that will join its subtree will offer a low path cost in return and thus, lures more sensor nodes to join the subtree of the malicious node.

6.2   Simulation Results of the Proposed Detection System

Next we discuss the simulation results of detecting the malicious node. To measure the success of each detection module independently, we have configured the simulator to run either detection module 1 or detection module 2.

Figure 6 shows the performance of the malicious node when detection module 1 is running. We can see that in sparse WSN, 25-node, the performance of the malicious node is not affected. First, the number of common neighbours between the malicious node and its parent is small so a small number of sensor nodes can detect the malicious node. Out of the small number of neighbours that can detect the malicious node a smaller number may be its children. Accordingly, most of the children of the malicious node cannot detect it and they do not change their malicious parent to a good one. As the WSN gets denser, the number of common neighbouring sensor nodes between the malicious node and its parent increases. In addition, the number of the children of the malicious node increases so a larger number of the common neighbours are children of the malicious node. These children that detect the malicious node switch their parents to good ones so the percentage of data delivery at the base station increases. Also, the location of the malicious node and its offered path cost affect the success of detection module 1. Since the malicious node is offering a low path cost, it can be easily detected in locations far from the base station. Figure 6(b) shows that the percentage of data delivery will rise from 78.36% to 81.65% if the malicious node is placed at (75, 75). Whereas, it rises from 72.95% to 86.51 % at location (85, 85), see Figure 6(c).

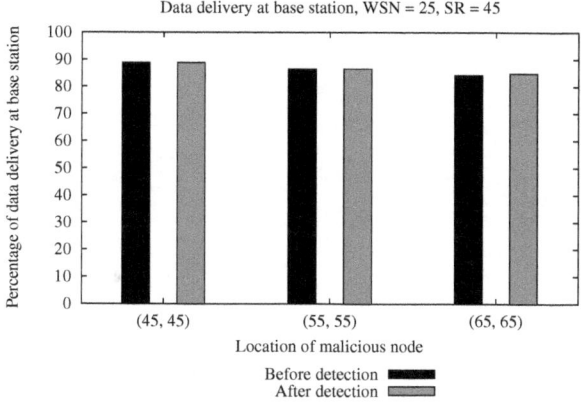

(a) Data delivery in 25-node WSN

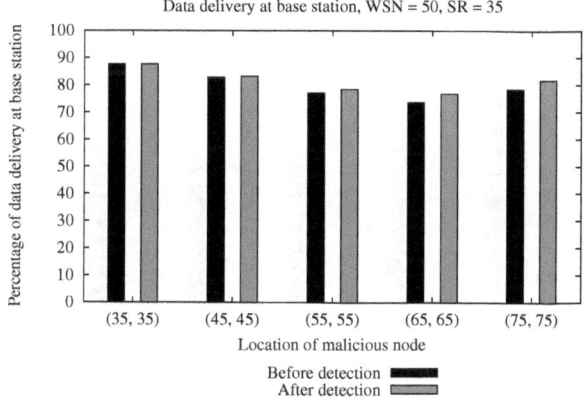

(b) Data delivery in 50-node WSN

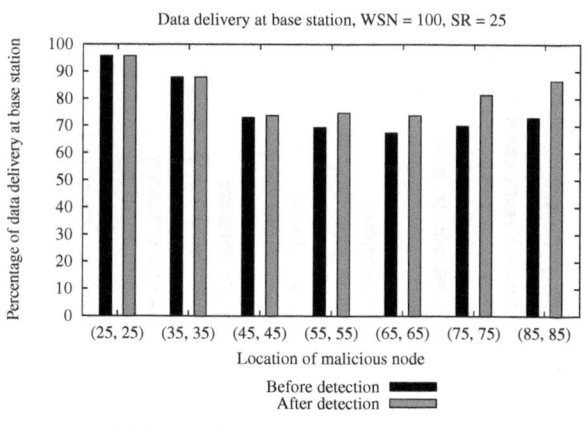

(c) Data delivery in 100-node WSN

Fig. 6. Performance of malicious node under detection module 1

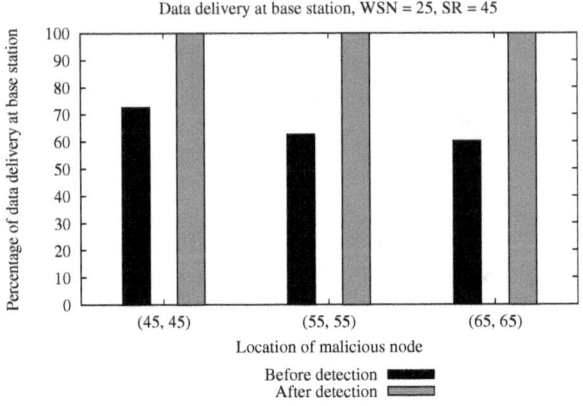

(a) Data delivery in 25-node WSN

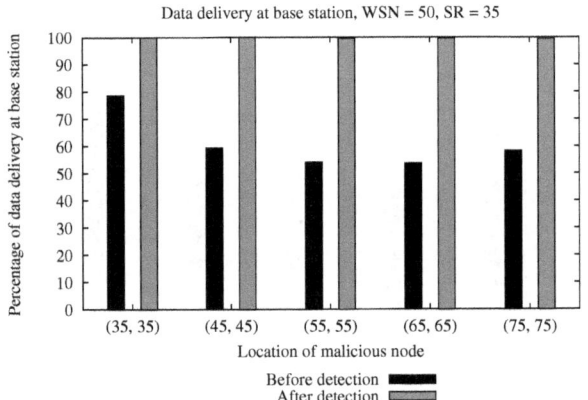

(b) Data delivery in 50-node WSN

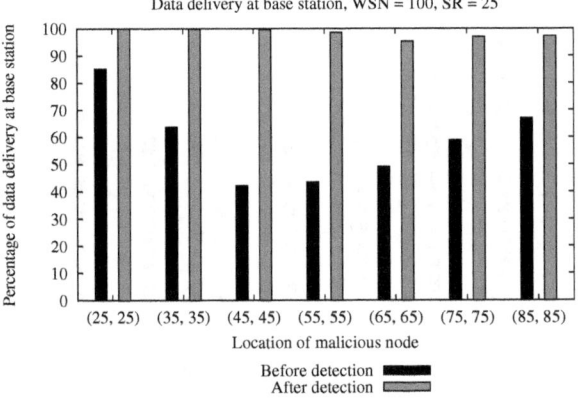

(c) Data delivery in 100-node WSN

Fig. 7. Performance of malicious node under detection module 2

The success of detection module 2 depends on the location of the malicious node and the size of the WSN. In the 25-node and 50-node WSNs, the percentage of data delivery is almost 100%, see Figures 7(a) and 7(b). However, in the 100-node WSN, the percentage of data delivery can be as low as 95% especially in locations far from the base station, see location (65, 65) in Figure 7(c).

By broadcasting a low path cost value in frequent beacons, the malicious node attracts more sensor nodes to its subtree as explained previously and as shown by the black bars in Figure 7. As a consequence of its success, more data packets are routed to the malicious node. This leads to higher packet collisions in the vicinity of the malicious node, which affects the computations of link qualities and path costs of its neighbours.

The high packet collisions lead to a phenomenon that occurred in dense WSN, 100-node. Between the centre of the WSN and its far edges from the base station, the parent of the malicious node forms a loop by joining the subtree of the malicious node. This happens because the parent sensor node suffers from high path costs due to packet collisions and it finds the best path through one of the children of the malicious node. This loop cannot be broken because the malicious node is configured to drop data packets passing through it. Therefore, the parent sensor node will never find its data packet returning back to it. We can see that the percentage of data delivery at the base station is as low as 95.27% when the malicious node is at location (65, 65), Figure 7(c).

7   Conclusion

We proposed a lightweight IDS that detects a malicious node that exploits the construction of routing trees in CTP. A malicious node may advertise a low path cost value in frequent beacons to lure other sensor nodes to choose its route. The proposed IDS is composed of two modules. The first module detects discrepancies in the advertised path costs of sensor nodes. The second module implements a state machine to check the frequency of beacons broadcast. Simulation results showed that the success of the first detection module was affected by the density of the WSN and the value of the path cost offered by the malicious node. The success of the second detection module was affected by the location of the malicious node and amount of traffic in the WSN.

Acknowledgement. This work is in part supported by the Informatics Circle of Research Excellence (iCORE) of the province of Alberta, Canada and NSERC ISSNet, Canada. Islam Hegazy is on leave from FCIS, Ain Shams University, Cairo, Egypt for his PhD.

References

1. Akyildiz, I.F., Su, W., Sankarasubramaniam, Y., Cayirci, E.: Wireless Sensor Networks: A Survey. Computer Networks 38(4), 393–422 (2002)
2. Al-Karaki, J.N., Kamal, A.E.: Routing Techniques in Wireless Sensor Networks: A Survey. IEEE Wireless Communications 11(6), 6–28 (2004)

3. Couto, D.S.J.D., Aguayo, D., Bicket, J., Morris, R.: A High-Throughput Path Metric for MultiHop Wireless Routing. In: Proceedings of the 9th Annual International Conference on Mobile Computing and Networking (MobiCom), pp. 134–146. ACM, New York (2003)

4. de Graaf, R., Hegazy, I., Horton, J., Safavi-Naini, R.: Distributed Detection of Wormhole Attacks in Wireless Sensor Networks. In: Zheng, J., Mao, S., Midkiff, S.F., Zhu, H. (eds.) ADHOCNETS 2009. LNICST, vol. 28, pp. 208–223. Springer, Heidelberg (2010)

5. Fonseca, R., Gnawali, O., Jamieson, K., Kim, S., Levis, P., Woo, A.: TinyOS Enhancement Proposal (TEP) 123: The Collection Tree Protocol (CTP) (August 2006)

6. Fonseca, R., Gnawali, O., Jamieson, K., Levis, P.: TinyOS Enhancement Proposal (TEP) 119: Collection (February 2006)

7. Gnawali, O., Fonseca, R., Jamieson, K., Moss, D., Levis, P.: Collection Tree Protocol. In: Proceedings of the 7th ACM Conference on Embedded Networked Sensor Systems (SenSys), pp. 1–14. ACM Press, New York (2009)

8. Hegazy, I., Safavi-Naini, R., Williamson, C.: Towards Securing MintRoute in Wireless Sensor Networks. In: Proceedings of the 2010 IEEE International Symposium on a World of Wireless Mobile and Multimedia Networks (WoWMoM), pp. 1–6. IEEE (2010)

9. Krontiris, I., Benenson, Z., Giannetsos, T., Freiling, F.C., Dimitriou, T.: Cooperative Intrusion Detection in Wireless Sensor Networks. In: Roedig, U., Sreenan, C.J. (eds.) EWSN 2009. LNCS, vol. 5432, pp. 263–278. Springer, Heidelberg (2009)

10. Krontiris, I., Dimitriou, T., Giannetsos, T., Mpasoukos, M.: Intrusion Detection of Sinkhole Attacks in Wireless Sensor Networks. In: Kutyłowski, M., Cichoń, J., Kubiak, P. (eds.) ALGOSENSORS 2007. LNCS, vol. 4837, pp. 150–161. Springer, Heidelberg (2008)

11. Krontiris, I., Giannetsos, T., Dimitriou, T.: LIDeA: A Distributed Lightweight Intrusion Detection Architecture for Sensor Networks. In: Proceedings of the 4th International Conference on Security and Privacy in Communication Networks (SecureComm), pp. 1–10. ACM, New York (2008)

12. Network Simulator, ns-2, http://www.isi.edu/nsnam/ns/

13. TinyOS, http://www.tinyos.net/

14. Tseng, C.H., Wang, S.-H., Ko, C., Levitt, K.N.: DEMEM: Distributed Evidence-Driven Message Exchange Intrusion Detection Model for MANET. In: Zamboni, D., Krügel, C. (eds.) RAID 2006. LNCS, vol. 4219, pp. 249–271. Springer, Heidelberg (2006)

15. Woo, A., Tong, T., Culler, D.: Taming the Underlying Challenges of Reliable Multihop Routing in Sensor Networks. In: Proceedings of the 1st International Conference on Embedded Networked Sensor Systems (SenSys), pp. 14–27. ACM, New York (2003)

Author Index

GPSR Compliance

*The European Union's (EU) General Product Safety Regulation (GPSR)
is a set of rules that requires consumer products to be safe and our
obligations to ensure this.*

*If you have any concerns about our products, you can contact us on
ProductSafety@springernature.com*

In case Publisher is established outside the EU, the EU authorized
representative is:

Springer Nature Customer Service Center GmbH
Europaplatz 3
69115 Heidelberg, Germany

Batch number: 09474011

Printed by Printforce, the Netherlands